IELTS   SPEAKING

All of you wish to use English freely during the IELTS Speaking Test, but making this wish a reality remains a puzzle for most of you out there.

雅思口语 剑10版

慎小嶷 / 编著

Pat's Ten-Day Step-by-Step Guide
to the Speaking Test

机械工业出版社
CHINA MACHINE PRESS

本书正文按照天数划分内容，在十天里紧密结合《剑10》对最新雅思口语考试的应试策略进行了详尽的剖析，并结合《剑10》的考题特点提供了富有针对性的语言点讲解。

本书作者 Pat 老师有多年的英语国家生活经历，在使用地道英语表达对 IELTS 口语题库进行透析的同时，还对中国考生容易陷入的误区进行了非常中肯的提醒。词汇学习手册汇集了地道口语常用表达法的精华，考生可以随身携带、随时学习。

本书的音频部分均由英籍专业人士朗读，便于考生模仿和练习。

本书作者对于真实的英语国家生活和中国学生的口语瓶颈均有极为深刻的了解，并著有畅销书《十天突破雅思写作》和《十天突破 IELTS 写作完整真题库与 6-9 分范文全解》。

图书在版编目（CIP）数据

慎小嶷十天突破雅思口语：剑10版／慎小嶷编著. —5版.
—北京：机械工业出版社，2015.6（2016.3重印）
ISBN 978－7－111－50735－2

Ⅰ.①慎⋯　Ⅱ.①慎⋯　Ⅲ.①IELTS－口语－自学参考资料
Ⅳ.①H319.9

中国版本图书馆 CIP 数据核字（2015）第 132286 号

机械工业出版社（北京市百万庄大街22号　邮政编码100037）
策划编辑：孟玉琴　　　责任编辑：孟玉琴　于　雷
版式设计：张文贵
责任印制：乔　宇
保定市中画美凯印刷有限公司印刷

2016 年 3 月第 5 版·第18次印刷
184mm×260mm·31.375 印张·2 插页·805 千字
标准书号：ISBN 978－7－111－50735－2
定价：67.90 元（赠学习手册）

IELTS 口语的"脉"

你是谁

对 the IELTS Speaking Test 的持续跟踪让 Pat 深感在考场里真实出现的雅思口试话题极为广泛。事实上,它们几乎已经涵盖到了英美日常生活里的所有领域。

以 2016 年 1 月 30 日下午为例,在中国大陆就轮换出现了从 a house you would like to live in 到 a traditional festival 等跨度很大的 28 道卡片话题,如果再加上当天出现的第一、三部分考题经过排列组合后的可能性则更会远多于此。

与 Cambridge ESOL 出题者们明显"有备而来"相比,多数国内口语考生(希望您是一个例外)则仍处在采取顽固拖延战术或者根本就没有战术、慌不择路的"非正规军"状态。下面的官方统计数据残酷展现了这支"非正规军"在 IELTS Speaking Test 中是怎样被剑桥击溃的:

Mean Band Score for the Most Frequent Countries or Regions of Origin

(Source: www.ielts.org)

Place of Origin	Speaking	Place of Origin	Speaking
Germany	7.3	Greece	6.5
Philippines	6.9	Colombia	6.4
Nigeria	6.8	Egypt	6.4
Sri Lanka	6.7	Iran, Islamic Republic of	6.4
France	6.6	Italy	6.4
Malaysia	6.6	Mexico	6.4
Russian Federation	6.6	Brazil	6.3
Spain	6.6	Sudan	6.2

Place of Origin	Speaking	Place of Origin	Speaking
Hong Kong	6.1	Vietnam	5.8
Indonesia	6.1	Korea, Republic of	5.7
Jordan	6.1	Iraq	5.6
Nepal	6.1	Kuwait	5.6
Pakistan	6.1	Libya	5.6
Bangladesh	6	Saudi Arabia	5.6
Taiwan	6	Uzbekistan	5.6
India	5.9	Japan	5.5
Thailand	5.9	Qatar	5.5
Kazakhstan	5.8	Turkey	5.5
Oman	5.8	China(People's Republic of)	5.4
Syrian Arab Republic	5.8	United Arab Emirates	5.3

结论 在 IELTS 考生最多的 40 个国家或地区中，大陆考生的口语成绩平均值（mean band score）仅高于 United Arab Emirates（阿联酋），而低于其他全部亚、非、欧国家，也包括不少文化被普遍认为比中国文化更加"内向"的国家。很显然，导致这种分数差距的根本原因并不是缺少肢体语言，也不是缺乏目光交流，而只能是实打实的语言能力问题。咱们也许真的应该反思一下：我们是不是一直都把错了 IELTS 口语的脉？

考官是谁

在中国的互联网上，雅思考官往往会被描述成黑洞般的暗物质。"印度大妈"、"光头杀手"、"灭绝师太"、"5 分中年男"、"扔身份证的不耐烦 MM"，"像 Nikita 里面一个 killer 的冷面 SG"，"热情、然并卵的笑面虎老爷爷"、"拒绝 eye contact 的杀马特"，"酷似 Breaking Bad 里 Mr. White 的眼镜蜀黍"……国内考生中关于口语考官的种种轶闻已经足以写成一本精彩的武侠小说（a swordplay and chivalry novel）了。但这些故事的盛传，恰恰证明了多数考官其实都是普通人。

事实上，不仅是雅思口试，世界上截至目前为止的任何一种口试（包括求职时要做的 interview）都难以实现绝对的标准化，IELTS 也确实难以排除存在评分不负责任的 examiners，但口语考官们总体来说是敬业的。Pat 自己在国内从事雅思培训期间接触到了十几位现任和前任的 IELTS 口语 examiners，我可以非常肯定地说他们/她们无一例外都是"正常"人。而且相对于英美社会的整体情况而言，客观地说这些考官的平均文化素质还是不错的，如果连这些人您看了都觉着"不顺眼"，那么真等到在国外长期学习、生活您恐怕就得"大跌眼镜"了。

而且在评分能力方面，他们/她们全都体现出了下面的 5 个共同点：

❶ They are native English speakers.

这确保了考官们能够使用并且充分理解在英美被大家普遍接受的英文，但同时这也意味着他们/她们也许无法理解"罕见"的英文。

❶ They at least have an undergraduate degree.

您肯定知道 degree 和 diploma 的区别，其实口语考官们的整体教育背景在英美社会中是不算低的，但脸长成什么样那是人家的自由……

❶ They have Teaching English as a Foreign Language （TEFL） qualifications.

这点说明口语考官们是把从事语言相关工作当成自己 career path 职业规划的一个重要部分，所以大多数考官其实并不像传说中的"口语杀手"们打分那么"潇傻"。

❶ They need to get re-certified every two years.

考官资质每两年都是需要再次重新认证的，除非彻底不想干了，否则一般没必要让自己的打分屡次被 remark 推翻。

❶ They have at least three years of English teaching experience.

三年英语教学经验也不算很短了。这一条事实上确保了多数考官对孩子们的

"症结"还是能适当有所体谅的，但这同时也往往意味着考官对常见的技巧其实玩儿得比你都熟。

结论 IELTS speaking 的本质就是和你的考官用英语进行一次尽可能充分的交流。对口语考官的过度恐惧或者过度谄媚（butter up the examiner）都是没有必要的，你只需要像尊重其他人一样去尊重考官就够了，考官注意力的真正焦点其实是你的语言。

怎样使用本书收效最大

正是基于以上这些原因，在创作本书的全过程里，Pat 始终希望能够把在我身边的英语母语者们每天正使用着的真实口语和他们/她们的实际生活状态介绍给中国的同学们。坦白地说，写这样一本书并不轻松，因为在评析每个 IELTS 话题时我其实都是在不自量力地扮演着"文化传播者"的角色。

但让我感到欣慰的，除了中国考生朋友们越洋寄来的 thank-you notes 之外，还有下面这个令人振奋的事实：

《剑 10》出版之前已经开始在中国大陆发行的《十天口语》上一版里 Pat 着力推荐的 cycle to work, a variety of, is supposed to, tend to, regularly, preserve, natural habitat, layout, membership, innovative, economical, harsh, precious, appealing, give priority to...等等实用表达均在《剑 10》文本里密集地现身，这强有力地证明了《十天口语》对剑桥官方所偏爱的口语风格的把握是准确的并带有一定前瞻性的。That's the best compliment a test-prep book author can possibly get, right?

对于备考时间比较充裕的同学，Pat 希望您能够经常翻阅您手中的这本书。请确保在这里回行我可以肯定地说本书里的每句话都是自己用心写的，值得您花时间细读，看这样的书不会浪费您宝贵的时间。即使只是每次浏览三、五分钟，您也能获取一些此时此刻正在英语国家被人们真实使用着的词句。出国之后您就会明白：真实的英文口语其实是简洁有效的，反而比用来"唬人"的英语好学。跟 native speakers 卖弄"大词"只能像跟一个思想传统的人炫耀你多么熟悉 Fifty Shades of Grey 一样不靠谱。

对于考试已经迫在眉睫但还没开始准备的同学来说（Pat 深知这样心理素质"过好"的同学虽然正在减少，但却永远不会彻底消失），请您立刻停止拖延战术，登录 blog. sina. com. cn/ieltsguru 打印出本月口语预测题，然后按照下面的顺序选读本书：Day1（esp. Question 3）→ Day 2（通读）→Day 4（第一节）→ Day 6（至少结合音频把单词发音的那部分练一练）→Day 8 & Day 10（不要背答案，但是应该熟悉高分答案的语言风格）→ Day 9（熟悉高分答案的语言风格）→ 附录 A → 本书附赠的《IELTS 口语高频词汇和短语速查手册》里标星号的词汇和短语。

结论　充分了解每个月的出题动向是必要的，同时我们必须注意积累地道的英文表达和对当代英美文化的适当了解。只有这样，您才能真实地提高自己的英语口头表达能力。也只有这样，您才算是真正把住了 IELTS 口语的"脉"。

☆ **致谢**

本书参与协助编写工作的人员有：朱燕麟、朱卡亚、朱卫红、张静、周晖、李梅、高路、董明明、魏林、王玲、李晨光、王向雨、董倩、谢冰、高峰、袁诗宁、刘盈、毛润卿、张哲、阎密、范喻欣、刘瑾辉、陈蕲春、尹东临、郭东岚、叶彤彤、陈宏、尚彬、孔梦洋、孟若冰、冉鹏飞、苏惠心、杨毅、张红燕、王军、黄洋、李纲、刘菲、陈洁、闫文健、于辉、张洪霞、汪洋、陈江升、沈刚、李玉亚、李杰、谷明义、毕骁、董月、齐函芝、苑茜、杨欣、衡珊、陈雷、陆云、孟建章、王玉丰、王硕、董登阁、邱天、郎巍、李万博、徐彤英、刘振新、韩晚亭、谷茂云、万礼真、邱茂林、杨雅琳、冉继华。

My deepest appreciation goes to my parents and my sister Meg, without whom I wouldn't possibly have embarked upon this " cottage industry". Your loving and unwavering support means everything to me.

Special kudos goes to Ms Meng Yu-qin，the editor of this book，whose intelligence and resourcefulness make a real difference in the creation of this book.

Most of all，I wish to dedicate this book to the students who made up my classes in the Global IELTS Institute（Beijing）. Their example has continually spurred me to keep working on this book. I hope it will be a nice reminder of our delightful time together.

小嵬

2016 年 1 月于新泽西

英文自序

Preface

The speaking section is often the most daunting part of the IELTS Test. Ironically, many IELTS candidates perform poorly in the speaking section because they over-prepare for it. The "error-free" templates and picture-perfect "model answers" committed to memory make the entire preparation process a strategic failure — few people would try to learn the piano if they were only interested in playing the Liszt Sonata in B minor, right?

To achieve a high score in the speaking section of the IELTS Test, you must understand what the examiner realistically wants. Personal preferences vary when it comes to words, structures and concepts, but all examiners value spontaneity. It is fairly easy for them to spot thoughtless spouting of prepared answers, because there are few or no natural pauses in answers given by rote. In addition, candidates tend to hesitate noticeably when the examiner asks for further elaboration on a prepared response. This dramatic hesitation seriously erodes the candidate's credibility in proving English proficiency, which often results in score penalties.

Unlike many other preparation materials available for the speaking section of the IELTS Test, this book is not designed to be memorized by rote; rather, it is intended to develop the readers' spontaneous English conversation skills. Accordingly, all chapters are structured around subjects that are not only IELTS-oriented, but also current and thought-provoking. The perspective offered on each subject challenges you to think beyond its common treatment. Each subject is also presented with a one-step-beyond component, serving as a springboard for addressing related topics at a more sophisticated level.

It is true that speaking a second language is partly a talent, but it is mostly a skill. It will, like any other skill, improve with practical guidance and continued practice. I encourage you to actively use the English and test-taking techniques you will learn from this book. That will not only help you retain what you learn but also make you a more confident and competent IELTS candidate.

Pat,

January, 2016

Contents
目　录

剑 10 时代致读者

英文自序

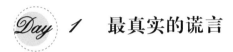

最真实的谎言

长期困扰中国口语考生的 10 个问题 / 2

Pat's Answers / 3

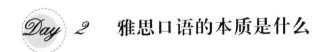

雅思口语的本质是什么

Part 1 的实质是什么？/ 19

Part 2 的实质是什么？/ 20

Part 3 的实质是什么？/ 22

Part 1 的话题有范围吗？/ 23

Part 1 的提问方式有规律吗？/ 24

Part 1 考什么？/ 24

近期亚太区 Part 1 真题库 / 24

Part 2 的答案还可以合理、合法地合并 / 39

Part 3 考什么？/ 40

Part 3 出题有规律么？/ 42

超短线 / 43

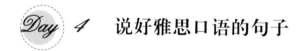

Day *3*　雅思口语的词

雅思口语中最常用的"小词" / 49

25 个更"痞"的雅思口试常用词（高分内容）/ 54

《那些花儿》/ 57

冰天雪地裸求都不给的 30 个"冻人"名词 / 63

曾让一个考官面部肌肉不停抽搐的动词短语 / 65

你早就认识却从不会想到去用的加分形容词和副词 / 68

对分数有野心的人应该熟记的关键反义词 / 73

Part 2 的 100 个核心词汇（7 分内容）/ 74

超短线 / 77

Day *4*　说好雅思口语的句子

怎样说出不"难"的长句？/ 81

Pat 总结出的地道口语里最常用的连接词 / 82

可以用来攒人品的词组和句型 / 86

雅思口语考试中到底有没有很特殊的句子？/ 89

超短线 / 90

Day *5*　雅思口语的段

怎样才能说出长段落？/ 93

Part 2 结构的 4 种选择 / 98

把段落说长的更多实用技巧 / 100

超短线 / 100

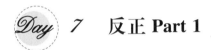

Day 6　练出 decent 的发音

练好句子的发音 / 106

超短线 / 110

Day 7　反正 Part 1

口语 Part 1 话题库索引 / 112

Pat 的 Part 1 完整素材库（时间太紧的读者只要结合我在博客里贴出的本月预测题准
　　备就好了）/ 113

超短线 / 156

Day 8　剑 10 时代的 Part 2 真题全集

IELTS 口语 Part 2 真题库全集索引 / 158

口语 Part 2 话题指南 / 159

考官给你的 Part 2 一分钟思考时间里你应该做的事 / 161

Part 2 要说多难? / 161

A 建筑与城市 / 166

B 组织与个人 / 192

C 人与自然 / 221

D 边玩边学 / 242

E 物质诱惑 / 284

F 曾经沧海 / 312

超短线 / 334

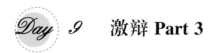

Day 9　激辩 Part 3

准备 Part 3 应该做什么？/ 337

Part 3 的高分答案长什么样 / 337

有效提高 Part 3 实力的 6 步 / 340

Pat 归纳的 290 个 Part 3 拿分词汇（7 分词汇）/ 345

超短线 / 359

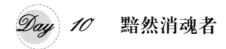

Day 10　黯然消魂者

（上）雅思口语卡片 10 大弱智话题 / 361

（下）雅思口语 10 大消魂卡片 / 367

超短线 / 385

附录

Appendix A　雅思口语考试十大经典错误排行榜 / 394

Appendix B　英语老话儿的新生 / 396

Appendix C　紧张的 120 个小时 / 399

Pat回北京最爱做的事就是下馆子，除了因为自己是真正的吃货（I'm a foodie.）之外，也因为在美国和加拿大的餐馆里实在没什么好吃的菜，生活久了特别深刻的体会就是享受肺、折磨胃。而英国菜嘛……更是出了名儿的不"给力"，除了 fish 'n' chips。

有次在北京的一家餐馆里，Pat突然发现英文菜单上很彪悍地写着"stir fly"（炒苍蝇）。我完全被老板的勇气震撼了，心想正常人胆儿再大也不至于连苍蝇都敢吃，而且居然还是炒着吃，《舌尖上的中国》里绝对没介绍过这种怪异的做法（This bizarre "recipe" was absolutely not featured in A Bite of China.），仔细研究之后才发现原来应该是 stir–fried（炒的）。

还有一次，Pat看到一家北京餐馆的菜单上对"干煸四季豆"这道菜的英文描述竟然是："This website is temporarily closed. Please check back later."这显然是因为餐馆老板在网上搜索这个菜的英文名称，但是网站却没有正常运行而得到的不是答案的答案，真正的 lost in translation。

Pat还见到过"四喜丸子"被叫做 four happy meatballs（四个快乐的肉球儿），"鸡肉"被翻译成 muscle，《一代宗师》里的"念念不忘"被译成 read, read and don't forget，而咱们中国的经典古语"知之为知之，不知为不知，是知也"竟被翻译成："Know is know. No know is no know. That's know."

本书就献给这些可爱的 glitches。

No sweat.

Day 1

 最真实的谎言
True Lies

Using lies as alibis
Is the same game
Played in different ways
It's just a waste of time
Made for gullible minds

长期困扰中国口语考生的 10 个问题

○ 口语考试是不是必须回答"积极"的答案？口试是不是一定要回答"新颖"的答案？

○ 口语考官打分到底依据什么？

○ 口语用词是越"奇葩"越拿分吗？

○ 口语要准备模板吗？

○ 发音在口语评分中到底有多重要？

○ 如何选择口语考点？

○ 看口语机经有用吗？

○ 口语考试要不要"套磁"？

○ 考官问的问题压根儿就没有听懂怎么办？

○ IELTS 口语考时事么？

Bonus Question

○ 怎样客观看待口试的 Predictions？

Pat's Answers

1　口语考试是不是只能回答"积极"的答案？口试是不是一定要回答"新颖"的答案？ (***Do I have to sound positive or optimistic? Do I have to give the examiner completely original or creative answers?***)

国内考生甚至一些培训教师普遍相信下面的错误观点：

A 不能给考官"I don't like..." "Actually, I don't know much about..." "Well, I disagree..." 这类否定语气的答案。

B 必须要给出非常有创意（original）、与众不同（unique）、引人入胜（engaging）的答案才能拿高分。

我们来看看一位真实的口语考官是怎样理解这个问题的（Clark: 29）：One important point to emphasize（强调）here is that the marking system does **NOT** include references to the following points:

* Interesting content
* Amusing or funny answers
* Body language
* The truth
* Appearance or dress

更加发人深思（thought-provoking）的是，这位考官同时还给出了自己评分的实例（Ibid，29）："I interviewed a young lady who was arrogant（傲慢的）, impolite, impatient and quite rude — but I awarded this lady a score of 8 only because her spoken English matched the descriptions in the marking system for band score 8."

像这样一个已经集所有讨厌于一身（obnoxious, intolerable）而且也并没有为了讨好考官而展示"事业线"（cleavage）的女士，因为英语说得并没有明显问题，还是从考官那里拿走了口语8分的高分。在真实考官的眼里，IELTS口试并不是"主要看气质"（It's not about whether the examiner finds the candidate attractive or not.）。

而我在环球雅思北京总校的同事，前任口语考官 Martin Renner 就更加直白地说："It's not what you say. It's how you say it."

这两位货真价实的考官的肺腑之言完全符合 Pat 自己对学生口语成绩的长期跟踪调查：口语的分数，只看你的英语水平和答案是否具体、充实，和所谓的"别出心裁"或者是否"积极"完全没有关系。说得更直接一点：考官坐到口试的小房间里的任务不是测智商，也不是搞"心理分析"，剑桥交给他/她的唯一任务是要确定考生的英语口语水平到底怎样。我们需要做好的，只是力争去说正确的流利的英文，但是实在没必要给自己设计更多的条条框框了（hard and fast rules）。

2 口语考官打分到底依据什么？（*How should I interpret the rating system?*）

大家都知道口语有四项评分标准，但是那个标准很学术，一般考生难以望其项背。通过下面这个表格，我们可以总结出一个更好理解的"草根版"口语评分标准。

Pat 总结的"草根版"雅思口试评分标准

	5 分	6 分	7 分
Fluency & Coherence 流利度和连贯度	句子中经常出现不必要的停顿，而且缺乏口语的衔接，还有些同学过度使用"er…""ah…"这些 fillers，甚至中间出现长时间没话说"干在那儿"（get put on the spot）的尴尬情况。而 5 分得主的另一个极端是超级流畅，说话完全没有轻重缓急，甚至已经听不出来喘气，看不到眨眼，同时答案里却充斥着像 moreover 这样在真实的英美生活里绝没有人说的"奥特曼"连接词，这种考生在说中文时都没有的灵异现象（supernatural phenomenon）只能被考官解读为是在背书	能说出完整的句子，但是每隔几句一定会有不连贯的地方。有可能出现较长时间的令人尴尬的停顿，但是次数不多	语速比较自然，有合理的衔接，只在很少的地方由于思考答案出现了不必要的停顿或者内容跳跃

（续表）

	5分	6分	7分
Grammar 语法	不能准确区分单词是否要加 ed 或者 s，甚至出现 he/she 不分的情况	每隔几句都有少量的时态或者单复数错误	基础语法错误已经基本消除，但仍存在一些高端的语法错误（比如少数介词或者连词使用不准确）
Pronunciation 发音 （本书 Day 6 将详解口语考试对发音的要求）	考官可以听懂你的内容，但某些地方他/她需要仔细分辨才能听懂，考官不会享受和你的对话，只希望考试时间快点过去	考官能比较容易地听懂你的内容，但仍然有些单词发音明显是错误的，语调上不是很自然	发音自然，但还是偶尔出现发音错误，考官已经开始享受和你的交谈过程
Vocabulary 词汇量	使用小学或初一单词过多，这是其中一种可能。 但对国内考生而言还有另一种更常见的可能，就是字典英语痕迹明显，使用大量在国外生活里从来不用的超级大词，Pat 管这叫作"词汇恐怖主义"（verbal terrorism）	用词已经比较准确，在适当的时候可以用出来一些有难度的词汇，但是遗憾的是，这些难词大约有 1/3 是被错误使用的	可以分辨在哪些地方应该用小词，哪些地方可以用大一点的词汇，偶尔有用词不当，但是不影响整体意思的表达

下面我们用《剑 10》Test 1 里面的一道题来说明低分与高分口语答案的区别：

Do you think your weekends are long enough? [Why / Why not ?]

典型的 5 分答案：

They're too short. I get up late on Saturday and Sunday. I need more time to have fun.

典型的 6 分答案：

No. My weekends are not long enough for me to do all the things I like, such as shopping and playing sports. And I still feel tired on Monday when I go back to school.

典型的 7 分答案：

Like most people, I have two-day weekends. But I have too much stuff to do at weekends — cleaning, doing the laundry, working out at the gym, hanging out with friends ... I just don't have enough time for them. Three-day weekends would be better.

再来看《剑 10》Test 2 的例题：

Do you think all children should learn to play a musical instrument？[Why？/ Why not？]

典型的 5 分答案：

All children should learn to play a musical instrument because they can enjoy music when they play it.

典型的 6 分答案：

I think they should. Studying is very stressful. Playing a musical instrument helps children relax. It's an important skill all children should have.

典型的 7 分答案：

Yes, they should because playing a musical instrument can reduce stress. It can also help children improve their memory and concentration. Playing a musical instrument, like the piano or a guitar, is also a good way for them to express themselves through music.

下面我们还用《剑 9》Test 2 里面的一道题来说明：

Do you enjoy looking for gifts for people? [Why / Why not?]

典型的 5 分答案：

Sure, because when I look for gifts, I want to show people I love them very much.

典型的 6 分答案：

Yes. I have many friends and I need to celebrate their birthday or other happy events. Finding the perfect gifts for them is exciting.

典型的 7 分答案：

Yes, I do because selecting the right gifts can be fun and enjoyable. *I always try to consider my friends'* interests and personality *when I select gifts for them. I* can't afford *expensive gifts，but I believe it's the thought that counts.*

再来比较一下《剑9》Test 3 里面不同分数段的答案：

Do you sometimes prefer to send a text message instead of telephoning? [Why?/ Why not ?]

典型的 5 分答案：

Sometimes，when I don't know a person very well, I send him a message first to show respect.

典型的 6 分答案：

I send more messages than I call people. They don't make people annoyed，and I spend little money sending text messages.

典型的 7 分答案：

Yes. I prefer to text when the message I want to send isn't an urgent one, *because that allows the receiver more time to think about how to respond. Texting is also much* cheaper *than calling.*

我们再以《剑8》Test 4 里的一道题为例：

Do you enjoy the advertisements on television?

典型的 5 分答案：

No，I don't. I think they are very boring.

典型的 6 分答案：

I don't like them. Advertisements on television just waste my time. They suddenly stop interesting TV shows and the things they try to sell are useless.

典型的 7 分答案：

I would say I enjoy some of them because they are creative and entertaining. But it's true most ads just spoil the fun of watching TV. Some ads are even misleading.

我们继续通过《剑 8》Test 1 的考题来体会低档、中档与高档分数之间的差异：

Do you think it would be a good idea for schools to ask students their opinions about lessons ?

典型的 5 分答案：

I think it's a good idea. That can make lessons more interesting. So the students will like their school much more.

典型的 6 分答案：

It sounds like a good idea. We can give the teachers our opinions and help them improve their lessons. This method will make us feel we are part of our school, too.

典型的 7 分答案：

It may be a good idea if the process is well managed. Students can get their opinions heard. Then the school will know how to meet their needs. On the other hand, some students' comments may be unfair, which may hurt their teachers' feelings.

我们还可以通过这道《剑 7》Test 2 的考题看看口语 7 分到底是怎样炼成的：

Do you like making other people laugh?

典型的 5 分答案：

Yes I do. I'm a funny person and I always tell my friends jokes.

典型的 6 分答案：

No, not really. I'm a serious person most of the time. Even when I tell some jokes, it seems other people don't find my jokes funny.

典型的 7 分答案：

Sure. I know lots of jokes and really enjoy sharing them with friends of mine. It seems like I just have a good sense of humor. I believe humor helps us reduce stress.

下面再用一个每场考试 Part 1 都会有人被问到的常考问题实例来说明一下 5 → 6 → 7 的飞跃（leap）：

What's your favourite subject at school?

典型的 5 分答案：

It's English because English is very useful and interesting.

典型的 6 分答案：

It's maths because maths makes us smart and maths is very useful for learning some other subjects such as chemistry.

典型的 7 分答案：

Humm, I guess it's PE, which stands for physical education. Sometimes we call it the gym class. PE not just helps us keep fit and stay healthy, it gets us more focused on academic subjects as well.

再看一个 5 → 6 → 7 的三级跳（hop, skip, jump）：

What's your favourite season?

典型的 5 分答案：

I like winter best. I enjoy the snow in winter. It's so beautiful.

典型的 6 分答案：

It's spring because everything is fresh in spring. Sometimes we have light rain. Spring is gentle and comfortable.

典型的 7 分答案：

Well, I would say… summer. Actually, the summer in Beijing is really hot… scorching! But in summer, my friends and I have lots of free time so we can hang out together in places like malls or Starbucks. And the coolest thing about summer is we can just wear casual clothes like tees and shorts…

我们的结论

☆ 5 分是挣扎着说出来的（或者另一个极端是无敌流利地"喷"出来的），和考官的交流要不然就是基本无效，要不然就是特生硬

☆ 6 分是思考着说出来的，和考官的交流开始有效，但是并不充分而且不很流利

☆ 7 分是快速思考之后较为连贯地说出来的，但中间会有呼吸和短暂思考所需要的自然停顿。和考官的交流比较充分，而且已经有一定的层次感，但是允许出现不会导致严重误解的语法、用词或发音错误

3 口语用词是越"奇葩"越拿分吗？（*Is the ability to use "unusual" or "weird" words an asset?*）

这绝对是中国孩子考 IELTS 口语的最大误区之一。

很多上过外教口语班的同学问我为什么外教讲雅思话题的用词总是比他们/她们自己的用词更浅显、更易懂，其实这种现象并不仅仅限于英语教学课堂。出国之后一下飞机您立马就会发现：在国外生活里真的没有人整天把"大词"挂在嘴上，因为那样去进行交流会很奇怪（That would be very odd.）。有些国内朋友在 21 世纪的第二个十年里所说的英文仍然带有明显的"文革英语"的痕迹，那些被频频用错地方的大词和畸形长句（convoluted sentences）难逃其咎。

请看下面这个由剑桥考官给出的真实口语 7 分实战案例：

What's your favourite colour?

Well, to be honest, I don't really have an actual favourite colour but I guess if I were buying clothes, then I'd usually go for something like blue or grey — kind of dull colours, nothing too bright.

也许您觉得这样的用词 "不配" 拿7，但其实这个考生的答案除了开始处的 Well, to be honest…还显得有点 "做作" 之外，风格已经接近于多数 native speakers 的真实交流风格了，而且内容也还算充实，所以得 7 并不过分。

这种英语风格同样也是 Pat 自己在上大学的时候天天都能听到的真实海外大学英语：

Sample
Rachel & Kyle

Rachel: *Kyle，are you ready for the <u>big exam</u> <u>coming up</u> this Friday?*

Kyle: *No. <u>I'm nowhere near ready.</u> I really have no interest in biology.*

Rachel: *So you should start studying right now.*

Kyle: *I have an idea. The test is on Friday，so maybe on Thursday night you <u>could</u>*（其实像虚拟语气这样国内孩子们压根儿就不敢用的特殊语法现象在真实的英美口语里反倒是用得不少，而且上面的那个 7 分实例里同样也用了，详情请看 *Day* 4）*<u>come over</u> to my apartment and help me <u>cram</u>*（突击学习）.

Rachel: *It <u>wouldn't be</u> smart to try and <u>rush through</u> half a semester's information in <u>just</u> three hours. I'll help you with that，<u>anyway</u>.*

Kyle: *I'm busy every night this week. I've got a date tonight and tomorrow I'm playing basketball. <u>I'll just pull an all-nighter</u>*（熬夜学习），*I guess.*

Rachel: *I don't think studying all night is going to <u>do you any good</u> if you <u>fall asleep during</u> the test.*

Kyle: *Hmm，<u>I guess</u> you're right. I'll change my date to after the test <u>and then</u> I'll be free to study this week.*

同时，Pat 还希望您不要轻视由一些简单词汇组成的短语（phrases）。经常跟 "老外" 聊天的同学们一定已经发现了，有很多小短语在真实的英文口语里面异常活跃，比如下面几个例子在雅思口试当中都有机会用到：

I work out（=exercise to keep fit）in the gym for an hour every day.

I'm studying hard because I don't want to let my parents down（=disappoint sb.）.

I couldn't figure out（= understand or find the answer to）how to do it well.

We played games to liven up the party. (=to make the party more fun)

Steven Chow's (周星驰) comedies never fail to crack me up. (=make me laugh)

Reading helps me wind down (=relax).

These photos bring back good memories of my childhood.

⚠️ **WARNING**   但是，Pat 反对您在雅思口试里使用 wanna, ain't, gal, yucky 这些在真实国外日常生活里其实并不太常用的过于口语化的表达。通读完本书后，您的口语用词风格将会非常接近受过良好教育的以英语为母语人士的用词风格：浅易、自然、平实，但也并非"痞话连篇"。

4 口语要准备模板吗? (*Will templates work?*)

近期刚听过一个口语模板，实在太经典了，必须记录在这儿：

……如果考官问你的问题你答不出来，可以深情地跟考官委婉地说，"Hmm, that is a very good question. Let me think about it..." 然后眼珠转两圈儿（而且还明确规定必须是"两圈"），假装沉思之后猛然惊醒，对考官大声说，"Ah, Sir! I finally found a good answer to your question. But I'm not sure if I understood your question correctly… So, could you please say your question again?"

I was dumbfounded by it. 这已经都不是卖萌了，这是真萌。如果学生敢在考场里用出这样的模板，后果肯定要比韩梅梅回答 "I'm fine. Thank you. And you?" 更严重。请鼓起勇气自己说吧，其实你没那么差。不论是中文还是英文，进行口头交流时如果频频使用模板会让 native speakers 觉得呆板甚至怪诞。

5 发音在口语评分中到底有多重要? (*How important will my pronunciation be during the actual test?*)

早在 2008 年 8 月，剑桥对口语考试的发音部分就推出了评分细则。这个标准听起来很美，但在实际评分过程中实施起来却很难 (The examiners will have a hard time putting it to good use.)。想把发音这样不可能量化的内容去量化，最后只能变成画蛇添足 (like gilding the lily)。我强烈建议各位: 不要因为考试对发音有评分细则而过度焦虑。另一方面，努力提高自己的发音水平还是有必要的，而且对您出国后的日常生活也会有实质帮助。本书的 Day 6 为您提供了实用的发音训练，可以帮助你在很短的时间内练出至少不让考官讨厌的发音（但是要达到让考官主动喜欢您的纯正发音确实需要一个比较长的学习和实践过程）。

6 如何选择口语考点？（ *Where am I supposed to take the IELTS speaking test?* ）

关于考点，我们可以明确三件事：

A｜考题难度在全国的各考点没有任何差异。这听起来很绝对，但这么说的依据是 Pat 自己近十年来持续跟踪不同考点考题的实践。想特别提醒大家：全国所有考点在同一天的考题都是同步的。很多同学不理解这一点。其实如果好好看看网络上的当天考生回忆，您就会发现全国当天考题确实是同步的。

B｜考官给你的打分会受其他考生水平的影响。口语考试是主观性考试，这就决定了它的评分必然带有主观性。完全标准化的口语评分不仅雅思没有，世界上也根本就不存在。Pat 也确实听到不少水平一般的北京孩子去外地考试考到 6.5 或者 7 分的实例，所以如果从总体来看，我们应该承认北京、上海、广州等大城市竞争更激烈一些。

C｜但具体到某一个考生，还是存在着不确定性（uncertainty）的。我们不能说他/她去外地就一定能比北京的口语考分高。比如，有可能给你考试的那个考官天性（by nature）就是"刺儿头"（very cranky），或者也许你的考官说英语时带有较重的"外地"口音，再比如你为了去外地而长途旅行，导致考前没能休息好等等。这些细节的不确定因素永远无法完全排除（can't be ruled out）。

结论：总体上二三线城市口语打分的大环境确实要好一些，但还要看自己的行程安排是否方便，而且考官自己的个性（individuality）与性格特征（personality traits）其实比区域大环境更重要。

7 看口语机经有用吗？（ *How can I use online collections of past test questions wisely?* ）

口语机经是对过去考题的总结，挺好，但美中不足的（a fly in the ointment）就是题目数量惊人，对于非专业人士而言最好还是结合近期动态来准备效率更高。各位可以随时查看 Pat 的博客 blog. sina. com. cn/ieltsguru 上面公布的最新口语预测，帮助您节约宝贵的备考时间。

8 口语考试要不要"套磁"？（ *Am I supposed to butter up the examiner?* ）

To tao or not to tao，that is the question.

　　像这类"第二十二条军规"（*Catch 22*）的问题其实永远都会吵个没完。但这样来看这个问题你就能看得更清楚：套磁并不会明显加分，但是如果套不好却可能导致扣分，因为考官被套一点也不影响他/她用英语提出问题，可集中精力用英语套磁却会让你没有精力去好好回答问题。再说，即使考官真的对你的套磁感兴趣了，他/她撇开考试真跟你聊起来了你吃得消吗？（Are you really up to it?）

　　比如，近期有个考生听考官是美国口音，为了"拉近距离"她就说自己的"偶像"——罗玉凤——也住在美国。没想到该考官正好看过 *People* 对凤姐的深度报道，追问了一大堆相关问题，直到考试结束还问该考生凤姐是不是已经在美国找到她的 dream guy 了。我们应该尊重考官，但像这种被动情况就纯属全力套磁而被"逆袭"（lost the upper hand）的结果了。

9 　考官问的问题我这土人压根儿就没听懂怎么办？（*What can I possibly do if I can't fully understand a question?*）

　　IELTS 口语里的 Part 1 和 Part 3 都是问答题。在这两个部分里，如果遇到有问题没听懂，国内考生的通常做法是说，"I beg your pardon?"（在英美日常口语里人们多数时候其实会直接说 "Pardon?" 或者 "Pardon me?" 或者 "Sorry, could you please repeat that?"

　　这两种说法对于话题轻松的 Part 1 是可行的，但 Pat 深入研究后发现：如果考生在话题比较正式的 Part 3 里面遇到一个问题没听懂，50% 以上的情况其实是因为问题里面存在着生词，那么即使考官真的 nice 到给你再重复一遍问题，重复之后多半也还是听不懂含有生词的部分，而这次如果还是答不出却要被扣掉 fluency 评分项的分数了。

　　下面两个方法可以确保您在 Part 3 即使遇到含有生词的问题也至少不会被严重扣分：

　　◆ 如果您的考官态度比较客气，那么请跟他/她说，"Could you please rephrase（转述）the question?" 或者 "Sorry, could you please explain what you mean by…（你听不懂的部分）?" 如果他/她愿意换种说法再说一遍，那么你就应该可以顺利地躲开原题里的生词了。

　　◆ 如果对方的态度不温不火，或者你根本就看不清他/她的态度，你没有信心他/她会愿意替你转述，那么请直接告诉他/她，"Well, my best guess would be…" 这么说的好处是诚实，坦白承认你确实就是在猜，那么即使后面你所猜测的内容有一点跑题，至少这道题他/她还可以原谅你，集中精神认真地听他/她的下一个问题就好了。

10　IELTS 口语考时事么？（*Am I supposed to constantly update my knowledge about current events for the speaking test?*）

最近有不少考生发来邮件问 Pat 如果近期考试的话是否要准备一些关于中美关系紧张（the rising tensions between China and the US）、蔡英文当选第一位台湾女性领导人（Tsai Ing-wen became Taiwan's first female leader）、"踢屁屁"协定（TPP，The Trans-Pacific Partnership Agreement）、克强经济学（Likonomics）、"小扎"的清华座谈（Mark Zuckerberg's Q & A session at Tsinghua University）、明星涉毒（celebrities who got arrested for using drugs）、甚至范爷和王思聪等名人的"网络骂战"（celebrity spats on micro-blogging websites）、AH 婚礼（the fairy tale wedding of Huang Xiaoming and Angelababy）等的相关信息，而且，每次到逢年过节的时候大家在来信问候之余也少不了要问问关于该节日的英语会不会在口试里被"盘查"。

这种担心是正常的，毕竟 IELTS 口试属于面对面的交流，很容易让人联想到考官是否会"实时"出题。但令人遗憾（也许是令人庆幸）的是，每一次 IELTS 口试的考题均是由剑桥统一提供的，整体来说考官个人并没有"出题权"，而且 IELTS 口语不考查最新的时事知识。

《剑10》里给出的官方真题最真实地展现了雅思口试"只考社会趋势，但不考具体时事"的明确定位：

❋ Which kinds of jobs have the highest salaries in your country?

❋ How do large shopping malls and commercial centers affect small local businesses?

❋ How important do you think spending time together is for the relationships between parents and children?

❋ What types of things do young people in your country most want to own today?

这种"只管趋势，但不管时事"的严格定位在一定程度上导致了口试话题的空洞与乏味，但想想考官一天下来要把有限的那几十个问题轮番问这么多不同的人肯定比你更郁闷，你心里也就平衡了。更最重要的是：考查范围明确也就保证了 IELTS 口语考题的难度对参加考试的全体考生来说是公平的，不会因为考官突然"逆天"而导致各考生之间出现明显的考题难度不公正。

所以，IELTS 口试的首要任务是考查你的英文口语表达能力。关注时事新闻（follow

current events in the news） 本身是一种很好的习惯，但你也不必为了准备口试而特意去突击时事新闻"涨姿势"了。

✳　　✳　　✳

怎样正确看待口试的 **Predictions?**

对于备考时间很紧的考生们来说，不论英语水平高低，提前看看口语预测里的题目都是高效率的备战方法。而且，由于雅思口试是分阶段更换题库而不是每次考试都更换题库，因此口语预测的命中率还是挺高的。客观地说：准备口语预测不算是浪费生命。但有3点 Pat 要特别请您注意：（a）对于那些过于简单、你肯定能回答出来的预测题，可以跳过去不必准备，有重点地备考是明智而非偷懒；（b）话题接近的考题完全可以合并。虽然你不是考官，但考官也不是你，考官就是一般人而不是 mind reader。当然，合并话题时必须自然，过于牵强那不叫合并，而叫无怨无悔地跑题；（c）Pat 坚决鼓励您把自己原创的想法加到预测题的答案里去，即使有点幼稚也比彻底放弃自我就地卧倒要可贵。至于如何扩展思路，您学完 Day 8 便知。

Okay，let's get the show on the road.

Day 2

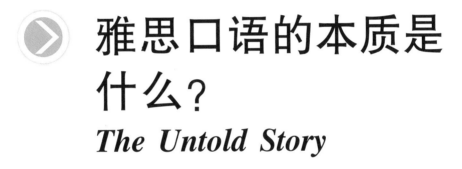

雅思口语的本质是
什么？
The Untold Story

Pat's Guide
To The IELTS Speaking Test

When I look into your big blue eyes,
I start to quiver and shake
Talk to me, talk to me,
All I want is just a nice little conversation

www.teachertube.com

　　对于从来没有近距离接触过外国人的那部分中国孩子,第一次进考场和考官面对面很可能会有"坐电椅"的感觉。经常点击上面这个网站上的 interviews（在页面上方的 search 栏里填入 interview 即可）,能让你更了解地道英语的交谈风格和"LW"们说话时独特的面部表情,帮助你从战略上藐视敌人。

▶ *We take the test very seriously, but we'll take a laid-back approach to it.*

Part 1 的实质是什么？

关键词：chat

　　雅思口语第一部分用剑桥的官方定义来说，是"关于你的背景、爱好、兴趣和习惯的基础问题"。但这听起来也太虚伪了吧？用普通人的话来讲，Part 1（俗称"趴1"或者"趴忘"）的本质就是一个 chat，跟考官聊聊你自己的基本情况。从答案长度上来讲，每道题平均能回答 3 句话左右就相当不错了。当然，如果确实遇到了准备充分的题目，您也不必"嘴下留情"，尽管发挥好了，只要能确保流利就成。

　　一般来说在国外聊天儿的时候人们是比较随意的（laid-back）。既然已经铁了心要去考官们的国家，那你就得按照他们的习惯来了。如果 Part 1 说得就跟背书（regurgitation）似的，人家就立刻会怀疑你跟他/她聊的诚意。因此，在 Part 1 里，请放松您的心态，跟 examiner 好好地聊一次吧！

　　而且，Part 1 的考题也是口试三个部分里最"欢乐"的一个部分，因为它最接近考生自己的生活。下面都是《剑10》给出的 Part 1 考题：

◆ How do you usually spend your weekends? [Why?]

◆ Which is your favourite part of the weekend? [Why?]

◆ Do you think your weekends are long enough? [Why / Why not?]

◆ How important do you think it is to have free time at the weekends? [Why?]

◆ What types of music do you like to listen to? [Why?]

◆ At what times of day do you like to listen to music? [Why?]

◆ Did you learn to play a musical instrument when you were a child? [Why / Why not?]

◆ Do you think all children should learn to play a musical instrument? [Why / Why not?]

◆ Do you enjoy travelling? [Why / Why not?]

◆ Have you done much travelling? [Why / Why not?]

◆ Do you think it's better to travel alone or with other people? [Why?]

◆ Where would you like to travel in the future? [Why?]

◆ Did you go to secondary / high school near to where you lived? [Why / Why not?]

◆ What did you like about your secondary / high school? [Why]

◆ Tell me about anything you didn't like at your school.

◆ How do you think your school could be improved? [Why / Why not?]

Part 2 的实质是什么？

关键词: description

对于 Part 2 (俗称 "趴 2" 或者 "趴吐")，剑桥的官方定义是 "In Part 2, the examiner gives you a topic card. You have one minute to prepare and make notes. Then you'll be required to talk about the topic for one to two minutes."

但现在在全球很多考点，考官其实都已经不再是发一个 card 了，而是发一张大纸，上面在一个很小的角落里印着一个 topic 和几点提示。

Part 2 的本质是要你做一个 description (描述)。为了更好地理解什么是 "description"，您可以回想一下自己小时候上语文课的时候，老师向你描述一个事物时和老师平时说话有什么不同。

"描述" 与 "闲聊" 至少有下面三个不同：

☆ 描述时一定会有适当的思考和停顿 (pause)。

我们说过，Part 1 基本可以看成是 chat，但是有些考生在 Part 2 因为正好遇到可以调动自己准备过的答案 (a prepared answer)，就直接把答案无比流畅地背出来。这明显不符合正常人描述的习惯。

☆ 描述需要有一定的规划，需要有秩序。

"描述" 需要更加精确的语言。而且和 Part 1 与 Part 3 不同，Part 2 需要在同一个话题的不同方面之间做数次转换，所以对答案的秩序性要求更高一些。不过既然是口语，毕竟与写作的严谨度要求不同，所以也不用太呆板 (rigid)。

☆ 句式会有一些变化(variations)，但是并不会像 Part 1 的 chat 那么多样(diversified)。

这一点听起来可能不好理解，但其实您自己试着用母语描述一个话题，1~2 分钟你马上就会发现其中的奥秘：这 1~2 分钟的过程并不是互动（interaction），而只是你自己一个人的独白，不像 Part 1 那样有考官不断给你信息的反馈（feedback）和新的提问（follow-up questions），所以你就不必再为了回应新信息去不停地修改你的句式了。

比如下面这道题是《剑 10》Test 1 的 Part 2:

> Describe someone you know who does something well.
>
> You should say：
>> who this person is
>>
>> how you know this person
>>
>> what they do well
>
> and explain why you think this person is so good at doing this.

下面这个则是《剑 10》Test 2 的 Part 2:

> Describe a shop near where you live that you sometimes use.
>
> You should say：
>> what sorts of product or service it sells
>>
>> what the shop looks like
>>
>> where it is located
>
> and explain why you use this shop.

再比如下面几个卡片话题也都是近期常考的：

◆ Describe a house.

◆ Describe a restaurant.

◆ Describe a successful small business.

◆ Describe an important stage in your life.

◆ Describe a park.

◆ Describe a good place to relax（not your home）.

◆ Describe a foreign country you want to visit.

◆ Describe a famous singer.

◆ Describe a vehicle.

　　如果这些"邪门儿"的 topics 让您感到无所适从，没关系，我们将在后面的 Day 8 和 Day 10 对它们以及整个完整卡片真题库进行深入探寻。

Part 3 的实质是什么？

关键词: discussion

　　"趴 3/趴睡"的本质是一个 discussion（讨论）。多数时候 Part 3 的问题与 Part 2 所考卡片的话题有关，但有的题目也可能会离开（deviate from）卡片的话题。其实这部分和 Part 1 的深层区别就是更加"博爱"：Part 1 的多数题是关于"you / your life"，而 Part 3 的多数题目则是关于"people"，"society"或者"your country"，甚至"the world / global issues"。

既然是 discussion，那么 Part 3 在语言上就必然有下面三个特点：

☆ 会用到很多表示逻辑关系的连接词。不过您尽可以放心的是：本书已经为您总结出了雅思口语乃至海外日常口语里所需的全部常用连接词，详见 Day 4。

☆ 会要求考生的答案比 Part 1 和 Part 2 更正式一些，无论从用词还是从内容都会比口试前两部分更加 formal。

☆ The good news is there's no need for you to make it as formal as a job interview. 毕竟 Part 3 还是考口语水平而不是考写作能力，所以 Part 3 的答案也不必过难，而且 Part 3 考题与雅思作文题的难度相比还是有一定差距的。更具体的 Part 3 详情请见本书 Day 9。

　　比如《剑 10》Test 1 的 Part 2 卡片话题是 someone you know who does something well，相应的 Part 3 就出现了下列问题：

◆ What skills and abilities do people most want to have today? Why?

◆ Which skills should children learn at school?

◆ Which kinds of jobs have the highest salaries in your country?

◆ Some people say it would be better for society if everyone got the same salary. What do you think about that?

很显然，这些问题与 IELTS 写作里面的技能类（skills）话题有相似之处，但要简单一些。

再比如，《剑 10》Test 3 的 Part 2 卡片话题是 a child you know，相应的 Part 3 就出现了：

◆ How much time do children spend with their parents in your country?

◆ How important do you think spending time together is for the relationships between parents and children?

◆ Have relationships between parents and children changed in recent years?

◆ What are the most popular free-time activities with children today?

这些问题也明显与 IELTS 写作里关于教育的考题有相似之处，但难度比写作考题还是要低。

Part 1 的话题有范围吗？

Pat 认真总结了近九年里的全部口语 Part 1 话题。分析结果表明：不管是新题、旧题、半新半旧或者是半新不旧的题，都一定超不出下面的 20 个方面。其中颜色越亮的话题越放松（laid-back），颜色越暗的越"板"（stuffy）。希望大家对这个图示最好能在头脑里有个大致印象，这样你就将发现 Part 1 的具体问题虽然千变万化，但剑桥的总体出题规律却变得容易把握了。您还将在后面的 Day 7 看到更深入的 Part 1 话题分析。

The Part-1 Topic Areas				
Studies	Language	Food	Nature	Sports & Outdoor Activities
Work	Weather & Season	Media	Collection	Pets
Building	Hometown	Arts	Clothing	Festivals, Holidays & Parties
People	Reading & Writing	Colours	Travel & Transport	Shopping

Part 1 的提问方式有规律吗？

整整九年的考题跟踪下来，Pat 很想说其实雅思口语 Part 1 的提问形式是极度缺乏创意的，因为它永远只有两种形式：

① Yes / No 类题

下面一节的真题中使用斜体字的题目都是这种类型，这类问题全都可以用 Yes 或 No 来回答，然后展开。

② Wh- （What / Why / Which…） / How 类题

如此有限的提问形式，在一定程度上破坏了我们征服 Part 1 应该获得的成就感。It spoils our sense of fulfillment. ☺

Part 1 考什么？

每个月在亚太考区最新出现的新题，Pat 都会及时在自己的博客 blog. sina. com. cn/ ieltsguru 的口语预测中为大家及时公布。

下面的这些真题是近期亚太区的最新 Part 1 真题（对这些考题的详尽分析请看 Day 7）。

The Most Recent Part 1 Question Pool
近期亚太区 Part 1 真题库

（您还可以在 Pat 的博客blog. sina. com. cn/ieltsguru 上看到本月的最新口语预测）

The Start of the Test

Please switch off / turn off your mobile phone.

What's your full name? / Can you tell me your full name please?

Can I see your ID card please?

☞ ☆ What's your full name? / Can you tell me your full name please?

这是固定的题目，简单地回答 **My（full）name is**... 就很好。如果你还不放心，一定想要解释名和姓，大家都知道中文的姓名顺序和英文正好相反，所以最好别太具体地说你的 first name / last name 是什么，除非故意想在一开始就弄晕考官，而 surname 那个单词又是比较正式的。所以，如果你非要说姓字名谁，那就还是脚踏实地地说 **My family name is… and my given name is…** 吧。

☞ ☆ Can I see your ID card please?

这个也是固定问题，回答 **Here you are.** 或者 **Here you go.** 都成。

Hometown / Your House / Your flat / Housework

What do you like about your hometown?

What do you dislike about your hometown?

Do you think your hometown is good for young people?

What would you change about your city?

What types of public transport can be found in your hometown?

Do you do housework?

Do you live in a house or a flat?

Is there anything hanging on your bedroom walls?

☞ ☆ What would you change about your city?

这里的 would 表示只是你的希望，未必是能实现的。

☞ ☆ What types of public transport can be found in your hometown?

注意，很多同学爱说的 transportation 那个词其实是美国的说法，英国考官会用 transport。

☞ ☆ Do you live in a house or a flat?

flat 是英国人说的公寓，国内同学更熟悉的 apartment 其实是美式说法，如果你拥有公寓的产权（ownership）则可以称它为 condo。

☞ ☆ Do you do housework?

最常见家务的地道英文表达是：wash the dishes / do the dishes（洗碗），do the laundry（洗衣服，在英美极少有人 wash clothes by hand），take out the rubbish（倒垃圾，这是英式英语，而在美国则叫作 take out the trash），vacuum the floor（用吸尘器吸地板，在国内吸尘器都已经快成古董了，而英美的绝大多数家庭却都还在坚持使用），mop the floor（擦地板），clear the table after dinner（晚饭后收拾餐桌），water the plants（浇花，请注意这个固定短语里的 water 是动词），而且在英文里 spring cleaning（春季大扫除）也是常用的说法。

Your Studies / Your Work

Are you working or studying?

（对学生）What do you like about your studies?

What's your major? *Do you like it?*

Is there anything you don't like about it?

What did you do on your first day in this school / university?

（对已经工作的考生）What do you like / dislike about your job?

Which do you think are more important, art lessons or academic lessons?

☞ ☆ What did you do on your first day in this school / university?

国外学校的第一天经常被称为 Orientation Day，常见活动有 an orientation tour of the campus（其实也就是带着大家看看校园），a Welcome Meeting，a free lunch（但最近几年因为经济不行，有些学校已经赖掉了），在有些学校里还可以 meet the faculty and staff（和教职工见面）。

☞ ☆ Which do you think are more important, art lessons or academic lessons?

Pat's Answer: I think academic lessons, such as maths, language and science lessons, are more important than art lessons. Academic lessons teach students the skills that they'll need to find jobs. Although art activities are fun and enjoyable, and art lessons can help students develop art skills, like painting and drawing skills, it seems these skills won't really help students when they leave school and enter the job market.

Pat's Note:

（ⅰ）地道短语 fun and enjoyable 意思是 "有趣的而且令人愉快的"

（ⅱ）如果您认为艺术课可以鼓励学生们去创造性地思考，可以说 Art lessons can encourage students to think creatively.

（ⅲ）IELTS 口语并没有唯一正确的 "标准答案"，不管考官是白考官还是黑考官，只要你的答案英文地道就是好答案。

Hobbies & Habits

What do you usually do at weekends?

Do you think it's impolite to use mobile phones in public places?

Do you often do things in a hurry?

☞ ☆ What do you usually do at weekends?

注意英国考官说 "在周末" 会说 at weekends，而不说 on weekends。

☞ ☆ Do you think it's impolite to use mobile phones in public places?

Pat's Answer: Well, it's impolite to use mobile phones in a public place <u>like</u> a cinema, library or classroom where people are supposed to be quiet. But I guess it's kind of okay to use mobile phones in public places <u>like</u> shopping malls where it's always noisy anyway, <u>if</u> we don't mind others hearing our phone conversation. （您将会发现 conversation 不论在 IELTS 口试里还是在出国后都是一个很有用的名词）

☞ ☆ Do you often do things in a hurry?

Pat's Answer: I do. I'm not very good at making plans or managing my time, so I'm often in a hurry to get things done, which can be really stressful.

Pat's Note:

如果您觉得自己很少匆忙做事，那么不妨试试这些地道词汇和短语：No, I don't. I'm not a person who likes to leave things to the last minute. I like to plan ahead and start early, so I usually have plenty of time to get things done.

☞ ☆ Do you think sleep is important?

Pat's Answer: Sure. A good night's sleep makes people feel refreshed and energetic. Sleeping well also helps to reduce stress and boost the brain's efficiency. People who don't get enough sleep often find it difficult to concentrate.

Pat's Note:

（i）短语 feel refreshed and energetic 的意思是"感到焕然一新而且精力充沛的"，短语 boost efficiency 的意思是"提升效率"

（ii）find it difficult to do sth. 是英文口语里很常用的句型之一，意思是"感到做某事很困难"。例如，美剧《纸牌屋》（*House of Cards*）里的男主角 Kevin Spacey 就说过，"Sometimes I find it difficult to decide between two choices."

☞ ☆ Are cooking shows（or cookery shows）popular in your country?

Pat's Answer: They're very popular, especially with health-conscious people（健康意识很强的人们）and people who really enjoy preparing meals. Home-cooked food is much healthier than fast food. TV chefs（厨艺节目中的"大厨"们）teach the viewers a wide variety of healthy recipes and cooking techniques（做菜的技巧）. Food is always beautifully cooked on those shows, almost like an art form（简直就像是一种艺术形式）…

Pat's Thought: recipe 是一个很容易被国内同学们用错的词，甚至有些英汉词典也把它错误地译成了"菜谱"。其实在地道英文里专门讲做菜的书叫作 cookbook（在英国也有些人说 cookery book）。而 recipe 则是特指具体某一个菜的备料（prepare the ingredients）和具体制作的方法。另外值得一提的是 It's like an art form. 这个说法，如果您觉得在日常生活里某个人已经把一件事儿"都做到极致了"，就可以说：It's (almost) like an art

▲ 在英美广受欢迎的"电视食神"
之一 Jamie Oliver

form. 还有，厨艺节目里的"明星大厨"们（celebrity chefs，一定要注意：chef 的发音是/ʃef/ 而不是 /tʃef/ ✗，发音错就没有拿分儿效果了）提供给观众的做菜操作建议在地道英文里叫作 instructions。作为一个真正的吃货（a true foodie），Pat 对 cooking shows 的兴趣已经跟很多 housewives 有一拼了，但是真正到该做饭的时候还是妥妥地按自己的节奏。（I don't really follow TV chefs' instructions.）☺

☞ ☆ Why are gardens and parks an important part of cities?

Pat's Answer: They provide an oasis（提供了一片"绿洲"）from urban life. Gardens and parks are places where we can get away from the hustle and bustle（熙熙攘攘）of city life. They're peaceful and quiet, and the air in gardens and parks is always fresh.

☞ ☆ Do you think trees and forests are important to us?

Pat's Answer: They're extremely important. They produce oxygen（制造氧气）and tree leaves absorb（吸收）dirty air. They also provide shade（提供树荫）in summer. Forests are the main source of wood（是木材的主要来源）, which is an important building material. And of course, trees look beautiful and ornamental（很有装饰性的）in gardens and parks.

Pat's Thought: 这个答案给得比较长，因为关于树和森林可说的实在太多了，如果愿意甚至还可以再扯到 prevent soil erosion（防止土壤侵蚀）等环境问题上面，您选出其中的几个关键词自己说就好了。

在北京，玉渊潭公园每年都有樱花节，而温哥华（Vancouver）每年的樱花节（Cherry Blossom Festival）也同样会吸引大量的游客。每年秋天，在北京还有很多人去香山看秋天的红叶（view autumn foliage，注意：这个 view 是动词，而且 foliage 不能加 s）。而在加拿大东部和美国的 New England 等地区，每年秋天也同样会有大批的游客 go on fall foliage tours。可见是"爱 tree 之心，人皆有之"（The love for trees is universal.）。

Sports / Outdoor Activities

What sports are most popular in your country?

Do you like cycling?

Do you like swimming?

What games are popular in your country?

☞ ☆ Do you think it's important to play a sport?

注意：play a sport 是很地道的英文，不是"中式英语"。

☞ ☆ Do you like swimming?

Pat's Answer: I sure do. It's a great way to relax and helps me reduce stress and anxiety. Swimming is also good exercise and helps me keep fit.

Pat's Note:

(i) 地道短语 reduce stress and anxiety 的意思是"减少压力和焦虑"；

(ii) 地道英文里常说 Swimming is a good way to lose weight（游泳是减肥良方）. 如果您希望通过游泳练出像宁泽涛那样健美的体型，则可以说 Swimming is a great way to build up muscles.

☞ ☆ Where do you swim?

Pat's Answer: I often swim in our community swimming pool because it's pretty close to my home and is very clean and well maintained.

Pat's Note:

(i) 地道表达 is well maintained 的意思是"保养、维护得很好"；

(ii) 如果想说在湖里或者海里游泳可以"更加接近大自然"，地道英文里通常会用 get closer to nature 这个短语

［剑桥例句］Swimming in the sea helps me get closer to nature.

☞ ☆ Do you often play games?

英语国家的常见游戏：

tag（基本就是国内小伙伴们玩的"捉人"游戏），hopscotch（中文翻译成"跳房子"，其实是跳画在地上编有数字的方格），hide-and-seek（捉迷藏）和 I-spy-with-my-little-eye（这个游戏可是 Pat 小时候的户外活动最爱，但国内孩子似乎不太爱玩，请看 Day 8 的详细解释）。board games 在地道英语里是泛指各种棋类游戏，具体地说在英美很流行的有 chess（象棋），Monopoly（大富翁）和 Scrabble（Pat 自己小时候喜欢玩的一种拼字游戏，它对小朋友甚至成年人提高拼写能力都大有好处）等。card games（牌类游戏），spelling bee（拼字游

▲ 在英美的玩具店里，Scrabble 和 Monopoly 经常是邻居

戏）以及 math games。

另外还有两种 Pat 不清楚在中文里到底叫什么但是在英美特别常见，一种是 scooter，就是左边这种，riding a scooter 是 Pat 住的小区里面小朋友们的最爱活动之一，还有一种是 pogo stick，叫弹跳棍感觉很别扭，但总之就是下面右侧的这种东东了，小朋友们在上面跳（jumping on a pogo stick）总是很开心，但由于有一定的安全风险，在英美很多孩子玩的时候还会带上头盔（helmet）。

☞ ☆ What games are popular in China?

chess, mahjong, puzzles（拼图游戏）, Monopoly（大富翁游戏）, riddle games（猜谜语）, jumping rubber band（跳橡皮筋）, playing with marbles（玩弹子球）, kite-flying, Dota 2, Diablo Ⅲ（暗黑破坏神3，"大菠萝"3）, 2048, GTA 5（侠盗猎车手5）, Clash of Clans（部落战争）, League of Legends（英雄联盟）等等。

☞ ☆ Does the sky look more beautiful during the day or at night?

Pat's Answer: I would say the sky looks more beautiful at night，when it's dotted with（点缀着）sparkling stars. It's very peaceful, but lively too — because of the stars. They twinkle in the night sky.

Pat's Note: 形容词 sparkling 的意思是"闪烁的"，形容词 lively 的意思是"有活力的"。请一定注意：它的正确发音是/'laivli/ √，而不是/'livli/ ✗

Pat's Thought: 在英美，人们喜欢看星星的地点通常是 outdoor places with lots of open space and clean air。

The Media

What types of TV programme do you like watching?

Why do we need ads?

What types of film do you like best?

What are the differences between local newspapers and international newspapers?

☞ ☆ Why do we need ads?

最重要的原因肯定是 They give us information about new products. 而且很多广告的娱乐性也很强（entertaining），更不用说还可以在广告里面看到 superstars；而对于商家（businesses）来说，ads 则是 important marketing tools。

☞ ☆ What types of TV programme do you like watching?

 剑桥的惯例：在这类问题中剑桥考官通常会将 What types of / What kinds of 后面的名词使用单数形式，但注意听到时不要误以为考官只允许你说一种选择，详情请看 Day 7。

The Internet

How often do you use computers?

What are the differences between emails and letters?

☞ ☆ What are the differences between emails and letters?

在英美 letters 也经常被叫作 snail mail（蜗牛信），因为实在太慢了。

Reading & Writing

Do you like reading?

Do you think handwriting is still an important skill for young people?

☞ ☆ Do you think handwriting is still an important skill for young people?

Pat's Answer: Yes, I think so. We still often take notes, answer test questions or write birthday cards by hand. Good handwriting is easy to read, while poor handwriting can be really confusing and annoying.

Pat's Note:

confusing and annoying 是 "令人困惑而且让人心烦的"，如果要说 "书写仍然是一种重要的沟通技能" 那就是 Handwriting is still an important communication skill.

☞ ☆ Do you prefer to type things or to write things on paper?

打字的好处除了更快（faster），还可以编辑（edit）和剪贴（cut and paste things）。

Language and Numbers

Would you like to learn another foreign language in the future?

Why is it important for children to learn maths?

☞ ☆ Why is it important for children to learn maths?

Pat's Answer: That's because maths skills can help children better understand science and the world around them. Maths can also help them think in a more logical way.

Clothing

What kinds of clothing do you like wearing?

Do you often help your friends shop for clothing?

Food

How often do you eat out in restaurants?

When do you usually eat snacks?

Do you think children should learn how to cook?

Do you like fruit and vegetables?

☞ ☆ When do you usually eat snacks?

Pat's Answer: I usually eat snacks in the mid-afternoon, like 2-3 p. m. , because that makes me feel more energetic and less tired. Sometimes I also eat snacks after working out.

Pat's Note:

（ⅰ） 动词短语 work out 是 "健身" 的意思；

（ⅱ） 在英美最常见的零食有 cookies, crackers, pretzels, ice cream, popcorn, jelly beans, cheese sticks, chocolate bars 等等，中国同学们熟悉的 "MM 豆" 在英文里叫 M & M's （中间的 & 符号要读成 "and"）；

（ⅲ） 如果想说 "在两餐之间饿了的时候就吃零食"，英文说 I eat snacks when I feel hungry between meals. 而 "感觉压力山大的时候就吃零食"，在地道英文里则会说 I eat snacks when I feel stressed.

☞ ☆ Do you think children should learn how to cook?

"小盆友" 们学做饭的好处包括 It teaches them an important life skill and makes them more independent （更独立），而且还可以 keeps them away from junk food （让他们远离垃圾食品）。

☞ ☆ Do you like fruit and vegetables?

Pat's Answer: Yes, I like them a lot. They taste good and they're rich in vitamin C and fiber, so eating fruit and vegetables every day can improve my health.

Pat's Note: 短语 be rich in ... 是 "富含……" 的意思，vitamin C and fiber 是 "维生素 C 和纤维"，如果要形容水果 "多汁的"，请坚定地用 very juicy 来表达

People

Do you prefer to have elderly people or young people as your neighbours?

What do you usually do when you are with your friends?

☞ ☆ Do you prefer to have elderly people or young people as your neighbours?

年轻邻居的好处是 more sociable（更喜欢社交的），more open-minded（思想更开放的）并且 I find it easier to communicate with young neighbours 等；而老人做邻居的优点则可以强调 They tend to be quiet but helpful.

☞ ☆ In your country，where can you meet new people?

这里的 new people 指的就是你"新结识的人"，请看 Day 7 的详解。

Art

Do you think it's important for children to learn to play a musical instrument?

Do you like painting and drawing?

☞ ☆ Do you think it's important for children to learn to play a musical instrument?

这里的 a musical instrument 表示"乐器"，各种乐器的地道英文表达请看 Day 7 的 Topic 8。

Buildings

Do you often go to museums?

Do you think museums are important to young people?

☞ ☆ Do you think museums are important to young people?

Pat's Answer: Yes，I do. Museums can teach young people about history，art and science. Some museums are pretty entertaining（形容词：娱乐性很强的）too. They offer interactive activities（互动的活动），stories or even games as part of their exhibitions（名词：展览）. They can create great learning opportunities for young people.

Pat's Thought: 有些中国孩子出国之后天天在宿舍里宅着，每天接触到的英语还没有在国内准备雅思的时候多。Pat 认识的一个北京孩子在美国生活了两年，英语丝毫没见长进，反倒熟练掌握了两种国内的方言，"留洋"成了"留唐"。其实即使是性格实在内向不喜欢跟本地人进行语言交流的同学至少也应该多去 local sports centers，museums

和一些 cultural events，感受一下当地人真实的生活方式。否则当你离开的时候，可就真成了"挥一挥衣袖，不带走一片云彩"。

Weather & Seasons

What types of weather do you like best?

What is your favourite season?

Do you like the rain? Why?

☞ ☆ Do you like the rain? Why?

Pat's Answer: I like light rain because it makes me feel calm and relaxed. The sound of light rain drops（雨点儿）falling on the ground is very pleasant. Walking in light rain is pretty fun too. On the other hand, if the rain gets heavy, driving can be tough（困难的）and the traffic would be really bad. That would bother me a lot（让我很烦）.

Shopping

Do you like shopping?

Do you often shop online?

Collection

Why do some people like collecting things?

What do you like to collect?

☞ ☆ Why do some people like collecting things?

详解请看 Day 7 的 Topic 10。

Colours

Do any colours have special meanings in China?

Nature

Do any flowers have special meanings in your culture?

What's your favourite wild animal?

☞ ☆ What's your favourite wild animal?

除了 panda，koala，kangaroo 这些考官已经听得比人类都熟悉的动物外，moose（驼鹿），beaver（水獭）和 turtle（海龟）都是英语文化里人们相当喜爱的动物，而且这几个词最大的好处就是发音异常简单，考试时绝不会因为舌头"转筋"而说不出来。

Pets

Do you like pets?

Why do so many people keep pets?

☞ ☆ Why do so many people keep pets?

Pat's Answer: That's because pets can help their owners（宠物的主人）reduce stress or loneliness（减少压力或孤独感）. It seems people who have pets are happier and more active. Keeping pets is also a great way for children to learn about responsibility because they need to take care of their pets.

Pat's Thought: 人们"遛狗"叫 walk their dogs（注意：不是"走狗"），把东西扔出去让小狗捡回来的游戏叫作 play fetch with their dogs。

Travel

Do you like travelling?

Do you have a driver's license?

☞ ☆ Do you have a driver's license?

对于这种考题最好不要只用 Yes ／ No 一个词就把考官简单粗暴地顶回去，看在 1850 大洋的份上至少也要跟他／她多练几句口语，比如可以用在英美人所尽知的一句名言用来解释自己为什么要 "考本子"：Driving is not a right. It's a privilege（特许的权利）. 或者如果你觉得 privilege 这个词太难那就简单地说 Driving makes life easier for me. 也很好。

如果没有 driver's license 那也不要说自己一直都在无证驾驶，可以说 The traffic is always tied up so there's no point in getting a driver's license anyway. 喜欢玩儿深沉的还可以说家乡的司机们都严重缺乏责任感（There're a lot of reckless drivers out there.），或者就坦白地说开车有风险（very risky），会让自己很 "怕怕"（I'm afraid of getting hurt）也同样是合理、有效的答案。

Pollution

How can people control the pollution in your city?

What harm can noise do to our lives?

Festivals，Holidays & Parties

Do you like going to parties?

Do you think it's important for people to celebrate their birthdays?

Which birthday left you with the deepest impression?

Do you prefer to celebrate your birthday with your family members or your friends?

How do you spend holidays?

Do you think festivals are important?

What are the most popular gifts parents give their children in your country?

Part 2 的答案完全可以合理、合法地合并

仅从 2015 年 12 月 3 日至 2016 年 1 月 30 日短短两个月的时间内，在中国大陆累计出现的卡片题就超过了 60 个。现实地说，除非是有长期的备考时间，否则把 IELTS 口试卡片题库里面的每道题都准备得很熟练是不可能的（That would be out of the question.），所以才会有那么多孩子在准备 Part 2 的时候大呼"累觉不爱"。

恰当地"合并"卡片题答案的备考方法不仅是可行的，而且是必行的。请看：

Describe a teacher who has influenced you.	Describe a neighbor who helped you before.	Describe a person who can speak a foreign language well.
Describe someone who helped you before.	Describe an important person in your life.	Describe an old person who you admire.
Describe someone who you have studied or worked with.	Describe a family member.	Describe someone who gave you good advice.

很明显，通过准备 an old English teacher，我们不仅可以准备好左上角的一个题目，还可以很自然地覆盖这个表格里其他所有的 topics，甚至还可以把一部分内容借用到 Describe a subject you liked at school. / Describe the first day of a course you attended at school. / Describe an ideal job. 等看似"不搭界"的考题里。

又比如下面这个表格：

Describe a special meal you had recently.	Describe a difficult thing you can do well.	Describe a skill.	Describe an interesting thing you did in your spare time recently.
Describe a happy event in your childhood.	Describe a birthday party.	Describe a good cook.	Describe an exciting experience.

通过准备一个关于 cooking 的详细过程，会让我们对描述这些题目都有足够的信心。

下面请您自己感受一下合并 topics 的乐趣，练习下面的话题怎样快速搞定：

Describe an electronic device (not a computer).	Describe a gift you have received.	Describe an expensive thing you want to buy.	Describe something you lost.
Describe your favourite method of communication.	Describe something you saved money for a long time to buy.	Describe something you use every day.	**?**

一个 mobile phone 的答案就可以让这么多"闹心"的话题都迎刃而解了。

此外，您还可以在本书的 Day 8 中看到完整的雅思 Part 2 真题库详解。

Part 3 考什么？

下面的题目都是近期在中国大陆出现的 Part 3 真题，可以帮助您充分领略 Part 3 的出题风格，对 Part 3 的详解您可以在后面的 Day 9 看到。缩写"cf."是"参阅"的意思，出国之后您在大学论文里经常会看到这个缩写。

○ **What do you think is a healthy lifestyle?**

（思路提示：have a balanced diet / eat plenty of fruit and vegetables / drink 8 glasses of water a day "一天喝 8 杯水"也是英国国家医疗体系 NHS 提出的健康生活标准之一 / exercise regularly / early to bed and early to rise 这可不是"中式英语"，而是很地道的英文：早睡早起）

○ **Do you think TV programmes can teach us about history?**

（思路提示：There're lots of history programmes on TV. / some of them are educational and helpful / but others are not based on historical facts / they're entertaining but misleading just to attract more viewers）

○ **What are the differences between modern buildings and traditional buildings?**

（思路提示：traditional buildings are more eco-friendly 更有益于环保的 / traditional buildings look more attractive / modern buildings are taller and stronger / modern buildings lack character 缺乏鲜明的个性特色）

○ **What are the differences between Chinese movies and Hollywood movies?**

（思路提示：The violence in many Hollywood movies really bothers me. / Hollywood movies tend to be more entertaining and creative. / Even in China, most box-office hits are Hollywood movies.）

○ **What are the differences between fresh food and canned food?**

（思路提示：fresh food is rich in fiber（纤维）and vitamins / fresh food tastes better / canned food takes less time to prepare and cook）

◉ How do TV programmes affect education?

（思路提示：some TV programmes are fun and educational / they can provide young people with lots of useful information / some other TV programmes can encourage imagination and creativity / but on the other hand, there're also TV programmes that contain violent or sexual images / young people tend to copy the things they see on TV）

◉ What do you think of giving children gifts when they behave well?

（思路提示：That's like a reward for their good behaviour. / but on the other hand, children may be spoiled if adults always do that / it would be better to reward them with words than with gifts）

◉ What skills can be learned at home but cannot be learned at school?

（思路提示：cooking skills / gardening skills / sewing and knitting skills 这个基本上就是中文的"缝纫"了，国外的 grandma 们也都爱没事儿时打个毛衣什么的，其实出国后您就会发现西方人在生活里的很多方面并不像您想象的那么"前卫"）

◉ What's your idea of success?

（思路提示：It can be anything I really try hard to do. / just like … anything that can give me a sense of achievement / even something as ordinary as cooking a nice meal for my family or friends can be called a success / some people are very ambitious and always try to achieve success in their studies or careers）

◉ Who can give good advice to us?

（思路提示：our parents / our teachers / our friends who have had similar experiences / or other people who really care about us）

◉ How can we solve the global warming problem?

（思路提示：control the number of cars / make public transport cheaper and more reliable / encourage people to walk or cycle to work）

◉ What are the differences between individual sports and team sports?

（思路提示：We're more focused when we do individual sports like jogging and swimming. / Individual sports can give us a stronger sense of achievement. / Team sports can help to improve our teamwork skills. / Team sports are more fun because we work closely with our teammates towards our common goal. ）

Pat指南

Part 3 的题目不管听起来多么怪异（weird），也没必要把答案想得太"深邃"（profound）了。时刻牢记：雅思口语无论再高分的答案也还是说话（spoken English），而不是写作（written English）。

Part 3 出题有规律么？

☆ 除了那些与 Part 1 类似的问题之外，Part 3 的一个重要特色（feature）是经常会有 1~2 个讨论差异（differences）的问题。

例如下面的《剑10》考题实例：

★ Have relationships between parents and children changed in recent years?（现在和过去之间的对比）

★ How do you think children's activities will change in the future?（未来和现在之间对比）

下面这个表格展示了最近九年出现过的所有比较类型，其中的符号 vs（versus）表示"与……相比"：

Government vs The Public 政府与公众	Males vs Females 男性与女性	Traditions vs High Technology 传统与高科技	Individuals vs Teams 个人与团队	Elderly People / Adults vs Children 老人 / 成年人 与儿童	The Present vs The Future / The Past 现在与未来 / 现在与过去

★ 另外，在 Part 3 里考生也经常会被问到 1~2 个涉及利弊（advantages / disadvantages）的问题。比如，《剑10》中出现了如下考题：

Do you think the free-time activities children do today are good for their health?

Are there any disadvantages to running a business?

Some people say it would be better for society if everyone got the same salary.

What do you think about that? Why?

★ 此外，Part 3 中考生还经常会被问到 1 ~ 2 个要求分析原因或者解决方法（Why / causes / solutions）的题目。比如《剑 10》中出现了如下 Part 3 考题：

Why do some people want to start their own business?

Why do some people feel they need to own things?

我们将在本书的 Day 9 里对更为详尽的 Part 3 答题技巧进行讨论。

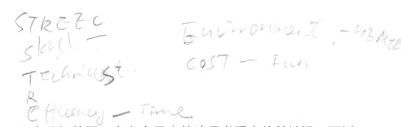

对于雅思口语 Part 1 和 Part 3 中的问答题，有六个用来快速思考理由的关键词，可以供备考时间过短或者口语基础太"潮"的同学在考试时实在想不出思路被"干"在那儿时突围使用：

Time	**Health**
Cost	**Safety**
Mood	**Knowledge**

∗其中 health 除了身体健康 physical health 也包括心理健康 emotional health

比如我们来看一道 Part 1 中比较"另类"的考题：

Do you think children should be allowed to drive?

这个题的视角很蹊跷，但是没关系，不妨来试试六字诀：

Time→ Children can get to school earlier if they are allowed to drive.

Cost→ It would cost more for children to learn to drive.

Mood→ Children would find driving very exciting.

Health→ If children got hurt in an accident, they would suffer even more than adults.

Safety→ Some children would not be able to drive safely.

Knowledge→ It would be nice if children could learn more about traffic rules through driving.

以上只是 Pat 给您的一点提示。当然，您也可以完全用这六个提示词想出属于自己的 ideas。

需要提醒的是：六字诀对口试的 Part 1 和 Part 3 问答题最有效，但是对于 Part 2 卡片题的思路来说，则还是沿着本书 Day 8 中每类话题里的展开思路表格思考更有效。

但是也有特例，比如最近在大陆考区有一只 Part 2 卡片熊经常出没：

Describe a TV show that you dislike（不喜欢）.

喜欢的电视节目比较好说，但描述自己不喜欢的节目却不太容易深入下去。

也用六字诀试试：

Time → Too late（around midnight）and terribly long.

Cost → It cost（注意 cost 的过去时还是 cost）a huge amount of money to produce.

Mood → It's too serious and heavy（话题过于沉重的）.

Health → It's filled with violent scenes and has harmful effects on young viewers.

Safety → It makes risky behaviour seem fun and cool .

Knowledge → The producers don't have any fresh ideas and the show is interrupted（中间被打断）by ads every five minutes.（如果内容俗套、毫无创意，则可以说 It's corny.）

像这样一个 TV show 足以让人做噩梦（bad dream / nightmare）了吧。

在头脑中使用六字诀需要对它们大量练习，熟练掌握才能在考场中运用自如。如果觉得自己已经很有把握了，那么可以再加上 View（美还是丑）作为备用理由。

Note：六字诀只是在实在没招儿了时作为救命稻草，对于能自己快速想出 ideas 的题就完全不必依赖它们，毕竟在 IELTS 口语里流利度是相当重要的一个指标。

Think hard. Speak softly.

Day 3

 雅思口语的词
IELTS Speaking Building Blocks

Talk in everlasting words,

And dedicate them all to you.

I'm here if you call me.

You think that I don't even mean a single word I said.

They're only words.

And words are all I can possibly have.

☆ http://www.topics-mag.com ☆

这个网站上的网友来自世界各地，大家可以经常上去看看。

它的英语风格其实就很接近雅思口语高分答案的风格：不是很难，但也并不是很"痞"；有一定的描述性，但绝不是背书。

▶ *We take the test very seriously, but we'll take a laid-back approach to it.*

考试的时候词汇用得好会加分，这是不争的事实。可到底什么叫好词？在培训界却很有争议。

英文有句名谚，"A man travels across the world in search of what he needs and returns home to find it."中文里叫"舍近求远"。

其实大家准备雅思口语备考的过程，也多半如此。我经常告诉自己的学生们："老师教的'亮点'词句，只是用来点缀（spice up）你的答案的。很多内容其实完全可以用简单一点的英文自己说。口语的本质是交流，而不是吓人的。"

请您仔细体会下面这个《剑10》Test 1 的高分答案：

> **Some people say it would be better for society if everyone got the same salary. What do you think about that? Why?**
>
> *I don't think it would be fair for everyone to get the same salary. There're always people who work harder than others. They should be rewarded for their hard work. Giving everyone the same salary will make these hard-working people feel frustrated.*

这样用词简洁的答案之所以会是高分答案，就是因为它并没有"语不惊人死不休"的难词怪词，但却意思清晰、内容充实。

再请看这个《剑9》Test 4 的高分答案：

> **Do you think bicycles are good for all ages?**
>
> *I don't think so. Cycling is a good way to keep fit for most ages. But for people who are too young or too old to have good balance skills, cycling can be dangerous.*

下面的《剑8》Test 1 高分答案同样用词平实，但能有效地传达意义并且层次清晰，请时刻牢记"交流"才是地道口语的唯一目的：

> **How do you think neighbours can help each other?**
>
> *There're a number of ways, such as helping elderly neighbours with their housework or walking their pets for them. When new neighbours move in, we can*

> *show them around the community*, *and give them important community service phone numbers.*

再请看下面的答案：

> **What's your favourite subject at school?**
>
> *I guess… it's history, especially world history. I like it so much because it broadens our knowledge and explains lots of things to us, like why America wanted to gain independence from Britain, and why Hitler wanted to attack other countries during the Second World War. Probably the most important reason I like this subject is the history tests are always so easy…*

> **Do you think it's possible to be friends with someone if you never meet them in person?**
>
> *That's possible. Sometimes even very good friendships can be formed this way. I've heard about pen friends or " pen pals" who didn't really meet in person but could still communicate well. And these days, it's very easy to make new friends on social networking websites like Facebook and Twitter.*

这样的答案，如果能够比较流利地说出来，至少会有 8 分，但它们却并没有刻意使用任何 "霸气" 的词汇，只是努力地想和考官进行一次实实在在的交流。

当然，并不是每个人都需要 8 分，再看这个回答：

> **What kinds of radio programme do you like best?**
>
> *Actually I don't really listen to the radio very often. But it seems I tend to prefer news shows and sports shows because they are fun and helpful. They give me information about what is happening around the world and in important sports competitions.*

说这样的答案，考生的目的显然是要和考官进行很真实的交流，而不是想把一堆大词和连自己都不明白的难句扔给考官之后就 "闪"。

即使非常抽象的考题依然不是必须要用那些所谓"高端、大气、上档次"的词汇才能拿到高分。

请再看这个常考题的高分答案:

Is laughing the same as feeling happy?

No, *they're different. It seems there's always some confidence behind our laughter because we've made the laughing sound*, *and it could be annoying to the people around us. Feeling happy*, *though*, *can be a private thing. We can just keep happiness to ourselves.*

像这样的答案,已经绝对是 IELTS 口试中的高分答案了,就因为它们合理(make sense),而且更像"人话"(human utterances)。

今天就跟您分享在 IELTS 口语考场上真正能打动考官的词。这些词汇多数貌不惊人,但当您亲身踏出国门之后就会真正明白它们在国外生活里发挥着何等重要的作用。

雅思口语中最常用的"小词"
Common Colloquial Words and Phrases

◇ 前面标"★"的词句表示极为常用,一定要熟练掌握。

◇ 对于没有标出"★"的词句,如果时间很紧的话那就不要记了。准备 IELTS 听说读写四项都有一个真理:不要为了那些在考场里你可能想不起来的东西去牺牲(compromise)掉那些考场里你一定会用到的东西。

◇ 此表格充分考虑了英、美两国的英语习惯。对于那些只在美国和加拿大使用,但是英国人并不常用的口语词汇在本书中一律不予推荐。对于没有十分把握的词句,Pat 还专门向我的英国朋友们做了确认。

序号	英文表达	讲解	用法举例
1	★ stuff	东西,口语里面等于 things,但同时必须提醒国内的同学们:stuff 永远**不能用复数**	The **stuff** in that store is very expensive.
2	★ pretty	= 副词 very	My new iPad is **pretty** fun.

（续表）

序号	英文表达	讲解	用法举例
3	★ fun	= interesting（请朋友们注意 fun 作形容词时其实并不是 funny "搞笑的"意思,但它在英美日常生活里的出现频率绝不比 funny 低）	There're lots of **fun** things to do in the classroom.
4	★ adore	非常喜欢	I **adore** that singer.
5	shortly	= soon	I'll get these things done **shortly**.
6	spot	（1）看见 = see ★（2）地方 = place	（1）I **spotted** some squirrels（松鼠）and woodpeckers（啄木鸟）in Stanley Park. 注：Stanley Park 是温哥华的一个大公园,离我家很近,非常美 （2）It looks like a nice **spot** for a picnic（野餐）.
7	★ eye-opening	不是中式英语,而是很地道的英文,"让人大开眼界的"	Trips to other countries can be reeeeeally **eye-opening**.（本词原为 really,此处系口语用法。本书里的"sooooo"也是同类用法）
8	★ decent	在国内上英语课时老师可能会语重心长地告诉你这个词是"体面的",但在国外真实生活里这个词远远更多的时候是表示"不错的,挺好的"意思 = quite good	This job offers a **decent** salary and an impressive set of benefits（工作的"福利"在地道英文里就直接用 benefits）.
9	★ hang out	玩儿。很多时候可以代替 play,但要注意这个词组后面不能直接跟宾语	（1）I often **hang out** in bars at weekends. （2）I often **hang out with** them at the park.
10	★ kind of = sort of	有点……, = somewhat	My boss is **kind of** hard to get along with.

（续表）

序号	英文表达	讲解	用法举例
11	★ like…	like 作为连词在口语中极度常用，可以表示"比如说"、"像是……"、"差不多是"	I bought lots of stuff, **like** carrots, beef and salmon. That programme is **like**, … boring.
12	in a row	= one after another 连续地出现或者发生，这个短语在英美生活里用来描述一系列连续的事物时都已经到了无孔不入的程度，但在国内孩子们那儿却悄无声息	（1）Jeremy Lin led New York Knicks to **seven wins in a row**. （请注意 in a row 通常都是放在它所修饰的复数名词后面） （2）Patricia passed **four exams in a row** last week.
13	★ entire	= whole / complete（谁都知道 whole 和 complete 常用，但有多少国内同学爱用 entire 这个地道英文里的绝对高频词呢？而且它的副词 **entirely** 也是在考试时替换 completely 的绝佳选择。牢记在口语里 entire 后面跟名词，entirely 后面跟形容词）	（1）Daniel ate the **entire** cake and made no apology for that. （2）Our situation is **entirely different** from theirs. （3）Jessica **is not entirely sure** if she can get a nice job after graduation.
14	★ … as well.	也…… = … too.	Beijing is exciting for its night-life. And it's culturally attractive **as well**.
15	… is a piece of cake. = … is a snap. = … is a breeze.	小菜一碟，后面这两个国内孩子普遍不熟悉，但在英美生活里却时常能听到	The IELTS speaking test is just **a breeze** if you know all the tricks about it.

（续表）

序号	英文表达	讲解	用法举例
16	know... inside out = know... backwards and forwards	精通……	He **knows** computers **backwards and forwards**.
17	I'm all for...	我完全支持某事物（＝I strongly support...，注意：这个句型在英美口语里很常用，但在学术写作里不要用）反义：I'm against...	I've got nothing against change — **I'm all for it**.
18	is no picnic = is a pain in the neck	很折磨人	Getting the homework done everyday **is no picnic**.
19	★ ... really bothers me. / ... is getting on my nerves.	让我很烦	The noise really **bothers me**. / The noise is **getting on my nerves**.
20	★ kick back and relax	放松	At parties, we just **kick back and relax**.
21	★ a couple of	几个	I stayed in France for **a couple of** weeks.
22	a bunch of	＝ some 一些	I went there with **a bunch of** new friends.
23	dozens of	几十	I just bought **dozens of** gifts online.
24	★ loads of ＝tons of	＝ lots of	I've got **loads of** work to get through before tomorrow.
25	★ make sense	＝ be reasonable 合理	The plot（剧情）of that movie didn't **make** any **sense**.

(续表)

序号	英文表达	讲解	用法举例
26	★ …, you name it. = and the list goes on and on	……应有尽有(常被放在列举出的几个名词之后表示其实还有更多,数不胜数)	Beijing has traditions, modern lifestyles, world-class universities, exciting night-life, … **you name it.**
27	By doing that, I kill two birds with one stone.	一举两得	When I travel around, I take photos and then sell them online. So you see, **I** just **kill two birds with one stone.**
28	★ … is the best + 名词, hands down.	……绝对是最……的	The new iPad is **the best** tablet(平板电脑) I've ever seen, **hands down.**
29	… would be the last thing I want to do.	……是我在人生里最不想做的事	Doing the dishes **would be the last thing I want to do.**
30	★ mess up…	把某件事给"弄糟了",这个短语在英美生活里实在太常用,尤其是生活在节奏紧张的大城市里的人们特别爱用 mess up …	(1)There are always people who come to a party and try to **mess things up.** (2) Julia **messed up her chances of** becoming a great singer.
31	get the hang of	基本了解怎样做某事	"I've never used a word processor before." "Don't worry — you'll **get the hang of** it shortly."
32	It's a shame!	"太可惜了"(在这里 shame 跟"羞耻"无关)	**It's a shame** that you have to leave so soon.

（续表）

序号	英文表达	讲解	用法举例
33	…is non-existent.	这个表达完全等于中文里所说的"压根儿就不存在"	Some scientists believe global warming **is non-existent**. Some of them even argue that the earth is actually getting colder.
34	★ end up verb +ing	这个短语后面经常接动词的 ing 形式，用来描述某人或某事物最终处于某种状态	**I ended up** having to do all the work myself.
35	★ suit someone very well / suit someone's needs	国内同学们普遍酷爱使用 suitable，简直是"用 suitable 成瘾"。但事实上，suitable 的语气比较正式，在英美口语对话里其实并不是经常听到，反倒是动词 suit 更常用。例如：suit someone very well / suit someone's needs 这两种说法在真实英美生活里的使用频率就非常高	The bustling city life **suits** Jeremy **better**.

25 个更"痞"的雅思口试常用词（高分内容）
Slang Words and Phrases

    这里我们不说 Eminem，Black Eyed Peas 或者 50 Cents 的歌词，只说雅思口语的常用加分俚语。其实中文里面也有很多俚语，比如"火"、"大腕儿"、"肿么"、"牛人"这些词，真的都"巨"常用对吧？但对于连在国外都不常用的那种英文，下表中坚决不予收录。而且如果您觉得自己本身就是比较"板"的人（a stuffed shirt），那么这个表格不适合您。Just skip it！

普通版	俚语限量珍藏版	中文解释	例句
fan	★ buff / freak / mania	"迷",这三个词的语气一个比一个强,到最后一个 mania 已经是喜欢到有点病态的"痴"了。雅思考试里… buff 的语气最合适,比如:a car buff, a music buff, a movie buff 等等。(注意:buff 在英美是指"粉"某种事物,但如果是指"粉"某一个人,则还是必须用 fan 或者 admirer)	(1) I am **a movie buff**. I go to the movies whenever I can find some free time. (buff 这个词的语气很像中文里的"……控") (2) I'm a big **fan** of Jeremy Lin.
bookworm	nerd / geek	书呆子,现在也已经被扩大到指各类宅男宅女(但如果是正面含义地说一个人"博览群书"则要说这人是 an avid /ˈævid/ reader)	**Nerds** are often laughed at.
be so surprised	freak out	很吃惊	I totally **freaked out** when I heard the news.
release pressure	let off steam	释放压力	I often go to the gym to **let off steam**.
feel ill /sick	feel under the weather	身体不舒服	Aaron's **feeling under the weather** and should get some rest.

（续表）

普通版	俚语限量珍藏版	中文解释	例句
expensive	★ pricey	很贵的	That car was **pricey**. But he bought it without batting an eyelash（想都没想）.
is better than…	★ beats…	在英美日常口语里很多时候动词 beat 并不是指"打败"，而是指比……强，优于	Having the newspaper delivered to your place **beats** having to go out and buy one, right?
not satisfactory	★ not up to par	不能让人满意的	Owen's work **isn't up to par.**
is boring	★ is a drag	单调的,烦人的	A nine-to-five job can really **be a drag.**
the boring things you have to do everyday	★ the daily grind	日常的辛劳	I'm sick and tired of **the daily grind** and want to get away from it all.
is totally unappealing	is totally gross	让人恶心的	The food in that cafeteria（自助餐厅）**is totally gross.**
is hard to understand	is over my head / is beyond me	对我来说太高深了,我理解不了	The professor's lecture **was way over my head.**
drive me crazy	drive me up the wall	让人抓狂 让人"爬墙"	The noise really **drives me up the wall.**
have fun / have a good time	★ have a ball = have a blast	玩得超级开心	The kids are **having a ball** building their sandcastles.
fancy	funky	新奇的	He's into **funky** outfits（服装）.
clothes	★ outfit	（一件）服装	This **outfit** looks gorgeous.
attention-getting	flashy	很"炫"的	Some young girls are into **flashy** accessories（饰品）.
beautiful and expensive	snazzy	华丽的,地道英文里这个词经常用来形容服装或者首饰	Superstars tend to wear **snazzy** clothes.

(续表)

普通版	俚语限量珍藏版	中文解释	例句
strange	★ weird / odd	怪异的	The noise sounds so **weird**.
old and uninteresting	corny	很俗的,没创意的	The lyrics（歌词）are meaningful but **corny** as well.
a person who likes playing video games	a gamer / a vid-kid	超级爱打游戏的人	I'm **a vid-kid**. I spend all my free time playing games.

Pat 指南

☆ way 这个词在口语里面很多时候作副词,表示"远远……",口语考试时用效果很好。

This movie is way better than the director's last movie.

The professor's lecture is way over my head.

The life in this city is way too stressful for people who grew up in tiny villages.

☆ 中文的"不错"到底怎么表达? quite good? fairly good?

请你和考官用这个词来表示"不错",看看他/她的反应:decent。这个词在口语里面和"体面的"没有关系,倒是很像中文的"不错的"。

I can't find a decent house in my price range.

A decent meal in that restaurant costs anywhere from 200 to 500 yuan.

I just need a decent salary without getting myself overworked.

《那些花儿》
Cool Alternatives to Some Excessively-used Words

有首歌叫《那些花儿》,唱的是年轻时特花心的一男人成熟之后突然反省的故事。当然媳妇儿不能总换,不过对于口语用词来说,能经常替换却绝对是好事儿。需要注意的是,这里说的替换,仅是为了考虑考试的效果,但其实很多意思在生活中使用得最多的就是每组左边那个最普通的词。比如一般在国外生活中说"巨大的",绝对是 huge 这个词用得最频繁。

但在 IELTS 考场里,这个词存在着被国内考生使用过度的可能,那么为了应试就可以试一试 enormous 这类在国外生活中同样很常用,但是大部分考生却不了解的词汇了。总之,一切 为了拿分!

	一般考生的表达	含义	更加分的说法
关于 **number** (数量)	lots of money	一大笔钱	a fortune
	there are so many	大量出现	... are sprouting up all over the city (or the country / or the world)
	lots of	大量的	loads of / tons of
关于 **activities** (活动)	play	娱乐,休闲	hang out
	finish	结束	wrap it up
	protect	保护(某种资源, resources / old buildings / wild animals 等)	preserve (但如果保护一个人那么还是要用 protect)
	destroy	破坏	ruin
	relax	休息	kick back and relax
	try my best	尽最大努力	give it my best shot
	easy	简单的	It's a piece of cake. = It's a snap. = It's a breeze.
	difficult	困难的	tough
	painful	痛苦的	grueling
	go to bed	去睡觉	turn in (有点像中文的"洗洗睡吧")
	make trouble	制造麻烦	make waves
	sit in the sun	晒太阳	catch some rays
关于 **things** (物品)	valuable	贵重的	precious
	strange	奇怪的	weird / odd
	expensive	贵重的	pricey
	cheap	便宜的	dirt-cheap
	fashionable	时尚的	stylish = "in"

(续表)

	一般考生的表达	含义	更加分的说法
关于 **things** （物品）	popular	流行的	"in" / big / well-liked（big 其实也是口语中很常用的一个"流行"）
	good taste	很有品位的，"很有格调的"	classy（地道英文里这个词跟上课一点儿关系也没有）
	bad products	劣质产品	rubbish（BrE）/ trash（AmE）
	old	老的	worn-out / beat-up
	new	新的	brand-new
	huge	巨大的	enormous
关于 **people** （人）	famous person	名人	celebrity
	beautiful / pretty	漂亮的	gorgeous
	fat	胖的	overweight
	thin	瘦的	slim（在地道英语里 slim 也完全可以很自然地用来形容偏瘦的男性，所以它其实并不完全等于中文里的"苗条"）
	honest	直率的	straightforward
	strong	强壮的	well-built
	kind	善良的	caring / thoughtful
	cute	可爱的	adorable
	funny	搞笑的	hilarious
	busy	很忙的	tied up
	relaxed	放松的	refreshed
	tired	疲劳的	wiped-out / worn-out / bushed
	rich	有钱的	wealthy / affluent
	expert	高手，"大牛"	pro
	high-quality	高素质的，高水准的	high-caliber（形容词） [剑桥例句] It's not easy to find **high-caliber** employees.
	become successful	成功	make it big

（续表）

	一般考生的表达	含义	更加分的说法
关于 **hobby** （爱好）	like	喜欢	be into / be fascinated by…
	like and dislike	又爱又恨	have mixed feelings about
	don't know any-thing about it	不了解	don't even have a clue about it
	depend on	依赖	count on
	not happy	不高兴的	in a bad mood
	decide	决定	determine
	can't decide	无法决定	be torn between A and B
	boring	枯燥的	It's a drag.
	moving	感人的	touching
	understand	理解	figure out
	make me angry	生气	It makes my blood boil.
	be surprised	吃惊	freak out
	feel afraid	害怕	get cold feet
关于 **weather** （天气）	cold	冷的	chilly（有点冷）/ freezing（很冷的）/ frigid（严寒的）
	cloudy	阴天的	overcast
	hot	热的	scorching
关于 **buildings** （建筑）	tall buildings	高楼	high-rise buildings
	big	宽敞的	spacious
	narrow	狭小的	cramped
	messy	混乱的	cluttered
	quiet	安静的	peaceful / tranquil / serene
	clean	干净的	tidy / neat
	ugly	丑陋的	It's an eyesore. / It's hideous.
	dirty	脏的	filthy

（续表）

	一般考生的表达	含义	更加分的说法
关于 **food**（食品）	delicious	好吃的	tasty / out of this world
	smells good	香喷喷的	aromatic（说 food）； fragrant（说 flowers 或者 plants）
关于 **time**（时间）	for a long time	很长时间	for ages
	always	总是	constantly

从**非常喜欢**到**极度讨厌**的地道英文表达

下面这个表格覆盖了从**非常喜欢**一直到**极度讨厌**的全部常见地道英文表达，在 IELTS 口试的 Part 1 中一定能用到其中的几种：

… is my biggest passion in life.（最喜欢）

I'm fascinated by…

I'm crazy about…

I adore…

I love…

I'm a… buff（……迷，在 buff 前填入自己特别喜欢的东东，比如 car, music 或者 movie，但要注意：这个句型不能用来说自己喜欢某个人）

I'm really into…

I like …

I'm not keen on…

I'm not very fond of…

It's a drag.

I totally dislike…

I hate…

I can't stand…

I loathe…（最不喜欢）

其实口语里还有语气更强的，不过基本就是骂人了，考试用就算了

从最频繁到最偶然的地道英文表达

下面的表达分别对应从**最频繁**到**最少发生**的各种频率,只要听到考官张嘴说 How often…的题就要条件反射地想到这个表格:

I… all the time. (总是……)

I constantly…(不间断地……)

I… daily. (其实 daily 不止是《日报》,在地道英文中它也经常作副词,表示"每天都……")

I… almost every day. (几乎每天都……)

I… every other day. (每隔一天都……)

I… on a weekly basis. (每周都……)

I often…(经常……)

I …regularly. (经常……)

I … on a regular basis. (经常)

I … every now and then. (时常…)

Sometimes I…(有时候……)

I … once in a while… (偶尔……)

I don't… very often. (不常……)

I rarely… (中国考生极其爱用的 seldom 在英美生活中用的却不如 rarely 多)

I hardly ever…(几乎不……)

Maybe once in a blue moon. (表示"极少",这是个成语,在英美生活里有时也能听到)

Do you know what amazes me more than anything else? The impotence of force to organise anything.

—Napoleon Bonaparte

冰天雪地裸求都不给的 30 个"冻人"名词
Top 30 Magical Nouns

名词	注释	举例
leisure	休闲 (= recreation)	**leisure** time / **leisure** magazines / **leisure** activities
mood	心情	Colours can really affect our **mood**.
ambience	氛围, 气氛 (=atmosphere)	The **ambience** there is pretty inviting.
efficiency	效率	Listening to music can actually boost our **efficiency** at work.
smog	雾霾(最常见的污染之一)	Shanghai is becoming **smoggy** these days.
necessity	必需品	A car is an absolute **necessity** in Canada since it's so sprawling (开阔的).
incentive	能给人去做某事的动力的事物, 激励物	There is little **incentive** for people to leave their cars at home when public transport remains so expensive.
the pace of life	生活节奏	**The pace of life** in Beijing is very stressful.
competition	竞争 (反义: 合作 co-operation /collaboration 这个词的语气更正式一些)	The **competition** is so fierce today.
encouragement	鼓励	My parents gave me a lot of **encouragement**.
enjoyment	享受, 乐趣 (= pleasure)	Some people play musical instruments just for the **enjoyment** and pleasure.
gallery	美术馆, 画廊	Art **galleries** are sprouting up over the CBD of Beijing.
artworks	艺术品 (= works of art)	This museum is rich with creative **artworks**.
excitement	激动的心情	The kids got filled with **excitement** at the thought of visiting Disney land.

（续表）

名词	注释	举例
preference	偏好	His girlfriend really changed his clothing **preferences**.
an approach	做某事的方法或途径(后面接 to sth. 或 to doing sth. ,这个 to 是介词)	（1）We've decided to take a different **approach to** the problem. （2）This is a new **approach to** teaching English as a foreign language.
nutrition	营养	**Nutrition** and exercise are essential to physical fitness.
cuisine	一个地区或者国家菜的统称,有点像中文的"菜系"	I'm really into Greek **cuisine**.
status symbol	身份的象征	Fancy cars are not just vehicles. They are **status symbols** in Hong Kong.
fragrance	芳香(饭菜和咖啡的香味儿则要叫 aroma)	The **fragrance** of the garden is fascinating.
family bonds	亲情	Sharing meals together can really make **family bonds** stronger.
potential	潜力	Individual sports help us discover our own worth and **potential**（潜力）.
employment	就业	**Employment** opportunities are rare（稀少的）these days, due to the financial crisis.
blockbuster	大片儿	That movie was a big-budget **blockbuster**.
a sense of achievement	成就感	Watching their children grow and develop gives parents **a sense of achievement**.
traffic congestion	交通堵塞（= traffic jam）,但要注意: traffic jam 允许用复数,而 traffic congestion 必须保持单数	**Traffic congestion** has become a major problem because of the increasing number of cars.

（续表）

名词	注释	举例
regulations	规章制度（经常连在一起说 rules and regulations）	It's essential to know the rules and **regulations** of safe driving.
the hustle and bustle	喧闹拥挤（这个词可好可坏,有人喜欢也有人不喜欢,是说 big cities 的必备词）	I'm tired of **the hustle and bustle** of big cities.
the daily grind	日常的辛劳	I'm sick and tired of **the daily grind** and it's time for a change.
tourist attractions	旅游景点	Many Vancouver **tourist attractions** are free with the Vancouver Pass.

曾让一个考官面部肌肉不停抽搐的动词短语
Phrasal Verbs

有个学生告诉我,她考口语的时候用了一些我上课讲的动词短语,那位 SG 考官的眼神里明显有惊奇感,而且面部肌肉开始不停地抽搐。不知道大家有没有发现,当学英语的同学倾向于使用某个单独动词的时候,地道英文里却经常会用一些动词短语来表达。其实,你也行!

动词短语	讲解	例句
check out	体验,感受	Be sure to **check out** those fun places.
★ figure out	理解 ≈understand	I just can't **figure out** the difference between them.
bring about	带来	These problems have **brought about** the American financial crisis（金融危机）.
carry out	从事（某事）	I always make sure our plans are successfully **carried out**.

(续表)

动词短语	讲解	例句
★ go about	从事(某事)	How you **go about** your work or studies may be asked during the test.
come up with	给出(答案或想法) ≈ present	I'm afraid I can't **come up with** a good solution to this problem.
face up to	承担	They should **face up to** their responsibilities.
★ pay off	有回报	All my hard work **paid off**.
★ take up	开始(一种爱好)	I've recently **taken up** jogging (慢跑).
think of	想到,想起	The only reason I can **think of** now is there are too many people and so few cabs (=taxi).
★ work out	锻炼身体	I go to the gym and **work out** regularly (定期地).
★ rip sb. off	口语里面说"买东西被骗了"时,大家总是用 cheat,真该学学这个短语了	The stall (摊儿) owners **ripped you off** — it's fake stuff.
★ take... into account	考虑到……	We should **take** the cost **into account** as well.
★ get rid of	去掉,消除	We should **get rid of** the sources of pollution (污染源).
★ sleep in	睡懒觉	I often **sleep in** on Sundays.
★ get so worked up	大惊小怪	There's no point in **getting so worked up** about the test.
adapt to	适应	It's essential for kids to **adapt to** their school life.
★ participate in	参与	Our professors often encourage us to **participate in** group discussions (讨论).
cope with	处理,应付 ≈ deal with	They have to **cope with** customers' complaints (投诉) every day.

（续表）

名词	注释	举例
★ get stuck	被……困住了，陷入……	When I was in Beijing, I often get stuck in traffic.
★ stick to	坚持	Stick to your plan. Don't give up so easily.
brush up on	突击复习……	You should brush up on your Spanish before you go to Spain.
★ burn out	累垮了	I'll burn out if I keep working like this.
★ wind down	放松 ≈ relax	I really need to wind down after such a hectic day（忙碌的一天）.
let... down	让……失望	I study hard because I don't want to let my parents down.
★ liven up	让某事物更有活力、更加活跃 ≈ brighten up	We played games to liven up the party.
下面这几个词虽然不是 phrasal verbs，但也是相当常用的动词短语		
open our minds / expand our minds	开阔我们的思维（open our minds 可不是"Chinglish"，而是在英美大学课堂里经常可以听到的地道短语）	Learning another language can open our minds.
can never hurt ≈won't hurt	不会有坏处的	Learning to speak another language won't hurt.
ease your mind release pressure	这两个很像，都是"释放压力"	Music eases your mind and helps you release pressure.

你早就认识却从不会想到去用的加分形容词和副词
Super-cool Adjectives and Adverbs

Adjectives 形容词

单词	注释	例句
independent	独立的（independence *n.* 独立）	Cats tend to be more **independent** than other pets.
energising	有很多单词（例如 uplifting, encouraging 等）的意思都接近于中文里说的"可以给人正能量的"，但 energising 则是最接近于中文"可以给人正能量的"英语形容词	（1）It was an outstanding speech, very **energising** and engaging（引人入胜的）. （2）Our holiday was refreshing（令人感觉焕然一新的）and **energising**.
amazing / awesome	极好的, 非凡的 ≈ great / wonderful	That garden is **amazing**.
genuine	真实的, 真正的（＝true），它的副词形式 genuinely（＝truly）用来修饰形容词也很常用	（1）The painting is a **genuine** masterpiece（杰作）. （2）These parents **are genuinely concerned about** teen violence.
pathetic /pəˈθetik/	查字典也许会得到"可悲的"或者类似翻译，但在真实的英美日常生活里它却经常表示 of poor quality	He made a **pathetic** attempt to explain the failure.
punctual	守时的（在涉及时间的话题里很有用）	Being **punctual** makes us more productive.
refreshed	精神很振奋的（"让人精神振奋的"就说 refreshing）	After a good night's sleep, I feel **refreshed**.
dynamic	有活力的（替换 active 很棒）	Hong Kong is one of the most **dynamic** port cities in the world.

（续表）

单词	注释	例句
precious	珍贵的(= valuable)	Some people collect **precious** stones.
inexpensive	挺便宜的(考试时代替 cheap 非常棒的选择)	I prefer **inexpensive** clothes.
efficient	效率高的(effective 则是指"效果好的")	Working in groups may be more **efficient** than working separately.
awkward	令人尴尬的, 让人很"囧"的(口试里的近义词：embarrassing)	There followed an **awkward** silence while we tried to think of something to say.
enjoyable	好玩的, 有意思的(它的名词 enjoyment 也很有用)	That trip was one of the most **enjoyable** experiences I ever had.
fancy	新奇有趣的 (反义词：tacky 俗气的)	Katie wants a simple black dress, nothing **fancy**.
exquisite	精美的, 精致的(在 Part 2 我们将会更多地用到这个词)	Some people who collect antique furniture (古董家具) have **exquisite** tastes (高雅的品味).
desirable	好的, 值得拥有的(很多时候可以代替 good)	That car is really **desirable**. But... now I'm broke (没钱).
encouraging / motivating	给人动力的	My boss never said any **encouraging** words to his employees.
appealing	吸引人的(≈ attractive)	The offer sounds very **appealing**.
intelligent	思维能力很强的	The students are very **intelligent** but it seems the teachers are not so good.
thoughtful	体贴的, 善解人意的	She's considerate and **thoughtful**.
state-of-the-art	非常先进的, 很尖端的(在当代英美口语里这个词和 art 其实并没有什么关系, 反倒经常被用来形容尖端的科技或者设备)	This PSP is definitely **state-of-the-art**.

(续表)

单词	注释	例句
user-friendly	方便好用的,"用户友好的"	This laptop is pretty **user-friendly**.
rewarding	很有回报的	This job is pretty **rewarding** financially as well as emotionally.
gorgeous	非常漂亮的	Vancouver is home to some of the most **gorgeous** scenic spots (景点) on earth.
flawless	完美无瑕的	His English is **flawless**.
nutritious	(食物)富含营养的	Raw vegetable salads are very **nutritious**.
original	原创性的,有创意的	The plot of this movie (电影情节) is pretty **original**.
messy	乱糟糟的,注意：它跟梅西 (Lionel Messi) 的拼写不同,除非你是"梅黑"	Jason's bedroom is always **messy**.
fascinating	迷人的	The fragrance (芳香) in this garden is **fascinating**.
informative	信息量大的	News shows are **informative**.
entertaining	娱乐性强的	Game shows are pretty **entertaining**.
authentic	地道的,正宗的	The difference between American-Chinese food and **authentic** Chinese food is huge.
posh / luxurious	奢华的,奢侈的	Tourists don't need to stay in **posh** hotels to enjoy a city.
atrocious	巨差的(= terrible)	Sometimes the traffic congestion (= traffic jam) in this city can be **atrocious**.
useless	完全没用的	These impractical suggestions are **useless**.
hideous	极丑的,丑得人神共愤的 (= extremely ugly)	Those **hideous** buildings seriously spoil (除了"溺爱",这个词也经常表示破坏本来很完美的东西) the view.

(续表)

单词	注释	例句
mediocre	平庸的,稀松平常的,"一般般的"(请注意:mediocre 和 regular 不是同义词。regular 是指常规的,语气是中性的,而 mediocre 则是指很平庸的,语气是贬义的)	That book was so **mediocre** I threw it away after reading the first 10 pages.
poisonous/toxic	有毒的	Car exhaust fumes(汽车尾气)can be **poisonous**.
memorable	很值得回忆的(在英美生活里当向别人介绍旅行、生日派对、观看现场表演等值得回忆的经历时这个形容词几乎是必用词汇,而 IELTS 口试恰恰经常涉及到这些领域)	The trip was very **memorable** and far exceeded our expectations.
exhausting	让人精疲力尽的	Rock-climbing can be **exhausting**.
frustrating	令人沮丧的	The career prospects(工作前景)are **frustrating**.
complicated / complex	复杂的	This is a **complex** issue. The plot of that movie was **complicated**.

Adverbs 副词

单词	注释	例句
Actually, … Basically, …	这两个词大家都认识,但 Pat 在国内期间却极少听到中国孩子使用它们,与真实英美生活里它们的超高频使用形成鲜明对比,应该力荐一下	**Actually**, these two words are old hat (老掉牙的) and I'm sure you guys know them already. But **basically**, they're still worth recommending.

(续表)

单词	注释	例句
Essentially, ...	经常用在句首,表示"本质上看,……"	**Essentially**, this problem is a problem about the conflicts(冲突) between development and tradition.
typically	多半(代替 mostly 是很棒的选择,另一个好选择是使用动词短语 tend to)	(1) Seniors(老年人) are **typically** more laid-back and more understanding. (2) July and August **tend to** be our busiest months. (3) We **tend to** get cold winters and warm, dry summers in our part of the country.
practically	几乎(代替 almost 的极好选择)	I have to work overtime(加班) **practically** every day.
immediately	立刻(= right away)	Measures should be taken **immediately** to cope with this problem.
constantly	比 always 语气更强的	As a salesperson, I'm **constantly** on the go.
currently	现在 (= now = at the moment)	I'm **currently** working at a design company.
unfortunately / sadly	不幸的是	**Unfortunately**, not so many people have meals with their family members today, due to the fast pace of life.
Honestly, ...	老实说……	**Honestly**, I don't know much about this topic.
Normally, ...	通常,考试时拿它替换国内孩子们使用过量的 usually 会很酷	**Normally**, I plan things one or two days ahead.
Hopefully, ...	希望能够……(意思很接近于 I hope…)	**Hopefully**, we'll get the noise controlled shortly.

对分数有野心的人应该熟记的关键反义词
Antonyms for Pros

单词		反义词	
spacious	宽敞的	cramped	狭小的
gorgeous	漂亮的	ugly / hideous	丑陋的（hideous 语气更强，相当于中文所说的"丑得人神共愤的"）
organised	整齐的,有秩序的	messy	混乱的
fun	有趣的	mundane	乏味的
extravagant	奢侈的	economical	省钱的（说事物）
		frugal	节俭的（说人）
adorable	可爱的（经常用来说小动物或者小朋友）	disgusting	令人厌恶的（可以用来描述任何让你感觉特别不爽的东东）
boost	促进、提升	restrict	制约
encouraging / motivating	给人动力的	frustrating	令人沮丧的
is speeding up	加速	is slowing down	减慢
is improving	改善	is deteriorating	恶化
delighted	高兴的	upset	"郁闷"的,很不高兴的

[剑桥例句]

(i) There're six desks in this room so it's rather cramped.

(ii) It frustrates me that I'm not able to put any of my ideas into practice.

Part 2 的 100 个核心词汇（7 分内容）
100 Building Blocks in Part 2

对于有很多同义词的词汇，这里都只剩下最拿分的一两个选择，为了考试咱们就赤果果的（cheeky）了。

☆ 100 个核心词汇按照感官（senses）分类

视觉词汇　Sight	
形容词	特漂亮的　gorgeous / breathtaking　壮观的　spectacular 精美的　exquisite　　　　　　　迷人的　enchanting（比 charming 更 charming） 很时尚的　fashionable / stylish　非常便携的　ultra-compact 耐用的　durable　　　　　　　　光亮的　glossy / sleek 巨大的　enormous　　　　　　　毛绒绒的　fluffy 可爱的　adorable　　　　　　　　胖乎乎的　chubby 干净整洁的　tidy / neat 独特的　unique（请您注意听音频里它的正确发音，有很多中国同学把它的 　　　　　重音位置读错了，它的正确重音是在 ni: 这个音节上） 整齐有秩序的　well-organised　竖固的　solid （人）笨拙的　clumsy（说物品"笨重的"则是 bulky） 敏捷的　agile　　　　　　　　　破旧的　beat-up / worn-out 凶猛的　fierce　　　　　　　　　圆形的　round 椭圆形的　oval　　　　　　　　　长方形的　rectangular 清澈的　crystal-clear
名词或者词组	建筑的外观　exterior　　　　　　　　　　建筑的内部　interior 形状规则的建筑　a regular-shaped building 形状不规则的建筑　an odd-shaped building 高耸的建筑　a towering building 建筑的入口　entrance　　　　　　　　　台阶　steps 砖墙　brick wall　　　　　　　　　　　玻璃幕墙　glass curtain wall 柱子　columns　　　　　　　　　　　　装饰　decorations

(续表)

视觉词汇　Sight

<table>
<tr><td rowspan="2">名词或者词组</td><td>

花纹　pattern

绿地　lawn

设施　facilities（设备则是 equipment）

瀑布　waterfall

（人造的）水池 pool（天然的池塘叫 pond）

有神的眼睛　sparkling eyes

浓眉　thick eyebrows

眼镜　glasses／a pair of glasses

强烈的好奇心　an inquiring mind
</td><td>

雕塑　sculptures

花坛　flowerbed

喷泉　fountain

亭子　pavilion

皱纹　wrinkles

闪亮的湖水　shimmering water

灿烂的笑容　a bright smile

花白的头发　salt-and-pepper hair
</td></tr>
</table>

听觉词汇　Hearing

鸟叫　birds chirping in the trees　　　　烦人的　annoying

悦耳的　pleasing to the ear　　　　轻松的音乐　soothing music

嗅觉词汇　Smell

花香　fragrance（of flowers）　　　　饭菜的香味　aroma（of food）

味觉词汇　Taste

非常好吃的　tasty／is out of this world　（delicious 仍然是最常用的"好吃的"）

感觉词汇　Emotional Perception

神圣的　holy／sacred　　　　特别棒的　awesome

信息量大的　informative　　　　娱乐性强的　entertaining

令人大开眼界的　eye-opening　　　　很值得回忆的　memorable

很有活力的　lively（请注意听 lively 的正确发音）／dynamic／vibrant

慷慨的　generous　　　　直率的　straightforward

可靠的　reliable　　　　乐观的　optimistic

无忧无虑的　carefree　　　　有吸引力的　attractive

开明的　open-minded　　　　举止优雅的　elegant

举世闻名的　world-renowned　　　　志向远大的　ambitious

遇事冷静的　level-headed　　　　顽强的　tough／tenacious

谦虚的　modest　　　　体贴别人的　thoughtful

（续表）

感觉词汇　Emotional Perception	
节俭的　frugal	喜欢社交的　sociable
很好接近的，不"摆架子"的　approachable	
反应快的，机智的　quick-witted	有远见的　forward-looking
多产的（指作家或者歌手）　prolific	有才华的　talented
势利的　snobbish	过于现实的　materialistic
很有回报的　rewarding	很有品位的，很有格调的　classy

休闲词汇　Leisure Activities	
唱卡拉OK　sing karaoke	练跆拳道　do taekwondo
滑旱冰　roller-skating	滑滑板　skateboarding
打太极　do taichi	做日光浴　sunbathing
遛狗　walk one's dog	慢跑　jogging
远足　go hiking	宿营　camping
烧烤　have a barbecue	
感觉焕然一新、精力充沛的　feel refreshed and energetic	

在本书的 Day 9 中我们还将分析 Part 3 所需的地道加分词汇。

★　　★　　★

今天的必备词汇学习结束之前，Pat 想再次认真地提醒各位：英语从来都不是"贵族语言"，它其实是一种极为看重实效（pragmatism）的语言。在欧洲，它不如法语那么"有格调"（classy），也没有德语严谨（rigid），但最后英语还是靠着自己的实用性（utility）征服了世界。实用永远是说英文的最高标准。

潜水去也。

Sleep tight.
Don't let the bed bugs bite.

超短线
The Ultra-Short Track

口语考试考的是一种综合素质，想仅靠背单词就通过雅思口语考试并不现实。但是对于备考时间过于紧张的"小盆友们"来说，熟练掌握下面的地道词汇并在口试时积极使用，虽然不能化腐朽为神奇，但至少能减少不做充分准备就去裸考的罪恶感：

名词：

approach 这个词是指用来做某事的方法，比如 a new approach to learning English。

动词：

participate in 参加……，比 take part in 稍正式一些，在英美口语里也很常用。

involve 涉及到……，在国外有些人只要说到将来的事儿就喜欢把这个词挂在嘴边。

It really **bothers** me. 只要一个东东让你"好烦"，就可以用这个动词描述它，从一个不喜欢的电视节目到一次没有安排好的 trip（过去时是 bothered）。

形容词：

stylish 形容"很时尚的"其实并不一定要用 fashionable。

entertaining 说一个东西娱乐性很强就是它了。

affluent 这是 rich 那个词的替身（"替身"目前在英美时髦叫 avatar 了，就因为 James Cameron 的那部电影）。

informative 这个词的意思是："信息量很大的"，用它来描述电视节目或者报纸杂志都不含糊。

appealing / attractive 可比 beautiful 更有韵味。

mind-numbing 就是比 boring 还枯燥 10 倍的。

efficient 高效率的，说得更直白那就是 It saves time，它的反义词 time-consuming 耗时间的，也是个挺拿分的词。

laid-back 考试时砸锅卖铁也不用 easygoing。

词组：

concerned about 关注……，比如 I'm very concerned about the air quality in my city.

类似的地道好词还有很多，但备考时间不够的同学还是先把这些搞定吧，时间充裕的同学可以再学习随本书附赠的《IELTS 口语高频词汇 & 短语速查手册》。

Day 4

> ## 说好雅思口语的句子
> ## *Why Convoluted Sentences Don't Work*

Why'd you go and break what's already broken?
I try to take a breath but I'm already choking
because everywhere I look, I can see
how you hold back.
How long till this goes away?

不知您是否熟悉 podcast 这种在国外已经相当流行的学习手段，比如在 google 上搜索一下 English as a second language（ESL）podcast，就会有上千个学习资源供你选择，而且都是标准的发音和地道的英文，真的该试一下了。

We take the test very seriously, but we'll take a laid-back approach to it.

词汇是砖，句子是墙。

如果墙太长，就变成了长城，会把你封闭起来，让人感觉你很 closed-off。

很多培训老师推荐学生说长难句。其实长难句有两层意思，一是要长，二是要难。环球的大班很多是我教的，我承认讲课的时候老师说长难句对大班授课的效果有好处，可以迅速让学生产生"仰视老师"的崇拜心理。但问题是，是否有必要在考口语的时候让考官"仰视"考生呢？

考雅思口语的时候，如果你想让自己的语言听起来不那么机械和怪异，就请尽量少用长、难、怪的句子。正常人在说话的时候是不可能像写作那样"处心积虑"的。

＼ 怎样说出不"难"的长句？

长期在国外学习和工作，Pat 可以很坦诚地告诉您：真实生活中的英语句子有一个明显的特点，就是虽然使用的动词、名词和形容词千变万化，但是最常用的连词却只有十几个。即使已经在国外住了很多年，积累了大量实词，但每天用到的连词也还是这十几个。而对于雅思口试而言，考生的分数很大程度上就取决于是否能够把这十几个连词准确、自然、流畅地运用好。

很多中国考生在口语考试里把像 Moreover, ...这样非常正式的连接词用到"也是醉了"。但 Pat 必须提醒您：在您的口试过程中请不要使用 Moreover, ... 否则将会导致考官感觉你是一个拘谨、较难接近的人。事实上，"其次"在国外日常生活里通常会用 also / as well 等自然的形式，或者更简洁地直接使用 and 来表达。

我们现在就来仔细看看地道英文口语里真正常用的连接词到底是哪些：

Pat 总结的英文口语里最常用的连接词

类别	内容	用法说明与例句
因果	... because ... so... therefore As a result	☆ 一句话里用了 because, 就不要再用 so, because 和 so 在同一个句子里"互不兼容" ☆ therefore 在地道口语交谈中用得并不多, 如果 IELTS 口试里使用的话, 最多也就是在 Part 3 里出现 1~2 次, 过多会让考官产生压迫感 ☆ As a result, ...（因此）也是更适合 Part 3 的讨论
让步	Although..., ... Even if..., ... ★ ... as long as...	☆ if 是如果, 而 Even if..., ... 则是"即使"的意思, 是对还没有发生的情况让步 例: Even if you take a taxi, you'll still miss the train... ☆ as long as 是 "只要……" 的意思, 例如 Backstreet Boys 的歌词 "I don't care who you are, where you're from or what you did, as long as you love me." 例: My parents don't really care what job I do, as long as I'm happy.
转折	But... However, ...	☆ 表示转折, 两个说法都可以, 在口语里 But 比 However 更常用
补充	Besides, ... ★ ... also ... ★ ... too. ★ ... as well. ★	例: I don't really want to go. Besides, it's too late now. 例: Olivia is fluent in Chinese and English. She also speaks a little French. ☆ ... too. 和 ... as well. 常用于句子结尾 例: The new system is more efficient, and it's cheaper too. 例: I need a ticket for *Tomorrowland*, and one for *Avengers* as well.

（续表）

类别	内容	用法说明与例句
修饰	… that… … who… ★ …, which… ★	☆ 定语从句在 IELTS 口语里还是挺常用的，不过 that 在口语里经常会被省略，而 which, who, when 和 where 则一般不省略： 例：I can't find the books（that）I got from the library. 例：A skilled workforce is crucial, which is why the training programme is so important. 例：Employees who work from home can have a better work-life balance.
对比	On the other hand, … ★ … while ★ … By contrast…	☆ On the other hand, …（另一方面），非正式口语里也可以说 But on the other hand, … 例：My job is boring. On the other hand, it pays well. ☆ … while 表示两种人或物之间的对比，英美日常生活里用得并不算多，但在口试中，特别是在 Part 3 里面使用 1~2 次完全可以，而且效果也相当自然： 例：I do every single bit of housework while Phoebe just does the dishes now and then. ☆ By contrast…在生活口语里用得不算太多，但可以在 Part 3 的深入讨论里用来引出两种人或者两种事物之间的对比： 例：The coastal areas have mild winters. By contrast, the central areas are extremely cold in winter.
举例和泛指	like… ★ such as… ★ For example, … ★ … and stuff like that. … and things like that. … or something like that.	☆ 举例和泛指同样可以帮你比较自然地说出更长一些的句子。举例除了 for example / such as 这些常用说法，其实"like…＋名词"是日常口语里最常听到的一个： 例：I'm into fantasy novels like *Harry Potter and The Chronicles of Narnia*. ☆ such as 在口语里也是 native speakers 谈话时举例的常用"例器"：

（续表）

类别	内容	用法说明与例句
其它	...as well as... ★ in terms of... ★ instead of / rather than ★ in particular ★	例：Lewis enjoys team sports such as basketball and cricket（板球，这是英格兰人相当迷的运动，和 Pat 的最爱 baseball 有一些相似之处）. ☆ 我们在前面说过：as well 常用于句子的结尾。而当用在句子中部时，则一般会用 as well as 的形式： 例：Jessie likes the bookstore as well as the reading club. ☆ in terms of 在……方面，就……而言，在意义上很像 talking about.../ speaking of...，但那两个词组多数时候出现在句首，而 in terms of 在句子里的位置则更加灵活： 例：Larry's last job was better in terms of salary. 例：The experiment didn't find any differences in terms of what students could learn. ☆ rather than 和 instead of 都表示"而不是……"的意思，这两个地道词组中国孩子们都耳熟能详，Pat 却很少听到各位在口语里面用： 例：Support was offered by the government rather than private companies. 例：We can deal with this chapter now instead of waiting until tomorrow. ☺ 例：People are mainly worried about traffic in the area, and, in particular, the increasing speed of cars near schools.
不是连词却胜似连词的表达	...tend to... ★ basically ★ actually ★ get ★	☆前三个在英美生活里极为常用的口语表达其实都不是连词，但仔细分析它们在句子里面又实在没起到什么实际的作用，主要功能还是让 native speakers 把自己的句子更自然地"串"起来。它们不应该再被无视了： 例：The gym tends to（一般会怎样，多半会怎样）get very busy after 6 pm.

（续表）

类别	内容	用法说明与例句
不是连词却胜似连词的表达		例：We tend to get freezing winters and dry summers in this part of the country. 例：Basically, the car is in good condition, but the paintwork needs a bit of attention. 例：Harrison is actually very helpful. ☆ 有些同学可能觉得 get 这样的词绝不会是拿分的词，但 Pat 却要很真诚地对您说：出国之后您对 get 的使用频率将会与您在国外生活的时间成正比。因为当您实在想不到一个合适的词去表达自己意思的时候，常常会发现其实就是这个异常方便的 get 一直在不离不弃地跟着自己： 例：Tyler's gone to the corner shop to get（=obtain）some milk. 例：I get（=receive）junk mail from this company daily. 例：Things are getting（=becoming）difficult in this country. 例：Katie got bored with her job immediately. 例：Ben'll get his suit dirty（cause sth. to become）in the park. 例：I'll get this paper finished by tonight.（get sth. done 在真实口语里同样极为常用）

也许你不愿意相信，上面表格中的这些连词，不仅仅是对付雅思口语考试的长句子足够了，甚至对付大家今后几年中的国外校园生活里的长句子也够了。英语口语里的动词、名词、形容词极为丰富，但是连词却真的是相当有限的。

仍然牢记：口语里的长句子是对短句子的使用非常熟练之后，再对这些最常用的连接词自然运用而形成的，而不是刻意去堆砌出来的（Don't just cram them into your sentences）。

可以用来攒人品的词组和句型

攒人品（RP）对于雅思考分的重要性已经越来越高。在一些城市的烤鸭当中正悄然兴起一股利用业余时间帮助公园里老奶奶回收农夫山泉塑料瓶的风潮，据说对提高分数很有效。

下面的这些考试时躲不掉的词组和句型，对于考前攒 RP 也有不可忽视的作用。

Absolutely Essential Words and Phrases for Boosting Your RP

可以攒人品的词组	As I see it, …/ I guess…/ I suppose… As for… = When it comes to… = Talking about（英式）= Speaking of（美式） tons of = loads of = lots of a wealth of… and stuff like that = and the like = and what not

☆ <u>As I see it, …/ I guess…/ I suppose…</u> 我想……

多数国内考生考口语的时候都是 I think 不断，连用 20 多个，听起来实在太像"思想者"的雕塑了。

I suppose… 也是口语里常用的"我想……"

I guess… 口语里其实有时并不是"我猜"，而只是很客气地说："俺脚着吧……"。

In my opinion 口试时可以用 1 ~ 2 次，但使用过多则会让考生听起来很"顽固"。

☆ <u>As for…（英美通用）= When it comes to…（英美通用）= Talking about（英式）= Speaking of（美式）</u> 说起……，谈到……

这几个词组大家都很熟悉，但是不要怕，它们在国外比在国内用得更多，坚决放心用，特别是前两个。

When it comes to traffic, I have to say living in this city is just like a nightmare（噩梦）.

☆ <u>loads of = tons of = lots of</u>

这三个口语词组的后面跟积极事物或者消极事物都很常见。

The Internet offers loads of free resources.

☆ a wealth of... 大量的

这个词组在国外生活里也很常用，注意：它后面跟的一般都是 knowledge / information/books 这类积极的事物。

Public libraries offer us a wealth of information.

☆ and stuff like that ＝ and the like ＝ and what not

是 "等等等等" 的意思，代替 and so on 不错。

I like suspense movies, action movies, funny movies and stuff like that.

可以攒人品的句型	tend to... ★
	I think of... as...
	is / are supposed to... ★
	are more likely to... ★
	not necessarily ★
	There's no sense in... ＝ It doesn't make any sense. ＝ It's pointless to...
	used to...
	is the norm ★
	is a luxury ★
	won't hurt ★
	enable sb. to do sth.
	have a hard time doing sth.

☆ tend to... ＝ for the most part 多半……

这两个是口语里经常用来代替 most of 的优秀句型，可惜真的极少在国内听到孩子们用。

例 1：Kids tend to be more active than adults.

例 2：The winter in Beijing tends to be freezing.（地道英文里还有个 frigid 更冷）

☆ I think of... as...

我把……看作是……

I think of photography as a way to express myself.

☆ is / are supposed to... ＝ should

在口语里代替 should 非它莫属。

Children are supposed to read more books because that can help them gain a great deal of knowledge.

☆ is / are more likely to... 更有可能去……

Children are more likely to copy the violence and bad language in movies.

☆ not necessarily 这个完全等于中文的 "不一定"、"未必"

Rich people are not necessarily happy.

☆ There's no sense in... = It doesn't make any sense. = It's pointless to... ……没道理

There's no sense in blocking（封杀）that extremely useful website.

☆ used to... 经常用来表示过去的某种习惯或者状态

有的朋友把英文名曲 "Somebody I Used to Know" 翻译成 "一些身体我用过才知道" 是很严重的翻译错误。

My reading speed is still quite slow, though I'm much better at dealing with vocabulary than I used to be.

☆ is the norm. ……是最普遍、最常见的做法

In traditional schools, rote learning（死记硬背）was the norm.

☆ make sense = be reasonable 有道理的

My tutor wrote me this note but it didn't make any sense.

☆ is a luxury 是一种奢望

Having your own garden is a luxury in cities like Beijing and Shanghai.

☆ won't hurt 不会有坏处

The house looks good. But a fresh paint job just won't hurt.

☆ enable sb. to do sth. 让某人可以去……

English abilities enable us to find more information on the information highway.（英美口语里经常用 the information highway 这个短语代替 the Internet，很酷）

☆ have a hard time doing sth. 很难去……

Graduates this year are having a hard time finding a decent job because of the financial crisis（金融危机）.（decent 这个词其实在口语里是 "还不错的" 意思，在国外生活中相当常用，但国内的孩子们宁可舍近求远地说 quite good 或者 fairly

good，也不愿意用 decent 这个既省事又拿分的说法）

☆ something is approaching / something is just around the corner 某件事情的发生时间越来越近了，即将发生

The IELTS test is approaching. / The IELTS test is just around the corner. ☺

雅思口语考试中到底有没有很特殊的句子？

Yes and No.

为什么这么说呢？因为口语的本质就是用来进行实时交流的工具，如果"处心积虑"地搞特殊那就一定不是正常人说的语言了。但是另一方面，下面两种句子还是有点特殊，如果恰当使用，在考试里还是明显会有拿分的作用的。

❶ 定语从句

用 that，who，which 引导的定语从句其实是中国同学们很熟悉的一种句式，但是对于以有效的沟通和交流为高分标准的 IELTS 口语来说，定语从句已经是一种很好的特殊句式了。《剑 10》的 Speaking 部分里就使用了定语从句：

Are there any other jobs **that** you think should have high salaries?

Describe someone **who** does something well.

❷ 虚拟语气

听起来很神奇，其实说白了就是用过去的时态表示现在或者将来的事情，表示比较客气的假设。雅思口语中很常用，而且在《剑 10》的 Speaking 部分里就有不少：

Some people say it **would be** better for society if everyone **got** the same salary. What do you think about that?

How do you think your school **could be** improved?

Where **would** you like to travel in the future?

　　定语从句和虚拟语气虽好，但也请您一定注意不要使用过度，因为用得太多它们压根儿就不"特殊"了。

超短线
The Ultra-Short Track

关于雅思备考，Pat 一直坚信而且确实被大量 7 分或以上的高分考生证明的真谛就是备考必须紧密地围绕剑桥官方所喜爱的英语风格进行，其他的不管听起来多漂亮至少对于雅思来说都是浮云。深刻领会剑桥官方提供的《剑 4》~《剑 10》是体会"剑桥风格"的最好武器。

备考时间已经彻底不够，甚至连书都已经看不下去了的"烤鸭"们其实不妨试试通过练习剑桥听力来提高口语语感的方法：多听剑 4～剑 10 每套题里的听力段子，并且把剑 4～剑 10 里听力试题的文本（tapescripts）也看上几遍，耳濡目染也能学到不少地道的口语句子。退一步说，即使这样做之后你的口语还是一点进步都没有，那至少也熟悉了剑桥听力的常考词汇和句型，并没有浪费时间。

比如，《剑 9》里的这个听力段子就用到了不少我们已经学到的关于地道英文连词的知识，证明了这些内容的实用性：

As well as that, wherever possible, recycled materials have been used. For example, the floors are made of reclaimed floor. And the owners haven't bought a single item of new furniture ... So the occupants of the house won't pollute the land or use any damaging chemicals. It's true that the actual construction of the house was harmful to the environment, mainly because they had to use massive amounts of concrete — one of the biggest sources of carbon dioxide in manufacturing. And, as you know, this is very damaging to the environment.

下面这个剑桥"段子"同样也调用了很多本书里 Pat 推荐的让您的说话风格更接近受过良好教育的 native speakers 真实口语风格的表达：

At a UK university, as I'm sure you know, you will be in an environment where independent learning is the norm, which takes most students a while to adapt to, and at a time when you'll be separated from your normal surrounding and, in most cases, your family.

不过 Pat 要特别提醒这部分同学的是：一定要先把官方提供的剑 4～剑 10 听力题都做完 1～2 遍之后再把它们当成口语资料，而绝不要先把它们当口语书学习，然后再当成听力题来练习，否则你会发现自己每次练都是满分……

Day

> # 雅思口语的段
Bricks versus Concrete

Are you listening?

We write a thousand pages

They're torn and on the floor

Headlights hammer the windows

We're locked behind these doors

And we are never leaving

because this place is part of us

And all these scenes repeating are just so cold to the touch

　　这个相当酷的辩论网站几乎覆盖了所有的常考口语讨论话题。在页面中部选择 Education，Culture，Environment & Animal Welfare 等主题后，您就可以在 This house believes that 的后面看到各种各样的辩论话题。点击辩论话题之后，您就可以立刻找到自己需要的各种支持和反对理由(points for & points against)。

▶ *We take the test very seriously, but we'll take a laid-back approach to it.*

怎样才能说出长段落?

(本章适合备考时间充裕的同学学习)

如果您上过培训课,那么口语老师一定给自己的方法起了一个新奇有趣的(fancy)名字,通过它来使自己的方法在学生的心目中产生一种神秘感和敬畏感(get you mystified and put you in awe)。这种作法可以增强教师授课的综合效果,但其实如果看穿了,雅思口语 Part 1 和 Part 3 的答案不管多么有创意,却一定是沿着两条思路展开的:顺承与对比。

中国的传统艺术讲究"起承转合"四个字,咱们就用这四个字来形象地分析一下顺承和对比的区别。

结构1 "起—承—(合)"

这种结构的特点是:

(1)先直接回答考官提出的问题(起),(2)再具体展开自己的回答(承),(3)如果愿意还可以在答案的结尾总结一句(合),但这句话并不是必需的,如果感觉不自然那么就不要说。

具体展开的方式有:

• 使用 because, so, for example, such as, like(比如 ……),if, and, also, even 等逻辑关系词

• 使用 they, I, we, it, that 等代词

• 再次使用前一句话里使用过的关键词

以上三种方法并不互相排斥,一个答案里往往会同时用到其中的两种甚至三种方法。它们既可以确保你说出的答案完全扣题,而且又可以让你的句子之间产生自然的承接。

请看《剑10》Test 3 的这个问题:

Do you enjoy travelling?

下面的 7 分答案就是典型的"起—承—合"结构。

(起:回答考官提出的问题)Yes, I do. (承:具体展开)Travelling is fun and enjoyable. I can see new things when I travel. I can **also** make lots of friends during trips to other places. **And** of course, travelling expands **my** mind and helps **me** learn about other cultures. (合) I guess that's exactly why I really enjoy travelling.

我们再来看《剑 10》Test 2 的这个问题：

At what times of day do you like to listen to music?

下面这个 7 分答案同样是典型的 "起—承" 结构：

(起:回答考官提出的问题) I like to listen to music in the late afternoon and at night. (承:具体展开) I tend to feel tired in the late afternoon after work, **and** music can make **me** feel refreshed. Listening to music at night before bedtime makes **me** feel calm and relaxed, **so** I can sleep well.

《剑 10》Test 4 这个问题的 7 分答案也是 "起—承" 结构：

Are there any benefits to society of people wanting to get new possessions?

(起:回答考官提出的问题) Yes, there are. (承:具体展开) People need to work hard **if** they want to get new possessions. When people buy new possessions, **like** new phones, new clothes or new furniture, **they also** contribute to the economy. **And their** demand for new things often leads to inventions and innovations.

再来看这道常考题：

Why do some people like collecting things?

下面这个 7 分水平的答案也是用了 "起—承" 结构。

(起:回答考官提出的问题) Different people may collect things for different reasons. (承:具体展开) Some people collect things **because they** have too much spare time and need more personal pleasure. Others may think of collecting stuff as a good way to make investments. **I even** know people who collect things just to show **them** off to friends.

再看这道常考题：

Do you like shopping?

一个 6 分水平的 "起—承" 式答案可能是这样的：

(起:回答考官提出的问题) Yes, I like it. (承:具体展开) I have lots of free time. **So** when I feel bored, I go shopping with friends. Shopping is **also** a good way to reduce stress.

"起—承—(合)"式的优点:逻辑简单明白,向着同一个方向展开内容就可以了。

"起—承—(合)"式的缺点:口语不太好的同学有时候会发现答案说不长。但客观地说如果您的口语目标只是 6 分,答案本来也不需要很长,平均起来 2 ~3 句话已经足够(当然答案长度只是一个方面,更重要的还是看内容和英文是不是地道)。

☆ "起—承—(合)"结构的常用词汇和句型
(不要都背,否则……肯定记不住!)

(1) 起

Yes / No 题		Wh- / How 题	
词汇及句型	说明	词汇及句型	说明
Yes / Yeah / Yep ☆ Sure. You bet. Absolutely. Certainly. Definitely. *No / Nope.* *Not really.* *Not necessarily.* *No way!* ☆	☆ Yep 这个词英美年轻人很常用,而且通常用升调 ☆ No way! 语气很强,除非你真的想表示强烈的否定,否则不要用	Obviously, … ☆ Apparently, … I'm pretty sure… *To be honest, …* *In fact, …* *As a matter of fact, …* There are a variety of… ☆ There are a wide range of… ☆	☆ Obviously, … 和 Apparently, … 都表示"很明显" ☆ 斜体的词汇可以用来引出否定的答案 ☆ There are a variety of … 和 There are a wide range of… 也表示"有多种多样的……"

(2) 承

词语和句型	备注
… because… … primarily because… ☆ Besides, … … also…	☆ … primarily because…(首先是因为……) ☆ … plus…(而且) e. g. Beijing is a gorgeous (非常漂亮的)city, plus it has such an amazing history.

（续表）

词语和句型	备注
… plus… ☆ …, too. And … as well. In other words, … That is to say, … I mean … By the way, …	☆ as well 经常出现在句尾, 而当用在句子中部时则会改为 as well as 的形式。在英美生活里有时候也能听到有人把 as well 放在句首, 但并不是每个人都喜欢这样使用: 例: I'll visit Andrew, and Martin as well. 例: I need to go to the bookshop as well as the post office.

⚠ WARNING   请注意:在雅思口语里极少有机会使用"In a word, …"。这是很多中国考生, 甚至教师频繁出现的错误。in a word 在英文里面后面永远只跟一个单词, 而不能跟一个句子, 比如 She is, in a word, lying.

结构2 "起—承—转—(合)"

"起—承—转— (合)" 式就是先回答考官提出的问题, 然后开始说其中一方面, 接下来再说另一方面。每方面各说多少其实是比较随意的, 没必要太机械, 只要确保不说空话 (rambling) 就可以了。最后的 "合" 部分如果觉得不自然也可以省略。

请看《剑10》Test 2 的这个问题:

How do large shopping malls and commercial centers affect small local businesses?

下面这个 7 分答案就是典型的 "起—承—转" 结构:

(起:回答考官提出的问题) They can have both positive and negative effects on small local businesses. (承:展开其中的一个方面) Large shopping malls and commercial centers can provide consumers with more choices and often lower prices. So they take a lot of business away from local businesses. (转:展开另一个方面) **On the other hand**, the competition can make local businesses improve their goods and services to better meet local people's needs.

> "起—承—转—(合)" 式的优缺点和 "起—承—(合)" 式正好相反:它的内容比较容易说得更多, 因为毕竟两方面都可以展开。但是相应地, 它的结构也要更复杂一些。

☆ "起—承—转—(合)"式结构的常用词汇和句型

(不要全背，否则……还是记不住!)

(1) **起**

Yes / No 题	Wh- / How 题
Yes and no. I can't say for sure. (注意和起—承结构里的"起"不同)	It's kind of complicated.（kind of 是"有点儿"，complicated 是"复杂的"） … may vary from person to person.

(2) **承**

可以参考前面的"起—承—(合)"结构的承接部分，因为两种结构里的"承"部分是相似的。

(3) **转**

On the other hand, …

But…

By contrast, … ☆

If… didn't…, …would… ☆

Without…, … would… ☆

☆ By contrast, …

表示用它后面的内容和它前面的内容去对比。可以用它在 Part 3 里进行过去与现在、现在与将来、男性与女性、成年人与儿童、城市与乡村等之间的对比时使用 1~2 次。

例句：Men like the Internet for the freedom it gives them to try new ways of doing things. **By contrast**, women like the new opportunities the Internet gives them to interact with others.

☆ If… didn't…, … would…

当 If 在"转"的部分里使用时，常会用 If… didn't…, … would…的虚拟语气形式，假设一种和现实相反的情况。

例句：**If** governments **didn't** provide museums with financial support, they **would** have to rely on admission fees.

☆ Without..., ... would...

它也是一种虚拟语气形式，假设某个实际存在的事物如果不存在将会怎样。

例句：The Internet is an important source of information. **Without** the Internet, we **would** have great difficulty finding the information we need.

Part 2 结构的 4 种选择

Scenario 1：对于"牛人"，Pat 建议您不要太担心卡片答案的结构，只要确保自己的答案能够覆盖卡片上的每一个提示要点，并适当补充确实与话题相关的内容即可。雅思口语其实没有太"奇葩"（wacky）的卡片，否则就不是口试而是有奖问答了。

Scenario 2：对于有一定的英语表述能力的考生，Pat 建议您看到卡片之后有一个大致（rough-and-ready）的顺序安排就好了，也不必过于机械（mechanical）。

Scenario 3：对于完全没有口语功底但是又有"野心"想考高分的苦孩子们，也可以考虑背一些结构性的句子。下面是一些不错的结构性句子，每组知道一句就够：

❶ I'm going to talk about...

    I'd like to talk about...

    Well, let me talk about...

    I'd like to describe...

    省略号填入你要描述的话题，比如 Beijing, my favourite sport, my cousin...

❷ I'll start off by talking about...

    To begin with, I'll talk about...

    省略号填入卡片上第一个提示中的问题。

❸ Moving on to...

As for..., ...

省略号填入卡片上第二个提示中的问题。

❹ Concerning with the next question of...

Now let's look at...

省略号填入卡片上第三个提示中的问题。

❺ Maybe I could wrap up my description with my thoughts about...

Now, I'm going to explain to you...

省略号填入卡片上 Explain... 后面第四个提示中的问题。

Scenario 4：下面的几个词组，适合从"大牛"到"菜鸟"（rookies / newbies）的全部考生，因为它们可以帮助你在不同话题之间快速转换。

▶ **in terms of...**（谈到……，关于……）

= regarding = concerning = when it comes to

e. g. In terms of price, this car would be a nice choice.

▶ **What I need to emphasize here is that...**

= The fact I need to highlight here is that...（我需要特别强调的是……）

= What I need to stress here is that...

e. g. What I need to emphasize here is that he did that all by himself.

▶ **Specifically, ...**（具体地说，……）这个经常用来进一步地深入说明

e. g. He made great contributions to China. Specifically, he donated（捐献）lots of money to various charities（慈善组织）in China.

▶ **By the way, ...**常用在答案快要结束的位置

e. g. By the way, some parrots can be used as alarm clocks.

▶ **In other words, ...**

= I mean...

e. g. In other words, people go there not for pleasure, but on business.

把段落说长的更多实用技巧

① 下面的表达都表示"更具体地说":

Specifically, …

In particular, …

② 口语里最有效的举例方式:

For example…

like…

such as…

③ 如果你感觉已经实在没什么可再展开的了可考官却还意犹未尽,那么可以试试:

In other words, …

I mean…

… that is to say, …

然后所有你要做的,就是很"流氓(cheeky)"地把前面一句话换个说法再说一遍……

超短线
The Ultra-Short Track

对于备考时间严重不足的同学们来说,如果本来就没兴趣深入研究口语的段落结构,但又奢望能把自己的回答说得"跌宕起伏",那么就只能靠下面的六种关系了:

a 因果	b 举例
c 假设	d 让步
e 对比	f 补充

如果您现在在图书馆或者自习教室里,请把它们默念五遍,然后再看看本书 Day 4 里分别对应这六种关系的连接词,并且在说英文时积极使用它们,您就会发现自己说的内容已经有了一些层次感。

Day

练出 decent 的发音
Taken at Face Value

I take it you already know.
Of tough and bough and cough and dough.
And now you wish, perhaps,
To learn of less familiar traps.

*_http://www.bbc.co.uk/worldservice/learningenglish/grammar/pron_*

　　要练出不错的发音，除了积极模仿音频里的英国 SG 和 MM，还可以登录上面的这个 BBC 官方网站，里面的发音部分相当酷。

*_www.howjsay.com_ 与 _www.inogolo.com_*

　　如果你遇到即使通过词典还是拿不准发音的单词，请立刻登录左边这个网站，它会带你朗读所有的英语常用词。而右边这个网站则专门提供对人名、地名等专有名词的朗读。

▶ *We take the test very seriously, but we'll take a laid-back approach to it.*

前文已述，地道英文口语里有个相当常用的单词，其意思与中文里的"不错"极为接近：decent。native 的发音需要长期积累，attractive 的发音需要专业训练，但 decent 的发音是有可能在短时间内就练成的。

多短呢？也许，一天……

三大纪律

☆ 少看理论 ☆

关于英语发音的书面理论不管听起来多么玄妙，它们其实只会让你的中文 reading 能力越来越强，靠研究书面理论去提高英语发音要比让老外分清张馨予、张予曦、张雨绮的名字更难。

☆ 集中精力 ☆

只要开始练习你就必须把 TV set，PC，laptop，tablet，PSP，smartphone 等干扰源全部关掉，完全投入到战斗中（Throw yourself into it.），唯一允许留在你身边的电子产品是一个录音装置（a recording device）。

☆ 听自己说 ☆

身边放一个录音笔，这样进步更快。实在不好意思就把你身边的人都赶走，并且规定一个小时之后才能回来。

适合国内同学的英文单词发音测验
A Pop Quiz on Pronunciation

请各位先做三个小测验，都是 Pat 总结的中国考生常见发音错误，看看现在你属于哪种水平。

☆ TEST 1 — EASY

If your English is every bit as good as the average English learner in China, you will have no difficulty pronouncing the following words correctly.

这个测试很简单，是看你能不能达到中国学生发音的平均水平，如果错 5 个以上，那你的英语现在就肯定处在中国人能听懂你的意思，但是外国人完全听不明白你在说什么的状态。测试的时候请随时对照音频里的录音。

❶ beach ❷ because ❸ yesterday ❹ famous

⑤ invite   ⑥ library   ⑦ night — light   ⑧ slow — snow

⑨ thick — sick   ⑩ said — sad

☆ TEST 2 — HARDER

Your English pronunciation skill is distinctly above average here in China if you can pronounce the following words properly.

这个测试难度大一些，如果这些单词你的发音都正确，你的发音就处在 native English speakers 能轻松听懂的状态。测试的时候请随时对照音频里的录音。

① newspaper   ② industry   ③ quite — quiet   ④ temperature

⑤ sandwich   ⑥ thought   ⑦ clothes   ⑧ kind

⑨ comfortable   ⑩ loose — lose

☆ TEST 3 — HARDEST

Now you can discover how close you are to native English speakers in pronunciation. The next ten words are no cinch — you will be acquitting yourself creditably if you pronounce eight of them correctly.

这个测试最难，是看你英语发音的可爱指数。如果这 10 个词你都能正确发音，不用我说，肯定有老外夸过你发音好。测试的时候请随时对照音频里的录音。

① atmosphere   ② celebrity   ③ affluent   ④ synthesize

⑤ photography   ⑥ economic   ⑦ gorgeous   ⑧ unique

⑨ resources   ⑩ sunbathing

单词发音的七宗罪

听来听去，国内的考生发音其实只有 7 种常见错误（您不是要告诉我刚才的测试里 7 种错误您全都犯了吧?）。如果 7 种错误都能改掉，发音虽然还不完美，但是已经完全可以让老外轻松听懂你的英语了。

1. 应该是长音还是短音?

Pat 经常听到学生会把 meal 说成 mill，把 sheet 读成 shit，甚至还有人把 beach 说成

bitch。请您仔细跟音频朗读下面的单词：

heat   extreme   miss   peak   pick

2. 力度够不够?

北京话讲究轻快，所以很多北京考生在说英语的时候发音力度不够，例如把 because 发成"笔铐子"，sorry 说成"骚瑞"，apple 念成"挨剖"，都是因为发音的力度不够。请来自北京的读者仔细跟音频朗读下面的单词：

net   Patrick（有无数北京孩子把 Pat 英文名字里的 Pa 轻轻松松地发成了"拍"的音）
family   kind   easily   because   sorry   apply

3. 有没有儿化音?

北方话，特别是北京话，儿化音超多。像"公主坟儿"，如果说成"公主坟"，或者把"冰棍儿"说成"冰棍"，就会让人不寒而栗。但是来自中国北方的同学一定要注意：对于不含 r 这个字母的单词，即使在美国，也是不会有儿化音的。

请来自北方的读者仔细跟音频朗读下面的单词:

famous   panda   grandpa   gorgeous   difficult

4. th 音到底怎么发?

中文里面没有 th 这个音，所以要发好这个音还真要好好练一练。关键是舌尖儿要伸到上牙的外面一点点（不要太多，否则很难看哦），轻轻地碰到上牙，然后轻轻吹口气，效果就出来了。如果是 these 里面的 th，就把舌尖伸出来一点点，轻轻地在上牙上摩擦一下，就可以了。请大家仔细跟音频朗读下面的单词:

those   thought   synthesize   thread   throw

5. l 和 n 怎么区分?

这两个音在中国南方的一些地区经常有考生分不清，因为一些方言里面没有 n 这个音。另外我还发现一些说粤语的同学，有时候把 fat 里面的 t 省掉了，把 report 里面的 t 也省掉了，也请务必注意改正。请南方的读者仔细跟音频模仿下面单词的发音:

night   light   slow   snow   money（有些南方同学会把这个词说得像英文里的女孩名字 Molly，如果您也有这个问题请一定注意跟着录音积极模仿）

6. 重音究竟在哪儿?

把重音位置发正确是比较高端的要求了。重音的位置发错,小则会听起来别扭,大则会导致考官难以理解你的意思。请读者仔细跟音频模仿下面单词的发音:

comfortable   newspaper   atmosphere   celebrity   photography
yesterday   temperature

7. v 和 w 的区别

这两个音区分的关键是牢记发 v 的音牙齿会碰到下嘴唇,但是发 w 的音牙齿不碰下嘴唇。请大家仔细跟音频模仿下列单词的发音:

invite   wife   swim   win   visit

☆ TEST 4 — TONGUE TWISTER PRACTICE

下面的三个绕口令都是帮助你巩固今天学习的效果的,请跟录音好好练习朗读一下。

❶ If Peter Piper picked a peck of pickled peppers, where's the peck of pickled peppers Peter Piper picked?

❷ We will wish to visit their wives.

❸ I think this thin thread will go through the eye of this thick needle.

★   ★   ★

好,单词的发音我们先练习到这里。打开手机看看有没有彩信。

★   ★   ★

练好句子的发音

现在我们再前进一步,突破句子的发音。还是强调我们练习的三大纪律:

★ 少看理论

★ 集中精力

★ 听自己说

高分考生的发音凭什么拿高分?

经常有学生跟我抱怨,为什么看 *Gossip Girl* 或者 *The Big Bang Theory* 的时候没有几句话能听懂。其实除了很多国内同学所习惯的词汇与当代真实英语的常用词汇严重脱节外,另一个重要原因就是不熟悉连读、弱化这些发音规则,所以导致很多你认识的单词却听不懂。

不信您试试这个:

http://www.oprah.com/oprahs-lifeclass/What-Oprah-Learned-from-Randy-Pauschs-Last-Lecture-Video

这个 Randy 教授在英美可是鼎鼎大名的,号召力甚至超过 Obama 和 David Cameron,你能听懂 Oprah Winfrey 对他的最后一次演讲的思考吗?

几年来的教学实践告诉我,发音能真正接近 native English speakers 的考生,一定会注意下面四个方面:

★ 连读	★ 弱化
★ 句子重音	★ 语调

A 弱化与连读 Weak form and Liaison

弱化与连读是区分发音高手和菜鸟的重要依据。这两个技巧效果相似,都是让你的句子更流利更连贯,所以我们把这两项放在一起练习。请仔细听音频的朗读,认真模仿下面的发音。

part-time

but now

I'll

He'll

what's

Where is she?

Do you want a beer?

Want to go shopping?

give me an answer

three hundred years

but that word is hard

it used to be

You should take care of them.

kick back and relax

the gap between the urban area and the rural area

B　句子的重音 Sentence Stress

一般来说，名词、动词和形容词会倾向于重读，而介词、连词和代词会倾向于轻读。但是要注意别太机械地使用这个规则，其实很多时候最重要的是看你的句子要强调哪一个单词。比如下面的句子，强调的内容不一样，重读的单词就不同。

I don't know where he is now. (Maybe someone else does.)

I don't know where he is now. (So don't keep asking me.)

I don't know where he is now. (But I know where Nancy is.)

I don't know where he is now. (But I saw him last week.)

C　句子的语调 Sentence Intonation

大家都知道，一般来说，疑问句用升调，陈述句用降调。但实际上可没那么简单，native English speakers 说话，每句话里面都会有几次升降调的变化。只是陈述句一般句尾落在降调，而疑问句句尾落在升调。请仔细听录音，体会下面一段话每个句子的升降调，并注意模仿。(放心，这个段落一定不会白模仿的，里面的很多句子在雅思口语 Part 1 和 Part 2 我们都可以用的)

(Please pay close attention to the word stress sentence intonation.)

Three Great Reasons to Learn a Foreign Language

☆ Improve your Chinese

As a person who speaks only one language, you have no basis for comparison; all you know is Chinese. In different languages the same idea is often expressed in different ways. There is a reason most great writers and poets are students of many languages.

☆ Enhance your travel experiences

Traveling is one of the great joys of life and also one of the most expensive. Why not get the most out of your experience? As a person who doesn't know the native tongue you are completely excluded from the culture. Knowing even a few phrases of the language will make a huge difference. You will meet many more people and find it much easier to get around.

☆ Languages are beautiful

Language is what makes us human. It is the medium we use to share our thoughts with the world. Could you imagine thought without language? Great language also has a wonderful musical quality. Learning a new language is like learning a new way to think and a new way to sing.

这一节给大家重点讲的是，如何让你的口语发音进一步接近老外的地道发音。其中最重点推荐的是连读和弱化这两个技巧。今天的最后，给各位介绍几段生活化的口语，这段话体现了地道英语发音的全部特点，请大家认真听，认真模仿。

(Familiarize yourself with the way native English speakers actually speak in daily life, particularly how some consonants and vowels are fused or omitted.)

Larry: Hi, Harry. Great to see you again. I heard you've traveled a lot recently.

Harry: Yup. Actually, in the past three months I traveled to tons of countries in Africa.

Larry: I really envy you, man! Did you pet a zebra?

Harry: Well, I didn't get to pet a zebra, but I was once chased by an elephant, and it was pretty scary!

Larry: Serious?

Harry: Nope, just kidding.

Larry: You really scared the heck out of me, buddy.

Harry: I really missed the comforts of home. And now I just want to take a break. A long break in my super comfy home!

The Ultra-Short Track

　　对于备考时间紧但又对自己的单词发音没有信心的同学，如果你对某个词甚至句子的发音不确定，也许你会选择查字典。其实可以试试 www. oddcast. com/home/demos/tts/tts_ example. php。它甚至允许你自己选择英音还是美音、男声还是女声，而且屏幕上的大脑袋盯着你也特有考试的感觉 ☺。

Day

▶ 反正 **Part 1**
Opposites Attract

Polar opposites don't push away
It's the same on the weekends as the
rest of the days
I know I should go but I'll probably stay
I'm trying to drink away the rest of the day

☞ **口语 Part 1 话题库索引**

Topic 1: Studies（Including learning English） ① 学习（含学习英语）   P113

Topic 2: Work   ② 工作   P115

Topic 3: Hometown（Including Traffic & Pollution） ③ 家乡（含交通和污染） P117

Topic 4: Entertainment（Including the movies, ④ 娱乐（含电影、电视、广播
TV, the radio, and other Leisure Activities）   以及其他休闲活动）   P121

Topic 5: Reading & Writing   ⑤ 报纸、杂志、阅读和写作
                                                                        P124

Topic 6: Clothing   ⑥ 服装   P127

Topic 7: Weather & Seasons   ⑦ 天气与季节   P128

Topic 8: Arts（Including Music, Painting,   ⑧ 艺术（含音乐、绘画与摄影）
Drawing and Photography）   P130

Topic 9: People（Including Family, Friends   ⑨ 人（含家庭、朋友、邻居与
and Meeting New People）   新认识的人）   P133

Topic 10: Collection   ⑩ 收藏   P136

Topic 11: Buildings（Including Museums, Libr-   ⑪ 建筑（含住所、博物馆、图
aries, Hotels, Houses, Flats 英式英语／Apart-   书馆和宾馆）   P137
ments 美式英语）

Topic 12: Sports, Other Outdoor Activities,   ⑫ 运动、其他户外活动、骑自行
Biking & Games   车以及游戏   P140

Topic 13: Shopping   ⑬ 购物   P143

Topic 14: Pets   ⑭ 宠物   P144

Topic 15: Age   ⑮ 年龄   P145

Topic 16: Travel   ⑯ 旅行   P146

Topic 17: Food（Including Restaurants,   ⑰ 食品（含餐馆、三餐、健康
Meals, Healthy Eating and Cooking）   饮食与做饭）   P147

Topic 18: Colours   ⑱ 颜色与数字   P150

Topic 19: Nature（Including Gardens, Parks,   ⑲ 自然（含花、花园、公园、
Birds and Flowers）   鸟类）   P150

Topic 20: Festivals, Holidays & Parties（Including ⑳ 节日、假期与派对（含生日、
Birthday, Gifts and Dancing）   礼物与跳舞）   P152

Pat 的 Part 1 完整素材库（时间太紧的读者只要结合我在博客里贴出的本月预测题准备就好了）
Pat's Idea Pool for the Part 1 Test

　　口语 Part 1 的话题都是生活中常见的，ideas 并不难想。但如果一边想思路，一边又想英语怎么表达，就可能导致 fluency 严重下降。其实正反两方面都说一说是个不错的选择，肯定比只说一方面内容多点。因此本章里的话题都按照正反两方面给大家提供思路，把它们串起来的方式可以参考本书前面的 Day 4 和 Day 5。不过实战的时候也没必要太机械，如果一方面已经够了那就没必要再正反都说。

　　请充分熟悉下面素材库里的句子，不要 100% 照背，多看看就行。时间紧的同学按照 Pat 在博客 blog.sina.com.cn/ieltsguru 里贴的最新口语预测题进行准备就够了。

Topic 1: Studies（including learning English）
学习（含学习英语）

★ I'm sure my hard work will pay off（会有回报）.	
AFFIRMATIVE（正方）	**NEGATIVE（反方）**
My university has a great reputation（名誉）. 注：IELTS 口语中也经常可以用 excellent 来代替 great	The curriculum（课程）is too hard for me. 注：hard 在地道口语中也经常可以用 tough 或 difficult 代替
★ This is a pretty promising field（有前途的领域）. 注："领域" 在口语里还可说 area 或者 sphere	I guess I will have a hard time finding a job when I graduate. 注：地道英文中 "找到工作" 也经常会用 land a job 这一固定表达
★ It enables me to fulfill my potential.（让我发挥我的潜力） 注：enable sb. to do sth. 让某人可以去做某事	We are not encouraged to exchange（交换）ideas with other students.
例：The new student loan will enable the undergrads as well as grad students to continue their studies. undergrads 是国外大学校园里对本科生	I hate the force-feeding approach to teaching.（填鸭式教学）

(undergraduates) 的更常见说法, 而研究生 (graduate students) 在实际校园生活里则通常被简称为 grad students	
My professors are really thoughtful and considerate (关心人的).	But sometimes what they teach in class is over my head (听不懂). 注: "听不懂" 在地道口语里也常会说成 It's beyond me.
My teachers are pretty lenient (要求不是很严的). 注: 在国外一般私立学校 private school 的老师要求得严一些 (strict / demanding) 而公立学校 public school 的老师相对比较 lenient	My teachers are so strict. It seems very few Chinese teachers encourage their students to explore (探索) areas that are beyond academic boundaries (超出学术课程界限的).
★ On top of that, there's a wide variety of extracurricular activities (课外活动), like the debate club, the chess club, the school newspaper, the basketball team, the choir (合唱团) and even a rock band. 注: "学校的社团" 在地道英文中一般就叫作某某 club, 这里并非指俱乐部	But extracurricular activities can be time-consuming (很耗时间的). 注: time-consuming 是 "很耗时间的" 意思, 它在地道英文中的反义词有两个, 一个是 efficient (高效率的), 另一个则是 rewarding (回报丰厚的)
I volunteer at the university library / school library. 注: 其实做 volunteer work 是 "LW" 考官们相当喜欢听到的一种经历; 而且 volunteer 的用法很灵活, 可以用做 verb, adjective 和 noun	I have a heavy class load this term. 这学期课业负担很重。注: 在学校里当你听到别人说 workload 时其实也是指课业负担
★ The canteen / cafeteria (食堂) serves great food.	The canteen / cafeteria food is atrocious (差得出奇的). 注: 说食物极其难吃还可以用 gross, 但雅思口试时请不要用 yucky ✗

（续表）

It's important to be bilingual（双语）today.	
AFFIRMATIVE（正方）	**NEGATIVE（反方）**
★ Understanding English enables you to understand the English-speaking cultures better. 注："双语的" bilingual 很多考生认识，但口试时却往往会忘记你自己其实就是 bilingual	You are considered "left behind" if you can't speak English.
Reading English novels and online magazines is an excellent way to boost your vocabulary（扩大词汇量）.	Learning a foreign language takes time and energy. 注：地道英文中还有 an arduous process（是一个艰苦的过程）的说法
English abilities give you a competitive edge and improve your chances of employment.	There're plenty of test-taking techniques（应试技巧）. But as a matter of fact, there're no shortcuts（捷径）to learning a foreign language.
★ We can travel the world with few language barriers（语言障碍）if we speak good English. 注：travel the world 是地道英文里的一个固定短语，这里 travel 后面不一定要加介词	中文字幕叫作 Chinese subtitles，中文配音的电影则叫作 movies dubbed in Chinese。
★ Singing along to English songs can help you acquire（获得）this language as well. 注：acquire 是教育类的地道加分词，后面可以跟某种知识或技能，比如 acquire languages skills	

Topic 2: Work
工作

FOR（正方）	AGAINST（反方）
It's well-paid. 注：同义表达是 The pay is good. 请国内同学注意这里的 pay 不要说成 payment	I'm really tired of working for peanuts（挣钱少）.

（续表）

★ My boss treats everyone equally.	I have to work overtime（加班）practically every day. 注：practically 在口语中经常代替 almost
The working environment is pretty friendly.	It doesn't offer the opportunity for quick promotion（提升）.
★ It offers me a whole lot of benefits（这里不是好处，而是福利，在英美员工们提到自己的工作福利时很少用 welfare 那个词，反倒是更常用 benefits），like paid vacation, a pension（养老金）plan and, on top of all that, a company car.	My boss is a slave driver（真不把员工当人）。"同事"英语怎么说呢？在多数公司里叫作 colleagues 或者 co-workers，在英国有时也能听到 workmates 的说法，但在美国通常只有蓝领工作者才管自己的同事们叫 workmates
I'm learning new skills to help my career prospects（事业的前景）.	It's a dead-end job（没有前途的工作）。
Sometimes I have to take charge of the whole team. 注：下次当您下意识地想到 be responsible for 的时候，请考虑是否可以用 be in charge of 去替换	I'm constantly on the go. 注：constantly 这个副词在地道口语中经常代替 always
★ Employees are paid time-and-a-quarter（125%）if they work on weekends. time-and-a-half（150%） double time（200%）	This job is back-breaking work.

Pat 指南

☆ 请已经工作的朋友们注意：你回答的工作并不一定是你的真实工作，只要英文正确就很好了。绝不用担心后面会问和你的工作相关的技术（specialized）问题。

☆ 下面几种工作回答起来更有特色：

I'm a freelancer（自由职业者）. (freelance writer, a freelance photographer...)

I'm self-employed.（自己有 business）

> a surgeon（外科医生）, a photographer（摄影师）, a pastry chef（面点师）,
>
> a veterinarian（兽医）, a biologist（生物学家）, geologist（地质学家）

但如果您对自己的口语没有足够的自信，就请不要说自己是一位 translator（翻译）或者 interpreter（口译员）。原因？It's plain as the nose on your face. ☺

☆ 在国外工作中凡是可以给员工带来动力的东西都可以称为 an incentive。

☆ "事业的发展方向" 在地道英语里有个特别常用的词组 career path，例如：It gives me a positive work environment（如果说 working environment 也是对的，在英美说 work environment 的人略多一点）with a promising career path.

Topic 3: Hometown（Including Traffic & Pollution）
家乡（含交通和污染）

AFFIRMATIVE（正方）	NEGATIVE（反方）
★ My hometown is a coastal city（沿海城市）. It offers some of the best beaches in China. 请一定注意 beach 中的 ea 是长音，绝不要说成短音，否则会把考官惹 "毛"）	The air is so smoggy（烟雾重的）.
	Lots of people there suffer from respiratory diseases（呼吸系统疾病）.
★ My hometown is an inland（内陆的）city best-known for the gentle, rolling hills surrounding it.	The traffic is always bumper-to-bumper（= tied up）during the rush hour. 注：表示在……期间时 during 在地道英文中用得极多，但国内考生都不太爱用，遗憾
This city is steeped in（沉浸在）time-honored（历史悠久的）traditions.	The cost of living is sky-high.
It's prosperous（繁荣的）.	"经济不景气" 英文：The economy is in a slump.
★ There's a real sense of community（社区）.	There's no sense of community.（邻居间缺少交流）
★ This city is well-known for its architectural heritage（建筑遗产）.	I can't stand the hustle and bustle（拥挤，喧闹）there. 注：can't stand... 无法忍受……
The cityscape（城市景观）is gorgeous and there are tons of towering skyscrapers（摩天楼）there.	Most of the buildings there are two to three storeys（层）high.

（续表）

★ High-rise buildings are sprouting up all over the city.	Some areas are pretty run-down（破旧的）.
It's pretty sprawling.（宽阔的，建筑分散的，比如美国的 Arizona 州）	It's densely-populated.（人口密集的，比如中国的香港）
★ I enjoy the peace and quiet there. 注：在这里 quiet 是名词	The noise really bothered me（烦人的）. I didn't sleep a wink last night.（一夜没睡）
This city is like a magnet（磁铁）for the tourists.	It's not so well-known, not even in China.
★ town→small city→medium-sized city→big city→metropolitan area（规模越来越大） ★ 城市里的 leisure facilities（休闲设施）: concert halls, opera houses, movie theaters, art galleries, coffee shops, sports stadiums, gyms	
★ The sky is always crystal-clear. = The sky's clear as a bell.	The car exhaust fumes（汽车尾气）are poisonous（有毒的）.
★ We enjoy a great climate（气候）all year round.	The climate is harsh.（气候恶劣） 注：有个稍大的词 inclement 也经常被受过良好教育的英国人用来形容天气恶劣：inclement weather
My hometown has a dynamic and vibrant（有活力的）nightlife with countless bars and clubs. Young people often go partying, clubbing and bar-hopping（体验不同的酒吧）at night. 注：请注意本句里的 nightlife 其实是特指一种生活方式，所以前面需要加 a 家乡适合年轻人居住的理由除这些之外还可以有 It's a university town / college town（是一所大学城）. The economy is thriving.（经济发展快）和 There're plenty of job opportunities around.（就业机会多）	The rising unemployment rate is driving up the crime rate. 注：家乡如果不适合年轻人生活的另一个重要原因则可能是 It lacks variety.（生活缺乏变化）

（续表）

★ At night, it's tranquil and serene（宁静的 = peaceful）.	It's close to an airport（机场）and the noise really bothers us（烦人的）. At night, we have a hard time falling asleep and wake up tired in the morning.
★ People there are pretty laid-back（放松的）.	The pace of life（生活节奏）is fast and stressful（压力大的）.
★ Going to concerts is a popular pastime there.（pastime 是指在某个地区很多人共同拥有的业余爱好，例如 Baseball is America's favourite pastime）	People in this city don't have much leisure time（休闲时间）.
In many cities, a driver's license（驾照）is a necessity for finding a job. 注：a necessity 是指必要条件或必需品。 在英国、美国和加拿大的不同地区驾照的说法略有不同，Pat 至少见到过 driving license、driver's license 和语法上并不正确的 driver license，但它们都是在实际生活中被使用的地道英文。	There're an awful lot of reckless drivers out there. 注：reckless drivers 指开车完全不考虑后果的危险司机，也可以说 They drive like crazy. 或者 They're offensive drivers. 它的反义词则是 defensive drivers（善于自我保护的司机）。不过今年年初在美国最新公布的一项民意调查则显示大家一致认为最可怕的司机其实是 slow drivers
Driving makes life much easier for me and for my family members. 注：除了上班可以开车 drive to work 之外，当然也可以为了休闲而开车 drive for pleasure	Driving is not a right. It's a privilege（特权）. 注：这是在欧美极为有名的一句话，意思就是必须要符合法律对驾驶的规定你才能有权开车。 形容某事"有风险的"可以使用 risky，不过在国内城市里让 Pat 感到最恐惧的并不是 cars，而是 mopeds（电动自行车），每次都是悄没声息地就杀出来了（very sneaky）

（续表）

It's vital for us to **drive safely**. 注：这三个词的重要程度依次递增： important → essential → vital	**Drunk driving** can kill. 注：酒后驾车也经常被简称为 DUI （Driving under Influence）
The written test was just a piece of cake and then I passed the road test without a hitch. 注：a piece of cake 大家应该很熟悉，就是 "小菜一碟"，而 do sth. without a hitch 则是对轻松过关的地道说法，出国后您在学校里则常会听到人说 I passed the test with flying colours！	I failed my road test twice before I finally passed it.
I don't have a car so I'm free of all the burdens of car ownership：having to keep the car maintained and filled with gas, the parking fees and of course the insurance 😊 注：the burdens of car ownership 作为车主的负担；maintain 在说到车时是维护、保养的意思；而 insurance 当然就是保险了	I frequently find myself sitting in my car stuck in traffic for hours. 注：get stuck in...　国外生活中相当常用的一个短语：被……困住 有关 biking 的英文知识请看本章中的 Topic 12

Even public transport is not so dependable（不是很可靠的）these days.

AFFIRMATIVE（正方）	**NEGATIVE**（反方）
It's fun to ride around on a bus because you get to see many interesting people.	I take the bus so I can take a nap（睡一小觉）.
When I'm in a hurry, I take the subway（= the underground / the Tube）.	I often get stuck in traffic.
比较拿分的交通工具（即使你可能从来没有乘坐过也放心说吧）： minibus（中巴）；shuttle bus（班车和机场巴士）；ferry（轮渡）；light rail（轻轨）	Sometimes the traffic can be obnoxious（= terrible）. The cab fare（打车费）is expensive in Beijing and Shanghai.（任何车费都叫 fare）

Pat指南 🔊

☆ "打车"除了 take a taxi 在国外生活中还经常有人会说 flag down a cab / hail a

cab / grab a cab。

Topic 4: Entertainment（**including the movies，TV，the radio，and other leisure activities**）娱乐（含电影、电视、广播以及其他休闲活动）

All work and no play makes Jack a dull boy.	
Just escape reality for a couple of hours and watch a movie.（逃避现实几个小时去看场电影）	
FOR（正方）	**AGAINST**（反方）
★ I'm into animated movies（动画片 = cartoons）. I'm a movie buff.（影迷，你是不是又想到了 fans？那至少也得改成单数）	The plot of that movie was too far-fetched.（情节太牵强）
I enjoy movies with a fun plot（情节 = storyline）. 注：当形容词时，fun 是有趣的而 funny 则是搞笑的	你一定已经知道 comedy 是喜剧，但是你有没有试过用 slap-stick 这个词代替 comedy 呢？
Suspense movies（悬念片）keep me on the edge of my seat.	I dislike gangster movies（警匪片），because they are so violent. 英雄当然是 heroes，反派是叫 villains
★ I prefer movies with great acting（演技）.	I hate movies with a predictable storyline.（看了开头就知道结尾的那种）
In that movie, Angelina Jolie（安吉丽娜·朱莉，认真听录音，Jolie 的发音超级容易错）played the lead（演主角）. And Brad Pitt played opposite of her.（演对手戏）	The soundtrack（电影音乐）from that movie was just mediocre（比较一般的）. 注：如果想把欧美名星一网打尽就要熟记一个网址：www. thefamouspeople. com/
★ I like movies with a happy ending.	I can't stand romantic movies because they are so corny（没创意的）.
Good movies are always thought-provoking（引人深思的）.	The special effects（特效）in that movie were not very impressive.

（续表）

★ That movie has a strong cast.（演员阵容强大） My favourite star had a cameo role（客串）in it.（也可以说 He / She just had a bit part（小角色）in it.）替身演员叫 stuntman / stuntwoman	
Good movies can be really entertaining（娱乐性强的）.	That movie was too serious. It was a drag（ = it was boring）.
That movie was a blockbuster. Its box office take was incredible（让人难以置信的）.	I adore（喜欢）movie stars with a "bad boy" or "bad girl" appeal（吸引力）. 注：adore 就是 like 的加强版，跟 LW 们谈电影时尽管多用
★ 低成本电影地道英文叫作 low-budget movies，而上座率很高的电影则叫 a smash / a box-office hit	

THE MOVIE THEATER / THE CINEMA （电影院）	HOME（家里）
It has a better atmosphere（气氛）. 注：better 在雅思口语中可以用 more desirable 这个常用表达代替	You have more choices. 注：choices 也常用 options 代替
★ You watch a movie on an enormous（巨大的）screen.	Pirated DVDs are dirt-cheap.（盗版碟超便宜）
The sound and visual effects are way better.（视听效果好多了） ★ You share the viewing experience with a large audience.	比 sound effects 更大的说法叫 acoustic effects 或者 audio effects，但后两个在口语里都不如第一个常用
★ Watching TV is fun, no doubt about it.	But on the other hand, it can be totally time consuming（消耗时间的）.
Some TV programmes are educational while others tend to be more entertaining.	Some TV series are not all they're cracked up to be.（有些电视剧并不像宣传的那么好） I'm tired of watching the boob tube（TV 的通俗说法）every night. 注：厌烦在地道英语里也可以说成 I'm fed up with… 或者语气更强的 I'm sick and tired of…

（续表）

★ Sometimes I just flick through the channels because there're too many channels to choose from.	Actually, televisions are barriers to strengthening families. （是增进亲情的障碍）
TV programmes 的常见种类（genre）有：TV series（连续剧），reality show（真人秀），quiz show（问答节目），variety show（综艺节目），sports show, news show, sitcoms（情景喜剧），game show, documentaries（纪录片，在 Discovery Channel 和 National Geographic Channel 上经常放的那些），脱口秀（这个英文自己说吧，嘿嘿）	Watching too much TV gives you square eyes. （在英美有一种说法：看电视太多眼睛会变方）
	★ Many people eat their evening meals sitting in front of the TV set, which is very unhealthy. 这种现象在国外太普遍了，以至于英文里已经出现了一个极为常用的词叫 TV dinner，说不健康的生活方式时也别忘了跟考官说这个词
	I'm a bit of a couch potato on Sundays.
	There're too many commercials（电视广告）during prime-time（黄金时段）viewing.

Pat 指南

☆ 以下这些闪光的人名都是 Pat 发现国内同学们最容易念错的明星名字，请仔细听录音：

Leonardo DiCaprio 环保主义者（a committed environmentalist）莱昂纳多·迪卡普里奥的名字稳居读错榜榜首，比亲身解释"岁月是一把杀猪刀"还要让他痛心

Beyoncé Knowles 其实这位美女的名字准确发音并不是"碧昂斯"

Anne Hathaway 她演的公主日记很多同学应该都看过

Avril Lavigne 这位太火了应该不用解释大家也知道是谁，但她的名字却经常被人读错

Nicole Kidman 妮可·基德曼这么简单的英文名字其实也很容易读错

Cameron Diaz 连影坛大姐大的名字都有人敢说错

Keanu Reeves 基努·里维斯有 1/8 的印第安人血统所以有一个原住民的名字

Robert Downey Jr. 连钢铁侠（*Iron Man*）和复仇者联盟 2（*Avengers: Age of*

Ultron）里的男主角也会惨遭误读

Miley Cyrus 如果谁生活在欧美却没听说过 Hannah Montana 那这人真的很难再混下去了

Matt Damon 拯救大兵瑞恩里的男主角，最近几年有越来越火的趋势

Halle Berry 黑珍珠哈里·贝瑞的名字同样是一个考验

David Beckham 小贝虽然不是影星，但他的姓总是被国内同学念错，也放进来吧

说来说去，最不容易发错音的还是超模 Kate Moss 和成功地摆脱了"单身男神"称号的 George Clooney 的名字，所以他俩一定会红。

☆ 恐怖片叫 horror movies，动作片叫 action movies，Titanic 那种就叫 romance/romantic movies，sci-fi 就是科幻，外星人地道英文叫 aliens。

☆ 另外，和考官聊的时候如果说到电影，一定别忘了 flick 是口语里经常用来代替 movie 或 film 的拿分表达。

☆ 电视剧的一集叫 an episode。

☆ 电视节目中间插播的广告除了叫 TV ads，也经常被称为 TV commercials，专门播放广告的时段叫 ad slot / commercial slot，"黄金时段"是 prime time，而"让我很烦"最拿分的表达则是 bothers me。

Topic 5: Reading & Writing
报纸、杂志、阅读和写作

★ I'm always on the lookout for a good book.（我总是在寻找好书）	
AFFIRMATIVE（正方）	**NEGATIVE（反方）**
★ When you read a good book, you communicate（交流）with a great mind.	I can't stand motivational books（励志书）because essentially（本质上），they're pretty much the same.
Reading English novels is an excellent way to boost your vocabulary（扩大词汇量）.	Some biographies（传记）are false.
★ Reading expands your thoughts.（开阔思路）	I don't put pen to paper very often.（很少用笔写东西）
Many coffee shops and restaurants offer free wi-fi（无线上网）now.	

（续表）

Children can improve their handwriting（笔迹）by imitating（模仿）nice examples of hand-writing online before developing their own style.	Practice makes perfect.（熟能生巧，虽然俗但确实地道，忍了吧）So kids should try not to type everything.
★ Email is free.（It costs nothing.）	I hate writing letters simply because my handwriting is always so messy（混乱的）. But letters convey our feelings more effectively.（更有效地表达情感）
The information highway has put a wealth of information at your fingertips.（考试时请体验一下用 information highway 代替 the Internet 的感人效果）	But kids often get addicted to online games.（对网络游戏上瘾）
★ On the information highway, everything is just a click away from you.（距离你只有点击一下鼠标的距离）	Lack of computer skills is a handicap（严重的缺陷）today. 注："精通电脑的"最常用的表达是 computer-savvy

Reading newspapers helps us keep up with the world around us.	
★ Newspapers get us updated on daily events. 注："时事"则叫 current events/current affairs	Compared with newspapers, magazines tend to specialize in certain subject matters.
★ Local newspapers focus on the local happenings. 注：如果您对不停地重复使用 events 感到厌倦，那么 happenings / occurrences 就是不错的选择	Local newspapers tend to be somewhat biased.（有偏见的）
★ International newspapers are more comprehensive, which means they deal with a wide range of issues.	报纸的头版叫 the front page，头条叫 the headline

As I see it, magazines make you more knowledgeable while newspapers make you more worldly（精通世事的）.	
The articles（文章）are well-written.	But the layout（排版）is kind of messy.

（续表）

Some magazines are geared towards an adult audience while others cater to the teenage readership.	When I feel bored, I just flip through some magazines. （随便翻翻）

Pat指南

☆ 说"一本书好看"在地道英文里有个说法，国内同学很少用，因为觉得语法貌似是错的，但其实它是很常用的英文。话说 Pat 上学时曾在图书馆找到了一本 *On the Road*（在路上），拿给图书管理员准备 check out 时，librarian 突然就来了句：It's a good read.

☆ 请注意"书虫"bookworm 这个词在地道英文里并没有贬义。

【剑桥例句】Bookworms spend most of their spare time reading and are interested in collecting books.

☆ 有几种书值得一说（虽然并不一定值得一看）：

best-sellers （畅销书，可以是任何种类的）

literary classics （文学经典）

motivational books （励志书）

fiction books （大致就等于中文里的小说）

suspense novels （悬念小说）

cookbooks （菜谱，注意单词 recipe 是指一个菜的做法，而不是一类书）

travel guides （旅行指南）

☆ newspapers 常见的栏目 （sections）

business section （贸易栏目）

financial section （金融栏目）

international news （国际新闻）

national news / domestic news （国内新闻）

local news （地方新闻）

cultural section （文化栏目）

classified ads （分类广告）

☆ 不止是音乐会的听众，报纸和杂志的读者群其实也可以叫作 audience，或者叫 readership，报纸和杂志的销量则叫作 circulation。

e. g. The newspaper has a daily circulation of 60,000.

☆ 如果说某种媒体"面向"某种群体，有三种表达，大家至少应该掌握一种，而且说到 TV 和 advertising 也经常用到：be geared towards = cater to = target (*v.*)

☆ 杂志的出版时间可以这样介绍：

It comes out once a week. 或者 It's published monthly.

☆ 订阅杂志英文叫 subscribe to a magazine，失望地取消订阅则是 cancel the subscription 或者 unsubscribe to a magazine。

Topic 6: Clothing
服装

Clothes make the man.	
FOR（正方）	**AGAINST（反方）**
These days, baggy clothes（肥大的服装，就跟面口袋似的那种）are really "in"（= popular）.	I'm into stylish stuff. 注：stylish = fashionable = trendy
★ Nice clothing enhances appearance.（美化形象）	A poor taste in clothing spoils the impression that you make.（破坏你给别人的印象）
I prefer a classy, mature style, like suits.（有格调的成熟的风格） 注：suit 就是套装，比如 business suit 就是"西服"	Half of my clothes are out of style（过时了）.
I prefer a youthful, casual style, like tees and jeans.（青春休闲的风格） 注：T-shirt 很多时候在地道英语中会被年轻人用 tee 这个词代替	They look pretty outdated（过时的）.
★ I prefer the athletic（运动的）look, just like a baseball tee, gym pants and sneakers（运动鞋）.	说服装有一个词请一定记得和考官用一下：outfit，复数是 outfits，其实就是 clothes 的意思，这个词在国外年轻人中用得极多，几乎已经过多

（续表）

★ Fashion has become an important way for us to **express ourselves**.	
These days fashion is very diverse（多样化的）. /There are different styles to match our individuality（意思是个性，而不是性格 personality）.	I'm a fashion victim.（一心追随时尚的人）
Name-brand clothing is often considered a status symbol.（名牌服装经常被看做是身份的象征）	Some people just prefer to go against the norm and don't pay any attention to the trends.（不走寻常路，美特斯·邦威……）
I just stick to（坚持）my own style. 注：如果说一个人很有个性，地道英文可以说：He/She has character.	Some people are just conformists（盲从的人）.
★ We should follow our own paths.	Some people prefer fashion over comfort.
卖服装的小店叫什么？国外生活里最常用的是 boutique，请您一定仔细听音频文件中这个单词的发音	

Pat 指南 🔊

☆ 虚荣心的地道英文是叫 vanity。比如：Vanity makes a person unrealistic.（不现实的）

☆ 如果真考到 fashion 话题不妨跟考官提一下 *The Devil Wears Prada*（穿普拉达的恶魔）这部 flick。

☆ casual clothing 的反义词是 formal clothing 或者有时也说 dressy clothing。

Topic 7: Weather & Seasons
天气与季节

Weather affects our mood.	
AFFIRMATIVE（正方）	**NEGATIVE（反方）**
I really enjoy the glistening snowflakes（闪亮的雪片）in winter.	The monsoon season（梅雨季节）in Shanghai is pretty long.

（续表）

The winter is pretty mild （温和的）.	The summer is scorching （热得不行的）. 您要是夏天去过美国的菲尼克斯就能最深刻地领会 scorching 的本质含义。
Hong Kong is pretty warm all year around.	I can't stand the muggy weather. （闷热的天气）
★ I like autumn best because we can see the colourful foliage （也是树叶的意思，但 foliage 不能加复数）.	Overcast weather （阴天） gives us a bad mood. 注：考试时"阴天"不一定非要再用 cloudy weather
I feel comfortable when it drizzles in summer.	But I feel upset when it pours. （drizzle 下小雨，pour 下大雨） 注：描述心情不好时 upset 极为常用，很像中文里的"郁闷"
The rain washes away the pollution. 注：wash away 不是洗走而是冲走	Heavy rain often results in flooding. 注：雨下得大也可以说 It often rains heavily during the summer months.
Everything feels so fresh in the spring. 注：地道口语中还经常可以用 refreshing 这个词来形容事物让人感觉焕然一新的	还可以说 Many plants bloom in the spring. 注：bloom 在这里是动词：开花
My birthday is in the spring / summer/ autumn winter. That's exactly why it's my favourite season. 注：That's exactly why…正因为如此……，同样的意思有时也可以改说 That's precisely why…	Autumn is the back-to-school time for students. That's why I kind of dislike it… 注：kind of 是常用的副词短语，有点儿……的意思。dislike 的语气没有 hate 那么强，还算比较客气
Christmas is my favourite time of the year and that's during the winter. 注：during 是地道英文中表示"在……期间"时极为常用的介词，可惜国内的同学用得过少	The long and harsh winter makes me feel miserable. 注：harsh 是"严酷的"，而 miserable 在口语中则经常用来形容一切可怜兮兮的人或者东西，连《悲惨世界》的英文版标题都叫 *The Miserable World*

（续表）

关于冬天有几个词提示大家一下： 中文里的"雪花"在地道英语里不能说 snowflower，而要说 snowflakes 建筑物都被大雪覆盖了英文可以讲 Buildings are buried in snowdrifts. 而超大的暴风雪则是 blizzard	The winter there is not necessarily very snowy. But when it snows, the snow is blown around by strong winds, which makes things inconvenient for people. 注：is not necessarily... 是一个颇为常用的口语句型，表示"不一定是……"的意思
对于夏天那种湿热的天气，瞄准机会还可以用这句地道的英文跟考官抱怨一下：It's not the heat. It's the humidity（潮湿）that feels unbearable. 注：unbearable 是令人无法忍受的常用说法	The winter is like, ... freezing, or ... frigid!（这两个词可一个比一个冷） Pat 在国内时注意到有的老师教学生用 chilly 这个词表示"很冷的"，其实在地道英文里 chilly 只是"凉嗖嗖的"，而不是严寒。 例：In October, the days will still be warm but the evenings will get chilly.

Topic 8: Arts（including Music, Painting, Drawing and Photography）艺术（含音乐、绘画与摄影）

Beauty is in the eye of the beholder.
有些人说这句话是中文的"情人眼里出西施"，其实在地道的英文中这句话完全可以用来说 artwork，意思是每个人对艺术的理解都不尽相同

FOR（正方）	AGAINST（反方）
★ Music makes us more imaginative and it molds our temperament as well.（也塑造我们的性格）	Downloading music off the Internet for free is a very controversial issue today. 免费下载音乐现在是一个很有争议的话题。
Nice music infuses our lives with joy.（让我们的生活充满乐趣）	The lyrics（歌词）of her songs are too mushy for me（太肉麻了）.
Good music makes everything around us come to life.（让生活活跃起来）	Pop music doesn't have much depth.（没深度）

（续表）

Classical music tends to calm you down.	Most pop songs get us excited. Sometimes wild.
★ I like Beethoven, Mozart and Tchaikovsky. 其实地道英文就是用音乐家的名字表示他们的音乐，猜猜这三人是谁？	I'm into music with a strong beat（强烈的节奏感）.
★ Research has proved that playing musical instruments makes kids / babies more intelligent（聪明的稍正式说法）.	Learning to play a musical instrument（乐器）takes time and energy, and… lots of money, for that matter（＝as well）
★ Some music makes us feel inspired（受到激励的）. 英文里有种很地道的说法还算比较常用：Music is a mood enhancer（是调节情绪的好方法）. 从没听国内的朋友们用，不妨学起来	Some catchy songs（一听就会的那种歌）are actually pretty annoying（烦人的）.
Nice music calms the nerves and restores the soul（放松精神）.	说 music 对精神的影响还有一个更好记的短语叫 lift our spirits，它的形容词 uplifting 也较为常用，意思很像中文"给力的" 例：For Olivia, this was an uplifting concert.
Some paintings make us feel calm and peaceful.	Honestly, I can't understand abstract paintings（抽象画）.
★ Painting skills give us a better appreciation（欣赏）of art.	
Some other paintings are thought-provoking（令人深思的）.	
Photos bring back memories.	
★ Lighting, composition and a good subject are important to taking good photos（对一张好照片来说，光线、构图和所拍摄的内容都非常重要）	People in the background can really ruin a photo. 注：ruin 表示"破坏"，在口语里很常用
You can just slip a compact camera（卡片机）into your pocket.	

（续表）

★ Photos capture（捕捉）precious（珍贵的）moments for us.	Some people are camera-shy（不喜欢照相的）.
★ Photos record memorable（值得回忆的）experiences.	portrait, landscape and still life 分别是人像、风景和静物。我们随时随地拍的"快照"地道英文叫作 snapshots
Going through a photo album is like a trip down the memory lane. 看相册就像回到了过去的一次旅行。	I'm not so photogenic（上镜的）.
Some people look better in photos.	Others look better in person.
★ Some photos are candid（真实的）.	Some pictures are very flattering（比真人好看的）.
★ We can use Photoshop to touch up（改善）digital photos.	So these days, photos can really lie about their subjects.
Twilight（黄昏，前两年在英美大红特红的《暮光之城》当然也是这个词）and sunrise are the best times for photography because the light is gentle.	

Pat指南

☆ 在国外说音乐的种类除了 kinds/ types，还有一个超酷的词叫作 genre，在地道英文里这个词其实可以用来说任何艺术品的种类，相当拿分，但它的发音请您仔细听录音文件，如果发音不准那可就没有震撼力（overpowering effect）了。

☆ 一首歌的歌词叫作 lyrics / words，曲子则叫作 melody / music。

☆ Part 1 里描述音乐只要记住三个形容词 touching（感人的），mushy（肉麻的）和 corny（老掉牙的）就已经挺厉害了。

☆ 关于音乐的种类如 country, classical, rhythm & blues 考生们说得都太多了，或许还剩下点新鲜感的是 heavy metal 和 Latin music。

☆ 令人放松的音乐，除了 relaxing music，还可以说 soothing music。

☆ Beethoven, Mozart and Tchaikovsky.（英文里就用音乐家的名字来指代他们创作的音乐，请仔细听录音文件，这几个人是谁应该没什么悬念吧）

☆ 乐器的英文名称千变万化，真不知道为什么大家都要口径一致地告诉考官自己会

piano 和 violin。其实 flute（长笛），saxophone（萨克斯）和 keyboard（电子琴）不是更好记吗？而 violin 的近亲 viola（BrE /vaiˈəʊlə/；AmE /viˈəʊlə/）中提琴和 cello（/ˈtʃeləʊ/）大提琴也是简单易记却被受过良好教育的英美人士所偏爱的 instruments。

☆ 如果你实在记不住 LW 音乐家们的人名那就说 Lang Lang 吧，用汉语拼音就行而且还特地道，但同时要知道他是 an award-winning pianist。

☆ 谈到 paintings 应该知道三个形容词：realistic（真实的），representational（具体的）和 abstract（抽象的）。

Topic 9: People（including Family，Friends，Neighbours and Meeting New People）人（含家庭、朋友、邻居与新认识的人）

★ I grew up in a very close，loving family. And I still keep in touch with my family regularly（定期的）.

AFFIRMATIVE（正方）	NEGATIVE（反方）
★ China has a one-child policy.	Overpopulation（人口过多）led to this policy.
My family consists of my parents and me.（consists of = is made up of）	Sometimes I feel lonely because I have no siblings（兄弟姐妹的总称）.
★ I'm the / an only child.	Sometimes I wish I had a bunch of（= some）siblings.
My parents are pretty lenient（不是很严厉的）.	Just like most other Chinese parents，my parents are really strict.
★ I had a very strict upbringing（家教很严）.	Some kids never do housework at home. 常见的 housework：do the dishes / do the laundry（洗衣服）/ take out the trash（倒垃圾）
★ My parents can always give me good advice when I need it from them.	We shouldn't take our parents for granted.（不要把父母的爱当成无所谓的事）
Eating together as a family has a particular significance（重要性）in children's lives.	We're so busy these days even eating together as a family seems like a challenge for us.

(续表)

★ Sometimes a good neighbour can make a house a home.	
When we moved in, they respected our privacy and didn't ask us any question that would be too personal for us. 注：欧美人多数都不喜欢 nosy people（喜欢打听事儿的人），跟考官说这个他/她会很认同的	Our neighbours never return things that they borrow from us. 注：如果打算说这个那就要满腔悲愤的
Sometimes we invite our neighbours over for a get-together. 注：get-together 小型的聚会	They make an awful lot of noise. 注：在地道英文里表示不好的东西很多经常会用 an awful lot of... 来形容
Knowing our neighbours well brings us a sense of security（安全感）.	邻居发出的噪音可能有 loud music, blaring TV sets 或者 The couple fight every day.
We often invite our neighbours over for dinner.	I hardly know my neighbours. 注：hardly 几乎不，类似的意思也可以说成 I rarely（极少）see my neighbours.
There's a strong sense of community among us. 注：谈邻居时 community 是一个很常用的词，它不仅指所居住的小区，也指邻居之间的良好关系	We rarely see each other. 注：rarely，很少，表示频率低的常用副词
★ How do you meet new people, besides people you already know?	
Some people do volunteer work to meet new people. 注：很多国内同学误以为 volunteer 就等于中文的"志愿者"，其实这个词在地道英语里除了作名词"志愿者"之外，也还经常会用作形容词或者动词，比如：Max volunteers in the school library.	I didn't really like reading. I joined that book club just to meet new people. But when I realized I didn't share any common interests with other members, I just quit. 注：不再干某种工作地道英文叫 quit，退出某个社团也是 quit，而戒烟当然也是 quit smoking

（续表）

It's popular to meet new people online through chatrooms and social networking websites. 注：社交网站的英文是 social networking websites，例如国外的 Facebook，Twitter，Myspace 和国内的 Renren 网络社区则叫作 online community	I tend to feel nervous when I meet new people. 注：“社交恐惧症”的英文则是 social anxiety disorder
★ Friends are people you can count on（＝depend on）. A friend in need is a friend indeed.	
All friends of mine are intelligent, sincere and trustworthy（聪明的，真诚的而且值得信任的）.	They are just fair-weather friends（这个就像中文的酒肉朋友）.
We share a lot of interests with each other.	I hate back-stabbers（出卖朋友的人）.
We hit it off right away.（这个就是中文的"一拍即合"）	We drifted apart（逐渐疏远了）. ＝We just went our separate ways.
We really enjoy each other's company.（这里是"陪伴"）	
Share and share alike. 这是个 proverb（谚语），意思很像中文的"有福同享"	很忠实的朋友叫 loyal friends，不忠诚的则是 disloyal friends。朋友除了 friends，也可以说 companions 或者更口语化的 buddies
★ We're really tight ＝ We're really close.（说两个人关系很"铁"）	I've lost touch with most of my childhood friends. 注：lose touch with 意思是"失去联系"，它的反义词组当然就是您熟悉的 keep in touch with
I have long-distance friends as well, like friends living in France and Finland.	We meet up in chatrooms and play online games against each other. But … we've never met in person. That's a shame.（太可惜了，That's a shame. 是固定用法，与"羞耻"无关）

Pat指南

☆ 中文名字常见的含义：

It means strength（力量）／loyalty（忠诚）／courage（勇气）／prosperity（兴旺）／good health（健康）／purity and nobility（纯洁与高贵）／beauty（美丽）／honesty（诚实）／honour（荣誉）／wisdom（智慧）／sincerity（真诚）／humility（谦逊）／tranquility（宁静）／peace（和平）／good luck（好运气）／happiness（快乐）．

需要特别注意的是：国内朋友们爱用的 stand for 这个词组在地道英文里其实通常指"是……的缩写"，所以如果您的名字并不是任何中文词汇的缩写，那么就不要说 stand for。

☆ 介绍家庭的时候，如果你能够正确地区分下述两组词汇，考官将会非常惊讶（a nice surprise）。

在口语里说一个人的 family，或者很正式地说 immediate family，相当于中文里所说的"家人"；而 relatives 在口语里则相当于中文所说的"亲戚"

siblings 是泛指"兄弟或者姐妹"，而 cousins 是泛指"表兄弟或者表姐妹"

☆ nuclear family 是指父母和孩子两代一起的家庭，而 extended family 是很多代人一起住的大家庭（three or even more generations live together under the same roof）。

☆ 如果说"孩子像父母"，英文怎么讲呢？最地道的说法就是用短语 take after，如 They take after their parents.

Topic 10: Collection
收藏

It's my greatest passion in life. ……（从事某项活动）是我人生当中的最爱	
AFFIRMATIVE（正方）	**NEGATIVE（反方）**
★ Some people collect antiques and old coins（古董和老钱币）while others collect new things like toys, CDs, novels and souvenirs（纪念品）．	Collecting things can be an expensive habit.
People who collect antique furniture（古董家具）have exquisite taste.（高雅的品味）	Different strokes for different folks. 这个是 proverb（谚语），意思非常像中文的"萝卜白菜，各有所爱。"

（续表）

★ Collecting stamps can be a lifetime hobby.	Some people collect artworks as investors. （投资者）
Some people collect things for personal pleasure.	Others collect stuff in order to increase their wealth （财富）.
Some people collect precious stones. （宝石）	

关于 collection 还有三个词很酷，一个是 valuable artifacts，基本上等于中文的"工艺品"，另一个是 an avid /ˈævid/ collector of ... ，在地道英文里是指特别热衷于收藏某种物品的人，第三个是 connoisseur，就是"鉴赏家"了。

Topic 11: Buildings（including Museums，Libraries，Hotels，Houses，Flats 英式英语 / Apartments 美式英语）
建筑（含住所、博物馆、图书馆和宾馆）

Home sweet home.	
HOUSE / FLAT（住所）	**ITS SURROUNDINGS（周围环境）**
★ The rooms feel pretty spacious （宽敞的）. 注：狭小的叫 cramped	It's not in a convenient location.
★ The big windows let plenty of natural light in.	It's hard to get around if you don't have a car.
The whole place feels light and airy （通风好的）.	There's a wonderful view outside the window.
I decorated（装饰或者装修，这两个意思这个单词都可以表示）my flat all by myself.	
AFFIRMATIVE（正方）	**NEGATIVE（反方）**
★ There're some Chinese ink paintings （水墨画）and a family photo on the wall.	My flat / apartment looks pretty cluttered （乱糟糟的）.

（续表）

★ It has a roomy kitchen. （宽敞的厨房）	My flat has a balcony （阳台）. But it's pretty messy as well. 注：messy 的反义词是 organised
The hardwood floors are in good condition.	The floors are worn-out （陈旧的）.

★ 对于打算说自己住在 house 里的孩子们，不妨试试这两句然后看考官的反应：
I grow organic （有机的） vegetables in the yard. ／
I can almost taste the freshness of the air.

Pat指南

☆ 常见 housework 的地道英文表达：wash the dishes ／ do the dishes （洗碗）, do the laundry （洗衣服，在英美生活里比较少有人说 wash the clothes）, take out the rubbish （倒垃圾，这是英式英语，在美国则叫 take out the trash）, vacuum the floor （用吸尘器吸地板，英美多数家庭都铺地毯所以 vaccum 很关键）, mop the floor （擦地板），而 spring cleaning （春季大扫除） 也是三四月间经常能听到的说法。

Libraries hold a wealth of knowledge.	
Some people think of libraries as a haven, a place where they can get away from the busy city life. （haven 是避风港）	There's plenty of parking around.
★ I enjoy the quiet atmosphere there. （安静的气氛）	But there's a limit on the number of books you can check out. 注：check out （books） 借阅，也有些借书人会说 sign out books，意思相近
★ Libraries offer you a wealth of books. Good libraries put tons of resources at your disposal. （任你支配） 注：一个设施完备的图书馆叫 a well-equipped library	
Museums are buildings where historical, cultural or scientific stuff is kept and shown to the public.	

（续表）

★ There're tons of fossils on display（展出）in that paleontological museum.（这个要好好听音频文件，古生物博物馆）	比较少有考生说但是很拿分的 museums： folk art museum 民俗艺术博物馆 marine museum 海洋博物馆 wax museum 蜡像馆 planetarium 天文馆
★ Children's museums offer many hands-on activities（实际操作的活动）. 注：也可以很形象地说 Visiting a museum brings history, science and arts alive for the kid.	
★ I just enjoy wandering around（到处走走）in this museum because... the tickets are free.	"大饱眼福"的地道英文是 It's a feast for my eyes.
★ In 5-star hotels, there're usually tons of entertainment facilities.（娱乐设施） Each room has Internet access, which is commonplace（= very common）today.	高档的宾馆叫 posh / luxurious / upscale hotels；经济性宾馆叫 motels 或者 B&B（bed and breakfast），motel 国内翻译成汽车旅馆很不合适，因为其实你不开车去一样可以住
★ 服务很完美怎么说呢？ The service is perfect. 是个一般的答案 The service is flawless. 是个有意思的答案 The service is impeccable. 是个很棒的答案	"拆老房子"英语有很多说法，IELTS 口试里面推荐：knock down old buildings / demolish old buildings

Pat 指南

☆ 有两个词要分清，一个是 exhibition 展览，另一个是 exhibit，这个词也可以表示展览 = exhibition，但是它也可以表示单独的一件展品。

☆ 宾馆的类型很多，按星级有 three-star, four-star, five-star 甚至 7-star，比如逐渐没落的迪拜（Dubai）Burj Al Arab。

☆ 注意地道英文里住宾馆动词不用 live，而是用 stay in a hotel。

☆ 关于 libraries 我们在 Day 8 还将会有进一步的发掘。

Topic 12: Sports, Other Outdoor Activities, Biking & Games
运动、其他户外活动、骑自行车以及游戏

It's important to balance our time wisely between our work / studies and leisure.

FOR（正方）	AGAINST（反方）
Jogging（慢跑）and swimming are excellent ways to get fit.	Some sports, like marathon and hurdle-race（跨栏）, are too strenuous（累人的）for average people.
★ Exercise gives me a feeling of accomplishment（成就感）.	Some sports require months of training.
Many elderly people in China practice tai-chi（太极）in the morning.	average people 在口语里面比 ordinary people 更常用
★ I work out regularly（经常锻炼）at a gym, which helps me lose weight.	Jogging every day is too hard on my knees.
Individual sports boost our confidence in ourselves（增加我们的自信）.	关于 sports，有两个形容词请一定记清：strenuous（消耗体力的）和 laid-back（放松的）。如果能再记住三个名词就更好了：strength（力量），flexibility（柔韧性）和 endurance（耐力）
★ Individual sports train self-discipline.（训练自制力）	
★ Individual sports help us discover our own worth and potential（潜力）.	
★ Team sports require（需要）team spirit（团队精神）.	
★ Extreme sports can be really adventurous / risky（冒险的）.	表达"需要"，主语如果是人还要说 need，如果主语是事物就可以用一次 require 了
I can soak up（吸收）some Vitamin D when I do outdoor activities.	It seems sunbathing（日光浴）is not very popular in China.
★ You feel the wind in your face when you go hiking（徒步旅行）.	
★ At / On weekends, we often have a picnic（野餐）out in the open air.（注：at weekends 是英式的表达）	

（续表）

Riding a roller coaster （过山车） can be totally thrilling （非常刺激的） and you can hear passengers （乘客） scream at the top of their lungs （尖叫）.	

I'm into a variety of outdoor activities, like hiking （徒步旅行）, biking, camping, walking dogs （遛狗）, going to amusement parks （游乐场） and rafting （漂流）.

★ I just love the Great Outdoors. （就是 nature，大自然）

I'm quite the outdoorsman / outdoorswomen. At weekends, I often spend hours watching wildlife.

★ We can enjoy the beauty of nature by doing outdoor activities like camping, biking, hiking and fishing. （注意 nature 作大自然的意思讲时前面不加 the）

PLUSES （喜欢的理由）	MINUSES （不喜欢的理由）
★ Kite flying （放风筝） is great fun.	Some games, like chess and card games, challenge your intelligence. （智力）
Biking: I just appreciate the simple pleasures in life.	
★ Good games give you a youthful heart and positive attitude （年轻的心和积极的人生态度）.	Some people like to gamble （赌博） when they play mahjong and card games. （麻将和扑克）
★ Biking is very eco-friendly. （有益环保的）	But in big cities, biking can be risky （冒险的）.
In the West, people ride a bike for pleasure and recreation （= leisure）.	In China, biking is more like a mode of transport. （交通方式） 注：大家爱说的 transportation 其实是美式英语，而在英式英语中 transport 的名词和动词形式都是 transport
I love the feel of the breeze （微风） on my face.	
★ You can see more when you pedal （蹬） a bike.	
I use my bike every day, though not for long distances.	As a student, I can't afford to take taxis often.

141

（续表）

When riding my bike through the city, I always enjoyed stopping to taste the snacks cooked and sold by the roadside vendors. 注：roadside vendors 就是地道英文里对"路边小贩"的说法	I really hate it that cars spew fumes that I have to breathe in. 注：spew fumes 是拟人化的"喷尾气"说法
The bike doesn't pollute or cause traffic jams. It just helps people stay fit. 注：Pat 发现很多考生误以为 stay / keep fit 是指保持身材苗条，其实它在地道英文里的真实含义是"保持良好的身体状态"，而不仅指身材	But my hometown is not very biker-friendly. Bikes must share the road with cars and buses. 注：类似的合成词还有 user-friendly

Pat指南

☆ 要说好 sports，我们应该知道：

什么是 individual sports（个人运动），比如 jogging, skating, swimming, skiing 和 sports car racing；什么是 team sports（团体运动），比如 basketball, American football（橄榄球）和 baseball（棒球）；什么是 extreme sports（极限运动，也可以叫 X-sports），比如 bungee jumping, white-water rafting（漂流）和 skateboarding（滑板）。

在 www. buzzle. com/articles/list-of-extreme-sports. html 上有对十几种极限运动的详细解释。

☆ 常见中国传统游戏的英文表达：

tug of war，也可以叫作 rope-pulling（拔河） mahjong（麻将）

rubber-band jumping（跳橡皮筋） kite-flying（放风筝） riddle games（猜谜游戏）

playing marbles（玩弹子球） hide-and-seek（捉迷藏）

☆ 近期国内流行的游戏

Diablo Ⅲ（暗黑破坏神3，"大菠萝"3），Dota 2，League of Legends（英雄联盟），2048，GTA 5（侠盗猎车手5），Clash of Clans（部落战争）等等

☆ 英语国家的常见游戏：

card games（牌类游戏），board games（棋类游戏），tag（基本就是国内小朋友玩

的"捉人"游戏），puzzles（拼图游戏）

I-spy-with-my-little-eye（这个游戏可是 Pat 小时候的最爱，但国内孩子似乎不太爱玩，请看 Day 8 的详细解释），spelling bee（拼字游戏），math games and hide-and-seek（捉迷藏），riding a scooter 和 jumping on a pogo stick（后两种游戏的图片请看 P. 31）

关于游戏，我们会在 Day 8 中分享更多的地道英文。

Topic 13: Shopping
购物

People go shopping for different things, like clothing, toys, tools, books and groceries.

AFFIRMATIVE（正方）	NEGATIVE（反方）
Shopping is a good stress-reliever. a stress-reliever 是指减压的方式，在忙碌的现代社会里每个人都需要一些 stress-relievers，否则压力非"爆表"（immeasurable）不可	It's a pricey（=expensive）habit.
	I tend to buy things on impulse.（冲动的）
Shop till I drop.（生命不息，购物不止。）你甚至还可以说 It's my motto.（它是我的座右铭）	I'm a real shopaholic（如假包换的"购物狂"）.
★ I do a lot of comparison shopping.（这句完全就等于中文的"货比三家"）	Actually, I'm a last-minute shopper. I go shopping only when I really need something.
It's dirt-cheap.（便宜到极点了）	It cost me an arm and a leg. = It cost me a fortune. = It was really pricey. = It was very expensive.（注意 cost 的过去时还是 cost）
I love name-brand stuff.（名牌儿）英语里还有一个词叫 brand name，两个词用法很像，如果非要区分，brand name 是指品牌，但并不是所有品牌都能叫 namebrand products "名牌儿货"	shop assistants 就是"售货员"
★ Window shopping（只看橱窗而不买的行径）doesn't cost me anything.（对比：browse around the shops 浏览商品，既有可能买也有可能不买）	scam artists 是从事哪种艺术的人呢？哪种也不是，这种人叫"奸商"，在国内还有个网名儿叫 JS，而骗局就叫 a scam

Pat 指南 🔊

☆ 说购物有两个非常拿分的表达一定记得用一下：一个是 an item，就是泛指商店里出售的一件物品，还有一个是 boutique，就是"女僧"们特爱去的那种小型精品服饰店。

Topic 14: Pets
宠物

To some people, their pet is their constant companion（从不离开的伙伴）.	
AFFIRMATIVE（正方）	**NEGATIVE（反方）**
A dog is man's best friend. 请注意这里的 man 是人类的意思，前面不用加 a，是个 idiom	Pets may take up too much of your attention, at the expense of（以……为代价，牺牲）your family members.
★ Pets are good for our emotional health.	Sometimes pets may pee on the floor or chew up your shoes. 注：pee 是不正式地说小便，chew up 是咬碎的意思
Raising pets can boost our confidence and self-esteem（增进自信和自尊）.	We need to make sure our pets are well-behaved.
★ I brush my puppy every day.	Some owners mistreat（虐待）their pets.
Owning a pet can reduce stress and loneliness（减少压力和孤单的感觉）.	

Pat 指南 🔊

☆ 常见的 pets 包括 puppies 小狗, kittens 小猫, parrots 鹦鹉, tropical fish 热带鱼和 rabbits 兔子。

☆ 更有创意的答案包括 lizard 蜥蜴, pony 小马和 hamster，最后一种是胖胖的比老鼠大点的动物，Pat 本人可是不太喜欢（They rub me the wrong way.）。

Topic 15: Age
年龄

YES	NO
I grew up in… = I was raised in…	I'm not a person who hangs on to old memories. （总留恋过去） I prefer to look to the future.
I go back home during winter break and summer vacation.	I wish I could do so but I can't afford the plane ticket.
It has been a year since I left home.	I'm reaaaaaally homesick. （这个可不是在家养病，而是形容词，想家的）
I'm from / I come from… （这里如果只是介绍自己的个人背景那么就不要说came）	I'm having a hard time adapting to the way of life here. = Getting used to the way of life here is pretty hard.

Pat指南

☆ 说年龄，咱们要知道这几个词的分别：

baby / infants（大致是1~2岁的小朋友，不过在国外有时候7、8岁的孩子了还能听到有adults指着这些孩子说babies）

toddlers（走路摇摇晃晃的那种孩子，也就是差不多2岁的样子）

teens / teenagers（准确地说是13~19岁的孩子，不过也没有人算得那么清楚）

kids / children，对这两个词其实每个人的定义都并不完全一样，在美国甚至经常有人说college kids，基本上就是中文的"孩子"了（在法律上叫minors）

people in their 20s / 30s / 40s…（这个应该一看就能明白，还可以更具体地说people in their early 20s / mid 30s / late 40s）

middle-aged people（差不多就是中文的"中年人"，大概40多到50多）

seniors / the elderly / elderly people（老年人）

Topic 16: Travel
旅行

Traveling can be especially fun when you feel sick and tired of the daily grind（日常的辛劳）and want to get away from it all.

AFFIRMATIVE（正方）	NEGATIVE（反方）
★ We can explore（探索）new places and meet new people.	跟团旅行叫 take group package tours，旅行社叫 travel agency，自助旅行叫 independent travel，背包族则是 backpackers
★ Most importantly, we can try new foods（表示不同种类的 food 可以用复数）.	
I prefer to travel light（少带行李）.	Luggage（行李）can be really cumbersome.（不方便携带的）
Travel frees us from the grind of daily routine（日常的辛劳）.	
People from all walks of life enjoy traveling. 注：这是一个英文里的固定短语，但并不是指各行各业的人，其实就等于中文"各种各样的人"	跟年轻人 travel 最密切相关的三个名词是：exploration 探索，discovery 发现和 adventure 探险。 说旅行带来的好处时还可以用到一个词组叫"充电" recharge our batteries，但要注意这个词在地道英文里一般指对体力或者精神的恢复，而不是周末上辅导班
Traveling with friends is a great way to spend time with people who share interests with us.	Time and money are two major factors that will determine where we travel, when and for how long.
Traveling together helps to strengthen family bonds. 其中的 family bonds 是指亲情	major 在这里不是专业，而是主要的；determine 是一个口试常用动词，确定、决定的意思，接近 decide
I was fascinated by the villages, the islands, the deserts, the forests and the valleys that I visited. valley 是山谷的意思，be fascinated by 是指被……彻底迷住了，比如 She was fascinated by Brother Sharp（Xi Li Ge）.	旅行时的行程英文叫作 itinerary，安排行程就叫 plan the itinerary，跨越国界的友谊叫 friendship across borders

Topic 17: Food（including Restaurants，Meals，Healthy Eating and Cooking）食品（含餐馆、三餐、健康饮食与做饭）

You're what you eat.（This means if you want to be fit and healthy，you need to eat good food）

AFFIRMATIVE（正方）	NEGATIVE（反方）
★ I'm a vegetarian，so I'm really into things like tomatoes，carrots，cucumbers and broccoli.	Junk food is very fattening.（让人发胖的）
★ It's essential to have a healthy diet.（健康的饮食）	
Fish dishes are high in protein（蛋白质）and low in fat.	
★ Steaming（清蒸）is healthy because no vitamins are lost.	Fast-food restaurants tend to offer high-calorie（高卡路里的，即高热量的），high-cholesterol（高胆固醇的）but low-fiber（低纤维的）food.
Grilling（烤）is healthy too because no extra oil is used.	
★ I love Chinese cuisine.	
Our staple（主食）is rice.	
★ I like to start my day with a hearty（丰盛的）breakfast.	I often skip（略去，不吃）breakfast.
I always eat three square meals（吃好三餐，每顿饭都不对付）a day.	When I've had a big breakfast，I just skip lunch.
We all need some variety in our diets.（饮食应该多样化）	
★ People socialize（社交）at restaurants.	
Sometimes we have corporate（公司的）dinners at restaurants.	The food that restaurants serve can be very unhealthy，no matter how good it tastes. unhealthy = unwholesome
★ They offer a wide selection of foods（表示种类时 food 可以加复数）.	It's so greasy and fattening（油腻的，让人发胖的）
★ In Shanghai，classy（有品位的），upscale（高档的）restaurants are always packed（挤满了人）on Friday nights.	餐馆的客人叫 customers，餐馆里的气氛叫 atmosphere，或者学着餐饮业的内行们更专业地说 ambience 这个词吧。
The portions are so big.（菜量给的多）	Sometimes you have to wait for ages（等很长时间）for your food.

Pat 指南 🔊

☆ 说一种食物"有营养的"最常用的英文单词就是 nutritious。

☆ I'm a vegetarian, so I'm really into things like tomatoes, bamboo shoots, carrots, cucumbers and broccoli. 说自己是素食主义者是个挺拿分的选择，毕竟考官不能跟着你去看你晚餐吃什么，五种蔬菜分别是西红柿、竹笋、胡萝卜、黄瓜和西兰花，broccoli 的复数还是 broccoli，不需要加 s。

☆ 除了 pears（梨），grapes（葡萄）和 peaches（桃子）之外，雅思口试中更拿分的水果（fruit）名称包括：watermelon（西瓜），mango（芒果），cantaloupe /ˈkæntəluːp/（哈密瓜），kiwifruit（猕猴桃），papaya（木瓜发音挺逗的，请注意听音频文件），还有很多种梅子，比如 raspberries（这个不知道中文怎么讲，是一种暗红色的梅子）和 blueberries（蓝莓），有个性的人也可以说 durian（榴莲）☺。说水果还经常会用到 juicy（多汁的）这个词。

☆ 蔬菜和水果的营养价值类似，基本也就是 rich in vitamin C, minerals and fiber（富含维生素 C，矿物质与纤维），如果非要说得特别高深那么可以试试 They give us a wide range of valuable nutrients（营养物）.

☆ 指 food 的时候，healthy 这个词还有一个很棒的替换形容词叫 wholesome。organic food（有机食品）一般都被认为更 wholesome。

☆ 另外，在谈到健康的 diet 时，well-balanced（均衡的）这个词在英美生活中也相当常用。

☆ 如果您的英语基础比较好，那么不妨再掌握这两个相当拿分的词汇：trans fat（反式脂肪）和 sodium（钠）。在英美生活里当谈论饮食健康话题时它们两个属于绝对的高频词，英美超市里的很多食品为了宣扬自己很健康也喜欢在外包装上面用特大号字写上：0 trans fat（zero trans fat）或者 low sodium。

☆ 白面包是 white bread，全谷物面包是 whole-grain bread，全麦面包是 whole-wheat bread。后两种真心不太好吃，但是更健康。

☆ 我考过一些国内同学"买菜"的英文是什么，回答无一例外都是 buy vegetables。但"买菜"应该也不是只能买 vegetables 吧？其实 get groceries 才是真正最接近中文所说的"买菜"的地道表达。

☆ 要把 food 这样好吃却不好说的话题说得生动，需要知道三个词：

一个是 cuisine，指一个地方所有菜的总称。在英美经常吃到的 cuisines 有 Spanish（西班牙的），Italian，Indian，Mexican，Thai，Japanese，Korean，Vietnamese... 各种风味都有的餐馆叫 fusion-style restaurants。其实在美国基本都是 fusion-style，因为太不正宗（unauthentic），去尝尝美式中餐馆的 Kung Pao Chicken 或者 Ma Po Tofu 吧... Yuck！

另一个是 recipe，指一个菜的做法，比如 Many people have secret recipes that they don't share with others.

最后一个是 ingredient（原料），比如 Fresh ingredients make meals healthier.

☆ 英文里的酸甜苦辣咸分别是 sour，sweet，bitter，hot（英文经常把 hot and spicy 放在一起说）and salty。如果太淡了根本没味儿，就说 It's too bland for me.

☆ 在国外住久了，多数人都深感西餐要吃的其实根本就不是菜本身的味道，而是吃各种各样的 sauce/seasoning（调味酱）的味儿。

☆ 下面三个词汇都经常用来形容美食：mouth-watering（指色、香让人流口水，但是还没尝味道）< delicious（非常好吃）< out of this world（好吃到已经都不是人类吃的了。英美人就是喜欢夸张，从小随便干点事儿就能得到 excellent，great，amazing 等一堆称赞，文化如此，没办法）。

☆ 跟考官谈到你的日常习惯的时候，有三个地道的英文句子会非常拿分：

I rise and retire early.（早睡早起，请注意这个固定句型里的 retire 并不是指退休）

I usually turn in at midnight.（晚上 12 点才睡）

I'm a night owl.（我睡得很晚，是个"夜猫子"。注意 owl 这种动物在地道英语里并不带有贬义，从 *Legend of the Guardians* 里勇敢的 Soren 到小熊维尼 *Winnie the Pooh* 里的 Owl 都是特正面的形象）

☆ 一顿丰富的饭还可以很地道地称为 a hearty meal。

☆ 现在在英美人们开始越来越多地使用 TV dinner 这个有意思的表达，但它并不一定要看电视才能吃，而是用来泛指一切 frozen food（速冻食品）和 prepackaged food（即食食品）这类怎么吃不健康就怎么吃的食品。

☆ a good selection of... 是说服务行业，比如商店和餐馆等地方极其常用的一个句型，e. g. That store has a good selection of stuff.

Topic 18: Colours and Numbers
颜色与数字

Colours tell a lot about your personality and they affect your mood as well.	
FOR（正方）	**AGAINST（反方）**
I prefer catchy colours（抢眼的颜色）like bright orange, silver and black.	I hate loud colours. 我这个人就讨厌抢眼的颜色
★ Bright colours are considered outgoing and friendly.	Dark colours convey authority（体现一种权威）
★ Soft colours like cream（淡黄色）, and brown are gentle and graceful（优雅的）.	鲜明的色彩叫 vibrant colours / vivid colours
There's truth in numbers.	
We tend to think of 6, 8 and 9 as lucky numbers because they sound similar to some Chinese words that have positive meanings. 注: similar to（相似的）, 请注意介词用 to	Some numbers can be really tough to remember. Normally, I just make up a sentence with words that sound similar to these numbers to help me remember them. 注: tough 在地道口语里经常用来代替 difficult, normally 是口语里相当常用的一个副词，口试时可以用来替换现身过度的 usually。而 make up 则是"编故事"。 例: The 2012 doomsday（世界末日）was made up.

Pat指南

☆ 有些颜色说起来比 red/ blue 之类有意思多了，比如说 cream（淡黄色），lilac（淡紫色），maroon（一种比较暗的红色，你肯定听说过 Maroon 5，虽然那个乐队的成员现在已经不止 5 个人了），或者 navy（深蓝色）。

Topic 19: Nature（including Gardens, Parks, Birds and Flowers）
自然（含花、花园、公园、鸟类）

I love the Great Outdoors.（= nature）
★ I prefer parks that have their own unique atmosphere（独特的氛围）.
You can almost taste the freshness of the air.

（续表）

AFFIRMATIVE（正方）	NEGATIVE（反方）
★ I love the feeling of having my own garden and watching the plants grow.	Having your own garden is a luxury（奢望）in Beijing.
★ Gardens look gorgeous with all the flowerbeds（花坛）, lawns（绿地）and rockery.（假山）	
I like to watch the sunrise in the park.	
★ The flowers give off a sweet fragrance.（fragrance：香气） ★ The park is gorgeous when all the flowers are in bloom（开花）. Sometimes we give bouquets（花束）to our loved ones. I decorate my living room with fresh flowers. 注：decorate 是动词"装饰"，名词形式是 decoration，而 décor 则是泛指一个商店或者餐馆里的总体装修风格，请认真听录音文件里对 décor 这个词的发音	更拿分的英文植物表达： daffodil　水仙花 sunflower　向日葵 tulip　郁金香 violet　紫罗兰 orchid　兰花 lilac　丁香花 （P230 还有更全面的植物名称）
★ You can hear birds chirping（鸟叫）in the morning.	The serious pollution is driving birds away from this city.
Some birds have gorgeous feathers.（非常漂亮的羽毛）	Some birds are hideous.（= extremely ugly）
★ Magpies（喜鹊）are considered to be lucky birds in China.	Crows are often associated with（和……联系到一起）bad luck.
That's kind of a widely-held superstition.（迷信，kind of 是"有点像……"）	

Pat 指南 🔊

☆ 一些花在中国的文化中所代表的意义：

Lotuses（莲花）symbolize（是……的象征）purity（纯洁）and integrity（正直）.

The plum blossom（梅花）is a symbol of arduous efforts（艰苦的努力）and outstanding achievements.

Peonies（牡丹花）represent（代表）wealth and prosperity（兴旺）.

Lilies（百合花）represent one hundred years of love and devotion（love and devotion 是英文里的极常用固定搭配，爱与奉献的意思）.

Chrysanthemums（菊花）signify（代表）happiness and good luck.

☆ floral design 或者 floral arrangement 是插花，而花店除了可以直接叫 flower shop 外，在英美生活里也经常会被称为 florist's shop

Topic 20: Festivals，Holidays & Parties（including Birthday，Gifts and Dancing）节日、假期与派对（含生日、礼物与跳舞）

We socialise on these occasions（场合）.	
★ Chinese New Year is a nice time for family bonding.（家人增进感情的好机会）	喜欢音乐的朋友们肯定都熟悉 Katy Perry 的 *Firework*，不过在日常聊天时 firework 通常都是用复数形式，比如地道英文里的焰火表演就被称为 fireworks display（放鞭炮则叫 set off firecrackers）。如果非要跟考官说"中央电视台元旦联欢晚会"，下面这个表达会让他/她听得很舒服，尽管你自己会说得比较累：the nationally-televised gala on New Year's Eve
On Chinese New Year, people get together and catch up（叙旧）.	
★ On New Year's Eve, people watch New Year's specials on TV.（这里 special 是名词，特别节目）	
★ Chinese New Year is a festive time.	"喜气洋洋的"这个词英文怎么说？并不是 happy 或者 exciting，而是 festival 的形容词形式 festive 最地道，贴春联是叫作 stick couplets on doors
We visit relatives and exchange new year greetings.（互相问候）	

Pat指南 🔊

☆ 英美人非常重视的一个新年习惯是 make a New Year's resolution（做新年决定），通常是关于自己生活习惯的某种重要改变，但其实只有少数人能真正实施（Very few people can stick to their New Year's resolutions.），多数人都中途放弃了（fail to keep their New Year's resolutions）；

☆ 中国全年当中最重要的 public holidays 的英文说法：

the New Year holiday, the Spring Festival holiday（也可以说 the Lunar New Year holiday），the Qingming Festival holiday（也可以说 the Tomb Sweeping Day holiday），the Labour Day holiday, the Duanwu Festival holiday（也可以叫 the Dragon Boat Festival holiday），the Mid-Autumn Festival holiday 和 the National Day holiday

☆ 英国人最熟悉的 public holidays：

New Year's Day

Saint Patrick's Day 相当惊讶地发现很多学生误以为这个节日和 Pat 有关，让我受宠若惊，但其实这是传统的爱尔兰节日，现在在美国和加拿大也都相当重要，3 月 17 号这一天出门最好身上穿点带绿色的东西，否则朋友们 will pinch you 没商量。

Good Friday, Easter Monday 这两个假日分别在 Easter（复活节）Sunday 之前的周五和之后的周一，而 Easter Sunday 这天在大城市经常会有 Easter Parade 花车游行，而且满街都是真人扮的大兔子，相当好玩。

Christmas

Boxing Day 这个节在加拿大也有，圣诞节之后的第二天大家集体去超市疯狂抢购的"打包节"，全民总动员凌晨就到商店门口排队的盛况不亚于春运。

此外，当您在英国听人说 bank holidays，别去银行，乖乖放假休息就好了☺

It's always better to give than to receive.	
FOR（正方）	**AGAINST（反方）**
★ Parents give their kids gifts to celebrate major festivals. 注：major 在这里作形容词：主要的	It's not uncommon for people to give their boss pricey（= expensive）gifts to develop guanxi（这个其实已经是地道的英文词了，"搞关系"）.
★ On Valentine's Day, people give their lovers gifts to express their love and emotions.	注：It's not uncommon for sb. to do sth. 的意思就是：It's common for sb. to…
★ It's the thought that counts. 重要的是心意 注："给人印象深刻的礼物"的地道英文叫 unforgettable gift 或 memorable gift	常见的礼物可以准备一下，但最好不要只是很 general 地讲 toys 或者 flowers，可以试一试 a model car, bouquets（花束），a detective novel（侦探小说），a necklace（项链），candies, fashion magazines 或者 the *Harry Potter* Series

（续表）

At parties, we get rid of stress and meet new people.	

The more, the merrier!（人越多越好玩!）这句是国外有人说要开 party 时一句极度常用的话，记得也让考官听到你说

FOR（正方）	AGAINST（反方）
★ Some people are naturally the life of the party.	Some people just go wild and do silly things at parties.
★ Party games are often organised.	I'm NOT really into parties. They make me feel like a fish out of water.（感到很不适应）
Throw yourself right into it.	而非常喜欢参加 party 的人英文叫 party animal: I'm a real party animal.
There are different types of parties, like birthday parties, beach parties, housewarming parties, farewell parties… 最后这个是送别的 party，非常 sentimental（伤感的）	如果 party 不成功有一个很棒的中文词"尴尬的"，但它的英文怎么说呢？请记住 awkward 这个词不管在任何时候都完全等同于中文的"尴尬的"
At birthday parties, people can really let their hair down.（完全放松）	
★ We'll throw a surprise birthday party for the birthday boy / birthday girl.	Sometimes people get drunk at parties.
Sometimes presents are exchanged.	And this often leads to unwanted sex or drunk driving, which can be disastrous.（灾难性的）
★ Nice parties are fun, exciting and … memorable.（值得回忆的）	开 party 英文怎么说呢？你可能选择 hold a party，但考试时请一定记得用一下 throw a party 这个地道表达，然后就等着看 examiner 的反应吧
★ It's always fun to get wrapped up in（陶醉在）the exciting atmosphere.（气氛）	
We had a blast!（玩得非常开心!）这句是开完 party 后经常说的话	
★ We love attending dances（舞会）. ★ Some dances have a theme（主题）.	

（续表）

> Teens really enjoy costume dances（化装舞会）.
> I enjoy dancing to exciting music.
> ★ Dancing to slow music is more graceful, though（更优雅的）.

Pat指南

☆ 想说好 festival / party 有关的话题，请一定记住用一个词：reunion（团聚），比如 class reunion（同学聚会），family reunion（家庭聚会），do some catching up（聊彼此的近况）和动词 celebrate（庆祝）在这个话题也很常用。

☆ 唱卡拉 OK 英文叫 sing karaoke，请仔细听音频文件，英语里面的日文词最后一个 e 通常是要发音的。

☆ 您还可以在 dance. about. com/od/stepsandmoves/ 这个网站上看到对于英美人普遍熟悉的舞蹈舞步的详细介绍。鸟叔 PSY 的江南 Style（Gangnam Style）虽然曲调非常上口（very catchy），甚至能让人上瘾（addictive），但是说舞蹈还是不要说"骑马舞"（horse-riding dance）了。

☆ 传统舞蹈的动作与舞步（the moves and steps of traditional dances）很复杂，而且需要大量的练习才能掌握（are complicated and take a lot of practice to learn）；而现代舞蹈的动作与舞步则通常更有创意、更自发而且更有趣（The moves and steps of modern dances tend to be more creative, spontaneous and fun. ），而且现代舞蹈并没有固定的套路（don't really follow a routine），因而能够给人更多的自我表达的空间（allow for more self-expression. ）。

☆ 跳舞让人放松（is very relaxing），而且也是很好的健身方式（is good exercise for the body）。而对单身的年轻人来说，舞跳得好还能增加约会对象的范围（single young people who are good at dancing tend to have a larger dating pool）。考官只要是在英语国家上过大学就一定会心一笑或者面带坏笑（a wicked smile）。

☆ 地道英文里对于在 party 中和别的参与者进行社交活动叫作 mingle with other guests，更正式一点还可以叫作 socialize with other guests，而像 Facebook 和 Renren 这样的社交网站则被英美人称为 social networking websites。

☆ 亲友之间的小型聚会在英美口语里也经常被称为 a get-together。

☆ 关于 birthday，在西方有一个生日特别重要，就是 the 21st birthday，因为这天之后 adults 能享受的所有权利你都有了，再去酒吧也不用总被查 ID 了。地道英文里还有一个词组叫 paint the town red，经常用来形容庆祝生日时的疯狂活动。

超短线
The Ultra-Short Track

　　对于备考时间有限的同学来说，<u>先集中准备好本次考试中最可能出现的题目仍然是重中之重</u>。可以先把 Pat 博客 blog. sina. com. cn/ieltsguru 里本月口语预测中的 Part 1 考题结合本章语言点讲解准备好，如果还有时间再考虑系统学习相关词汇和句型。

Day

▶ 剑 **10** 时代的 **Part 2** 真题全集
The Whole Spectrum of Part 2 Topics

Pat's Guide
To The IELTS Speaking Test

How many roads must a man walk down
Before they call him a man
How many seas must a white dove sail
Before she sleeps in the sand
How many times must the cannon balls fly
Before they're forever banned
The answer, my friend, is blowing in the wind
The answer is blowing in the wind

IELTS 口试 Part 2 真题库全集索引

A　　描述与建筑和城市相关的话题 / p. 166

B　　描述与个人和组织相关的话题 / p. 192

C　　描述与自然界相关的话题 / p. 221

D　　描述与休闲娱乐活动相关的话题 / p. 242

E　　描述与物品相关的话题 / p. 284

F　　描述与经历和事件相关的话题 / p. 312

口语 Part 2 话题指南

A

酒店 / 170

一座现代建筑 / 170

购物中心 / 173

一个著名建筑 / 175

建筑师 / 189

别墅 / 175

理想中的住处 / 175

老房子 / 178 & 180

住所里的一个房间 / 365

童年时的家 / 180

宁静的地方 / 182

城市 / 182，184 & 186

图书馆 / 188

美术馆 / 368

音乐厅 / 375

被污染的地方 / 390

有噪声的地方 / 389

露天市场 / 366

餐馆 / 372

小商店 / 162 & 375

B

欣赏的运动员 / 197

健身俱乐部 / 198

小企业 / 198，372 & 375

成功的小公司 / 375

音乐人 / 200，202 & 204

乐队 / 204

一部小说 / 206

影星 / 206

电视节目主持人 / 385

艺术家 / 208

历史人物 / 209

历史事件 / 211

企业家/ 211 & 213

一个领导人物 / 211 & 213

普通人/教师 / 215

帮助你学习的人 / 215

理想的工作 / 391

老人 / 218

孩子 / 218

学校规定 / 163

C

有水的地方 / 168 & 223

近期的旅行 / 188 & 224

学校假期 / 224

公园 / 225，226 & 239

花园 / 228

安静的地方 / 228

散步 / 230

恶劣的天气 / 231

野生动物 / 234 & 235

宠物 / 236

植物 / 238

D

童年游戏 / 244 & 246

有趣的新闻 / 247

让你发笑的事 / 249

喜爱的电视节目 / 249，252，253，254 & 256

有教育意义的电视节目 / 385

问答节目 / 251

广播节目 / 251

电视剧 / 253 & 254

电影 / 258，259，261 & 263

歌曲 / 265

儿童歌曲 / 271

广告 / 267

童年时的故事 / 269

网站 / 271

外国文化 / 274 & 364

向往去旅行的国家 / 276

喜欢的运动 / 277

极限运动 / 280

一项技能 / 279 & 377

希望学会做的事 / 279 & 377

你想学的外国语言（非英语）/ 322

绘画 / 279

好的法律 / 364

E

汽车 / 285 & 288

电子产品 / 291，293，296 & 298

收到过的礼物 / 295

丢失的物品 / 295

照片 / 299

信件 / 302

手工制作 / 302

玩具 / 305

服装 / 305

首饰 / 308

贵重的东西 / 291，296，305 & 308

发明 / 309 & 310

老家具 / 365

雕塑 / 370

坏掉的物品 / 388

F

问卷调查 / 164

开心的事 / 313

别人向你表示祝贺的场合 / 313

让你气愤的事 / 366

体育事件 / 316

课堂活动 / 319 & 381

科学实验 / 381

成功的事 / 322 & 383

表演 / 322

音乐活动 / 322

听音乐的场合 / 322

婚礼 / 325

节日 / 328 & 363

近期的变化 / 330

用电脑完成的事 / 334

迟到的经历 / 361

交通堵塞 / 361

喜欢的科目 / 362

重大决定 / 362

一次谈话 / 362

人生里的重要阶段 / 363

购物经历 / 366

野餐 / 240

特殊的饭 / 377

友人的拜访 / 377

聚会 / 383

生日 / 383

淘气的事儿 / 386

对于考试当月最新出现的话题，您还可以在 Pat 的博客 blog. sina. com. cn/ieltsguru 的本月口语预测里看到。

考官给你的 Part 2 一分钟思考时间里你应该做的事

好消息是：在 Part 2 考官将会给你纸和笔（如果他/她居然很不敬业地忘了你就说 Could I have a pen and a sheet of paper?）。在六十秒的思考时间里，考官是允许你在纸上写一些 notes 的。还有几件事特别提醒口语基础不太好的考生朋友们注意：

☆ 卡片题必须注意时态，对于过去的内容一定一定一定要记得用过去时。

如果题目涉及到过去的内容，在思考的一分钟里干脆就直接在纸上写上 -ed 这个符号，以确保自己在描述的时候不会忘记时态。

☆ 卡片题名词的复数和谓语动词的单数很容易忘记加 -s。

基础不太好的童鞋也可以在纸上写出一个"大 S"来提示自己绝不要忘记单复数。

☆ 如果是描述 a person 的题，一定会有考生将 he/she 不分。

有些同学在指代一个人时，一会儿用 he 一会儿又改用 she，考官只能不断猜测这人是"以前是男的的女的"还是"以前是女的的男的"。如果您自己也犯过这类错误，请把 he 或者 she 在纸上写清楚……

☆ 记录 ideas 和 key words 时一定要写清楚，字可以写得大点。

在这方面考官完全管不着你，你也不用替剑桥省纸，但如果你在描述时因为看不清自己在纸上记录的 ideas 和 key words 而一再地停下来，把口语考试变成"阅读"考试，就很可能导致悲剧。

★　　★　　★

Part 2 要说多难?

对于绝大多数中国考生来说，口语卡片题是 IELTS 口试里最难斩将的一关，因为 Part 2 是"独白"，一旦开始描述之后全程都要自己说，而且还得面向考官，不能扭着脸儿说。更恶心的是很多雅思卡片题的 topic 在中国孩子的眼里压根儿就"不可理喻"。相当多考生的最后一道心理防线在怪异的话题、表面淡定内心狰狞的"独白"和考官的冷眼旁观联合夹击之下轰然倒塌了。

中国同学们在描述 Part 2 卡片题时的最常见误区就是总想让自己的答案产生"引人入胜"的效果，成为能震撼考官的"大杀器"。

但事实上，你的 examiner 真正希望听到的只是：

（1）清晰的答案，也就是听完你的描述后考官可以比较容易地明白你所描述的人物、事物或者事件是"什么样儿的"就很好了；

（2）扣题的答案，也就是确实覆盖卡片上面提示你介绍的要点，对卡片上面明确提示的要点一定不要偷工减料。同时，考官也允许你适当补充一些确实与话题有关的内容（牢记：自己补充相关内容的作用只是"锦上添花"，但不要"喧宾夺主"）；

（3）流畅的答案，也就是一个你确实能够自然、流利（但也不是"不喘气"）地说出来的答案。如果用词难度过大或者句子过于曲折，就很有可能在描述过程中出现长时间"卡壳儿"的窘状，导致在 fluency 评分项上被扣分，甚至进一步影响你回答 Part 3 时的心态。

我们以《剑 10》Test 2 的卡片题为例说明：

Describe a shop near where you live that you sometimes use.

You should say:

    what sorts of product or service it sells

    what the shop looks like

    where it is located

and explain why you use this shop.

英文里有两句著名的谚语叫作"Small is beautiful."和"Less is more."——"小就是美，少即是多"。咱们来看看能不能用浅显的英文把一个便利店（convenience store）描述清楚：

I'm going to describe a convenience store in my neighbourhood.

The store is on the south side of an old brick building. The store has large windows, and there's a sign with the name of the store, Kevin's Convenience, on top of the front entrance. There're three parking spots at the front of the store.

The store is small, but it offers a nice selection of goods, from food to magazines to birthday cards. And the coolest thing about this store is that it has some stuff that I can't find in bigger stores, like baked sweet potatoes.

The owners of this store are a middle-aged Chinese couple. The store is small but well managed, with friendly and helpful employees. The shelves are always clean and well organised, and prices are reasonable.

I sometimes buy stuff from this store because it's just a 2-minute walk from my flat, and it's open 24 hours a day, all year round. The service is always good. It really proves that "Small is beautiful."

这个答案很简单，但它描述得清楚、扣题，而且它的词汇和句式都很浅显，即使是英语基础很一般的孩子也能比较流利地说出来。这样的答案完全可以满足 Part 2 高分答案的要求。

我们再来看一个比较"偏"的卡片话题是不是也可以有清晰、扣题、流畅的答案：

Describe a rule in your school (that you agree or disagree with).

You should say:
    what the rule was
    whether you followed it
    whether you think it was good or bad.

这道真题让很多"烤鸭"还没出国就已经明显感受到了国外和国内教育的不同：国内考试通常并不鼓励考生对学校教育"吐槽"，如果"吐"得太狠甚至还可能遭到高考零分作文之类的惩罚。但这道卡片题却明明白白地告诉你不管是你赞同的还是反对的，只要是一条学校的规定你就可以放心说。

国内学校的 rules 跟国外学校的 rules 也并不完全一样，比如很多英美中小学都规定自己的校园是 nut-free zone（不允许学生携带坚果类食品的区域），这类 rules 在国内学校里就很少有。

Pat 自己对于英语国家的中小学教育很熟悉，所以我并不想去"神化"它，特别是英美公立中小学的教育，问题其实并不算少。但只从回答好这道考题的角度来说，school rules 的选择还是很多的，比如按时到校（always arrive at school on time），听老师的指令（follow the teachers' instructions），在校内禁止使用手机（no mobile phone use at school），在学校里不能嚼口香糖（no chewing gum on school grounds），头发保持干净整洁（Students' hair should always be neat and tidy.），遵守学校对于着装的要求

（follow the school dress code），例如有些学校要求穿校服（wear school uniform），不允许女生穿高跟鞋（no high heels are permitted in school）等等，这些也是很多英美中小学里常见的 school rules。

那么这道题到底要说到多"难"才能拿高分呢。Pat 就用在英美中小学里同样也有的规定 —— 上课举手回答问题 —— 来说明咱能不能用清晰、浅显的英文说出这道难题的高分：

I'm going to talk about the "hands-up" rule in the high school I attended. We were asked to put our hands up in class to answer questions.

I always followed this rule. But sometimes when I got chosen by the teacher, I couldn't remember what I wanted to say. That was kind of embarrassing.

This rule made us feel we could make our own choice to answer a question or not. And we were encouraged to put our ideas forward in a polite way instead of just talking over each other. We put up our hands only when we had an answer ready and were sure of the answer, so the rule also increased our self-confidence.

But some of my classmates were too shy to put up their hands even if they knew the answer. They were afraid they would get the answer wrong and get laughed at. And some teachers always picked the same people to answer their questions.

Anyway, this rule helped us a lot. Without it, we would have just shouted out our answers and ended up learning nothing at all …

除了标颜色的单词略难一点之外，这个答案里的所有词汇都非常浅显易懂，但是照样能够把这道题描述得清清楚楚。

下面的这个 Part 2 卡片题则是一道更加"变态"的考题：

> Describe a time when you were asked to give your opinion in a questionnaire or survey.
>
> You should say:
>   what the questionnaire / survey was about
>   why you were asked to give your opinions
>   what opinions you gave
> and explain how you felt about giving your opinions
> in this questionnaire / survey.

*D*o you know what amazes me more than anything else?
The impotence of force to organise anything.

—Napoleon Bonaparte

问卷调查？多数考生用中文恐怕都将难以下"嘴"。但其实如果遵守"清晰、扣题、流畅"的 3 个原则，用非常浅显的英文就足以把这个题讲清楚了。请看 Pat 怎样描述我自己上周刚寄出的一个问卷调查（同时请仔细听音频里的外教朗读）：

A couple of weeks ago, I bought a laptop at Best Buy. Then last Friday, I got an email from Best Buy, asking me if I could fill out their customer satisfaction questionnaire and send it back to help them improve their service. Since I felt pretty happy with the purchase, I decided to answer the questions for them.

The questionnaire was a PDF file… not a scanned one. It was divided into three parts. The first one was about the customer's personal information, like age, gender, address, phone number and email address. The second part was about the product — questions like what I bought and whether I was satisfied with it.

The longest part was the third one, which focused on the service I received at Best Buy. This part alone contained more than twenty questions, such as how I would rate the friendliness of the staff, what my overall rating was for this shopping experience with Best Buy and whether I would recommend their service to others.

It took me about half an hour to complete the form. I answered "Yes." to most of the questions and gave their service five stars. From the well-designed questionnaire, I could tell that they tried really hard to improve their service. So next time when I need electronic stuff, I'll definitely get it from them again.

而且不仅是这道题，事实上是所有的雅思卡片话题，对用词的难度要求其实并不高。卡片题的真正难点并不是词汇，而是紧扣卡片上给出的提示要点的思路。本章给出的全部答案和关键词全都是为了说明这个道理。对于 native speakers 考官来说，用只有韦式字典里才有的单词"武装"出的答案是怪异的甚至令人痛苦的，请对考官"嘴下留情"。

> 本章里的真题请您充分结合 Pat 在博客里贴出的本月预测来准备，把卡片题库在考前全都看一遍没有可能也没有必要。

A 建筑与城市

Pat 解题　Pat's Decryption

建筑师（architects）在西方社会的地位从历史上到今天一直是比较高的，属于 "professionals"（这个词在地道英文里有时是特指像 lawyers，doctors，accountants，architects 这样高收入的专业人士）。有些 architects 甚至已经成了文化明星，地位已经跟摇滚巨星差不多了（They have even attained the status of cultural heroes or superstars with their own followers.）。比如 Frank Gehry 就是其中的一个，下面这张照片是 Pat 本人在世界顶级的 MIT 校园拍摄的 Frank Gehry 作品，够另类（funky）的吧？

关于 建筑 ，有两个单词大家经常弄混：即 building 和 architecture。building 指的是一栋一栋的房子，而 architecture 一般作不可数名词，很少用复数，除非指很多不同种类的建筑风格，它其实指的是一个城市或者地区建筑的总称，而不是某一个单独的建筑。

关于 城市 ，也有两个词经常被用混：即 city 和 urban，其实 urban 不是 "城市"，而是形容词 "城市的"，如果要用 urban 表示城市，就一定要说 the urban area。

本节我们会学到各种不同类型建筑的英语表达，包括商场、宾馆、图书馆、别墅、四合院儿、寺庙等。此外还有对三个重要中国城市——北京、上海和香港的描述。

On top of all that，我们还将选出全球 beauties 最多的六大城市，严重期待 ing…

展开本类话题的思路线索　Brainstorming Techniques

（熟悉下图可以确保你在拿到任何本类卡片题时都能有话说）

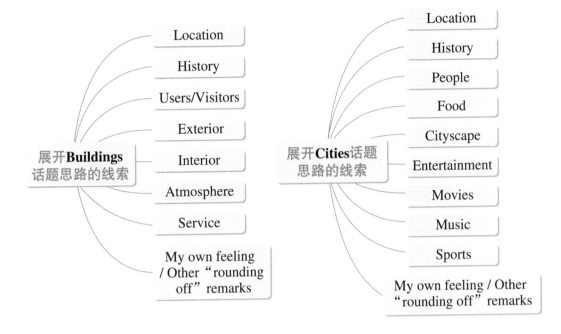

展开**Buildings**话题思路的线索
- Location
- History
- Users/Visitors
- Exterior
- Interior
- Atmosphere
- Service
- My own feeling / Other "rounding off" remarks

展开**Cities**话题思路的线索
- Location
- History
- People
- Food
- Cityscape
- Entertainment
- Movies
- Music
- Sports
- My own feeling / Other "rounding off" remarks

本类话题最新完整真题库　Recent Questions on This Topic

✷ Describe an old building.

✷ Describe a tourist attraction.

✷ Describe an educational trip.

✷ Describe an unusual building.

✷ Describe a shop you like.

✷ Describe a hotel.

✷ Describe a school / library you studied at before.

✷ Describe a building in your school / university.

✷ Describe your ideal house.

✷ Describe a quiet place.

* Describe a place that makes you feel relaxed.
* Describe a place near water.
* Describe an important city in China.
* Describe a city you would like to visit.
* Describe a long journey you made.
* Describe an interesting trip.

分级演示 A Spectrum of Sample Answers

1. 建筑（building）

☆ **一个有水的地方**

Pat 指南

这个其实不是 building，但是最近也总出现，不好分类，放在这里吧。如果您想描述自然界中有水的地方，还可以参考 C 类话题里的第 1，2 题

Describe a place where there is water. You should say: where the place is what this place is like what kinds of people go there and explain why people choose to go to this place.

难度指数：★★★★☆

Pat 的答案

Our neighborhood has a community swimming pool. Lots of people go there on hot summer days. Some of them just go to the pool to cool off. Others go there to exercise, which is really nice because swimming is a great way to keep fit.

But frankly, not all the people there can swim well. Yes, there are some who can swim like fish but I would say most swimmers there are just beginners who can only splash water around and are totally afraid of going under water. Some of them even have a hard time doing the doggy-paddle.

On any hot day in summer, the pool buzzes with kids. And sometimes there're instructors giving swimming lessons to them. Enjoying the sun and getting paid is a pretty good deal, huh?

And ... I don't have a girlfriend (for girls: boyfriend). So who knows? Maybe this pool'll give me a chance.

轮到你了   It's Your Turn.

▶ **Word Bank on This Topic**

社区　neighborhood / community　　放松，休闲　hang out

[剑桥例句] Sophie is well-known in the local community.

健身　exercise / work out

[剑桥例句] Andrew works out in the gym two or three times a week.

保持身体强健　keep fit		保持身体健康　stay healthy
坦白地说　frankly		完全的初学者　absolute beginners
溅起水花儿　splash water around		狗刨　doggy-paddle
教练　instructor		救生员　lifeguard
男式游泳裤　swim trunks		女式游泳衣　swimsuit / bathing suit(AmE) / bikini
拥挤的　crowded		热身运动　warm-up exercises

[剑桥例句] Warm-up exercises are important before a run so as not to strain any muscles.

蛙泳　breast-stroke		仰泳　back-stroke
蝶泳　butterfly-stroke		自由泳　freestyle
来回游　swim lengths		游泳好　swim like a fish
彻底不会游泳　swim like a brick		浅水区　the shallow end

请参考Pat的思路，并适当借鉴这个词汇表里的单词，思考如果是您会怎么说

Pat 的海外生活英语实录

上面这个工具箱里的词都挺不错的，但也没必要全搬。可下面的这个词要是考到这个话题您还存着不用那就将是"一不说成千古恨"的结果—— **spot**。这个单词作名词时在地道口语里完全等于中文的"地儿"。例如：

【剑桥例句】

（1）This park looks like a nice spot for a picnic.

相应地，下次说到"有水的地儿"，您就可以理直气壮地对考官说：This is a nice **spot** for swimming and playing water games.

（2）This museum is one of the region's best-known tourist spots.

☆ 一个现代建筑

（A）酒 店

> Describe a hotel you have stayed in or visited.
>
> You should say:
>
>   where the hotel is located
>
>   when you stayed there
>
>   why you went there
>
> and explain what you liked about it.

难度指数：★★★★☆

Pat 的答案

I stayed at the Yong-Fan Hotel while visiting Shanghai last July.

It's located at the southeast corner of the city and is renowned for its guests. I was

told many celebrities stayed there before, like Daniel Wu（吴彦祖）and Takeshi Jin（金城武）. It offers comfort, convenience, great service and … luxury！The room I stayed in was very spacious and the room temperature could be set with a digital thermostat, which I found pretty neat.

The hotel has a wide variety of rooms, from single rooms equipped with microwave, coffee maker and fridge to Presidential Suites which is reeeeeally luxurious. All rooms have wi-fi connection. The hotel restaurants offer a good selection of food.

The hotel employees were friendly and helpful, and the room rates were very reasonable considering the location of the hotel. I really enjoyed my stay there.

轮到你了   It's Your Turn.

▶ **Word Bank on This Topic**

著名的   renowned（在 IELTS 口试里用它代替 famous 很棒）   名人   celebrities

[剑桥例句] The region is renowned for its outstanding natural beauty.

恒温器（欧美建筑的房间里调节温度的常用设备）   thermostat

宽敞的   spacious   奢华的   luxurious（luxury 名词）

总统套房   presidential suite   高档的   upscale

提供……的丰富选择   offer a good selection of（英文口语里常用这个句型介绍商
                          业服务）

舞厅（不是"球房"）   ballroom   精美的   exquisite

（装饰等）有品位的   classy   员工   employees

员工的统称   staff   宾馆的房价   room rates

入口大厅，大堂   lobby   装饰   decorations

无可挑剔的   impeccable   标志性建筑   landmark

巨大的   enormous   功能   function

外观   appearance   扶梯   escalators

壮观的   spectacular

[剑桥例句] There was a spectacular sunset last night.

无线上网   wi-fi connection / wireless Internet connection

口碑好	enjoy a great reputation	位于	be located... / be situated...
豪华的	posh / luxurious	客房服务员	room attendants
桑拿	sauna	门童	bellhop / bellboy
提供洗衣和待客泊车服务	Laundry and valet service are also available.		
非常热情的	very helpful / go out of their way to help you		

> 请参考Pat的思路，并适当借鉴这个词汇表里的单词，思考如果是您会怎么说

Pat 的海外生活英语实录

如果要用英语说 "宾馆的服务设施"，基础不错的同学可能会想到 **hotel facilities**。但在地道英文中还有个更地道的 **hotel amenities** 才是表达这个意思的最佳选择：

【剑桥例句】The council has spare cash which it proposes to spend on public amenities, such as swimmings pools, gardens and parks.

Time to Branch Out.
推而广之

Describe a modern building in your city.

补充弹药

office building 写字楼

administration building 行政楼

glass-wrapped 用玻璃包裹起来的

energy-efficient 节能的

Extra Ammo

Do you know what amazes me more than anything else? The impotence of force to organise anything.

—Napoleon Bonaparte

（B）购物中心

> Describe a shopping center that you like.
>
> You should say:
>
> where it is
>
> what it is like
>
> how often you visit this shopping center
>
> and explain why you like this shopping center.

难度指数：★ ★ ★ ★ ☆

Pat 的答案

Let me talk about my favourite mall，Oriental Plaza. It's located right in the heart of downtown Beijing and is just a stone's throw away from the Tian'an Men Square.

The mall is huge... enormous. It's 20 storeys high and looks reeeeeally exquisite because it's wrapped in glass on all sides.

The interior is also amazing: very spacious and well organised — not like many other malls where you can easily get lost.

My friends and I are fascinated by this mall because all the stuff there is top-notch and well-priced. And the service is good too. We feel like we are treated as honored guests. The shop assistants always greet us warmly and try their best to help us find what we want. The service counter also provides a wide variety of services, like gift-wrapping，coupons as well as information on sales.

This mall is a landmark in Beijing，not just because of the size and location，but also because of the amazing shopping experience people can have there.

轮到你了　　　　　　　　　　　　　　　　　　　　It's Your Turn.

▶ **Word Bank on This Topic**

距离⋯⋯近在咫尺（地道英文习语）　just a stone's throw away from...

[剑桥例句] We were staying in a small flat just a stone's throw away from the beach.

精美的 exquisite	建筑的外观 exterior
把……包起来 wrap	巨大的 enormous
几层高 …storeys high	建筑的室内 interior
宽敞的 spacious	安排得当的,清晰有序的 well organised
顶级的 top-notch	定价合理的 well-priced / reasonably-priced
顾客 customers	售货员 shop assistants
问候某人 greet sb.	优惠券 coupon
标志性建筑 landmark	

[剑桥例句] The Rock of Gibraltar is one of Europe's most renowned landmarks.

购物体验 shopping experience	电梯 lifts(BrE)/ elevators(AmE)
扶梯 escalators	灯光 lighting
壮观的 spectacular	装饰 decorations
很有格调的 classy	全额退款 full refund
地铁线 Metro line	口碑好 enjoy a great reputation
受到追捧 enjoy a large following	精品(服装)店 boutiques

[剑桥例句] Rebecca has attracted a large following among the rich and famous.

化妆品专柜 cosmetics section	美食街 food court
特价 sales / special offers / promotions	全场打折 store-wide sales
百货店 department store	便利店 convenience store/corner shop(BrE)
花店 florist's(shop)	面包房 bakery
售后服务 after-sales service / post-sales service	
收据 receipt(请注意这个单词里的字母 P 不发音)	
特别热情 very helpful / go out of their way to help you	

> 请参考Pat的思路,并适当借鉴这个词汇表里的单词,思考如果是您会怎么说

Pat 的海外生活英语实录

在商场里"闲逛"的最准确英文表达不是 walk in the mall,甚至都不是 browse

through the stores 而是 **hang out in the mall** 这个地道的说法：

【剑桥例句】

（1）You still hang out at the pool hall?

（2）Who's Jonathon hanging out with these days?

Time to Branch Out.
推而广之

Describe a famous building in your city.

补充弹药

flock to （*v.*）涌向

celebrity 名人

packed 挤满人的

Extra Ammo

（C）别　墅

Describe your idea of an ideal house（理想的别墅）.

You should say:

what type of house it would be

why you would like to live there

what special features it would have

and explain whether you think you will ever live in a

house like this.

Pat 指南

在这道题里您可以向考官尽情地展示您会用虚拟语气这种貌似高深其实没什么的句式。

难度指数：★ ★ ★ ☆ ☆

:Pat 的答案:

Actually, my ideal house would be just like an **average** house, nothing too **fancy**. It would be conveniently located, have a couple of cozy bedrooms, a **spacious** living room, a roomy kitchen, some bathrooms and a **double garage**. Most importantly, it must have a big backyard for flowers and vegetables. I love the feeling of watching plants grow.

There should be plenty of **appliances** in the kitchen, like a **gas stove**, a **microwave**, a **fridge** and a **dishwasher**. Next to the kitchen there would be a **dining area** with a dining table and some chairs.

The living room must have **high ceilings**, a sofa, some **armchairs**, a **rocking chair** and a coffee table. As for the TV set, it should be a **high-definition** TV set with a large screen. And the big windows would let lots of natural light in.

What else?... Oh, the bathrooms! There must be a **bathtub** so I could relax in warm water after a busy day.

The garage would be for my cars, bikes and tools. Such a house would cost like 5 million Renminbi in cities like Beijing and Shanghai. So I guess it's nothing more than just a dream for me...

轮到你了   It's Your Turn.

▶ **Word Bank on This Topic**

几个　a couple of   普通的　average（注意在这里它不是"平均"的意思）

[剑桥例句] The food was fairly average（=not excellent, although not bad.）

阳台　balcony

家用电器　home appliances　在英美家庭里最常见的有 fridge 电冰箱, dishwasher 洗碗机, vacuum cleaner（生活里常被简称为 vacuum）吸尘器, microwave oven（生活里常被简称为 microwave）微波炉, washer / washing machine 洗衣机, dryer 烘干机等

*D*o you know what amazes me more than anything else?
The impotence of force to organise anything.

—Napoleon Bonaparte

（房屋或者房间）很舒适的　cozy　　　天花板　ceiling

宽敞的　spacious / roomy　　　　　长沙发　sofa / couch

单人沙发或者单人座椅　armchair　　花瓶　vase

摇椅　rocking chair　　　　　　　　壁炉　fireplace

高清电视　high-definition TV set　浴缸　bathtub（日常口语里常会简单地说 tub）

能停两辆车的车库　double garage　储藏室　closet

衣柜　wardrobe　　　　　厨房里的橱柜　cupboard（请注意听音频里的发音）

还房贷　pay a mortgage　　　　郊区　the suburbs

乡村　the countryside　　　市中心　the city center / downtown

社区　community / neighborhood

秋千　a swing set（指秋千这种设备，小朋友们在秋千上玩儿则叫 play on the swing）

我要自己去装饰它　I'll decorate it all by myself.

烧烤　barbecue / grill　　　花坛　flower bed　　　草坪　lawn

生活和休闲设施　amenities（such as stores, sports centers and parks）

除厨房和浴室铺瓷砖之外都是硬木地板　has hardwood flooring throughout, with ceramic tiles in the kitchen and bathroom（flooring 在地道英文里是特指地板用的材料）

非常近　It's just around the corner.（地道英文里面也经常用这个句子来形容一件
　　　　事情很快要发生了，比如 You test is just around the corner!）

这只是个幻想　It's just a fantasy.

[剑桥例句] Steve's favourite fantasy was to own a big house and a flashy（很"炫"的）car.

请参考Pat的思路，并适当借鉴这个词汇表里的单词，思考如果是您会怎么说

Pat 的海外生活英语实录

地板上铺的大地毯叫 **carpet**，小方毯叫 **rug**，床上盖的毛毯叫 **blanket**，但是墙上挂的挂毯应该叫什么呢？跟考官说 **a tapestry**/ˈtæpɪstri/，他/她将会对你刮目相看（He / She will be amazed.）。

【剑桥例句】It was hard to hang the tapestry on this curved wall.

Pat 指南

Describe a room that you use a lot.

IELTS 口试题库里有一道相关考题是描述你经常使用的一个房间。**uktv. co. uk/home/ dgiped/kw/236** 这个网站上有各种房间的布置思路（点击页面上方的 Rooms 可以看到各种房间名称），而且都配有图片，只要"看图说话"再适当描述自己的活动答案就足够了，远比你凭空想象出一个房间要简单得多。

☆ **一个历史建筑**

（A）民居（四合院儿）

难度指数：★★★★☆

Pat 的答案

As far as I know（国内孩子说卡片的一大问题就是口气总像该领域的权威似的，但其实听起来挺假的，因为并没有人会是所有问题上的专家），most Beijingers used to live in courtyard buildings called "Siheyuan". But now living in a courtyard building is kind of a status symbol in Beijing because it's so spacious and cozy at the same time.

A small or medium-sized Siheyuan usually has its main gate built at the southeastern corner of the courtyard with a screen wall just inside, which offers more privacy. And with all the plants and flowers, the courtyard is just like a garden for the family.

In the past, just from the size and style, one would be able to tell whether a courtyard house belonged to an average family or a rich one.

A Siheyuan is a pleasant building to live and work in. The courtyard itself can be a thing of beauty because it can serve as a "light-well" and allows lots of sunlight to pour into the rooms.

These days, a Siheyuan is like a private oasis away from the noise and the hustle and bustle of urban life...

轮到你了   It's Your Turn.

▶ Word Bank on This Topic

据我所知　As far as I know, ... / To the best of my knowledge, ...

过去曾经　used to...　　　　　　　宽敞的　spacious

[剑桥例句] Jason used to live in Glasgow.

（房屋或者房间）很舒适的　cozy

四合院建筑　courtyard buildings（courtyard 就是指围起来的院子）

属于　belong to　　　　　　　　中等规模的　medium-sized

隐私　privacy　　　　　　　　　身份和地位的标志　a status symbol

[剑桥例句] Among young people, this brand of designer clothing is the ultimate status symbol.

天井　light-well　　　　　　　　沙漠中的绿洲 oasis

喧闹拥挤（名词短语）hustle and bustle　　破旧的　run-down

[剑桥例句] The building looks run-down.

阳台　balcony　　　　　　　　　翻新（建筑）　renovate（v.）

宽敞的　spacious / roomy　　　　社区　community / neighborhood

郊区　the suburbs　　　　　　　乡村　the countryside

请参考Pat的思路，并适当借鉴这个词汇表里的单词，思考如果是您会怎么说

Pat 的海外生活英语实录

在喧闹（busy and bustling）的城市里，四合院给人感受最深的就是它的宁静安详。那么怎样用地道英文里来说一个地方是"宁静安详的"呢？**peaceful and quiet** 是个很棒的说法，而英语基础好的同学还可以用 **tranquil and serene** 这个同样很地道的短语。

【剑桥例句】This neighborhood is tranquil and serene, with a pleasant small town feel to it.

Time to Branch Out.
推而广之

> Describe your childhood home / a room you spent time in when you were a child.

补充弹药

childhood memory / childhood memories　童年的记忆

childhood buddies　童年时的玩伴

recall　（*vt.*）回忆

（B）寺　庙

难度指数：★★★★☆

Pat 的答案

I'm going to talk about a temple in my hometown.

The temple dates back all the way to the 15th century. Interestingly, although it's a holy place, it's located on the busiest street in my hometown.

But from the moment you enter the temple, you start to feel calm and peaceful. Like most Chinese buildings, the temple faces south and the front gate is guarded by two stone lions. Entering the front hall, you'll see four enormous wood sculptures. They're called "the Four Heavenly Kings".

The Great Hall is separated from the front hall with a courtyard where you can see lots of trees and plants. The roof of the Great Hall is supported by thick, tall columns. Inside the Great Hall, you can see a seated Buddha statue and the statues of some of his students. On the east and west walls of the Great Hall, you can also find some Buddhist works of art.

This temple is not just a place of worship. It offers cultural activities as well, including Chinese art classes. So you see, besides being a religious site, it's also educational and fun.

轮到你了 It's Your Turn.

▶ Word Bank on This Topic

一个神圣的地方　a holy place　　历史可以追溯到……　…dates back to...

[剑桥例句] This building dates back to the 17th century.

雕塑　sculpture	雕像　statue
庭院　courtyard	屋顶　roof
巨大的　enormous	柱子　column
神坛　altar	佛祖　Buddha
塔　pagoda	雕刻的文字　inscription
古董　antiques	艺术品　works of art

从事宗教活动的场所　a place of worship

文化活动　cultural activities	有教育作用的　educational
宗教的　religious	用于某个特定用途的场所　site
被与……隔开　is separated from...	许愿　pray and make a wish
烧香　burn incense sticks	尼姑　nuns
和尚　monks	通道　corridor / passage
让人顿悟的　enlightening	佛教徒　Buddhist

[剑桥例句] That was a very enlightening programme.

> 请参考Pat的思路，并适当借鉴这个词汇表里的单词，思考如果是您会怎么说

Pat 的海外生活英语实录

谈寺庙时很可能会用到"信仰"这个意思，很简短的一个小词 **faith**，当你对考官说出来的时候震撼力可一点都不小。

【剑桥例句】Britain is a multi-faith society.

Time to Branch Out.
推而广之

Describe a peaceful place.

补充弹药

worship 崇拜，敬仰

faithful 忠实的

followers 信徒

calm one's nerves 放松精神

Extra Ammo

2. 城市

> Describe a famous city in China.
>
> You should say:
>
>   where the city is
>
>   why it is important
>
>   whether you visited it before
>
> and explain whether you think it will be better in the future.

☆ *城市之 北京*

难度指数：★ ★ ★ ☆ ☆

> Pat 的答案

I guess all people, regardless of（不论，这是一个特棒的短语，可以代替被考生用滥的 no matter what）their background, have heard something about Beijing, not just because of its long history, but also because of the Summer Olympics eight years ago.

Apparently, Beijing is best known for its brilliant history. It's the capital city of China, not just now, but in five dynasties in Chinese history as well. Beijing is also renowned for its cultural diversity. Currently, there are over 200,000 foreign-born people living in Beijing. And as you probably know, Beijing is politically important because most of the national leaders live here.

What fascinates me most about Beijing is the interaction between traditions and modern lifestyles. modernity and tradition. Glass-wrapped buildings are popping up all over this 3000-year-old city…

轮到你了

It's Your Turn.

▶ **Word Bank on This Topic**

不论	regardless of	显然	apparently / obviously
辉煌的	brilliant	朝代	dynasty
著名的	renowned	文化多样性	cultural diversity

出生在外国的 foreign-born（出生在当地的英文里叫作 local-born 或者 locally-born）

相互的影响	interaction	让某人着迷	fascinate someone
传统	traditions	现代的生活方式	modern lifestyles

集中快速地出现 pop up

[剑桥例句] A lot of tall modern buildings are popping up.

用玻璃包裹起来的 are wrapped in glass / glass-wrapped

天际线	skyline	柔和的	gentle
小吃	snacks	庙会	temple fair / temple bazaar
豌豆黄儿	pea paste	直率的	straightforward

[剑桥例句] Just following the signs to Bradford — it's very straightfoward.

热情好客的	very welcoming	胡同儿	narrow alley
文物	cultural relics		

豆汁儿 bean juice（在北美其实只有 soy milk，很少听到有人说 bean juice，但我觉得北京的豆汁儿叫 bean juice 更准确）

请参考Pat的思路，并适当借鉴这个词汇表里的单词，思考如果是您会怎么说

Pat 的海外生活英语实录

要说某城市是一个"文化中心",您一定会脱口而出:a cultural center! 而且还自我感觉超好······唉,瞧你,一不小心又俗了不是? 请记得跟考官说:It's a **cultural hub**,然后等着看他/她可爱的蓝眼睛是怎么"变绿"的:

【剑桥例句】

(1) The City of London is the hub of Britain's financial world.

(2) Chicago is a major transport hub, with the busiest airport in North America.

☆ 城市之 上海

难度指数:★ ★ ★ ★ ☆

Pat 的答案

Shanghai is the largest city in China in terms of population — 24 million people live in Shanghai.

Shanghai is also a world-class city and an economic powerhouse.

The history of Shanghai is actually kind of short, like... I'm not sure ... maybe 200 years. In many ways, Shanghai was a Western invention. The Bund is the best spot to see its colonial past.

Now the city is a popular tourist destination, famous for attractions like the classy Xintiandi, the bustling City God Temple, the peaceful Century Park, the gorgeous gardens and lawns, and the breath taking Pudong skyline.

Every time I went there, I noticed something new. It's so dynamic. And the bar and club scene in Shanghai is amazing. There're endless things to see and do in this city.

By the way, the Shanghai dialect sounds pretty cute. I enjoyed mimicking it when I was there...

轮到你了　　　　　　　　　　　　It's Your Turn.

▶ **Word Bank on This Topic**

在……方面，就……而言　in terms of　经济中心　economic powerhouse

有点儿……　kind of / sort of　　　创造　invention

外滩　the Bund　　　　　　　　　地点　spot（名词）= place

看见　spot（动词）= see　　　　殖民地的历史　colonial past

旅游目的地　tourist destination

旅游景点　tourist attractions（日常口语里经常简单地说 attractions）

繁华的　bustling　　　　　　　　很有格调的　classy

特漂亮的　breathtaking / gorgeous（请注意听两个字母 g 的不同发音）

城隍庙　City God Temple　　　　有活力的　lively / dynamic / vibrant

[剑桥例句] Karen is young and dynamic. She'll contribute a lot to the team.

方言　dialect　　　　　　　　　金融中心　financial hub / financial center

模仿着说话　mimic　　　　　　　超好的　incredible / amazing

[剑桥例句] She was mimicking the people in our office.

精致的（形容人）　refined　　　精致的（形容物）　exquisite

（人）很有品位的　have exquisite taste　聪明的　bright / intelligent / smart（AmE）

自然地结合，融合　blend（v.）

"小资"　bobos（Bourgeois Bohemians）这个词的意思很像中文的"小资"

迪斯尼乐园　Disneyland

大城市的地铁系统　Metro

上海自贸区　the Shanghai free-trade zone

请参考Pat的思路，并适当借鉴这个词汇表里的单词，思考如果是您会怎么说

Pat 的海外生活英语实录

上海无疑是一个"国际化的都市"，但用英文怎么表达呢？**a cosmopolitan city** 就是最地道的选择：

【剑桥例句】London is a cosmopolitan city and a business hub.

☆ 城市之 香港

难度指数：★ ★ ★ ☆ ☆

Pat 的答案

In my view, the most striking thing about Hong Kong is... the people, no doubt about it. So many talented people work in this city. Not just the movie stars and the super singers, but gifted people in almost every area, finance, business, arts, fashion, education ... you name it.

Another thing that's really amazing about Hong Kong is, of course, the skyscrapers. It's fascinating how such a tiny island accommodates so many tall buildings. Hong Kong has the most beautiful skyline in the world, hands down (is + 形容词最高级 + hands down 不是 "举手投降"，而是 "最……" 很地道的强调表达形式). And the view of Hong Kong Island is breathtaking, especially when you take the Star Ferry across the Victorian Harbor.

Hong Kong is a mecca for fashion lovers like me because there's always name-brand stuff on sale.

Actually, I just returned from Hong Kong last week. Its economy was kind of in a slump and people were complaining about that. But it's still one of the best places to live in the world...

轮到你了   It's Your Turn.

▶ **Word Bank on This Topic**

惊人的 striking / amazing   有才华的 talented / gifted

[剑桥例句] Schools often fail to satisfy the needs of gifted children.

应有尽有…… you name it.

[剑桥例句] Everglades Camp offers horseback riding, tennis, water sports, you name it.

国际化的　international / cosmopolitan

[剑桥例句] London is probably the most cosmopolitan city in Europe.

容纳　accommodate　　　　　　巨大的　enormous

轻松胜出　the best..., hands down　　渡轮　ferry

维多利亚湾　Victorian Harbor　　是……的圣地　is a mecca for...

[剑桥例句] His own bookstore became a mecca for writers and artists.

名牌货　name-brand stuff　　　经济在衰退　The economy is in a slump.

抱怨　complain　　　　　　　密集的（建筑）　dense

经济中心　economic powerhouse　殖民地的历史　colonial past

旅游目的地　tourist destination　名望　fame

[剑桥例句] She moved to London in search of fame and fortune.

东西方相遇（英文固定习语）　East meets West.

中药　Chinese herbs / Chinese medicine

爱尔兰酒吧　Irish-style pubs　　大片儿　blockbusters

娱乐业　entertainment industry　叉烧包　barbecue pork buns / roast pork buns

成龙　Jackie Chan　　　　　周润发　Chow Yun-Fat

刘德华　Andy Lau　　　　　谢霆锋　Nicholas Tse

甄子丹　Donnie Yen　　　　财富　wealth

繁华喧闹　hustle and bustle（名词短语）

[剑桥例句] Nicholas wanted to escape the hustle and bustle of city life.

繁华的　bustling（*adj.*）　　很有格调的　classy

天际线　skyline　　　　　特漂亮的　breathtaking / gorgeous

旅游景点　(tourist) attractions

有活力的　lively / dynamic / vibrant

请参考Pat的思路，并适当借鉴这个词汇表里的单词，思考如果是您会怎么说

Pat 的海外生活英语实录

　　要介绍一座城市"很有活力的",地道英文里最常用的两个形容词就是 **dynamic** 和 **vibrant**:

【剑桥例句】New York is a dynamic city with many vibrant neighbourhoods.

Time to Branch Out.
推而广之

Describe a trip you took recently.

补充弹药

itinerary　行程安排	destination　目的地
check out... (*informal*)　体验……	
local delicacies　当地的特色佳肴	

Extra Ammo

3. 一个图书馆(双语感悟)**Random Reflections on Libraries**

> Describe a library that you have visited.
>
> You should say:
> 　　where the library is located
> 　　what you use it for
> 　　how often you visit this place
> and what people think of this library.

　　校园里可说的建筑很多,比如 cafeteria / canteen 食堂,dorm / dormitory / hall of residence 学生宿舍楼,gym 体育馆或健身房,administration building 行政楼,student union building 学生会大楼,recreation center 休闲活动中心(在有的国外大学里是和 student union building 放在一起的)。至于教学楼,在英语里一般不叫 teaching building ✗,而是叫某某 Hall 或者 faculty building。

中国学校里的 library 多数是形状很规则的，英文叫 It's regular-shaped。近年来英美的图书馆则有盖得越来越不规则（odd-shaped）的趋势，我个人最喜欢的是 Seattle Public Library（右图），真正属于 the Information Age 的建筑。

如果一个大学图书馆是校园里的标志性建筑，英文就要说 It's a famous landmark on campus。如果图书馆的外面全都是玻璃，英文会说 It's wrapped in glass on all sides. 如果还有曲线墙面，那么就是 curved walls。外观漂亮可以说 The exterior is gorgeous，室内也好看则说 The interior is pretty neat as well。入口处的门厅是 entrance hall 或者 lobby，大厅里的大柱子叫 enormous pillars / massive columns。借书柜台是 circulation desk，还书直接扔进 drop box 就好了。阅览室，说 reading room 考官就能听懂。还有一种 group study room 是可以进行集体学习和讨论的，但是一般要预订（reserve）。有些图书馆还设置了一些 study carrels，是木板的小隔间，可以自己坐在那里看书。

图书馆的书库分两种：一种叫 closed stacks，另一种是 open stacks。目录室叫 catalog room，复印室叫 photocopy room，计算机房是 computer lab，多媒体室可以叫 multi-media classrooms，图书管理员当然是 librarians，借书说 check out books，也有些人说 sign out books，还书就是 return books，过期不还要罚 late fee，有些图书馆还有 self-access center，也是类似多媒体教室的功能。如果你说图书馆里的气氛很让人放松，即是 The atmosphere there is really refreshing. 如果说它是智慧的宝库 It is a fount of wisdom，提供很多书籍 provide a wealth of books，是求知者的乐园 It is a mecca for knowledge-craving students！

临时抱佛脚

我们可以把下面这个不按常理出牌的卡片也放在本节一起准备：

Describe a famous architect（建筑师）.

让中国孩子们用中文描述一个建筑师都是难上加难，更别说用非母语了。

别急，其实你完全可以用几分钟就解决它。分两步走：

（a）牢记说艺术家的几个英文必备词：talented / gifted 不是"有礼物的"而是有才华的，prolific 高产的，作品源源不断的，creative / original designs 有创意的作品，trendsetter 引领潮流的人，be passionate about 对……满腔热忱的和 masterpiece

杰作;

（b）适当了解一个建筑师的大概生平，比如有个网站是世界顶级建筑师大全 www. greatbuildings. com/architects. html。人名都按照英文姓氏的首字母排列，点击其中一个然后下拉到 Biography 板块就成了。比如找找咱们华人的骄傲 I. M. Pei（贝聿铭）吧。

更棒的是，有了这道题我们就一起把最近常考的难题 Describe an artist 也轻松搞定了。

architects 在西方的社会地位很高，了解一些相关知识还是挺有必要的，重要性绝不低于参加"公测"（open beta testing）。

另类话题 Off-the-Wall Topics

Pat 的"驴友"杂志最爱 *Travelers' Digest* 今年评选出了全球美女最多的六大城市，可惜都不是英联邦国家的城市，雅思考生们可能暂时还去不了。不过你会发现：这本著名的旅游杂志（但请注意它绝对不是一本黄色杂志!）在描述这么让人流鼻血的城市时用的竟然都是这么简单的小词：

☆ Top 6. Moscow, Russia

Mother Russia is home to some of the world's most beautiful women. The Moscow subway alone has more beauties than most of the states in America. It's not only the tall, blonde hair, blue-eyed girls that make it so great, it's also the amazing level of friendliness that you will find. It's a definitely unique experience when what seems the world's most beautiful woman is looking your way, it leaves you wondering whether you have something on your shirt. But in fact you probably don't, they could very well think you're attractive.

☆ Top 5. Los Angeles, California

How much can be said about L. A. girls? Well I think you will find upon arrival that so much can be said you'll find yourself at a loss for words. The women of L. A. are on a level unlike most any other kind you may have ever seen. This is where the cool people come to live, to work, & to try to "make it"（= become successful）. This is what the Beach Boys had in mind when they wrote the song *California Girls*.

☆ Top 4. Varna, Bulgaria

Many of you may not have heard of Bulgaria, some of you may not know where to find it on a map, but you have all been there, in your dreams at night when you sleep.

It's the land of sunbathing. But more importantly, it's the land of the world's most beautiful, charming & affable women, oh how I love them so.

☆ Top 3. Buenos Aires, Argentina

Buenos Aires should be the capital of the Western Hemisphere, for it's wealth of beautiful women. Where else can an average person get invited to Fashion TV parties & kiss a 6'1 supermodel, well not too many other places let me tell you.

☆ Top 2. Copenhagen, Denmark

Copenhagen has surely got some of the world's most beautiful ladies & also some of the friendliest. For instance, I had just arrived at the Copenhagen train station. It was late. I was tired, but I must've been looking good, because I noticed a gorgeous Danish girl looking my way, so I looked hers, then I smiled, then she pointed me out to her friend. This alone is why I say Copenhagen is one of the best.

☆ Top 1. Stockholm, Sweden

Stockholm is a city filled with the best-looking women in the world, women so good looking that when you walk into a 7-11 you will swear that you have just walked into a reality TV show. The women are super friendly & well educated. They speak English with English accents. They start making you wonder whether England in fact had good-looking women but they're all on working vacations in Sweden.

描述建筑和城市的网址

下面的网址对骨灰级 DIYers 准备有关 buildings 和 cities 的卡片"灰肠"有用：

现代建筑：

www. guardian. co. uk/artanddesign/series/greatmodernbuildings（It's a website that features a whole lot of world-renowned modern structures…）

老建筑：

http://art. eserver. org/（This is a website that offers tons of info on Western architecture）

城市：

http://www. lonelyplanet. com/destinations（This is a leading website that is specifically geared towards travel info）

B　组织与个人

Pat 解题　Pat's Decryption

讲到关于人物的话题，我经常会想到 Akon 的那首 *Mr. Lonely*

Lonely I'm so lonely，

I have nobody，

To call my own…

其实人生有一半的时间是很孤独的，而另一半时间，是爱我们的人（those who genuinely care about you）和我们爱的人（our loved ones），让这个世界变得不再空旷（Love makes the world go around.）。

这一节我们学习对 organisation 和 individuals 的描述。

经常有学生问 Pat，到底什么是 organisation？给您一个权威的英语答案吧，根据 *Longman Dictionary of Contemporary English*: An organisation is a group of people with a special purpose, such as a club or business. 所以应该说 organisation 的选择还是很多的。

其实最好说的 organisation 就是一个 English learning club 了，说说自己最熟悉的 English lectures, English corner 和 the importance of English 就够了。不过这种内容确实有点 "鸡肋"（mediocre）。我想中国孩子们最感兴趣的 organisation 应该是 the NBA，所以今天我们会好好看看这个组织。

至于 individuals，当然就是 "个人"。每天咱们都和个人打交道，但其实描述个人并不容易。比如一个 "胖" 英语就有很多词，除了 fat（很贬义），还有 overweight（语气更客气一点），chubby（胖乎乎的），pudgy（又矮又胖的），stout（粗壮的）……

再比如 "外向的"，"内向的"，经常听到国内的孩子们用 extroverted 和 introverted，但这两个词其实有点大，在国外生活中确实偶有听到但用得不算频繁。日常口语说 "外向的" 其实可以说 He's very sociable.（= outgoing），而 "内向的" 则可以说 He's quiet around people he doesn't know well.（= not so outgoing）

本节咱们就要研究各种不同的人。

OK. Here we go.

展开本类话题的思路线索　Brainstorming Techniques
(熟悉下图可以确保你在拿到任何本类卡片题时都能有话说)

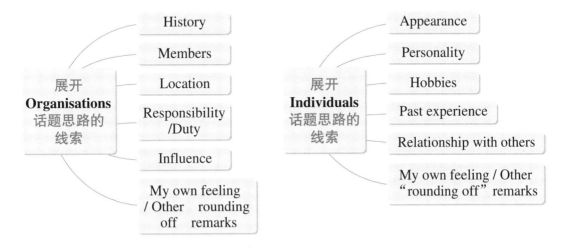

本类话题最新完整真题库　Recent Questions on This Topic

❈ Describe a famous person who you admire.

❈ Describe an elderly person.

❈ Describe an international celebrity / a famous person in a foreign country.

❈ Describe a teacher who helped you before.

❈ Describe a person who helped you before.

❈ Describe an ideal job.

❈ Describe a neighbour.

❈ Describe a singer / band.

❈ Describe a business leader.

❈ Describe a person who you want to be similar to in the future.

❋ Describe a sportsman / sportswoman.

❋ Describe a family member.

❋ Describe a friend.

❋ Describe a happy person you know.

❋ Describe a successful leader you admire.

❋ Describe a person who is good at speaking a foreign language.

分级演示　A Spectrum of Sample Answers

1. 组织（organisation）

> Describe an organisation.
>
> You should say:
>> which organisation it is
>>
>> what kind of organisation it is
>>
>> what people think of it
>
> and whether it is popular.

☆ **一个组织之** NBA

难度指数：★ ★ ★ ☆ ☆

Pat 的答案

I'm going to talk about the NBA, which stands for the National Basketball Association. It's probably the most renowned sports organisation in the entire world（entire 在口试里代替 whole 很不错，副词 entirely 在口试里则可以代替 completely）.

As far as I know, currently the NBA is made up of 30 teams from America and Canada. The organisation was founded in New York like 60 years ago. At first, things were kind of tough, but these days, it's one of the most influential sports organisations in the world.

There are tons of basketball buffs in China and that's why NBA has such a huge following here. Some NBA games are even played in China and the tickets always sell out in like 20 minutes.

I don't know why but sometimes in China, live broadcasts of the regular season or playoffs stop being aired all of a sudden. And that really bothers me. Well, it's good we still have the Internet.

My favourite basketball players are Jeremy Lin and Kobe Bryant. They are really cool. I admire them not just for their successes, but also for their spirit, you know, their sportsmanship. They have been named the MVP many times, which made them real legends in my eyes.

The NBA is a legend, too. No doubt about it, because it's so successful in terms of making money. And more importantly, it's entertaining. I hope more NBA players will come over to China and show us their amazing basketball skills.

轮到你了   It's Your Turn.

▶ **Word Bank on This Topic**

现在	currently / now	是……的缩写	stand for...

现在　currently / now   是……的缩写　stand for...

著名的　renowned   艰难的　tough

……迷　名词 + buff（复数：buffs，比如 music buffs, car buffs, movie buffs 等）

有影响力的　influential   （门票）卖光　sell out（这里不需要用被动）

[剑桥例句] The first issue of the magazine sold out within two days.

常规赛　regular season   受到追捧　enjoy a huge following

现场直播　live broadcast   播放　air

[剑桥例句] The game will be aired live on CBS at 7:00 tonight.

季后赛　playoffs   让人很烦　bother sb.

最有价值球员　MVP   运动精神　sportsmanship

团队精神　team spirit   团队成员非常团结　There's real team spirit.

传奇　legend

很有娱乐性的　entertaining

很激励人的，励志的　inspiring

关注他们最喜欢的球队　keep track of their favourite teams

热情　passion

在……方面　in terms of

激励人们　inspire people

[剑桥例句] Tennis arouses（激发）a good deal of passion among its supporters.

组织、管理得很好的　well-run / well-managed

达拉斯小牛队　Dallas Mavericks（地道英文里也经常简称为 the Mavs）

迈阿密热火队　Miami Heat　　　　休斯敦火箭队　Houston Rockets

波士顿凯尔特人队　Boston Celtics　　洛杉矶湖人队　L. A. Lakers

克里夫兰骑士队　Cleveland Cavaliers　奥兰多魔术队　Orlando Magic

底特律活塞队　Detroit Pistons

圣安东尼奥马刺队　San Antonio Spurs（简称 the Spurs）

由……组成　be made up of... = consist of（后面这个不要用被动语态）

俄克拉荷马雷霆队　Oklahoma City Thunder

菲尼克斯太阳队　Phoenix Suns（这个州的夏天超热，这大概也锻炼了
　　　　　　　　球员的顽强精神）

请参考Pat的思路，并适当借鉴这个词汇表里的单词，思考如果是您会怎么说

Pat 的海外生活英语实录

　　两支球队"棋逢对手"怎样表达呢？跟 chess 或者 opponents 都没关系，而应该用 **evenly-matched** 这个简单却地道的合成词。

　　【剑桥例句】The two teams were fairly evenly-matched.

　　请仔细听音频文件中这些 NBA 球星的名字怎么发音（并且猜一猜他们是谁）：

Blake Griffin

Derrick Rose

Rajon Rondo

Dwyane Wade

Russell Westbrook

Kevin Durant

Chris Bosh

Chris Paul

Kobe Bryant

LeBron James

Dwight Howard

Ricky Rubio

Rasheed Wallace

Dirk Nowitzki

顺着这道题的思路，我们把下面这道题一起快速准备一下。

☞ Describe an athlete / sports team you admire.

同时身为 one of the fastest-rising NBA stars，a Harvard graduate 和粉丝们心目中的 "Lin-sanity"，大男孩林书豪让不少老美主动把地道英文里的 "双赢"（win-win situation）改成了 Lin-win situation。虽然因为膝盖受伤（knee injury）不得不中途退出去年的常规赛（missed his team's last 14 games of the regular season），但他无疑是真心英雄（a genuine hero）。

Fast Facts about Jeremy Lin:

He's a Chinese-American NBA player，born and raised in California，and is proud of being Chinese.

His parents emigrated to the U. S. in the 1970s.

Both of his parents are just average height but Jeremy is well over 6 feet tall.（1 foot =30. 5cm）

Although Jeremy played basketball at a high school just across from Stanford University, he ended up in Harvard.

He got a degree in economics from Harvard and is now a professional player for the Charlotte Hornets.

Some sports reporters called him "the most surprising story in the NBA".

Jeremy is just 27, which is still pretty young for a famous NBA player, and he definitely has an even more brilliant basketball career ahead of him.

I really hope one day Jeremy Lin can become a point guard as great as Magic Johnson.

I totally love this quote from "Lin-sanity" (as many of his fans call him), "When I'm on the court, I try to play with all my emotion and heart."

您还可以在 **www. biography. com/people/groups/olympic-medal** 看到更多在英美大家都熟知的体育明星。

www. olympic. org/athletes 则专门提供奥运明星们的介绍。比如在右上角的 Quick search 一栏里输入 Dan Lin，点击 Go，然后点击右下角的 More About Dan Lin，您就能看到对林丹的详细介绍了。

☆ **一个组织之　健身俱乐部**

难度指数：★ ★ ★ ★ ☆

> Pat 的答案

I'm going to talk about the fitness club I belong to.

Last summer, I felt really out of shape. A friend of mine told me some exercise would get me back in shape. So I went to this fitness club. It was open from 9 a. m. to 10 p. m. , and it offered a variety of memberships. They also had a three-day guest pass for first-timers. I'd never been to a gym before so they recommended their "8-week beginner's plan".

It turned out that the club was pretty cool. It had lots of good machines like the treadmills, exercise bikes and steppers. All the equipment was brand-new. It also offered Pilates and yoga classes. And with the membership I could use the swimming pool for free.

When I first started working out there, my body hurt all over. But then I got used to the exercise, and now I'm feeling pretty good. Sometimes I ask the trainers for some advice. They are real experts and always give me sound advice.

My one-year membership cost me 1, 500 renminbi — kind of expensive, right? But I'm getting my money's worth…

轮到你了   It's Your Turn.

▶ **Word Bank on This Topic**

状态不好　out of shape（这个跟体型没关系，而是指身体状态，如果身体状态好就是 in shape）

会员资格　membership

[剑桥例句] You have to apply for membership of the sports club.

健身房　gym	推荐　recommend
设备　equipment	跑步机　treadmill
举重　lift weights	

"动感单车"，固定自行车　exercise bike / stationary bike（健身俱乐部里的"动感单车运动"叫作 spinning）

踏步机　steppers	普拉提　Pilates
崭新的　brand-new	瑜伽　yoga
锻炼　work out	肌肉　muscles
专家　experts	钱花得值　get my money's worth
尊巴舞　Zumba dance	

请参考Pat的思路，并适当借鉴这个词汇表里的单词，思考如果是您会怎么说

Pat 的海外生活英语实录

您出国之后立马会发现：健身对于年轻白人来说实在是生活里太重要的一个部分了，

我的很多朋友都是命可以不要，但是不能不去 gym，而且有几天没去健身就开始"hold 不住"甚至 feeling guilty（有负罪感）。参加健身俱乐部的目标多半是为了让自己变得"更有形儿"。用地道英语介绍这种健身目的绝不能说 give myself more shape ✗，而要说 **get toned** 或者 **tone my body**，假如你的考官正好也是一年轻白人，考试时你能在扣题的前提下用出这两个表达，将立刻让他/她"心有戚戚焉"，不信你就试试。

【剑桥例句】Leo is exercising regularly to get toned / tone his body.

2. 个人

> Describe a famous person.
>
> You should say:
>
>   who the person is
>
>   why he/she is famous
>
>   why you admire this person
>
> and explain what others think of him/her.

☆ *娱乐人物之　歌手a*

王菲对媒体出了名的不友好，作"王的男人"也是有目共睹的困难，前男友窦唯骑电摩穿行胡同儿的照片已经神似动漫里的大叔。但是，内什么，仍然还是有人喜欢王菲，正是因为她性格中的不完美吧（She's not a perfect person. But she's always been true to herself.）。不论怎样看待她，咱们都不能否认：她是传奇（She's a legend.）。

难度指数：★★★☆☆

Pat 的答案

I would say Faye Wong is still my idol, despite the complaints about her performance at the New Year's Eve gala.

Faye was born and raised in Beijing. Her father took her to Hong Kong when she was 18. At first, she went to modeling classes because she was tall and slim. But she soon lost interest in modeling. Faye enjoyed humming tunes because she felt it was relaxing. A songwriter noticed that and was really impressed by her voice. So he encouraged her to sign a recording contract. Faye released her first album at the age of 19. Then a very important album was produced. Several songs in this album became big hits and won awards for her. So far practically all her albums have been really well-liked.

Unlike other singers in Hong Kong, Faye ignores the press. And that gives her some bad-girl appeal, which I find really attractive.

Faye is not only a talented singer but also a great actress. A couple of years ago, she even won a best-actress award.

Although some people felt disappointed with her performance at last year's New Year's Eve gala, I still adore her "rebel" image. She never treats the press well but the press has to respect her for her incredible talent…

轮到你了   It's Your Turn.

▶ Word Bank on This Topic

王　Wong（大家出国之后经常可以看到一些香港或者广东移民的 last name 是 Wong，而不是 Wang）

抱怨　complaint   表演　performance

春节联欢晚会　（Chinese）New Year's Eve gala

（男性）偏瘦的，（女性）苗条的　slim

有神的眼睛　sparkling eyes

哼歌儿　hum（songs），在表示歌曲的时候除了说 songs，很多时候地道表达中也可以用 tunes 这个词

（歌手）签约　sign a recording contract / sign a record deal

出专辑　release an album   成功的作品　big hit

几乎　practically / virtually（代替 almost 很棒）

新闻界　the press   忽视　ignore

有魅力的　attractive / appealing   吸引力　appeal

[剑桥例句] Spielberg's films have a wide appeal.

多才多艺的 multi-talented / versatile　　有才华的 talented / gifted

叛逆 rebel　　　　　　　　　　　　　　特喜欢 adore

[剑桥例句] Don't you just adore lying in a hot bath?

模特班 modeling class

非常棒的 incredible / amazing / awesome

请参考Pat的思路，并适当借鉴这个词汇表里的单词，思考如果是您会怎么说

Pat 的海外生活英语实录

95% 以上的国内考生都知道 idol 是 "偶像" 的意思，但在地道英语里其实还有一个比偶像地位更高的词：**icon**，是指文化、艺术、娱乐、体育等领域里最具代表性的人。它在英美文化里是个非常地道的词，谈明星时使用将会给考官带来 "心灵的撞击"。

【剑桥例句】Kobe Bryant is a basketball icon and role model（榜样）to a lot of young athletes.

☆ 娱乐人物之　歌手 b

难度指数：★ ★ ★ ☆ ☆

Pat 的答案

I guess you heard a lot about Jay Chou too because he's so incredibly famous in China.

He grew up in a single-parent family. When he was little, Jay didn't get good grades at school. His mother was really concerned about him, but he just looked on the bright side. When he felt down or lonely, he looked for nice music to cheer him up.

He was kind of average-looking so no one really expected him to make it as a singer. He wrote songs for many popular singers like Karen Mok（莫文蔚）and Vivian Hsu（徐若瑄）.

Jay released his first album "Jay" fifteen years ago. His soft voice was so unique and this album turned out to be an instant hit.

His music is always original. That's why many young Chinese simply adore him. His latest album "*Opus* 12" (shi er xing zuo) is, again, a smash hit.

Jay's music blends many elements, like R&B, hip-hop, and folk music. Recently, it seemed like he was really into giving his songs some traditional Chinese appeal, like he did in "*The Porcelain*" (*Ching Hua Tzi*).

Young people are just crazy about him and tickets to his concerts always sell out in just a couple of hours…

轮到你了   It's Your Turn.

▶ **Word Bank on This Topic**

极度地…… incredibly (后面加形容词)   担心 be concerned about

看到积极的一面 look on the bright side

感到情绪低落或者很孤独 feel down or lonely (注意 feel down 并不是 " 中式英语 ", 而是表示感到情绪低落很地道的英文口语)

让人开心 cheer sb. up

外表普通 average-looking / ordinary-looking 成功 make it / succeed in doing sth.

出专辑 release an album   独特的 unique

刚出现就立刻热卖的作品 instant hit   原创的 original

超级喜欢 adore   结合 blend

[剑桥例句] Then you should blend the ingredients (原料) into a smooth paste.

元素 element   民俗音乐 folk music

作曲 compose (作曲人则是 composer)   编曲 arrange (编曲者则是 arranger)

创作型歌手 a singer-songwriter   独特的 unique

多才多艺的 multi-talented / versatile

[剑桥例句] Chris is a versatile young actor who's as happy in action films as he is in TV comedies.

专辑 album   单曲 single

歌词　lyrics（请注意这个词在地道英文里一般被当成复数名词来使用）

曲　music / melody　　　　　　　签约　sign a contract

有才华的，有天赋的　talented　　　很喜欢　be really into...

刚出来就卖光了　sell out（不需要用被动）

巨大的商业成功　smash hit

（Jay 的 squinted eyes 有很多美国和加拿大女孩特喜欢，韩国的歌手 Rain 和鸟叔 PSY 也是这种类型的眼睛）

请参考Pat的思路，并适当借鉴这个词汇表里的单词，思考如果是您会怎么说

Pat 的海外生活英语实录

周董已经不是"范特西"（*Fantasy*）年代的"小鲜肉"（a fresh-faced young man），但他的音乐不知不觉地火了十多年，而且始终保持着很高的质量，影响了整整一代人，堪称是音乐界的传奇人物，他与昆凌（Hannah Quinlivan）在 Selby Abbey 举行的婚礼更是占据了娱乐媒体的头条（made entertainment headlines）。"音乐界"的地道英文叫作 **the music scene**，而"传奇人物"则是 **a legend** 或者 **a legendary figure**。

【剑桥例句】Jazz legend, Ella Fitzgerald, once sang in this bar.

有时雅思口试里还会出现一道难度比较大的考题：**Describe your favourite band.** 知道了 band members 乐队成员，lead singer / lead vocalist 主唱，guitarist 吉他手，bassist 贝斯手，drummer 鼓手，keyboard player 键盘手，single 单曲，album 专辑，big hit 非常成功的作品等词汇之后，就可以看看这个网站：**today. msnbc. msn. com/id/4595384/ ns/today-entertainment/t/best-rock-bands-ever/#. UD06ZcHibBR** 全都是让任何一个真正喜欢音乐的人震撼的名字，其中有几个还在伦敦奥运会的 opening ceremony 出现了。

☆ *娱乐人物之　乐手马友友*（instrumentalist Yo-Yo Ma）

难度指数：★★☆☆☆

Pat 的答案

Yo-Yo Ma（马友友）is one of the most renowned cellists in the world. His father gave him lessons on the cello when he was just four. When Yo-Yo was nine he had the opportunity to study at the famous Juilliard School of Music in New York.

Now he's considered to be one of the greatest cellists in the world. He tours the world playing his cello. When he performs solo, he likes to play classical music. But he has recorded country music, traditional Chinese music and African music as well and actually, he's always looking for new ways to express himself. He also likes to perform on stage with other artists. Wherever he performs, people are moved by his music. Sometimes the effect is so powerful that many audience members are moved to tears. And he always receives thunderous applause and cheers at the end of his shows.

He's a reeeeeeally talented guy…

轮到你了   It's Your Turn.

▶ Word Bank on This Topic

著名的   renowned ("举世闻名" 的则是 world-renowned) / celebrated (在这里不是 "庆祝的")

[剑桥例句] Celia is a celebrated opera singer.

大提琴手	cellist	长号	trombone
在舞台上演出	perform on stage	深受感动	be moved by / be touched by
观众成员	audience members	雷鸣般的	thunderous
鼓掌和欢呼声	applause and cheers	鼓掌	applaud
长笛	flute	竖琴	harp
娴熟的	adept / skillful		
独奏	solo performance (n.) / perform (v.) solo		

请参考Pat的思路，并适当借鉴这个词汇表里的单词，思考如果是您会怎么说

guy 这个词似乎常被英汉字典翻译成 "家伙"，但其实单独这个词就是口语里面的 man，并没有任何坏的意思（除非你非要明确地说 a bad guy）。而且，虽然它的单数只能

指男性，但是在地道英语里它的复数 guys 却不一定只是指男性，男女都有的群体也可以叫 guys，比如很多时候在英美校园里一群男女学生相互打招呼时就会说 Hi, guys！

Pat 的海外生活英语实录

Yo-Yo Ma 五岁就开始登台演奏大提琴了，无论如何也得算是个"神童"（prodigy）。很多成功的国外乐手都是从小就被人们称为 prodigy，有趣的是剑 8 Test 3 的 Reading 题里也出现了 There has always been an interest in geniuses and **prodigies.** 这样的句子。所以请记住"神童"这个词，在 IELTS 口试中被考到 artist 的话题时你就可以做到"与狼共舞"了。

【剑桥例句】He read in the paper about a math prodigy who was attending university at the age of 12.

Time to Branch Out.
推而广之

> Describe your favourite book.

补充弹药

biography　传记	autobiography　自传
entertaining　娱乐性强的	informative　信息量大的

It's a truly original book. 它是一本极具原创性的书。

I found it almost impossible to put this book down. 这本书实在太吸引人了。

Extra Ammo

☆ **娱乐人物之　影星**（英美观众熟知的刘玉玲）

难度指数：★ ★ ★ ☆ ☆

Pat 的答案

Let me talk about my favourite Chinese-American actress, Lucy Liu. Having experienced some ups and downs in her career, now she is one of the most successful Chinese-American actresses in Hollywood.

Her straight black hair makes her so different from the blonde actresses. I think she really knows what she looks good in and wears clothing with so much confidence. For instance, she often wears slim pants to accentuate her long legs.

Her most famous role was in *Charlie's Angels* as a confident and stylish angel who looked so incredibly graceful fighting bad guys. Her style expresses a clear "Don't mess with me！" look. I like it！

The 21st century is often called the Chinese Century and I'm sure even more Chinese stars will break through Hollywood in the future...

轮到你了   It's Your Turn.

▶ **Word Bank on This Topic**

起起落落　ups and downs（这么复杂的概念，英文就这么简单）

事业　career　　　　　金发的　blonde（男性金发的是 blond，少一个 e）

自信的　confident（名词是 confidence）　（男性）偏瘦的，（女性）苗条的　slim

时尚的　fashionable / stylish / trendy　　强调，凸显　accentuate

[剑桥例句] The singer's dress was tightly belted，accentuating the slimness of her waist.

优雅的　graceful / elegant　　　　　　海报　posters

狗仔队　paparazzi（注意这个词本身就是复数概念，所以口语里不要再加-s）

[剑桥例句] Paparazzi follow famous people everywhere they go in order to take photographs of them for newspapers and magazines.

请参考Pat的思路，并适当借鉴这个词汇表里的单词，思考如果是您会怎么说

访谈　interview　　　　　　　　　魅力四射的　glamorous

名人　celebrity

Pat 的海外生活英语实录

在 Hollywood，Lucy Liu 是能够出演高上座率电影（box-office hits）的少数华

裔演员之一，这种显赫身份（prominent status）真够让人羡慕的。其实不仅是明星，对任何让你"羡慕"的人，比如拿到 Oxford 全奖的大牛或者复议之后单科提高了 1.5、人品爆棚的幸运儿，你都可以发自内心地说，" I really **envy** him／her！"

【剑桥例句】

I really envy her ability to talk to people she's never met before.

☆ 艺术家之 梵高

难度指数：★ ★ ☆ ☆ ☆

⌐ **Pat 的答案** ¬

Vincent Van Gogh（梵高）is now considered to be one of the greatest painters because of his profound influence on modern art. His most famous masterpieces were the Sunflowers and the Starry Night.

Van Gogh was born and grew up in the Netherlands. He was a compassionate person and had great sympathy for the poor people there. He even gave away most of his own things to the poor, but then got fired by his boss and had to rely on his brother for money.

Van Gough painted farmers and workers. He was incredibly talented and creative. Instead of trying to copy what he had before his eyes, he just used colours freely in order to better express his emotions.

Later he moved to Paris, where he sold none of his works. Van Gogh was poor and had serious illnesses. In the end, he suffered so much from his illnesses that he took his own life with a gun.

As a painter, he sold only one painting during his lifetime and was little known to the art world at the time of his death. But his fame grew fast after his death. I admire him not just because of his talent. Actually he's much more than a great painter. He's one of the greatest cultural heroes of modern times…

轮到你了   It's Your Turn.

▶ **Word Bank on This Topic**

深刻的影响 profound influence   荷兰 the Netherlands（形容词：Dutch）

有同情心的 compassionate   同情心 sympathy   名誉 fame

艺术家的作品 works（请注意在表示这个含义时 work 经常加复数）

（绘画的）笔触 brushstroke / brushwork   抽象的 abstract

具象的 representational（艺术家）   多产的 prolific

[剑桥例句] He was probably the most prolific songwriter of his generation.

受到好评的 receive rave reviews   名人 celebrity

一夜成名 an overnight success   叛逆的 rebellious（发音是/rɪˈbelɪəs/）

[剑桥例句] Julia's teachers regard her as a rebellious trouble-making girl.

天才 genius   珍贵的 precious

杰作 masterpiece

请参考Pat的思路，并适当借鉴这个词汇表里的单词，思考如果是您会怎么说

Pat 的海外生活英语实录

　　最成功的艺术家通常都会有独特的风格。基础一般的国内同学会用 He/She has a very special style. 来表达这个意思，而基础好的同学则多半会讲 He/She has a unique style.（请注意 very unique ✗ 是中式英语，因为 unique 本身就不能再比较程度了）但其实在海外英文里还有 **an instantly recognisable style**（一眼就能辨认出来的风格）这样更加形象而且地道的说法。

　　【剑桥例句】The Eiffel Tower in Paris is an instantly recognisable landmark.

Pat 指南 🔊

　　关于艺术家，这个网站最大的优点是内容相当专业，但英文却简单得跟玩儿似的：library. thinkquest. org/J001159/famart. htm

　　☆ *历史人物之　军事人物（风靡英美的孙武）*

　　难度指数：★ ★ ★ ☆ ☆

Pat 的答案

Sun Wu was one of the greatest military theorists in ancient China. I don't know about you, but I have read *the Art of War* many, many times. His theories have profound influence on today's military and business leaders' decision-making.

He lived in an age of war about 3,000 years ago. Sun Wu wrote loads of books about military theories. When the ruler of the state Wu asked Sun Wu to show his theories by training ladies of his court, those beauties kept laughing at Sun Wu as he gave them orders. Sun Wu had two of them executed immediately, then none of the others dared to laugh again. Finally they were trained well enough to go into battle.

Sun Wu was appointed as a general because of this. From then on Sun Wu led his armies with great success. His military theories covered a lot of ground, including the factors that decided who would be the winner, how to defeat the enemy without even fighting a battle, making the best use of the situations and guiding the struggle to victory.

His theories were created thousands of years ago but they are still very useful today. Amazing, huh?

轮到你了 ///////   It's Your Turn.

▶ Word Bank on This Topic

军队	the military	理论家	theorist
深刻的影响	profound influence	宫廷	court
立刻	immediately = right away	处决	execute
战役	battle	任命	appoint (v.)
胜利	victory / triumph	光荣的	glorious
正直	integrity		

[剑桥例句] No one doubted that the president was a man of the highest integrity.

战略	strategy	有远见的	forward-looking
权力	authority / power	勇敢的	courageous
无敌的	invincible / indomitable		

[剑桥例句] The indomitable lady said she would continue to flight for justice.

请参考Pat的思路，并适当借鉴这个词汇表里的单词，思考如果是您会怎么说

Pat 的海外生活英语实录

用英语说人 "很聪明的"，有些同学爱用 clever，也有人喜欢说 smart，但是在口试的 Part 2 卡片题里，使用比它们更正式的形容词 **intelligent** 描述效果会更好。

【剑桥例句】

(1) Helen had a few intelligent things to say on the subject.

(2) Noah is very intelligent, but dislikes studying.

IELTS 口语题库里还有一个相关话题 **Describe a historical event. / Describe an event in history.** 很多同学看到这道题时都感到特茫然，其实这个话题的可选择范围极为广泛。在英美中学里学习历史时，从古代史（ancient history），中世纪历史（mediaeval history）到现代史（modern history），当代史（contemporary history）当中发生的任何一个事件都可以叫作 a historical event。而且这道题目里也并没有明确要求必须是中国历史，所以中外历史事件都是可以的，并不需要太紧张。

对于多数中国同学来说，描述在中国发生过的历史事件相对更容易一些。history. cultural-china. com/34two. html 这个网站介绍了绝大多数重要的中国历史事件，页面右上角从 A 一直到 Z 覆盖得极为全面，而页面左侧的 History in Photos 则有点儿 "看图说话" 的感觉，即使不是为了考试就当休闲读物看都挺有意思的。

而 www. tostepharmd. net/hissoc/top100events. html 则提供了改编自美国 Life 杂志的对于最近一千年里人类 100 件重要历史事件的深入描述。需要特别提醒您注意的是：尽管每个历史学家都希望自己不带有偏见（completely unbiased），但是美国的历史学家和中国的历史学家即使在看待同一事件时也往往会意见相左。这个网站上的有些观点同样存在着明显的偏见，只有辩证分析技能（critical thinking skills）才能让我们不至于盲从。

☆ **人物之 企业家**（entrepreneur）/**有米的人**（a wealthy person）

Bill Gates

难度指数：★★☆☆☆

Pat 的答案

Let me talk about one of the richest guys in the world, Bill Gates. Actually, I guess you know more about him than I do. But... anyway, let me give it a try.

When Bill was little, sometimes when his mother asked him what he was doing, he simply replied he was thinking. An unusual answer for a little kid, huh?

At age 13, Bill Gates started programming computers. Later he went to Harvard Law School, only to drop out in his junior year. He started a computer software company called Microsoft. He hoped there could be personal computers in every home and every workplace. His dream was to create software technology that would be inexpensive and easy enough for everyone to use. Bill Gates also wrote a famous book called The Road Ahead, which clearly explained the value of computer technology in modern life and made predictions about the future of computers.

Microsoft has become the leading business in the world, which had made Bill and his wife the richest couple in the world. But they did much more than just becoming rich. They established a foundation to help people suffering from poor health...

轮到你了　　　　　　　　　　　　　　　　　　　　　　　　It's Your Turn.

▶ Word Bank on This Topic

不平常的　unusual　　　辍学　drop out of school　　　编程序　programming

创业者　entrepreneur（英美生活里还有个固定说法叫 He's a self-made man. 或者 She's a self-made woman. 也是用来形容一个成功的男人或女人"白手起家"）

[剑桥例句] Ramon was one of the entrepreneurs of the eighties who made their money in property.

便宜的　inexpensive（比 cheap 听起来客气一些）/ economical

建立　set up / establish　　　　　基金会　foundation

榜样　role model　　　　　　　　慈善事业　philanthropy

慈善组织　charitable organisation　　激励人的　inspiring

勤奋的，敬业的　industrious / diligent / hard-working

完美主义者　perfectionist　　　　崇拜　worship（语气比 admire 强）

工作地点　workplace　　　　　　预言　prediction

远见　vision　　　　　　　　　　一个有远见的幻想家　a visionary

反垄断法（也翻译成反托拉斯法） antitrust law

官司 lawsuit 垄断 monopoly

（相当地道的英文习语）他／她从不停止思考 He / She has an inquiring mind.

（人或者企业）是某一领域里的领军人物或企业 lead the pack

请参考Pat的思路，并适当借鉴这个词汇表里的单词，思考如果是您会怎么说

☆ 苹果前领袖 Steve Jobs ／ 记一个成功人物

难度指数 ★ ★ ★ ☆ ☆

Pat 的答案

To many people, Steve Jobs, the former CEO of Apple, was the most creative businessman in the world. He co-founded Apple in the late 1970s and had served as its CEO since the late 1990s. Actually, he was also a large shareholder of Disney. So he was like… super rich.

But to Apple buffs, myself included, Steve Jobs was much more than a successful businessman. To us, he was more like an artist. Over the years, Apple has brought us loads of beautifully-designed high-tech gadgets such as iPod, iPhone and MacBook Pro.

He was a great public speaker as well, and I remember him saying in a speech, "Don't waste time living someone else's life, or living the result of someone else's thinking."

Steve Jobs showed us the importance of the courage to follow our own heart. Many friends of mine totally worship him and study the way Steve Jobs did almost everything. They want to be just like him. When he went on a medical leave from Apple because of a rare form of cancer, we were deeply shocked and worried. And when he passed away in October 2011, we were so saddened by this deep loss. His biography became the #1 bestseller immediately…

轮到你了   It's Your Turn.

► **Word Bank on This Topic**

有创意的   creative / innovative   共同建立   co-found

大股东   large shareholder   迪斯尼   Disney

……迷   buff（出国后您会发现这个 "……迷" 相当常用，例如经常能听到的 I'm a car buff 和 I'm a movie buff，语气很像中文里的 "……控"，但请注意：buff 一般都是说某种事物的 "迷"，但如果说某个人物的 "粉丝" 在英美则还是要说 I'm a big fan of... 或者 I'm an admirer of...）

也包括我自己在内   myself included（常见的句中短语，意思和 including me 一样但语气更正式一些，一般它的前面会是表示某类人的复数名词）

大量的   loads of / tons of   设计很优美的   beautifully-designed

高科技的   high-tech

很好用的小东西   gadget（在英美生活里常用 gadget 指小型工具或者小型电子产品）

苹果笔记本系列中的一款超轻薄机   MacBook Air

苹果笔记本系列里的一款高端机   MacBook Pro

公共演讲   public speech   勇气   courage / bravery

崇拜   worship（这个动词的崇拜程度比 admire 还要强很多）

病假   medical leave   罕见的   rare   辞职   resign

董事会主席   chairman of the board（在英美生活里经常被简称为 chair of the board）

尽快好起来   Get well soon!（很多国内朋友们知道 Have a speedy recovery. 这样祝病人痊愈的说法，但在国外生活里 Get well soon! 却更为常用）

去世   pass away / pass along（英美口语里用来替换 die 的委婉语）

传记   biography   自传   autobiography

最畅销作品 bestseller   天才   genius

直觉   intuition

[剑桥例句] Often there's no clear evidence so you just have to base your judgment on intuition.

精通的　savvy（例如"精通电脑的"就是 computer-savvy）

[剑桥例句] Matt bought the laptop on the advice of a computer-savvy friend.

不走寻常路（英文习语）　　go against the grain

"保持对新事物的渴望，并且敢于承担风险。" "Stay hungry. Stay foolish."

阿什顿·库彻（传记电影 *Jobs* 的主演）　　Ashton Kutcher

以乔布斯的生平为依据的传记电影　　a biographical film based on the life of Steve Jobs

请参考Pat的思路，并适当借鉴这个词汇表里的单词，思考如果是您会怎么说

Pat 的海外生活英语实录

　　真正成功的领袖必然是有魅力的，但"魅力"一词如果用国内朋友们使用过度的 charm 来表达却实在是相当地没有"魅力"。请改用 **charisma** /kəˈrizmə/ 来描述政治家、企业家或者明星们等公众人物的"范儿"吧，考官对这个词的反应绝不会让你后悔。

　　【剑桥例句】How did a man of so little personal charisma get to be a leader?

☆ 人物之　普通人（教师）

难度指数：★★★☆☆

Pat 的答案

Let me talk about my favourite teacher — my mother（英美人普遍"童心较重"，Pat 和自己身边的朋友聊天的时候提到父母时我们都是用 my mom，my dad 这样的说法，绝没有问题，但您自己是否想用看自己的性格而定吧）. She's a high-school teacher, a reaaaaally good one. Her classes are always well-liked and she's great at sharing knowledge with her students.

In terms of appearance, my mom is kind of average. She just looks like any other lady her age, with some wrinkles on her face and gray hair. But she always wears a friendly smile on her face,

which makes her very approachable. I guess that's partly why her students are so crazy about her lectures. And… she's really elegant and has exquisite taste in clothing.

She's articulate, knowledgeable and most importantly, patient. I would say she's a teacher who's never cramped her students' style.

The most impressive thing about my mom as a teacher is, of course, how much knowledge she has. She read tons of books in her college years and has been always on the lookout for a good book. By the way, she often told me interesting and educational bedtime stories when I was little.

My mom has amazing cooking skills as well. The hot and sour soup she makes is second to none. And you know what? She often takes snacks she makes to class and shares them with her students.

My mom is not just a wonderful teacher, but a great wife and a great mother as well. And everyone says I take after her…

轮到你了　　　　　　　　　　　　　　　　　　　　It's Your Turn.

▶ Word Bank on This Topic

皱纹　wrinkle

受欢迎的　well-liked（这个词并不是中式英语，恰恰相反，其实它在地道英语里和 popular 一样地 popular）

[剑桥例句] A colleague（同事）described him as well-liked and respected by all.

好接近的　approachable

讲课　lecture（注意这个其实就是国外学校里的讲课，而不一定是"讲座"）

优雅的　elegant

表达能力很强的　articulate

知识丰富的　knowledgeable

阅读　read（注意过去时还是 read，但是发音变化了，请听录音）

有品位　has exquisite taste　　限制某人的发挥　cramp one's style

睡前故事　bedtime stories　　最好的　second to none / top-notch / the best

热情　passion　　让学生们敢于发言　get students out of their shells

[剑桥例句] Kyle used to be very withdrawn but he has really come out of his shell since Leah took an interest in him.

态度　attitude

孩子像父母（固定短语）　take after（my mother / my father）

投入　commitment　　　　不听讲的学生　unruly / disruptive students

激励　inspire　　　　　　开阔视野　expand one's outlook

很有启发的　enlightening / illuminating

把学生分组　divide students into groups / pairs

鼓励　encourage　　　　成绩　grades

表扬　praise / compliment（其实后面这个在国外生活里用得非常多，但国内同学却普遍只用第一个）

[剑桥例句] I must compliment you on your handling of a very difficult situation.

给老师的苹果　an apple for the teacher（国外的学生经常用一个苹果表示对某个老师的喜爱）

某种品质或者外表的特征在一个大家庭里一代代地延续。

　　It runs in the family.

请参考Pat的思路，并适当借鉴这个词汇表里的单词，思考如果是您会怎么说

Pat 的海外生活英语实录

在英美文化里，大家公认的一个好老师应该具有的素质除了 patience, confidence, leadership skills 等之外，"表达能力强"也是必不可少的要求之一（事实上，不仅是对教师，英美教育从 nursery / junior kindergarten 阶段开始就极为重视对于学生 public speaking 能力的培养）。所以当准备 a teacher 这个题目的时候，请务必记牢 **articulate** /ɑːˈtikjələt/ 这个单词，因为它就是在国外生活英语里形容一个人口齿清晰、表达能力强最常用的那个词。

【剑桥例句】

（1）Daisy gave an entertaining and articulate speech.

（2）This lady was an intelligent and articulate spokeswoman for a lot of causes（公共事业）。

Time to Branch Out.
推而广之

Describe a person who helped you before.

Describe a person who speaks a foreign language.

Describe your ideal job. (理想的工作)

补充弹药

intelligent	思维能力很强的	encouragement (*n.*)	鼓励
creativity	创造力	energetic	精力很充沛的

Extra Ammo

3. 人物之 老人与孩子 (双语感悟) **Random Reflections on Elderly People and Kids**

对于老人身体很好，我们可以说 He / She's hale and hearty. 或者 He / She's healthy and active. 白发可以说 white hair，而 "花白的头发" 则叫 salt and pepper hair，皱纹如果实在不想再说 wrinkles，那么说 lines 也成。说老年人很乐观，除了大词 optimistic 之外，还可以简单地说 He / She always look on the bright side。老人下象棋是 play chess，打太极除了 practice taichi 之外还可以叫 go through the tai-chi routines，老太太舞扇子就可以直接说 wave fans。"跳广场舞" 可以说 practise their square dance routine 要说老人 "睿智"，那么仅仅用 smart 就不够了，应该说 wise 或者 intelligent and sophisticated。

对于孩子，如果长个儿快，就是 is growing like a weed (野草)。小孩个子小则有一个有趣的说法叫 is knee-high to a grasshopper (只到蚂蚱膝盖那么高)，小孩皮肤好，就是 His / Her skin is smooth as silk，小孩胖嘟嘟的叫 chubby，小朋友特别好动，叫 hyperactive，或者说 is a perpetual motion machine (永动机)，小孩安静，说 tends to be quiet around people，扰乱课堂纪律的学生叫 unruly students / disruptive students，小孩成

绩好则常说 get good grades at school；是别人的楷模地道英语叫 is a role model for his / her classmates，门门儿功课都特棒要说 He / She is a straight-A student. 在某方面有天赋就说 has a talent（or has a gift）for music（或者 painting，maths 等）；而如果要强调人家成绩好是因为努力而不是靠运气，则可以说 It's all about hard work, not luck. 小朋友可爱除了 cute 还可以叫 adorable，小孩是父母的掌上明珠叫 the apple of his / her parents' eye（单数！），拧一下小孩子的脸叫 pinch his / her face，不过需要注意，在国外如果跟家长不熟就去碰孩子的脸很容易被起诉（taken to the court），因为 It's a litigious society！（什么事情都能打官司的社会）

临时抱佛脚

在亚太区时常露一小脸儿的人物卡片话题是：

Describe an international celebrity / a famous person who lives in another country.

▲ Adele

对于周六就要考了周一还没开始准备、根本没有可能系统学习本章关键词和句子的人来说，这道题也可以用一种很"寓教于乐"※的方法来准备：

先牢记 4 个用来描述大腕儿的拿分好词：talented 有才华的，dedicated 全身心投入的，fame and wealth 财富和名望（"淡泊名利"可以叫 does not seek fame and wealth）和 charisma（这个词的意思很像中文说名人时常用的"范儿"）。

▶ Katy Perry

然后就先去做雅思 L，R 或者 W 的练习吧，当实在累了的时候，抽空儿浏览一下这个娱乐性极强的网页：

www. imdb. com

这个网站一网打尽了现在所有在欧美当红大牌明星的 biography，只要在放大镜旁边的 search box 里填入要找的明星名字，再点击 All 菜单找到 Bios，然后点击放大镜，你就"到站"了。

※ 近年来在英美教育界还出现了一个挺时髦的新词叫 edutainment，等于 education + entertainment，虽然在一些过时的英文词典里还不一定能查到，但它确实已经是"寓教于乐"在当代英文里最地道的说法了。

另类话题　Off-the-Wall Topics

　　Joe Wong（黄西）这位 "70 后大哥" 的英语并不 native，而且他在说英语时的发音还带有浓重的东北口音。但他却登上了美国最著名的 late night TV talk show —— The Late Show with David Letterman，并且成了近期最受美国观众注意的 stand-up comedians 之一。Joe Wong 的成功故事再次告诉我们：英语说得简单易懂，反而能让你和 native speakers 进行更加充分的沟通。

　　I（Joe Wong）came to the United States when I was 24, to study at Rice University in Texas ...

　　Like many other immigrants, we want our son to become the President of this country and we try to make him bilingual（双语的）, you know, Chinese at home and English in public, which is really tough to do ...

　　In America they say that all men are created equal, but after birth, it kind of depends on the parents' income, or early education and health care ...

　　I'm honored to meet Vice President Joe Biden here tonight. I actually read your autobiography（自传）, and today I see you. I think the book is much better ...

　　So to be honest, I'm really honored to be here tonight, and I prepared for months for tonight's show. And I showed the White House my jokes about President Obama, and that is when he decided not to come ... And I started to think maybe I should run for president myself ...We have a president who is half black half white, it just gives me a lot of hope, because I'm half not black and half not white. Two negatives make a positive ...

So guys, you still think IELTS is scary? Give it your best shot, then you won't have any regrets at all.

C 人与自然

Pat 解题　Pat's Decryption

natural beauty 这个词在英文中其实有两个意思，一个是指自然景色，一个是指用天然的化妆品（cosmetics）。当然两个意思都挺好，不过这一节咱们只说第一个。

中国文化很强调"天人合一"（unity of nature and humanity），但是由于自然资源长期被过度开发（over-exploited），我们反而离自然越来越远了（more and more disconnected from nature）。

北美的生活离自然还是挺近的。Pat 在 BC 开车时还见过一只灰熊（grizzly bear）妈妈带着两只小熊（bear cubs）慢悠悠地违章横穿马路，如果真的不小心撞到（run over）它们，可就要被动物权益主义者（animal rights activists）告上法庭（be taken to court）了。

北美的生活中最重要的娱乐也是 fishing, camping, hiking, skiing 这些接近自然的活动。需要强调的是：如果你在北京爬香山，一定不要说 climb the Xiang Shan Mountain，因为在地道英文里 climb the mountain 是指全副武装地到山里去攀岩，挑战会很大，正确的说法应该是 go on a hike in Xiang Shan Park。

雅思口语里还有一道挺常考的卡片题是 **Describe a walk with a friend**。本节的大量内容都可以用来准备这道题，只要再知道两个关键词：stroll（散步）和 scenery（风景，请注意：这个词不可以加复数），然后再和朋友谈谈学业（studies）或者事业（career）就行了。

北美的国家公园很多，Pat 个人最喜欢 Alberta 的 Banff，那里的雪真的把人的呼吸都带走了（It took my breath away.）。

除了自然景色，在本节我们还会谈到动物。在北美，不仅野生动物、宠物很多样化，比较好玩的除了 dogs，还有 hamster, parakeet, tropical fish, pony 甚至 iguana。

展开本类话题的思路线索　Brainstorming Techniques
(熟悉下图可以确保你在拿到任何本类卡片题时都能有话说)

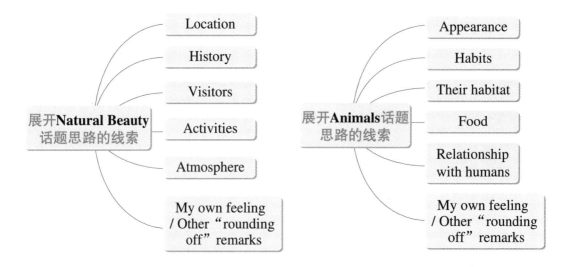

本类话题最新完整真题库　Recent Questions on This Topic

❉ Describe a garden/park.

❉ Describe a tourist attraction.

❉ Describe a meal/picnic in a park.

❉ Describe a place of natural beauty.

❉ Describe a good place to relax（not your home）.

❉ Describe a peaceful place.

❉ Describe a short trip.

❉ Describe a river / lake / sea.

❉ Describe a place where there is a lot of water.

分级演示 A　Spectrum of Sample Answers

1. 一个有水的地方

☆ **西湖**

> Describe a river, lake or sea you have visited.
>
> You should say:
>> why you went there
>>
>> what you liked about this place
>>
>> whether you would like to go there again
>
> and explain why it was nice.

难度指数：★ ★ ★ ★ ☆

Pat 的答案

It had long been a dream of mine to travel to the West Lake. This past spring I had that dream come true during a trip to Hangzhou.

It was a breezy, shiny day and the water in the lake was shimmering in the sunlight. I also saw some rolling hills in the near distance. The breeze on my face felt calm and refreshing.

Obviously, the Hang Zhou government had spent lots of money developing the West Lake as a tourist attraction. The trees were well-trimmed and the grass was neatly-mowed. There were many picnic tables and benches by the lake. Birds were chirping around me as I strolled around.

I also checked out the "Ten Scenes of the West Lake", you know, the ten most famous scenic spots nearby, like the Lei Feng Pagoda. It offered an amazing view of the lake and the hills …

轮到你了　　　　　　　　　　　　　　　　　　　It's Your Turn.

▶ **Word Bank on This Topic**

| 微风 | breeze | 刮着微风的 | breezy |

阳光明媚的　shiny

平缓的小山　rolling hills

令人感觉焕然一新的　refreshing

闪亮的　shimmering

泛起波纹的　rippling

旅游景点　tourist attraction

（枝叶）修剪得很整齐的　well-trimmed

（草坪）修剪得很整齐的　neatly-mowed

长椅　bench

鸟叫　chirping

漫步　stroll

体验　check out（informal）

[剑桥例句] Kevin's going to check out that new club.

风景点　scenic spot

塔　pagoda

壮观的　spectacular

非常美的　breathtaking / gorgeous

宁静的　tranquil and serene

安静的　peaceful / quiet

微风　breeze

掠过湖面　sweeps across the lake

> 请参考Pat的思路，并适当借鉴这个词汇表里的单词，思考如果是您会怎么说

Pat 的海外生活英语实录

"风景如画的"，如果说 It looks like a picture. 并不严格对应，因为 picture 其实也可以很丑，但 picture 的形容词形式 **picturesque** /ˌpɪktʃəˈresk/ 在地道口语中却是一个纯粹的褒义词。例如：

【剑桥例句】It was a picturesque cottage on the edge of the Yorkshire Moors.

句子里的 cottage 在当代英美生活里是指度假用的小屋，中老年中产们如果有点闲钱的话往往就喜欢去海滨、湖滨或森林里买个比较便宜的 cottage 供度假时住。

Time to Branch Out.
推而广之

Describe a trip you took recently.

Describe a school holiday.

补充弹药

Extra Ammo

refreshing 让人焕然一新的   rewarding 有回报的

well-planned 计划充分的   tiring 让人疲惫的

memorable 很值得回忆的

2. 公园/花园

Describe a park/garden.

You should say:
> where it is located
> what you do there
and whether many other people go there.

☆一个公园之 瀑布

难度指数：★★★★☆

Pat 的答案

I'm going to talk about the Falls Park, one of the most renowned national parks in China. Over two million people visit it each year.

The park lies in southwestern Guizhou. It's best known for its natural beauty, especially the spectacular waterfalls. The park also has a wide variety of wild plants and animals.

I went there last summer. The trees there reached so high that they reminded me of the skyscrapers in Hong Kong. And as I hiked around the park, I saw quite a few waterfalls, which roared over the rocks into the Baishui river. The scenery was very natural and seemed to change every few meters.

When I felt tired, I just sat on the ground

and enjoyed the natural beauty all around me.

Everything was good and the waterfalls were incredible.

The park is absolutely a must-see for nature lovers.

| 轮到你了 | It's Your Turn. |

▶ **Word Bank on This Topic**

著名的	renowned	位于	lie in / be located in
壮观的	spectacular	瀑布	waterfall
摩天楼	skyscraper	徒步旅行	hike
风景	scenery	特别棒的	incredible
非常美的	breathtaking / gorgeous	一定要看的地方	must-see
热爱自然的人	nature lover		

自然界里的天然草地　meadows（城市里需要人工维护的草地叫 lawns）

山谷	valley	宿营	camping
野餐	picnic	烧烤	have a barbecue
宁静安详的	tranquil and serene		

请参考Pat的思路，并适当借鉴这个词汇表里的单词，思考如果是您会怎么说

Pat 的海外生活英语实录

从多伦多开车两个小时就可以到举世闻名的 Niagara Falls. 瀑布当然壮观，但动静儿更大，从很远就能听到"隆隆的瀑布声"。用地道英文该怎么表达这个意思呢？绝不可以说 long long waterfall sound ✗，而要说 **thundering waterfall**。

【剑桥例句】The thundering waterfall plunges hundreds of meters to the river below.

☆ 一个公园之　海洋公园

难度指数：★★★★☆

Pat 的答案

The Ocean Park is about 20 minutes away from downtown Hong Kong by car. Or you can go on foot along the scenic Seawall Walk. The park is made up of many different sections. There's a lot to see and do as you wander through these sections.

In the Strait, sharks, turtles and seahorses are just some of the thousands of creatures waiting for you. They can be seen through the underwater windows. My favourite part is when divers feed the creatures underwater. It's an amazing sight because you can see the whole thing so clearly without wearing diving gear.

In the outdoor Wild Coast, you can see the exciting performance of the high-flying dolphins and the super active otters. Such shows take place several times each day. And the Amazon Rainforest is home to lots of exotic birds and fish.

In Children's World, the play area, kids can even touch some of the sea life they are interested in, so they can really experience sea life first-hand.

Trips to the Ocean Park are always eye-opening, even for those who already have a good understanding of the ocean...

轮到你了   It's Your Turn.

▶ **Word Bank on This Topic**

风景优美的，景色宜人的	scenic	部分	parts / sections
漫步	wander / stroll	海峡	strait
鲨鱼	shark	海马	seahorse
海狮	sea lion	龟	turtle
海象	walrus	海豚	dolphin
海豹	seal	虎鲸	killer whale
水母	jellyfish	水獭	otter
潜水员	diver	工具	gear

表演　performance　　　　　　　　超级活跃的　super active / hyperactive

[剑桥例句] Hyperactive children often have poor concentration（注意力）and require very little sleep.

发生，进行　take place　　　　　　珍奇的　exotic

直接地体验　experience… first-hand　让人大开眼界的　eye-opening

[剑桥例句] Living in another country can be really eye-opening.

野生动物园　safari park　　　　　　山谷　valley

风景　scenery（请注意：这个词不可以加复数）

一定要看的地方　must-see　对……来说是一个圣地　is a mecca for…

[剑桥例句] The bookstore has become a mecca for booklovers.

请参考Pat的思路，并适当借鉴这个词汇表里的单词，思考如果是您会怎么说

Pat 的海外生活英语实录

说到"海洋生物"，大家一定会本能地想到 sea life 或者 sea animals。这些当然也是地道的英文，但不妨试试 **marine life** 吧，它会让考官紧皱着的眉头舒展开。

【剑桥例句】

（1）The oil slick threatened marine life around the islands.

（2）The kids were amazed by the enormous variety of marine life.

☆ 花园

难度指数：★ ★ ★ ☆ ☆

Pat 的答案

My favourite garden is the Classical Chinese Garden which is just a 10-minute walk away from where I live. It's always a perfect place to visit. The covered walkways provide shelter so the beautiful views can be appreciated in any weather.

And the garden is breathtaking in every season. In spring, everything in the garden turns green and the flowers bloom. In summer, the trees are pretty shady so we can watch fish play in the glistening ponds. The trees change colours in autumn and the foliage looks absolutely fascinating. The garden is brilliant even in winter because snow makes it pure and neat.

This place is very peaceful, almost like a window on another world. Many elementary-school teachers take their students there to discover the secrets of the Chinese culture and the garden is often rented for filming...

轮到你了 　　　　　　　　　　　　　　　　　It's Your Turn.

▶ **Word Bank on This Topic**

遮风挡雨的地方　shelter 　　　　　　欣赏　appreciate

开花　bloom 　　　　　　　　　　　　阴凉的　shady

闪亮的　sparkling / glistening 　　　　池塘　pond

漫步　wander / stroll

树叶　leaves / foliage（请注意后面这个单词在地道英语里不能用复数）

[剑桥例句] The dense foliage overhead almost blocked out（遮挡）the sun.

岩石　rock(s) 　　　　　　　　　　　发现　discover

小学教师　elementary-school teachers 　　水墨画　ink painting

学者　scholar

诗歌　poetry（poetry 是泛指诗歌而 a poem 则是指一首具体的诗歌）

[剑桥例句] She started writing poetry at a young age.

让心灵平静　calm（或者 sooth）your nerves

抚慰人的精神　restore the soul

放松　unwind / wind down（请注意听音频里对它们的读音）

感到焕然一新、精力充沛的　feel refreshed and energetic

亭子　pavilion / gazebo

请参考Pat的思路，并适当借鉴这个词汇表里的单词，思考如果是您会怎么说

> **Pat 的海外生活英语实录**

　　"宁静的"，我知道你一定会想到 quiet, calm, peaceful 这些词，但估计您却想不到 **serene** 这个在地道口语里形容一个地方宁静相当常用的词，而且它还经常会被与另一个近义词 tranquil 连在一起来构成词组 **tranquil and serene**。

　　【剑桥例句】The guest house is set in a tranquil and serene garden.

常见植物英文名称（多数的发音都比较 tricky，请您认真听录音）

tulip　郁金香	lily　百合
chrysanthemum　菊花	peony　牡丹
daisy　雏菊	petunia　喇叭花
daffodil　水仙花	orchid　兰花
sunflower　向日葵	violet　紫罗兰
oak tree　橡树	palm tree　棕榈树
willow　柳树	holly　冬青
pine tree　松柏	maple tree　枫树

申加拿大学校的读者们今后可一定别忘了 check out the maple syrup，超级好喝！

poinsettia　一品红，很红很漂亮的一种花，Christmas 的时候经常作装饰用。

poplar　杨树，查字典的中文翻译是叫"杨树"，但 Pat 在国外看到过的 poplar 却都是树干上全部长满叶子，一排排（rows）的，装饰性很强（very ornamental）。

Time to Branch Out.
推而广之

Describe a walk that you regularly take.

补充弹药

soothing 让人放松的	breeze 微风
stroll 漫步	
feel refreshed and energetic 感觉焕然一新、精力充沛的	

Extra Ammo

3. 天气

> Describe an experience you had with bad weather.
>
> You should say:
>
> what kind of bad weather it was
>
> when it happened
>
> where you were when it happened
>
> and explain how it affected you.

☆天气之　恶劣的天气

Pat 指南

说恶劣天气的选择很多，比如 snowstorm 暴风雪（高强度的暴雪还可以称为 blizzard，喜欢打 Diablo Ⅲ "暗黑破坏神 3" 的朋友肯定很熟悉这个词，在灾难片儿里这词也特常用），heavy fog / thick fog 浓雾，typhoon 台风，flood 洪水，extreme heat / extreme cold 酷热或严寒等等。甚至在地道英语里连 earthquake 地震（口语里常被简称为 quake）和 tsunami 海啸也都算 bad weather。但是，如果这题说得过于恐怖反而有 "炒作" 的嫌疑，就说个 "一般坏" 的天气听起来反倒会更真实。

难度指数：★ ★ ★ ☆ ☆

Pat 的答案

Last August, some friends of mine and I had a very unpleasant camping experience. We listened to the weather forecast before we set off. It said it would be sunny and breezy over the next two days, just perfect for camping and picnics. So we were totally unprepared for nasty weather.

In fact, we really enjoyed the first couple of hours of the trip. The sky was nice and

clear. The camping spot was at the base of a mountain and the view was fantastic. We had a barbecue picnic and then started playing card games.

All of a sudden, dark clouds filled the sky, strong winds blew through the campsite and it started to pour. The temperature dropped to, I would say, probably just 8 or 10 degrees. Some friends of mine even started shivering. By the time we set up our tent in a terrible hurry, all of us got soaking wet.

We didn't expect any rain or chilly weather, so the sudden change put everyone in a bad mood. The rain continued through the night and into the next morning, which made all of us frustrated. We just packed our stuff and left the campsite.

The lesson we learned from it? Sometimes Mother Nature can be reaaaaally unpredictable. So when it comes to weather, always hope for the best and prepare for the worst …

轮到你了   It's Your Turn.

> ▶ **Word Bank on This Topic**
>
> | | |
> |---|---|
> | 令人不快的　unpleasant / upsetting | 天气预报　weather forecast / weather report |
> | 启程　set off | 刮微风的　breezy |
> | 野餐　picnic | 没有准备的　unprepared |
> | 很差的天气　miserable weather / nasty weather | |
> | 在山脚下　at the base of a mountain （规模较小的山则叫 hill） | |
> | 打牌　play card games | 突然地　all of a sudden （固定短语）/ suddenly |
> | 宿营地　campsite / camping site / campground | |
> | 下大雨　pour / rain heavily | 发抖　shiver |
> | 搭帐篷　pitch a tent / set up a tent | 全身湿透　get soaking wet / get drenched |
> | 令某人心情很糟　put someone in a bad mood | |
> | 沮丧的　frustrated | 收拾行李　pack someone's stuff |
> | 自然界　Mother Nature （地道口语里的常用说法） | |

不可预料的 unpredictable   紧急情况 emergency

可怕的 scary   能见度低 poor visibility

(浓雾等)笼罩 shroud something

[剑桥例句] The fog shrouding the city had lifted by eight o'clock.

导致开车必须减速 force the drivers to slow down

严寒的 freezing / frigid

挤在一起取暖 huddle together to stay warm   被冻住的 frozen

被卷走 be swept away   呼啸的风 howling wind

雷声隆隆 loud peals of thunder

闪电 lightning (请注意它比 lighting 采光，照明多一个字母 n，Pat 发现很多国内考生无法正确区分这两个词)

暴雨 torrential rain   大雨倾盆 The rain fell in buckets.

暴风雨 thuderstorm   暴风席卷而至 A storm rolled in.

(下)冰雹 hail (和 rain 一样，它也是既能当名词也可以当动词)

[剑桥例句] It hailed for a few minutes this morning.

受到严重破坏 be severely damaged

悲惨的 miserable (在英美日常对话里它很像中文"可怜兮兮的")

[剑桥例句] The forecast is for miserable weather today.

热浪 heat wave / extreme heat   炎热的 scorching

持续了……天 for … days in a row (in a row 是连续几个的意思，在英美生活里极度常用，但国内考生却很少有人熟悉这个短语)

请参考 Pat 的思路，并适当借鉴这个词汇表里的单词，思考如果是您会怎么说

4. 动物

Describe an animal.

You should say:
    what the animal is
    where it can be found
    what is special about it
and explain how people feel about it.

☆ **野生动物之 大象**

难度指数：★★★☆☆

Pat 的答案

Elephants are fascinating creatures.

They are huge, enormous! African elephant can stand as tall as 4 meters. Actually, they are the largest four-footed animals in the world. But they are pretty gentle and slow-moving. They never "bully" other animals.

Elephants use their trunk to "grab" food and they use their tusks to dig for water.

They are social animals. The mothers lead the whole family group.

People say that elephants never forget. Trainers can even teach them to use signs and pictures. For thousands of years elephants have been trained to carry heavy loads and carry people through the jungle. They are like hard-working employees for their masters. But they ask for bananas instead of cash…

轮到你了   It's Your Turn.

▶ **Word Bank on This Topic**

巨大的	enormous (=extremely large)	大象的鼻子	trunk
森林	jungle	大象的牙齿	tusk(s)
濒危物种	endangered species	偷猎	poaching (n.)
交易	trade	野生动物园	safari park
驯服的	tame (adj. & v.)	现金	cash

请参考Pat的思路，并适当借鉴这个词汇表里的单词，思考如果是您会怎么说

Pat 的海外生活英语实录

考到动物的话题，如果只是不停地说 animals 其实挺郁闷的。有两个办法：一是

把动物分类，IELTS 口语里用到的三大类动物就是 **fish**，**birds** 和 **mammals**（哺乳动物），但更难的像 reptiles ✗（爬行类）和 amphibians ✗（两栖类）至少最近 9 年里还没考过，就没必要记了。口试里绕开 animal 这个词的方法之二则是用 **creatures**。这个词，或者可以叫 **living creatures**，这个词也经常用来指动物（但注意不要用来指plants）。

【剑桥例句】Blue whales are the largest creatures ever to have lived.

☆ 野生动物之　狮子

难度指数：★ ★ ☆ ☆ ☆

Pat 的答案

Just like the tiger, the lion is also a member of the cat family and … in many ways lions are just big cats. Humans have been so amazed by the lion's size and strength that we call them the king of beasts. And a lion's roar can be heard from up to 10 kilometers away.

In Africa, lions live in groups called prides. Adult females take good care of their cubs, hunt and eat together, and defend their hunting grounds together. But the males tend to be really lazy and some of them are even troublemakers. Some cubs even get hurt by adult males when the adult females are away.

I like lions not really because they are strong, but because my girlfriend (for girls: boyfriend) is a Leo. So it's kind of "love me, love my sign" …

轮到你了　　　　　　　　　　　　　　　　　　　　　　It's Your Turn.

▶ **Word Bank on This Topic**

猫科动物	the cat family	力量	strength
兽中之王	the king of beasts	吼叫	roar

狮群　pride（在地道英文里一群狮子常被叫作 a pride of lions，可能跟雄狮看起来很"骄傲"有关）

小狮子／小老虎／小熊等　cub　　　捕食　hunt

保护　defend　　　　　　　　　　狮子座　Leo

星座　sign　　　　　　　　　　　凶猛的　fierce／ferocious

猎物　prey（请注意它是不可数的）

[剑桥例句] A hawk hovered in the air（在空中盘旋）before swooping（俯冲）down on its prey.

请参考Pat的思路，并适当借鉴这个词汇表里的单词，思考如果是您会怎么说

Pat 的海外生活英语实录

要表达"群居动物"，除了可以说 They live together. 之外，还有个很地道的说法：**gregarious** /grɪˈgeəriəs/ **animals**。而且这个词在口语里也经常用来形容某人"合群的"。例如：

【剑桥例句】

（1）Gregarious animals and birds live in groups.

（2）Emma's a gregarious, outgoing sort of person.

☆ **宠物之　鹦鹉**

难度指数：★★☆☆☆

Pat 的答案

Parrots have gorgeous feathers and a big tail. They are skilled at mimicking human sounds. When you visit a pet shop, you'll probably find some parrots repeating "Hello! Hello!" all day long. The ability to copy others serves parrots well. And parrot owners often notice that their birds say words like "goodnight" and "snack" at the right

moment. And some parrots even have the vocabulary of a two-year-old. But be careful! Sometimes parrots attack people around them. Most of the time, they are very friendly and adorable, though…

轮到你了   It's Your Turn.

▶ **Word Bank on This Topic**

羽毛　feathers	模仿……说话　mimic
重复　repeat	对……很有好处　serve… well
攻击　attack	可爱的　adorable / cute
烦人的　annoying	没创意的　uncreative / unoriginal

……岁的孩子　a …-year-old（省略号里填入数字就行，地道英文在这个短语里经常可以省略 child）

请参考Pat的思路，并适当借鉴这个词汇表里的单词，思考如果是您会怎么说

Pat 的海外生活英语实录

如果要用英文表达某人总是"喋喋不休"，除了可以说 **He's / She's very talkative.** 之外，**He / She is a windbag.** 也是经常听到的说法。这个说法比较逗，你的考官听到也将会心一笑。

【剑桥例句】The TV show host is not really a windbag, but some of his guests are.

Pat指南

<u>Describe an animal / pet you saw in your city.</u>

无论走到哪一个英美城市，在城市里见到最多的宠物永远都是 dogs。下面这个网站给"爱狗控"提供了各种狗狗最详尽的描述：www. terrificpets. com/dog_ breeds/

5. 重要的植物

> Describe an important plant in your country.
>
> You should say：
>
> what the plant is
>
> what you know about it
>
> whether you like it
>
> and explain why it is important in your country.

Pat 的答案

I'm going to talk about bamboo, which is one of the most important plants in China.

Bamboo is a kind of grass, but it can grow as tall as 30 meters. That's even taller than many trees. It grows very fast, like a couple of centimeters a day. Another amazing thing about bamboo is that the bamboo stem is not thick at all, but it's quite strong. It may bend in a storm, but it doesn't break.

Because bamboo is evergreen and upright, it's been a symbol of vitality and honesty in the Chinese culture. Actually, as it can survive cold winters, it's known as one of "The Three Friends of Winter" in China, the other two being the pine and plum.

Bamboo is also an important economic crop. The use of bamboo ranges from furniture making to building construction. China has long been a large producer of bamboo products, so apparently the bamboo goods industry can contribute a lot to the Chinese economy.

And as you probably know, bamboo is the panda's main source of food. Bamboo shoots are actually also used in a variety of Chinese dishes. They have a mild flavor and taste reeeeeally good. I love dishes that have bamboo shoots in them ...

轮到你了　　　　　　　　　　　　　　　　　　It's Your Turn.

▶ **Word Bank on This Topic**

厘米	centimeter	茎	stem
弯曲	bend	常青的	evergreen
直立的	upright	是生机的象征	a symbol of vitality
松	pine	梅	plum
经济作物	economic crop	范围包括从……到……	range from ... to ...
建造	construction	主要的食物来源	main source of food
竹笋	bamboo shoot	各种各样的	a variety of
清淡的味道	a mild flavor	菊	chrysanthemum
牡丹	peony	柳	willow
莲	lotus		

请参考Pat的思路，并适当借鉴这个词汇表里的单词，思考如果是您会怎么说

6. 公园（双语感悟）Random Reflections on Parks

a park，这么美的话题，当然要用一些比较吸引人的词，比如 This park is reaaaaaaaaaally tranquil and serene. 就是说这个公园/花园真是很宁静。而如果你说 It's pretty sprawling. 则是说各景点都铺得很开，不是很密集的那种。

如果有一条小溪穿过公园，就可以说 A gurgling stream traverses this incredible park. 如果说喷泉，当然用 fountain（天然的用 spring）。说优美的雕塑，就说 elegant sculptures，或者更"虚伪"的说法叫 breathtaking landscape designs。

如果是 amusement park 游乐场一类的公园，那就可能有 Ferris wheel（摩天轮）和 roller coaster（过山车）了。小孩子们可以爬上去的铁架子叫 jungle gym，滑梯在地道英文里就很简单地说 slide，旋转木马是 merry-go-round，沙坑叫 sandbox，秋千是 swing，跷跷板就叫 seesaw。公园里的"小径"可以称为 paths，但更长一些的则要叫 trails。"凉亭"的地道英文是 gazebo，不过英美公园里面的凉亭一般在形式上要比中国传统的凉亭简单太多了。崭新的设备则叫 brand-new equipment，而陈旧的设备则叫 worn-out equipment。如果要说一大片水面，就说 an enormous expanse of water，如果说公园里点缀着一些湖泊和池塘，就说 The park is dotted with lakes and ponds. 而如果要说小孩子可以在草坪上"嬉戏"，英文就是 Kids can frolic on the lawn.

公园里空气新鲜，我们说 We can almost taste the freshness of the air. 如果要说你的朋友们也经常在这里休息放松，就说 Many friends of mine like to hang out there. 而如果你自己也在这里休闲，那就是 just kick back and relax there 了。

临时抱佛脚

近期在亚太区有一只卡片熊经常出没：

Describe a picnic / an outdoor meal.

而且这个答案如果能说得比较有特色就可以合并解决另一道高频难题**Describe a special meal.** 所以就更值得关注。

这道题的 park 部分用本节前面的内容可以很容易就说到几十秒了，但关键的难点是同学并不太了解如何用英文去描述野餐（picnic）。Pat 用下面的列表帮您瞬间掌握英文的野餐：

中文	地道英文表达
景色	scenery
如诗如画的（当然也不一定非要说得这么酸，更多选择请看 Day 3 里的 Part 2 核心词）	picturesque
家庭聚会	family reunion
几家人一块儿聚餐（一般是每家都带些吃的，然后大家一起 share）	a potluck
公园里提供的野餐桌	picnic table
长椅	bench
小板凳儿	small stool
野餐时铺在地上的毯子（夏天则经常用 plaid sheet 格子布代替）	picnic blanket
铺开	spread out
背包	backpack
纸盘／纸杯	paper plate / paper cup
装食品和餐具的篮子（这在国外野餐时是常用的，考官听到会觉得很亲切）	picnic basket
烧烤（注意 barbecue 既可以做名词也可以做动词）	have a barbecue
烧烤用的碳	charcoal

（续表）

中文	地道英文表达
烧烤的（后面加上肉类或者海鲜就行了）	grilled ／ barbecued（chicken, shrimp, salmon…）
调味酱	sauce
沙拉	salad
糕点	pastry
甜点（特别要注意它的发音和沙漠 desert 可不一样）	dessert
水果（比如草莓和葡萄）	fruit（like strawberries and grapes）
垃圾袋	garbage bag
宿营	camping
再加上对公园景色和心情的描述，早就够了……	

另类话题　Off-the-Wall Topics

Nature, nature…

英文里面有个地道的说法叫 in your birthday suit，意思其实就是 not wearing any clothes。最接近自然的方式恐怕就是什么都不穿吧，这类人还专门有个名称叫 naturists。不爱穿衣服，跟 newborn babies 一样。很多学生好奇地问过我，国外的 nude beaches（裸体海滩）是什么样儿。温哥华很棒的大学 UBC 旁边有个著名的 Wreck Beach，向大家隆重推荐（We proudly present the Wreck Beach.），但照片在此略去，未满 N 岁禁止观看。

Wreck Beach sits directly west of UBC. It enjoys its fame as one of the largest nude beaches in the world. For safety reasons, the "nude" section（=part）of the beach is clearly marked. For the fact that the surroundings are absolutely gorgeous, Wreck Beach continues to be a very popular place to visit in Vancouver. Family groups, seniors and young people, anyone who want to be nude sunbathers in public goes there. It's a landmark, a very special, unique place in Canada. Yes, there are people who hate this beach and try to destroy it. But the community there just stick together to make their voice heard because they feel they're so fortunate to have it. They just want to protect its naturalness and the nakedness, for that matter（used to add a comment）.

D　边玩边学

Pat 解题　Pat's Decryption

很多同学在出国前，都爱幻想（fantasise）国外是不是比中国好玩。

这个……那得看你喜欢什么了。

如果你喜欢 sports，那绝对应该出国。连 golfing 这样国内的贵族运动（high-class sports），在美国也不过只是大众运动（popular sports），因为价格并不贵（not so pricey）。

但 Pat 这里要澄清（clarify）两件事，一是 Pat 在国内时发现有些考生甚至老师谈运动时说自己经常去 scuba diving。这个可能性其实比较小，因为在国外这个活动一般要经过专业训练的，偶尔玩玩还可以，经常去就比较有风险（risky）了。

还有一个常见误区是 bowling，这个一般在西方还是蓝领（blue-collar workers）玩得比较多，如果要强调自己很有品味（have exquisite taste），一般人就不大会去 bowling。比如最近美国总统 Barack Obama went bowling for the first time in 30 years, which was part of his effort to get closer to working-class people. 这可就是典型的美国式"作秀"了（That was just for show.）。

很多国内的朋友觉得 American football（橄榄球）很"暴力"，但其实美国的 football stars 却是美国智商最高的运动员群体（平均智商达到了 120 多）。您可能没看过 ice hockey（冰球）比赛，那才叫最暴力的运动，一半以上的观众基本就是抱着看打群架的心态去看冰球比赛的。

如果您既不喜欢 sports，也不喜欢 partying，甚至都不喜欢 going to the movies，那么真有可能你会觉得国外的生活挺单调的。西方人最喜欢的休闲活动除了 sports，基本上就是 fishing, hunting, camping, road trips, going to the movies, partying, clubbing, bar-hopping… 甚至连"看鸟儿"（bird-watching）也算是一种常见休闲活动。至于"洗脚城"（foot

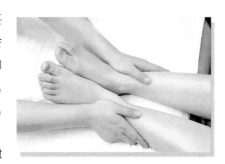

massage parlors) 则少之又少，而卡拉 OK（karaoke）也没有国内这么"火"（"in"）。所以由于练习的机会不多，像 Susan Boyle 那样自学成才的大娘歌手还真得有点天赋（gift）才行。

不过国外的购物狂（shopaholic）也很多，而且他们/她们还有一句座右铭（motto）叫 Shop till I drop.（生命不息，购物不止）。

到底哪种娱乐最好玩儿？那只能说是"萝卜白菜，各有所爱"了（Different strokes for different folks.）。

展开本类话题的思路线索　Brainstorming Techniques
（熟悉下图可以确保你在拿到任何本类卡片题时都能有话说）

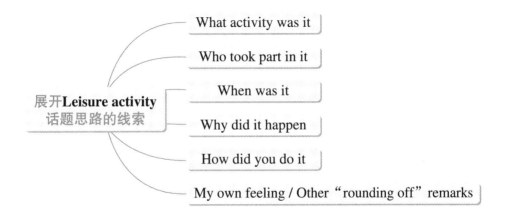

本类话题最新完整真题库　Recent Questions on This Topic

✽ Describe a piece of interesting news.

✽ Describe a story from your childhood.

✽ Describe a childhood game.

✽ Describe an outdoor activity.

✽ Describe your favourite foreign culture.

✽ Describe a foreign country you wish to travel to.

✽ Describe a TV programme that you like / dislike.

243

❈ Describe an advertisement that helped you buy something.

❈ Describe a film you like.

❈ Describe a book.

❈ Describe a childhood song.

❈ Describe a website.

❈ Describe your favourite sport.

❈ Describe an extreme sport.

分级演示　**A Spectrum of Sample Answers**

1. 游戏 / 户外活动

> Describe a game you liked to play when you were a child.
>
> You should say:
>   where you played this game
>   how it was played
>   how it influenced you
> and explain why you liked it.

☆ *游戏之　捉迷藏*

难度指数: ★ ★ ★ ★ ☆

Pat 的答案

I played hide-and-seek many times as a child. We usually played this game in a park or in a building with lots of rooms.

The game was like this: one of us, called the seeker, searched around for the hiders. It started with the seeker covering his or her eyes and counting to 100 while everyone else ran off and quietly found a place to hide.

After the counting was finished, the seeker opened his or her eyes and began a

search for the hiders. And that was my favourite part of the game. The hiders tried their best to keep quiet, being afraid of getting caught. But then, there was always someone who got caught and this person would become the next seeker...

Hide-and-seek was really fun because it was so simple. These days we play PSP games and play mobile games on our iPhones. But sometimes I really miss the simple pleasures of life...

轮到你了   It's Your Turn.

▶ **Word Bank on This Topic**

寻找　seek (*v.*)　　　　　　　　　躲藏　hide (*v.*)

生活里的简单乐趣　the simple pleasures of life（英美人说这个短语里面的 pleasure 时一般习惯加 s）

拔河　tug-of-war / rope-pulling　　　　跳绳　jumping rope / skipping rope

荡秋千　play on the swings（这个可不是中式英语，而是一个很地道的说法）

玩弹子球　play marbles

玩得特别开心　have a great time / have a blast

团队精神　team spirit

请参考Pat的思路，并适当借鉴这个词汇表里的单词，思考如果是您会怎么说

Pat 的海外生活英语实录

小朋友玩户外游戏除了"好玩儿"（fun 在口语里经常用作形容词）之外，另一个很重要的作用是可以锻炼孩子们的身体协调能力 **coordination skills**。

【剑桥例句】

（1）There are lots of fun things to do in this class.

（2）Gymnastics（体操）is a sport that requires good coordination skills.

☆ 游戏之 "*I spy with my little eye.*"

Pat 指南

注意这里 "eye" 不用复数，这个游戏一直是 Pat 在游戏中的最爱，中文名字却真的不知道该怎么说，不过它在国外小孩子当中极度有名，长途旅行的时候一家人在车里经常可以玩。前两年还有一部 Eddie Murphy 拍的搞笑电影就叫 "*I spy*"。这里给大家简单介绍一下：

It's like one person, often an adult, picks an object that he or she can see, and asks the kids, "I spy with my little eye. What is … (round / square / red / black / smooth…) ?" Then the kids try to identify this thing. Just as simple as that. The person who asks the question can even choose an object to spy that begins with a certain letter, like "something beginning with R / S / T …".

What makes this game really fun is there can be multiple answers. So when the kids choose the wrong thing, the adult should tell them "No." until they finally find the exact answer.

I remember once I asked a boy with black frames, "What is black?" Obviously, it was almost impossible for him to find the right answer…

轮到你了   It's Your Turn.

▶ **Word Bank on This Topic**

确定   identify   眼镜框   frame (s)

[剑桥例句] The research will be used to identify training needs.

Some other games I can think of now:
math games, spelling bee (拼字比赛), guessing games, Bingo, Blackjack (这个在 Las Vegas 的赌场里挺常见的), hopscotch (跳格子), Pin the Tail on the Donkey (补上驴尾巴，是很常玩的 party 游戏之一)

请参考 Pat 的思路，并适当借鉴这个词汇表里的单词，思考如果是您会怎么说

Pat 的海外生活英语实录

凡是涉及到"猜"的游戏，比如 riddle（谜语）和 puzzle（拼图游戏），一定都会给小朋友很多的悬念。"悬念"在地道英文中叫作 **suspense**，而让人保持悬念的英文则是 **keep sb. in suspense**。

【剑桥例句】Ruby kept William in suspense for several days before she said she would marry him.

2. 有趣的新闻

☆ *一条有趣的新闻之　银行劫匪*

> Describe a piece of interesting news.
>
> You should say:
>
> when you heard the news
>
> who was/were involved in the news
>
> why it was interesting
>
> and explain how you felt after you heard the news.

难度指数：★ ★ ☆ ☆ ☆

Pat 的答案

Let me share with you a piece of interesting news I heard last weekend.

Last Friday a guy went to a bank in New York and tried to rob it. Actually I thought he was kind of a nice guy. Just that he lost everything in the financial crisis: he got fired, he lost his house and his wife. The only thing he had was debt. So he decided to rob the bank and get some money… or maybe to get his revenge on society.

"Fill the bag up?.. With what?!"

But the problem was he didn't have a gun. So this guy just took a banana and put it in his pocket. He thought that could fool the bank tellers.

Then, he entered the bank, approached a teller, told her he had a gun and asked her to give him cash. Of course the police came. This guy got so scared and he pulled out his "gun", I mean, his banana...

The news was interesting. But actually, it was a sad story. Obviously many people have lost their jobs in this crisis. I feel sorry for them.

轮到你了　　　　　　　　　　　　　　　　　　　　It's Your Turn.

▶ **Word Bank on This Topic**

金融危机	financial crisis	债务	debt
复仇	revenge	愚弄	fool (v.)
银行柜员	bank teller	走近	approach
现金	cash	害怕的	scared
记者	journalist	报道	report / cover (v.)
丑闻	scandal	夸张	exaggeration (n.)

[剑桥例句] Paul said over sixty people were there but I think that's a slight exaggeration.

非常及时的	up-to-the-minute	轰动的	sensational
引人深思的	thought-provoking	面具	mask

[剑桥例句] This is a truly thought-provoking film.

荒唐的　absurd / ridiculous

请参考Pat的思路，并适当借鉴这个词汇表里的单词，思考如果是您会怎么说

Pat 的海外生活英语实录

　　再好笑的笑话听的次数多了也就没意思了，说话也是一样。要说一件事情是"搞笑的"，人人都用 funny，出国之后这么说话倒没问题，但考口语一个半天近四个小时里考官连着听将近20名考生不停地说 funny，实在是一件非常不 funny 的事情。其实 **hilarious** 的语气要比 funny 更强，很像中文"超级搞笑的"。

　　【剑桥例句】The joke he told us was hilarious.

Time to Branch Out.
推而广之

Describe something that made you laugh.

补充弹药

laugh one's head off　这是个非常地道的成语，指某人笑个不停

crack sb. up　让某人大笑（我自己最喜欢的一部 comedy 叫 *The Nutty Professor*. Check it out！）

hilarious　超级搞笑的

punch line　一个笑话最后的那句话，"包袱"

3. 电视节目

> Describe your favourite TV programme.
>
> You should say:
>
> 　　what kind of programme it is
>
> 　　what it is about
>
> 　　why you like it
>
> and explain whether it is popular in your country.

☆　**电视节目之　家庭滑稽录像**

难度指数：★ ★ ★ ☆ ☆

:Pat 的答案:

I'm really into the TV show *America's Funniest Home Videos*. It's a famous comedy series, not just popular in America, but in China as well.

It's like… people send in some funny moments recorded by their video cameras.

The host gives his amusing comments about these

videos, which often show wedding or party-planning mistakes. Sometimes the videos are organised around themes such as Christmas, Easter (Easter "复活节" 其实是英美极为重要的节日之一，但国内同学们往往不太熟悉。Easter 通常是在三到四月的某一个周末，而且在很多英美城市有大型的 parade 花车游行) or Thanksgiving.

And the coolest thing about it is the top videos of the week are selected for prizes. The host has a great sense of humor and often says to the audience, "Remember, if you get it on tape, you could get it in cash."

I like this because it's about family life, which is really a subject that all of us can relate to.

轮到你了   It's Your Turn.

▶ **Word Bank on This Topic**

喜剧 comedy	系列 series	摄像机 video camera
主持人 presenter / host	评语 comment	组织 organise (v.)
主题 theme	观众 audience / viewers	录像带 video tape

[剑桥例句] The theme of sadness runs through most of her novels.

现金 cash	有认同感 can relate to…	优雅 elegance (n.) / elegant (adj.)
真人秀 reality show	竞赛节目 game show	综艺节目 variety show
问答节目 quiz show	纪录片 documentary	

(故事、笑话等) 很搞笑的 funny / amusing (但如果搞笑到让观众 "爆笑不止"，则要改用 hilarious)

婚恋节目 date show	非诚勿扰 *If You Are the One*
嘉宾 guests	追求者 suitor

非你莫属 *Only You*

求职类节目 a human resources (or recruitment) reality TV show

吸引 attract	是街谈巷议的话题 is the talk of the town

[剑桥例句] The daring sculpture in the park is the talk of the town.

有争议性的节目 a controversial TV show   穿越剧 time-travel drama

请参考Pat的思路，并适当借鉴这个词汇表里的单词，思考如果是您会怎么说

Pat 的海外生活英语实录

想说电视节目"引人入胜的"，国内同学一般会想到 interesting / attractive 等词汇，其实最准确的应该是 **engaging** 这个词。

【剑桥例句】A good radio show script is always able to engage the listener.

此外，时常露一小脸儿的话题 Describe a quiz show.（有奖问答节目）也可以通过 www. dooyoo. co. uk/discussion/top-ten-quiz-shows/385040/ 和 www. dooyoo. co. uk/discussion/top-ten-quiz-shows/ 上大量真实的英国观众逐一点评他们/她们心目中的十大 quiz show 轻松搞定。

Time to Branch Out.
推而广之

Describe a radio programme.

描述一个广播节目

补充弹药

talk show　聊天节目　　　　a panel of guests　嘉宾团队

interviews with guests　与嘉宾进行的访谈　call-in show　观众打电话参与的节目

live phone calls　节目进行过程中由观众现场打进的电话

listener participation　（名词短语）听众的参与，这个短语里的 listener 可以不加复数或所有格

lively conversations　气氛很活跃的对话　　broadcast　播放

regularly / on a regular basis　定期地

radio host / radio presenter　广播节目主持人

talented　有才华的　　　　　witty　说话很机智的

attract a lot of listeners　吸引很多的听众　well-received　（节目）很受欢迎的

discussion about topical issues　围绕热点话题展开的讨论

Extra Ammo

补充弹药

weather information　天气信息	traffic information　交通信息
informative　信息量很大的	entertaining　富于娱乐性的
educational　很有教育作用的	
engaging　非常能吸引听众注意力的，引人入胜的	

Extra Ammo

Pat 指南

《中国好声音》节目引起了很多关注，让 Pat 想到了在美国大行其道的歌手选秀节目——*The Voice*。您不妨比较一下这两个节目的形式（the format of the two shows）之间到底有哪些相似之处：

"*The Voice*" is a reality singing competition（or you can call it a vocal competition show）. It's made up of three stages: the blind auditions, the battles, and the live performance shows. Only people with real

vocal talent are invited to the blind auditions, during which the decisions from the musician coaches are based on voice rather than on looks — the coaches can hear the singer perform, but they can't see the singer because of the rotating chairs. If a musician coach is impressed by the singer's voice, he or she pushes a button to select the singer for his or her team. Then the musician coach's chair turns around. Once the teams are formed, the battle is on. During the battles, the musician coaches focus on developing their singers' singing techniques.

They also have two of their own team members compete against each other by singing the same song together in front of a studio audience. Then the musician coaches decide which singers can advance. At the end of the battles, only the strongest members of each team go on to the live shows. In this final stage of the competition, the top singers from each team compete against each other during a live show. The audience vote to save their favourite singer. In the end, each coach has one singer ready to compete against the other teams' finalists（＝people who take part in the final game in a competition）. The winner of this competition is then named "The Voice" and receives the prize of a recording contract.

☆ 电视系列剧之 欲望都市

Pat 指南 🔊

试了几次想写一段描述 *The Walking Dead* 或者 *Nikita* 的，但是每次发现内容都写得太复杂，实在不适合当作卡片题的答案（because they were so full of twists and turns）。只好改为描述比较容易说的 *Sex and the City* 和 *The Big Bang Theory* 了。

难度指数：★★★★☆

Pat 的答案

I'm going to talk about *Sex and the City*. You probably watched it too.

It is a sitcom about four ladies who live in New York. They are close friends. Carrie is a columnist who enjoys talking about views on sex. Miranda is an ambitious lawyer. Charlotte is a lady who has old-fashioned ideas about love, while Samantha is a PR agent who believes women should have sex just like men.

The conversations in this sitcom are very funny because the four ladies are totally different in personality. The soundtrack is pretty good too.

It has won many awards because it is about an interesting subject: the influence of men on women and women on men.

But for ladies, the most attractive thing about the series is probably not the ladies, but the trendy clothing and the high heels...

轮到你了　　　　　　　　　　　　　　　　　　It's Your Turn.

▶ **Word Bank on This Topic**

情景喜剧	sitcom	专栏作家	columnist
志向远大的	ambitious	公关经理	PR agent
谈话	conversation	性格	personality

电影或电视剧的原声音乐　soundtrack　　　　　奖项　award

[剑桥例句] The best thing about the film is its soundtrack.

有吸引力的　attractive　　　　时尚的　fashionable / stylish

高跟鞋　high heels　　　　　（电视系列剧的）一季　season

一集　.episode　　　　　　娱乐性很强的　entertaining

有很多明星的演员阵容，强大的演员阵容　a strong cast /
　　　　　　　　　　　　　　　　　　　　a star-studded cast

请参考Pat的思路，并适当借鉴这个词汇表里的单词，思考如果是您会怎么说

Pat 的海外生活英语实录

　　电影版的 *Sex and the City* 更是把纽约的时尚生活展现到了极致。而 "时尚的" 这个词，其实并不只有 fashionable 一种表达。**trendy**，**stylish** 和 **chic**（请特别注意它的准确发音是 /ʃiːk/）都是在国外生活里描述某东东很时尚的地道常用词。

【剑桥例句】

（1）Jake writes for some trendy magazines for the under-thirties.

（2）The ladies in the film were stylishly dressed.

（3）I like your haircut — it's very chic.

☆ 电视系列剧之　生活大爆炸

难度指数 ★★★☆☆

Pat 的答案

　　Let me talk about my favourite sitcom *The Big Bang Theory*. The central characters in this show are Leonard and Sheldon. Both of them are Caltech physicists and they share an apartment. Leonard has an IQ of 173 but basically has no problem communicating with the "average" people. Sheldon is even smarter with an IQ of 187, but always sticks to routines and often has a hard time interacting with the "ordinary" people. Penny, their next-door

neighbor, is a waitress who dreams of being an actress. Leonard has a crush on her but they just seem to be completely different people. So Penny starts to show the two geniuses what "real life" is all about.

The show is funny… hilarious！ And most of the conversations are not just amusing, but very witty as well. I totally recommend it！

轮到你了   It's Your Turn.

▶ **Word Bank on This Topic**

情景喜剧　sitcom　　　　　　　　　电视系列剧　TV series

中央的，核心的　central / core

[剑桥例句] People have to pay more for flats（公寓）with a central location.

影视剧中的人物 character（全体演员阵容的地道说法则是 cast）

加州理工　Caltech（The California Institute of Technology，美国的顶级牛校，去年该校物理专业的排名全美第一）

物理学家　physicist

基本上　basically（它可是地道英文中灰肠常用的一个其实并没有实质意思的插入语）

[剑桥例句] "So what's the difference between these two TV sets?" "Well, they're basically the same，but the more expensive one comes with a remote control.

坚持，执着于　stick to　　　　　交流　interact with

[剑桥例句] Olivia's teacher says that she interacts well with the other children.

梦想做某事　dream of doing sth.

暗恋某人　have a crush on someone（不明白这个词组的意思在 Facebook 上就是绝对的"土人"）

[剑桥例句] It wasn't really love，just a schoolboy crush.

天才　genius　　　　　　　　　书呆子　nerd / geek

(故事、笑话等)很逗的　very amusing(在地道口语里这个词组比 very humorous 更加常用)

很机智的　witty　　　　　　　　推荐　recommend

[剑桥例句] Holly tried to think of something witty to say.

绿箭侠　*Arrow*（这部 TV series 是在 Pat 最喜欢的城市之一 Vancouver 拍摄的☺）

绝命毒师　*Breaking Bad*	破产姐妹　*2 Broke Girls*
罪恶黑名单　*The Blacklist*	实习生格蕾　*Grey's Anatomy*
权利的游戏　*Game of Thrones*	特工卡特　*Agent Carter*
纸牌屋　*House of Cards*	绝望主妇　*Desperate Housewives*
英雄　*Heroes*	绯闻女孩　*Gossip Girl*
女子监狱　*Orange Is the New Black*	广告狂人　*Mad Men*
迷失　*Lost*	吸血鬼日记　*The Vampire Diaries*
尼基塔　*Nikita*	办公室　*The Office*
美少女的谎言　*Pretty Little Liars*	行尸走肉　*The Walking Dead*
皮囊　*Skins*	梅林传奇　*Merlin*

娱乐性很强的　entertaining

（电视系列剧的）一季　a season

请参考Pat的思路，并适当借鉴这个词汇表里的单词，思考如果是您会怎么说

Pat 的海外生活英语实录

　　《生活大爆炸》里的 Sheldon 给人的感觉是个"愤世嫉俗者"，用当代英语里很常用的一个词 **cynic** 来描述他真是量身定做，而这个词的形容词形式 **cynical** 也是当代英美生活口语里的高频词之一。

【剑桥例句】

（1）I'm too much of a cynic to believe that he'll keep his promise.

（2）Adam is always deeply cynical about politicians.

　　☆ 喜欢的电视节目之　海贼王

难度指数 ★★★★☆

*Do you know what amazes me more than anything else?
The impotence of force to organise anything.*

—Napoleon Bonaparte

Pat 的答案

Let me talk about *One Piece*. I'm a huge fan of OP.

The main character of this anime series, Luffy, is the leader of the Straw Hat Pirates. He and his crew sail the seas in search of the treasure called "One Piece", which can help him become the next King of the Pirates.

Luffy is unstoppable not just because he can gain superhuman abilities by eating the "devil fruit", but also because his crew members are very helpful. Together, they defeat strong opponents such as Crocodile and Rob Lucci.

The action in *One Piece* is fast-paced and exciting. But *One Piece* is not just about fighting. It's also about friendship, teamwork and ambition.

In many other anime series, it's like… the main character does everything. But in *One Piece*, the crew members, like Zoro, Sanji, Nami, Robin, Usopp and Chopper, are all COOL, which makes the team extremely powerful.

One Piece is a very long series, but it's not boring at all, because it makes me think and inspires me a lot.

轮到你了   It's Your Turn.

▶ **Word Bank on This Topic**

影视剧里的人物　character	影视剧里的主人公　main character / protagonist 影视剧里的反面人物，"反派" villain
日本动漫　anime	日本漫画 manga
系列剧　series	船员（或者飞机机组成员）的统称　crew members
海盗　pirate	在海上长时间地航行（固定短语）　sail the seas
恶魔果实　devil fruit	打败　defeat
敌人　opponent / enemy	快节奏的　fast-paced
志向，抱负　ambition	动作动漫片　action anime

鼓舞，激励   inspire sb.

[剑桥例句] After the trip to the UK, she felt inspired to learn English.

尾田荣一郎	*Eiichiro Oda*	创作者	*creator*
妖精的尾巴	*Fairy Tail*	家庭教师	(*Hitman*) *Reborn!*
通灵王	*Shaman King*	七龙珠	*Dragon Ball Z* (在英美有时被简称为 DBZ)
火影忍者	*Naruto*	银魂	*Gin Tama*
周刊少年 Jump	*Weekly Shōnen Jump*		
死神	*Bleach*	犬夜叉	*InuYasha*
叛逆的鲁鲁修	*Code Geass*		

请参考Pat的思路，并适当借鉴这个词汇表里的单词，思考如果是您会怎么说

4. 电影

> Describe a film that you enjoyed watching.
>
> You should say:
>   what type of film it was
>   what it was about
>   why you enjoyed it
> and explain whether this film was popular in your country.

☆ **卡通电影之   怪物史瑞克**

难度指数：★ ★ ★ ☆ ☆

Pat 的答案

My favourite animated movie is *Shrek*, no doubt about it!

Actually, at first I didn't expect much from it, because I wasn't really into animations back then. But this one turned out to be a really good one.

The plot is like this: Lord Farquaad wishes to marry Princess Fiona. But the princess is held in a castle by a dragon. So Lord Farquaad talks Shrek, an ugly ogre, into saving the princess. Shrek fulfills this task but he falls in love with the princess too. At first, the princess is not impressed. But eventually, Shrek wins Fiona's heart.

The movie is full of famous fairytale characters like Snow White, Cinderella and the Three Little Pigs.

The soundtrack is good too...

轮到你了   It's Your Turn.

▶ Word Bank on This Topic

期望   expect（动词）/ expectation（名词）

卡通片   animation / cartoon / animated movie

剧情   plot / storyline   城堡   castle

像 Shrek 那样的怪物   ogre   最终   eventually

[剑桥例句] It might take him ages（ages 是口语里表示"很长时间"的常用说法）but he'll do it eventually.

童话   fairytale   灰姑娘   Cinderella

原声音乐   soundtrack   续集   sequel

不能以貌取人   Don't judge a book by its cover.

票房很成功   a box office hit   完成任务   fulfill the task

请参考Pat的思路，并适当借鉴这个词汇表里的单词，思考如果是您会怎么说

☆ **童年时看过的电影之   狮子王**

难度指数：★ ★ ☆ ☆ ☆

Pat 的答案

I saw *The Lion King* quite a few years ago but I still remember the plot clearly. It is about a lion prince named Simba. When Simba was a cub, his uncle murdered his father and made himself the ruler. But Simba was held responsible for the death. So Simba ran away out of guilt.

Many years later, Simba is told that the kingdom is in serious trouble. So he faces up to his responsibilities, returns, defeats his uncle and saves the kingdom…

The animation is awesome and the soundtrack is amazing. I particularly like the song " *Can You Feel the Love Tonight.* " by Elton John.

And I've learned lessons from this movie. It is about living up to our responsibilities, no matter how hard it is…

轮到你了　　　　　　　　　　　　　　　　　　　It's Your Turn.

▶ **Word Bank on This Topic**

很久以前　quite a while back	卡通片　animation / cartoon / animated movie
剧情　plot / storyline	王子　prince
统治者　ruler	让某人负责任　hold sb. responsible

[剑桥例句] She held Larry responsible whenever anything went wrong in the project.

小狮子（小老虎、小熊等）　cub	打败　defeat

内疚　guilt

票房很成功　a box office hit / a box office smash

特棒的　awesome / amazing	原声音乐　soundtrack
蓝精灵　Smurfs	格格巫　Gargamel
阿兹猫　cat Azrael	电影里的"反派"　villain
男性正面人物　hero	女性正面人物　heroine

一部电影或小说里的主人公　protagonist（*formal*）

三维立体的　3-D（它的地道读音就是 three – D）/ three-dimensional

[剑桥例句] These animations rely heavily on 3-D graphics（图像）.

请参考Pat的思路，并适当借鉴这个词汇表里的单词，思考如果是您会怎么说

Pat 的海外生活英语实录

美版的卡通片（animation）与日版的卡通片（anime）不同，美版不论故事情节多么紧张都一定会有一两个很可爱的卡通形象出现在电影里，但日系的则不一定。"可爱的"大家都用哪个词咱就不啰嗦了，但 **adorable** 在考试时其实更值得推荐。

【剑桥例句】

(1) Erin has the most adorable two-year-old girl.

(2) Theo is an absolutely adorable child.

☆ 搞笑电影之　失恋33天

难度指数：★★★★☆

Pat 的答案

My favourite movie is *Love Is Not Blind*, a well-acted and well-directed romantic comedy.

It tells the story of Huang Xiao-xian, a wedding planner who finds out that her boyfriend has cheated on her with her best friend. Xiao-xian is deeply hurt she starts keeping a diary about her painful recovery from the emotional loss. Her colleague, Wang Xiao-jian, has a crush on her but often gets laughed  at by Huang Xiao-xian. Still, he helps her pull through the 33 tough days after her breakup with her ex and eventually wins Xiao-xian's heart. His role reminds me of a famous saying: "Love is not blind. It just helps someone see things that others fail to see."

This hugely-successful movie is in fact low-budget and only cost 9 million yuan to produce. But it made 200 million yuan in the first week of its screening. Amazing, huh?

It turned out to be such a big hit partly because many singles who experienced breakups before found the story really touching. Another reason why it was an enormous box-office success was it was filled with hilarious conversations that kept the audience in stitches.

The movie was adapted from a popular web novel of the same name. And the right mix of humour and sorrow made this movie really enjoyable...

▶ **Word Bank on This Topic**

表演得很精彩的 well-acted

导演得很出色的 well-directed

情感喜剧 romantic comedy

出轨 cheat on someone（with another person）

[剑桥例句] Joanna finished with her boyfriend when she found out he was cheating on her.

写日记 keep a diary / keep a journal

从……当中恢复过来 recover（*v.*）from

感情的 emotional

同事 colleague

暗恋某人 has a crush on someone

熬过艰难的时期 pull through the tough days

分手 breakup

前任男（女）友或者前任配偶 ex

最终 eventually

低成本的 low-budget

放映 screening（*n.*）

巨大的成功 a bit hit

单身人士 singles

感人的 touching

巨大的票房成功 a box-office hit

特别搞笑的 hilarious

让观众大笑不止 keep the audience in stitches

剧本儿 script

改编自…… be adapted from

网络小说 web novel / online novel

准确的结合 the right mix of（在地道口语里也常把 mix 当成名词来用）

[剑桥例句] "Edward is studying physics and philosophy." "Oh, that's an interesting mix."

令人愉快的 enjoyable / delightful

结束一段恋爱关系 end a relationship（在英美年轻人的日常谈话里，relationship 常被用来指恋爱关系）

报复 get（or take）revenge on someone

是关于……主题的 deal with …

*D*o you know what amazes me more than anything else?
The impotence of force to organise anything.

—Napoleon Bonaparte

是由……扮演的　be played by …

（电影音乐）很容易记住的，上口的　catchy soundtrack / catchy movie tunes

夸张的　exaggerated

剪刘海儿　trim bangs（AmE）/ trim someone's fringe（BrE）

（电影或者电视剧）大受欢迎的　well-received / well-liked（比 popular 稍新鲜点儿）

广受好评的　receive rave reviews

[剑桥例句] The show has received rave reviews in all the papers.（在英美日常生活里谈到 papers 往往并非指论文，而是对报纸 newspapers 的"爱称"）

在某天放映　be screened on …　　　引起共鸣　resonate with sb.

《左耳》　*The Left Ear*　　　　《少年班》　*The Ark Of Mr. Chow*

《匆匆那年》　*Fleet of Time*　　　《栀子花开》　*Gardenia in Blossom*

《那些年，我们一起追的女孩》　*You Are the Apple of My Eye*

半自传体小说　semi-autobiography

取自一个真实的故事　is based on a true story

> 请参考 Pat 的思路，并适当借鉴这个词汇表里的单词，思考如果是您会怎么说

☆ 外国电影之　少年派的奇幻漂流

难度指数 ★★★☆☆

Pat 指南

《少年派的奇幻漂流》的艺术价值没有争议，但李安导演在奥斯卡颁奖仪式（the Oscar Awards ceremony）上向全世界说的那句"谢谢"却引起了人们的好奇。其实现在英美只要是对中国文化多少有点了解的人全都会说这两个字，普及率极高，只是有些白人说的腔调很怪，听起来像"鞋鞋"。在全球化的年代里，每个人都应该是 bilingual 甚至 multilingual。

Pat 的答案

My favourite foreign movie is *Life of Pi* directed by Ang Lee.

The main character is an Indian boy named Pi Patel, whose dad is a zoo owner. His family wants to move to Canada, and decides to take some of their animals along with them. But their ship sinks in a heavy storm. Pi ends up sharing a lifeboat with a zebra, an orangutan and a hyena. The hyena kills the zebra and orangutan. Then a tiger suddenly appears from the bottom of the boat, kills and eats the hyena.

In order to stay at a safe distance from the tiger, Pi builds a raft for himself. He also starts fishing to feed the tiger. A couple of weeks later, they reach an island, but then discover that the island is extremely dangerous. So they return to the lifeboat. Finally, they reach the coast of Mexico, and Pi is rescued and taken to hospital. But the insurance agents find his experience completely unbelievable, so they ask him to tell them the "true" story …

This movie is visually stunning, and tells a great tale of hope and courage. It's based on a book of the same title. I'm sure I'll read the book very soon because I like the story sooooooo much!

轮到你了   It's Your Turn.

▶ **Word Bank on This Topic**

由……执导	directed by …	李安	Ang Lee
拍摄得很美的	beautifully-shot	风暴	storm
猩猩	orangutan	鬣狗	hyena
筏	raft	发现	discover
援救	rescue	保险代理人	insurance agents
在视觉上让人震撼的	is visually stunning		
故事	tale	基于	is based on
勇气	courage	标题	title
角色	part / role	独特的	unique
特别喜欢	adore	爱情片	romantic movie
动作片	action movie	搞笑片	comedy / funny movie
历史片	historical drama	传记片	biopic / biographical film

[剑桥例句] A biopic is about the life of a real person.

科幻片　sci-fi movie / science fiction movie

奇幻电影（像 *Harry Potter* 和 *The Lord of the Rings* 那种）　fantasy movie

恐怖片　horror movie　　　　　　　贺岁片　new-year celebration movie

心理惊悚片　psychological thriller　　悬念片　suspense movie

扮演　play　　　　　　　　　　　　跌宕起伏的　full of twists and turns

很有悬念的结尾　a cliffhanger ending

强大的演员阵容　a strong cast / a star-studded cast

紧张感　tension（在英美生活里对于强烈的紧张感还有个形象的说法：
The tension is so thick you can cut it with a knife.）

请参考Pat的思路，并适当借鉴这个词汇表里的单词，思考如果是您会怎么说

Pat 的海外生活英语实录

　　总体来看，*Life of Pi* 无疑是一部出色的电影（an outstanding movie）。可 Pat 有个老美朋友偏偏就是不喜欢它的故事情节，甚至放言，"It's just an okay movie. The storyline is just mediocre！" 虽然看法完全不同，Pat 还是要本着 "I disapprove of what you say，but I will defend to the death your right to say it." 的精神认可这个 "毒舌" 的英文没有错：**is just mediocre**/miːdiˈəukə (r)/ 就是 "很平庸、并不出色" 的最地道的英文说法。

　　【剑桥例句】The film's plot is too predictable（剧情一看开头就知道结尾的那种）and the acting is just mediocre.

5. 歌曲之　加州明信片

Describe a song or piece of music.

You should say:
　　　　what the song or piece of music is
　　　　when you first heard it
and explain why you like it.

难度指数：★ ★ ★ ☆ ☆

Pat 的答案

I'd like to describe my favourite song, *picture postcards from LA.*

Of course, LA stands for Los Angeles, a city best known for its entertainment industry on the West coast of America. This song is about an average-looking waitress who always dreams about becoming a superstar in Hollywood. But whenever she shares her dream with the singer of this song

(Joshua Kadison), he's like, " So send me picture post cards from LA. And if you find me one, I'd love a picture of the California sun. " The melody of this song really calms me down, very very peaceful. And the lyrics are totally touching.

It's all about the average people's lives... our joys and sorrows. Maybe all of us, at least at some points of our lives, have dreamed about making it big. But very few of us manage to make our dreams come true. Few of us have the good fortune to become a super star. The singer has a deep and rich voice. I simply adore him and I love this song sooooooo much. It's just so moving because it's about us, the average people who wish to make it big someday.

轮到你了　　　　　　　　　　　　　　　　　　　　　It's Your Turn.

▶ **Word Bank on This Topic**

是……的缩写	stand for	洛杉矶	Los Angeles
外表普通的	average-looking	女服务生	waitress
一首歌的词	lyrics / words	一首歌的曲	melody / music
成功	make it big	喜怒哀乐	joys and sorrows

[剑桥例句] The sorrows of her earlier years gave way to joys in later life.

舒缓的，让人放松的	soothing	感人的	moving / touching

[剑桥例句] I put on some nice, soothing music.

国歌	national anthem	令人振奋的	uplifting

（歌或者音乐）很容易记住的，"很上口的"   very catchy

节奏　rhythm   热情奔放的　is full of passion

舒缓的　gentle and calm   拍子　beat

……说，   ... he's / she's like, "..." （这个表达在国外日常交流中转述别人说的某句话时比 he/she said 更常用，真可惜 Pat 居然就没听一位国内考生用过）

[剑桥例句] I told her it was dangerous and she was like, "What do you know about danger?"

请参考Pat的思路，并适当借鉴这个词汇表里的单词，思考如果是您会怎么说

Pat 的海外生活英语实录

       Pat 有时会在线收听来自国内的音乐节目。最近很流行说一首歌"给力"，对应的英文就可以这么说 "It's an **uplifting / inspiring** song." 而如果您想说一个故事（story）或一次谈话（conversation）"给力"，则不妨说 " It was an **engaging** story / conversation." 介绍一种最新的科技"给力"，地道的英文可以用 It's very **empowering**. 而一部电影或一次表演（performance）"给力"则要说：It was **phenomenal**.（phenomenal /fəˈnɒmɪnl/ 这个词貌似很书面，但其实在当代英美日常口语中的使用已经相当普及）。如果觉得一篇剑 10 范文里的论证"给力"，您则可以说 a **compelling / convincing** argument。

       较真儿的话，在当代英文口语里与中文"给力"最为酷似的一个表达其实是 It's a knockout.。但这个表达的语气已经比较"痞"了，容易导致烤鸭朋友们在考场里误用，所以不记也罢。此外尚有 two thumbs up 等表达，都是地道英文里的"给力"之选。

6. 广告

Describe your favourite advertisement.

You should say:
      what it advertised
      where you saw it
      what it was like
and explain why you like it.

难度指数：★★★★☆

Pat 的答案

My favourite commercial is a shoe commercial I saw on TV.

It's like … a guy rushes to the airport in a taxi, hops onto an airplane and flies to another city for a job interview.

Having arrived at an office building, he gets into the lift and rides up to the 20th floor, looking very nervous. He looked down at his shoes, only to notice that they don't match at all. But he completed the interview anyway.

The guy seems very disappointed. He looks sadly at his mismatched shoes. All of a sudden, his mobile phone rings — he gets the job. He's sooooooo excited and jumps into the air. Then the narrator says calmly, "Converse can always take you there."

I like this commercial because it's creative and fun, and the information is very clear and easy to understand.

轮到你了　　　　　　　　　　　　　　　　　　　　It's Your Turn.

▶ **Word Bank on This Topic**

电视、广播或者互联网上的广告　commercial

跳　hop　　　　　　　　　　乘电梯上楼　ride up in the lift (BrE) / elevator (AmE)

不相配的　mismatched　　　失望的　disappointed / frustrated

[剑桥例句] Is Sophie feeling frustrated in her present job?

旁白　narrator　　　　　　　匡威　Converse

大幅的广告牌　hoarding / billboard

广告传单　flyer　　　　　　有效的　effective

拍摄得很漂亮的　beautifully-shot

可信的　reliable

顾客群　customer base

请参考Pat的思路，并适当借鉴这个词汇表里的单词，思考如果是您会怎么说

Pat 的海外生活英语实录

"有创意的" 大家都知道是 creative，部分同学也知道 **innovative** 那个不错的词。但在英文口语里还有个固定短语叫作 **think out of the box**，也是用来形容人在思考或设计时充分发挥自己创造力的常用表达。例如：

【剑桥例句】People who can think out of the box usually run their own companies rather than manage others' companies.

7. 故事

☆ *童年听过的故事之　三只小猪*

> Describe a story from your childhood.
>
> You should say:
>   what the story was about
>   how you first heard this story
>   why you remember this story
> and explain whether it is still popular today.

难度指数：★ ★ ★ ☆ ☆

Pat 的答案

Let me share with you the Three Little Pigs.

Once upon a time there were three little pigs. They moved to a new village and built their homes.

The first little pig built a straw house simply because that was easy. But the house was not sturdy at all.

The second little pig built a stick house for himself. He didn't spend much time building it either.

The third little pig was pretty hard-working. He built a brick house, which was very sturdy.

Then of course, the wolf came along, blew the first house down and ate the first little pig.

And then in the same way, the wolf ate the second piggy.

The only house the wolf couldn't blow down was the house built by the third little pig because he built the house as well as he possibly could. The wolf gave up. And the third piggy just lived happily ever after.

My grandma told me this story when I was just 5 or maybe 6. But I still remember it because it taught me an important lesson: Hope for the best, but prepare for the worst.

轮到你了   It's Your Turn.

▶ Word Bank on This Topic

很久很久以前 once upon a time 从此之后幸福地生活着 lived happily ever after

(这两句基本是英文童话的固定开始和结尾，英美小孩子们都会背的)

坚固的 sturdy

[剑桥例句] They put up a sturdy defence of their proposal.

白雪公主和七个小矮人 Snow White and the Seven Dwarfs

灰姑娘 Cinderella   皇帝的新装 The Emperor's New Clothes

美人鱼 The Little Mermaid   安徒生 Hans Christian Andersen

丑小鸭 The Ugly Duckling   孙悟空 The Monkey King

童话 fairytale

请参考Pat的思路，并适当借鉴这个词汇表里的单词，思考如果是您会怎么说

Pat 的海外生活英语实录

童话故事的 "寓意" 英文怎么讲？只说 meaning 可不够准确，**moral** 才是 the right word for it，请注意当用作这个意思时 **moral** 是名词。

【剑桥例句】The moral of/to the story is that honesty is always the best policy.

Pat指南

如果您喜欢其他的儿童故事，可以看看这个网站 www. kidsgen. com/stories/ ，故事

巨多而且都很有意思，会让你的雅思备考变得十分"欢乐"。

从今年年初开始，雅思口试还时常偷着考这个卡片题 **Describe your favourite childhood song.**

下面这个很轻松的网站提供了大量的儿歌，www. mamalisa. com。您登录后点击地图里的 Asia，再点击 China 就看到中国的儿歌了，从"小燕子"到"两只老虎"都有。

8. 自己喜欢的网站

☆ **网站之 雅虎**

> Describe your favourite website.
>
> You should say:
>
>   which website it is
>
>   when you first visited this website
>
>   how often you visited this website
>
> and explain why you like it.

难度指数：★ ★ ★ ☆ ☆

Pat 的答案

My favourite website is Yahoo. I'm sure you've heard a lot about this website because it's definitely one of the most popular websites in the world.

I like this website so much primarily because it's very informative and entertaining. It offers loads of information like the latest world news, changes in the financial market and reports about sporting events. It also gives us the latest stories about the showbiz, you know, the movie stars, famous singers and TV programmes. And the layout of the web pages is very organised and user-friendly.

Another reason I really adore Yahoo is its founders are like heroes to young people. Jerry Yang and David Filo started Yahoo! back in 1994, when they were both just 24. So you see, Yahoo! is more than a leading website. It's also an inspiring success story to us.

Sadly, the number of Yahoo! users has been declining since Jerry Yang resigned from the Yahoo board…

轮到你了 ▮▮▮

It's Your Turn.

► **Word Bank on This Topic**

首先是因为　primarily because

信息量大的　informative

娱乐性强的　entertaining

金融市场　financial market

娱乐圈　showbiz

排版／格局　layout

[剑桥例句] Application forms vary greatly in layout and length.

有秩序的　organised

超级喜欢　adore

创建者　founder

激励人的　inspiring

[剑桥例句] She is the founder and managing director of the company.

辞职　resign

董事会　board ／ board of directors

点击率　hits

方便使用的　user-friendly

电子商务　e-business ／ e-commerce

收购　acquisition ／ takeover

[剑桥例句] If the company doesn't make any big acquisitions this year, it will hand back cash to shareholders.

合并　merger

社交网站　social networking website （口语里也常简称为 social networking site）

视频共享网站　video-sharing website，例如 YouTube

图片共享网站　photo-sharing website，例如 Instagram

盗用用户名　ID theft ／ identity theft

请求加好友　send a friend request

用户个人信息　profile

微博　micro-blog

名人之间的骂战　celebrity spat

"僵尸粉"　"zombie followers"

获得很多个"赞"　get many "likes"（过去时是 got many "likes"）

在（互联网上）疯传　go viral（它是近几年来在英美口语里非常流行的一个新短语）

[英美例句] A YouTube video called "David Cameron（英国首相卡梅隆）Thug Life" has gone viral in the UK.

上传　upload

热门词汇　buzzword

沉迷于　be addicted to ／ be hooked on

请参考Pat的思路，并适当借鉴这个词汇表里的单词，思考如果是您会怎么说

[剑桥例句] William is completely hooked on computer games.

Pat 的海外生活英语实录

21 世纪谁都知道网站叫 website，可网络公司的英文是……? 出乎您的意料，答案居然就是多数网站域名的最后部分：**dotcom**。惊奇，但是事实。**dotcom** 的确就是英文口语里对网络公司最地道的称呼。

【剑桥例句】

（1）A survey found that 20 of the top 150 European dotcoms could run out of cash within a year.

（2）Connor is a dotcom millionaire.

☆ **关于网站的双语感悟**

Random Reflections on Websites

The Internet is such a miracle!

互联网真是神奇! 说到 the Internet，就想起上大学的时候 Pat 教班里的同学说"互联网"这几个中文字，结果说成哪国文字的都有，就是没有说得像中文的。所以你永远不要说"My English is very poor."很多老外说他们的外语可比你的英语说得差多了!

首先，要知道"点击率"英文叫作 hits。This site gets tons of hits every day. 就是说这个网站点击率很高。网页的布局叫 layout。The layout of this website is pretty neat. 就是说网站布局很清晰。Users follow the links. 就是说用户只要逐个点击就可以到达目的地了。This website is very user-friendly. 就是说这个网站用户使用起来很方便。This site is very entertaining. 是说网站娱乐性很强。It is incredibly informative. 就是说信息量超大。I can get tons of cool stuff from it. 是说我可以从上面下载很多酷毙了的东东（当然下载也可以说 download），如果是一个专门关于流行音乐的网站，就说 It specializes in popular music.，如果要说是关于新闻时事的 www. cnn. com 或 www. foxnews. com 这类的网站，就说 It's all about current events（时事）.，要是如果说新闻都很及时，就说 It offers up-to-the-minute coverage of events.，如果要说一个网站给你的生活带来了极大的乐趣，就说 It really brightens up my life.，如果说它独一无二，就是 It's unique.，如果说你对它彻底着迷了，就说 I am really hooked on it!

9. 最喜欢的外国文化

☆ 最喜欢的外国文化之 英国文化

> Describe a foreign culture you're interested in.
>
> You should say:
>
> which culture it is
>
> why you like it
>
> how you get information about this culture
>
> and explain how you'll try to learn more about it.

Pat 指南

其实完全可以说是因为你会去那里学习，因此特别关注那里的文化，即使你其实正在玩儿命地申另一个国家的学校。不过英国文化即使在已经略显没落（declined）的今天也确实还是有它的优秀之处，否则老美们也不会对威廉王子与凯特的婚礼那么兴师动众地报道（It dominated the headlines.），而且一听说哪个朋友打算去英国旅游就妒忌得不行（get green with envy）。

Pat 给这个答案标了五星级，因为毕竟 culture 还是一个相对抽象的概念。但在这个答案里我还是尽可能多地用了一些简洁的表达来让它变得更清晰易懂。请您重点体会说清一种文化的思路，以及"小词们"的逆袭。

难度指数：★★★★★

┌ **Pat 的答案** ┐

Well I'm planning on studying in the UK, so I'm going to talk about the British culture.

I've heard and read a lot about the Houses of Parliament, the Tower of London and Buckingham Palace ... So I guess Britain would be a perfect place for sightseeing because of the gorgeous architecture there.

And ... Britain is the birthplace of sooooo many great minds, like Shakespeare, Newton and of course J. K. Rowling, the author of the Harry Potter series. She's my idol!

And what else?...I'm a music buff, and almost all of my favourite bands are British bands, like Coldplay and Keane. There're so many musically-talented people in the UK!

Another thing I really like about the UK is there're so many world-class universities there, like Oxford, Cambridge and LSE. That's exactly why I'm planning on studying in this great country…

In terms of personality, the British people are probably kind of reserved, but still friendly and polite. But it also depends on which part of the UK they're from I guess.

I don't really know much about the British food. I heard fish and chips was very popular there. But what it tastes like … I have no idea.

I used to think British cities were pretty foggy all year round, but some British friends of mine told me that was not the case anymore.

So far, most of the information I have about the British culture has been from magazines or TV programs. I really hope I'll get into one of the top universities there. That way, I will learn a lot more about this brilliant culture…

轮到你了   It's Your Turn.

▶ **Word Bank on This Topic**

打算去做某事   plan on（plan on doing sth. 在英美日常口语里面其实与 plan to do sth. 一样很常用）

议会大楼   the houses of parliament（这里的 house 要用复数，在伦敦也有称它为 the Palace of Westminster）

观光   sightseeing   作者   author

有音乐天赋的   musically-talented   世界级的   world-class

[剑桥例句] He's regarded as a world-class athlete.

性格内敛的   reserved   炸鱼土豆条   fish and chips

（在英国超级常见的快餐食品，在 Vancouver 偶尔有人也吃，但在 California 就比较少有人吃这个了，所以总的来说还是一种很英式的东东）

有雾气的   foggy   并非那样   that's not the case

被……录取   get into … / get admitted to …（在英美口语里第一个说法占绝对优势）

那样的话　That way, …

了解　learn（在日常口语里很多时候这个词其实并不是"学习"，而是"了解到"）

"伦敦眼"　the London Eye（伦敦很有名的一个摩天轮 Ferris wheel）

大本钟　Big Ben

伦敦著名的一家高端百货商店　Harrods（不过这家店由于坚持卖
　　　　　　　　　　　　　"皮草" real animal fur 而时常遭到
　　　　　　　　　　　　　animal rights activists 的批评）

> 请参考Pat的思路，并适当借鉴这个词汇表里的单词，思考如果是您会怎么说

Pat 的海外生活英语实录

　　说起英国人，同学们往往容易想到"温文尔雅的"这个词，尽管这个词并不适合所有的英国人，但总体而言还是比较准确的。Pat 在北京时问过学生们"温文尔雅的"英文该怎么说，大家全都异口同声地回答 gentleman（晕，连词性都不对）。其实如果在口试时要说一个人的言谈举止有风度，除了 polite / well-mannered 这些词之外，**refined** 也是一个好选择。

【剑桥例句】

Refined people tend to be very polite and show knowledge of social rules.

Time to Branch Out.
—— 推而广之

> Describe a foreign country you wish to travel to.

补充弹药

by air　乘飞机

travel half way around the globe　到地球的另一侧

check out…　体验……　　　　　　　　explore　探索

tourist attractions　旅游景点

Extra Ammo

10. 最喜欢的运动

☆ 最喜欢的运动之 游泳

> Describe your favourite sport.
>
> You should say:
>> what the sport it
>>
>> when you took up this sport
>>
>> what benefits it brings
>
> and explain whether this sport is popular in your country.

(男生女生都可以说的最常见运动的应该就是 swimming 了)

难度指数：★ ★ ★ ★ ☆

Pat 的答案

My favourite sport is swimming. Actually it's my favourite hobby.

I think swimming is a good way to work out because it exercises every muscle in my body. And I guess swimming skills are so important also because sometimes it can really save lives.

The fun it gives me is another reason I'm into swimming. Actually, when I was a young child, I didn't know how to swim. Some friends of mine even laughed at me for that. So my parents decided to send me to swimming lessons.

The instructor was very nice. At first, I just swam like a brick. My instructor showed me patiently how to kick my legs and put my face in the water, which was a good way to "get my feet wet." Then he taught me how to control my breathing. Little by little, I began to feel comfortable with the water in the swimming pool. Eventually, I could control my breathing perfectly and do the swimming strokes very well.

I'm a pretty good swimmer now — I can swim like a fish, and I can swim twenty laps and still feel great. I swim almost every day, and that really helps me keep fit and relax.

I'm still thankful to my childhood swimming instructor — for all of his help and support. He was awesome. His swimming lessons gave me so much confidence in myself…

轮到你了   It's Your Turn.

▶ **Word Bank on This Topic**

锻炼 work out   肌肉 muscle

游泳教练 swimming instructor（这里不要叫 coach）

完全不会游泳 swim like a brick   超级会游泳 swim like a fish

感激的 thankful

（经过很曲折的过程之后）终于 eventually

信心 confidence   保持身体强健 keep fit

热身运动 warm-up exercises   蛙泳 breast-stroke

仰泳 back-stroke   蝶泳 butterfly-stroke

自由式 freestyle   狗刨 doggy-paddle / dog-paddle

潜水 dive   浮板 kickboard

增强力量 build strength   增进耐力 boost endurance

改善平衡能力 improve balance

请参考Pat的思路，并适当借鉴这个词汇表里的单词，思考如果是您会怎么说

Pat 的海外生活英语实录

在 IELTS 口试里，谈到体育运动时往往会说到一项运动很"耗费体力的"，多数同学都是用 tiring 或者 exhausting。但在地道口语里还有个常用词叫 strenuous，口试时是个拿分效果挺明显的表达：

【剑桥例句】

（1）Lucas rarely does anything more strenuous than changing the channels on the television.

（2）Hannah's doctor advised her not to take any strenuous exercise.

Time to Branch Out.
推而广之

Describe a skill.

Describe something that you are good at.

Describe a difficult thing that you can do well.

Describe something you hope to learn.

补充弹药

tough	困难的	challenging	有挑战性的
overcome the difficulties	战胜困难	boost my confidence	提升我的自信
self-esteem	自尊	get used to	适应

Extra Ammo

11. 绘画（双语感悟）Random Reflections on Painting

我自己小时候学过五年油画（oil painting）。国外的 paintings 主要分成三种：景物画（landscape painting）、静物画（still life painting）和人像（portrait），自画像叫作 self-portrait，中国的水墨画我会把它叫作 Chinese ink painting。

画面的构图叫 composition，光线叫 lighting，画布叫 canvas，画框叫 frame，画室是 studio，而画廊当然就是 gallery 了。

一幅"杰作"叫 a masterpiece，而仿制品只能叫 a fake / a reproduction。具象画叫 representational paintings，抽象画是 abstract paintings，美术欣赏课在英文里叫作 art appreciation classes。

如果画的颜色很浓，说 It has intense colours.，画的颜色很鲜艳，叫 It has vivid colours.

全世界最有名的一幅画肯定是 *Mona Lisa*，它是一幅半身像（a half-length painting），是文艺复兴时期的作品（It dates back to the Italian Renaissance.）。Now it hangs in the

Louvre（挂在卢浮宫里）and attracts admirers from around the world（吸引来自于世界各地的崇拜者们）.

它的作者是 Leonardo Da Vinci（这个不用解释了吧?），What's really special about it 就是 Mona Lisa 神秘的微笑（her / mysterious smile）。

有的人觉得这幅画很真实（realistic / true-to-life），但是也有人认为它太虚幻了（so ethereal）。但是不管怎样，它一定会在你的心里产生强烈的感受（It evokes strong feelings.）。

临时抱佛脚

近期亚太考区的一道考题难倒了无数英雄:

Describe an extreme sport.

别说描述，估计至少有一半的 IELTS 考生长这么大都还没参加过极限运动，所以很多孩子感觉这道题本身就是他们/她们人生里参加的第一项极限运动。

这种题想说得"完美"当然不容易（如果真有所谓"完美"的话），但是介绍一下某种极限运动的基本情况其实还不算太痛苦，甚至可以变得有趣。我们先需要熟记 3 个关键词: risky（有风险的），adventurous（勇于冒险的）和 excitement / exhilaration / thrill（这 3 个词的程度依次递增，但记一个就够，名词: 兴奋）。然后再记住两个短句: It's an ultimate challenge（它是终极挑战）. 和 Overcoming such a challenge gives people a great sense of achievement（成功应对这样的挑战带给人极大的成就感）. 有空您还可以看看 BBC 是怎么介绍常见的极限运动的 news. bbc. co. uk/cbbcnews/hi/find_out/ guides/sport/extreme_sports，而且彩色图片可以进一步减少挑战这个话题给您带来的"极限感"。

更棒的是，近期的常见考题 **Describe an adventurous person.** 同时也就有的聊了。

另类话题　Off-the-Wall Topics

如果在国外生活中听到有人问你 What's your sign? 那是什么意思呢? 是在问你的星座是什么。如果说两个人的 signs are compatible，就是说两个人的星座配合度（compatibility）很高。

我小时候除了爱画画，还特喜欢研究星座（horoscope）。下面的星座描述，一定会让你更了解自己（get a fair and accurate self-image），满眼都是描述人的卡片能用得上的又简单又实用的英文。更棒的是，通过熟悉以下各种性格的英文描述还可以帮您准备好

Describe your personality. 这个题，而且其实多数人的性格都是以下各类性格特征（地道英文里叫作 personality traits）的 "混合物"（Most people are actually a rich blend of different personality traits. ）。

Capricorn（Dec 23-Jan 22）摩羯座

You are a practical Earth sign who is realistic and hard-working. You are filled with determination（决心）when you set your sights on something.

Aquarius（Jan 23-Feb 22）水瓶座

You are very creative, inventive and you take a unique approach（途径）to living your life. Many of your friends call you a true original（地道习语：确实有创意的人）. But you also tend to question your decisions and can lack self-confidence when suggesting something new.

Pisces（Feb 23-Mar 22）双鱼座

You love music and art and can get lost in a movie. You tend to be shy and quiet, but you have a great memory. However, you tend to blame yourself for everything that goes wrong and often have way too much self-pity.

Aries（Mar 23-Apr 22）白羊座

You are very generous and make an extremely loyal friend. Once you love somebody, you love them forever. But you sometimes test your friends to see if you can really trust them.

Taurus（Apr 23-May 22）金牛座

You are very loving and dependable and your calm personality always puts everyone at ease. You love nice things, but remember: you have to work hard to get them!

Gemini（May 23-Jun 22）双子座

You are an excellent communicator and you love to talk! Your wit（机灵）often help you persuade（说服）people to see things your way. You pay close attention to details and are very curious（好奇的）. But you can be known to have a dual（double）personality.

Cancer（Jun 23-Jul 22）巨蟹座

You truly care when friends tell you their problems. If you have a younger sibling

(brother or sister) , you are <u>very protective of</u> them because you love your family so much！ (The bad things are left out because this is my sign ho ho…)

Leo (Jul 23-Aug 22) 狮子座

You are fun and <u>playful</u> and enjoy being around people who are exciting. You always <u>liven up</u> a party and you make a great cheerleader for your friends. You give a lot of praise to others, and you expect it back in return.

Virgo (Aug 23-Sep 22) 处女座

Cleanliness and <u>a healthy lifestyle</u> are very important to you, which can sometimes make you nervous and worried.

Libra (Sep 23-Oct 22) 天秤座

You are an honest friend and people trust you with their deepest secrets. You are also very artistic and love drawing, painting, singing or anything else creative. Sometimes you are afraid of making the wrong choice, so you <u>mope around</u> (踱来踱 去) and worry about it much longer than you should.

Scorpio (Oct 23-Nov 22) 天蝎座

You love magic and <u>mystery</u> and <u>people are naturally drawn to you</u>. A Scorpio will always forgive — but will never forget. Once you break the trust of a Scorpio, things are never the same again.

Sagittarius (Nov 23-Dec 22) 射手座

You are kind and <u>caring</u> to those who need your help. You also love coming up with different ideas on how to solve a problem. But you also can be very <u>sensitive</u> and get your feelings hurt when friends don't view the world as you do.

It all comes down to how effective simple English can be. Guys, have a good one.

对本类话题有价值的网址

下面的网址对骨灰级 DIYer 准备关于 leisure activities 的答案会非常有用：

游戏：

http://www. tradgames. org. uk/ (It provides loads of info on traditional games from around the world.)

电影：

http://www.imdb.com/（This is by far the most comprehensive movie database online.）

图书：

http://www.amazon.com（Well, obviously all of you have heard a great deal about this site. Or maybe some of you have had shopping experiences with it already. Jeff Bezos, its founder, is an extremely talented guy.）

音乐：

http://www.unsignedbandweb.com/forum13.html（an online forum where you can get lots of info and thoughts about music）

运动：

http://www.justlanded.com/english/UK/Tools/Articles/Travel-Leisure/British-Sports（Actually, it's far more than that. You can find practically everything about the British culture there.）

E 物质诱惑

Pat 解题 Pat's Decryption

本节我们会学到很多描述物品的地道词汇和表达。

比如一般同学说衣服这个词都喜欢用 clothes，其实您身上穿的一套衣服国外生活中的很多时候也可以叫 outfit，而人身上戴的首饰则叫 accessories，比如 earrings，nose ring，belly-button ring（脐环）等，在国外总称为 body piercing。在北京的时候一次看报纸时发现有个作者居然误以为在国外戴耳环的男人都是 gay，这可就不靠谱儿了（way off base）。在英美戴耳环的男性很多，甚至连大学男教授也有戴的，但大部分人都只是把它当成装饰（stuff that enhances your appearance）。

本节我们还会学到很多 electronic devices，比如 digital cameras。不过最近 Pat 最感兴趣的电子东东是 iPad Air。英文里有一个超棒的词来形容这些电子小东西，叫 gadget，考试的时候不妨用 1~2 次。

当然我们还会学习更大型的 objects，比如 cars。我的学生当中车迷（car buffs）从来都不少。另外，咱们还可以看看两种这辈子还能买得起的车型。

handicrafts（手工制作的物品）一直是个难点，本节我们也得突破。

一口气谈了这么多 objects，希望我们不会变得 too materialistic（太物质化）！

展开本类话题的思路线索 Brainstorming Techniques

（熟悉下图可以确保你在拿到任何本类卡片题时都能有话说）

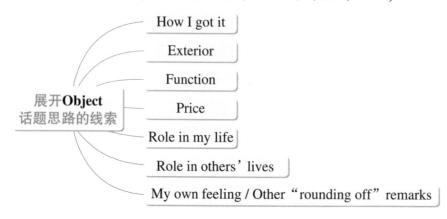

本类话题最新完整真题库　Recent Questions on This Topic

❊ Describe a vehicle.

❊ Describe a photo.

❊ Describe a piece of equipment you use every day.

❊ Describe an old piece of furniture（本话题请看 Day 10）.

❊ Describe an item of clothing/a piece of jewellery that you like.

❊ Describe a handicraft/something that was made by yourself.

❊ Describe something expensive you'd like to buy.

❊ Describe a gift or a present you have received.

❊ Describe an important conversation.（本话题请看 Day 10）

分级演示　A Spectrum of Sample Answers

1. 交通工具

☆ 交通工具之　*Mini-Cooper*

> Describe a vehicle you'd like to own.
>
> You should say:
>
> what the vehicle is
>
> why you would like to own it
>
> whether it would be expensive to buy
>
> and explain whether you think you'll buy it in the future.

这个题目 Pat 上课让孩子们练习时候大家总是会想到一大堆超级大词，真想试试用简单词能不能搞定它（sort it out）。

难度指数：★★★☆☆

Pat 的答案

A friend of mine bought a Mini Cooper last month. It cost her like 250,000 renminbi. But it looks like a 500,000 renminbi car, I have to say. (在真实的英文谈话里像 I would say... / ... I should say 这类小短语特别多，其实并不是真就"非说不可"，但说了却更像是人与人之间的交谈，而不是机器之间的互殴)

Back then（当时），that friend of mine was just looking for a small car with good performance and she got totally impressed by Mini. The exterior was sooooooo cute, like a chubby baby because it looked pretty compact. The car is sleek too. You know, shiny.

Unlike Beetles, Mini had a powerful engine, which makes it similar to other BMW cars. It can even handle the bumpy roads in the suburbs. It has good gas mileage as well. That's definitely good news when the petrol price（= gas price）is still sky-high here in China.

It looked small, but the interior turned out to be very spacious. The backseats were probably only good for kids, though. You can park it anywhere because of its small size, which is really nice in a city where there are not enough parking spaces.

I'm starting to envy my friend. I'm sure I'll buy a Mini too because it's just so fun. It's almost like if you test-drive a Mini, you'll buy it...

轮到你了   It's Your Turn.

▶ **Word Bank on This Topic**

性能　performance

性价比　performance to price ratio（日常生活里经常会更简单地说 It offers good value for your money.）

外观　exterior　　　　内部　interior

[剑桥例句] The car's interior is very impressive —— leather（皮革）seats and a wooden dashboard（dashboard 就是方向盘前方安装有很多仪表和空调开关等的那个控制板，在英美日常生活里有时也简称为 dash）.

胖乎乎的 chubby	紧凑的 compact
光亮的 sleek（大众的）	甲壳虫 Beetle
发动机 engine	类似的 similar
耐用的 durable	

坑坑洼洼的，不是一帆风顺的 bumpy（例如电影 *All about Eve* 里 Margo Channing 的那句著名台词：Fasten your seatbelts. It's going to be a bumpy night！）

可以承受 can handle...	油耗低 good gas mileage / good fuel economy
郊区 suburbs	宽敞的 spacious
汽油 petrol（BrE）/ gas（AmE）	很快 shortly / soon
羡慕 envy	方向盘 steering wheel
气囊 airbags	没有任何多余装饰的 no-frills

[剑桥例句] It's a no-frills shop supplying only basic goods at affordable prices.

装备齐全 It's loaded.	手动档 stick shift / manual
自动挡 automatic（transmission）	敞篷车 convertible
跑车 sports car	流线型的 streamlined

[剑桥例句] Streamlining cars can increase their fuel efficiency.

底盘 chassis（真正爱车的人都知道，engine 和 chassis 才是最重要的，exterior 其实真的不值多少钱）

商务用车（车正面是倾斜的那种长面包车） minivan / MPV

（一辆车）有 2（或者 4 / 5 / 6）个座位 It's a two（or four / five / six）-seater.（地道英文里说一辆车有几个座位最地道的说法就是说 It's a ...（填数字）-seater.

国内同学时常发错音的汽车品牌（请您注意听音频里的发音）

Mercedes Benz（其实在地道英文中说"奔驰"时经常会只说前面的第一个单词）

Land Rover 陆虎	Rolls Royce 劳斯莱斯
Volkswagen 大众	Hyundai 现代

Lexus	雷克萨斯	Lamborghini	蓝博基尼
Cadillac	卡迪拉克	Volvo	沃尔沃
Bentley	宾利	Renault	雷诺
Citroen	雪铁龙	Porsche	保时捷
Mazda	马自达	Nissan	日产
Saab	萨博	Toyota	丰田
Audi	奥迪		
Chevrolet	（生活里谈话时也经常简称为 Chevy） 雪佛兰		

请参考Pat的思路，并适当借鉴这个词汇表里的单词，思考如果是您会怎么说

Pat 的海外生活英语实录

　　最近中东局势不稳导致油价飙涨，Pat 在新泽西的加油站加油时每次都会听到不堪涨价之苦的哥们儿骂上几句。怎样用地道的英文来说一辆车"省油"或者"费油"。是不是您的脑子里已经飘出了 save oil 和 waste oil？堕落了哈。下次跟老外聊车的时候请您一定要记得用 **It gets good mileage**（发音/ˈmailidʒ/）. 或者 **It's pretty fuel-efficient.** 来形容一辆车很省油，而用 **It's a gas-guzzler**（发音/gæsˈgʌzlə/）. 来表达对喝油无极限的"油老虎"的无奈。

【剑桥例句】

（1）Smaller cars get better mileage and so cost less to run.

（2）Gas-guzzlers are expensive to drive because they use more fuel.

☆ 交通工具之　森林人

Pat指南

　　Mini-Cooper 和 Beetle 都是 MM 们的最爱。而 Pat 发现国内的男同学们一提起适合男性开的车就会立刻想到"悍马"（Hummer），可在油价飞涨而且全球都"Go green."的年代里，像 Hummer 这样

的 "油老虎" (gas-guzzler) 即使能买得起也不是谁都能养得起的。去年在美国和加拿大进行的一项最新调查显示，Subaru Forester（森林人）拥有很多受过良好教育的男性车主，而且性能不俗。Forester 左右对称的全时四轮驱动（symmetrical all wheel drive）正在悄悄地改变着英美传统观念中的 "猛男" 形象。

难度指数 ★★★★☆

Pat 的答案

I'm going to describe Subaru Forester 2015. I test-drove one last week and was quite impressed with it.

It has a nice exterior and the build quality feels good. The interior is spacious and comfortable, but not luxurious. The leg room and head room are perfect for me, and there's plenty of cargo room as well.

As for the performance of the car, the handling is very good and the acceleration is quiet and smooth. But the engine is a bit noisy.

There isn't much snow in my area. But during the summer it can rain hard so I guess the AWD feature of Forester would mean more safety on the road.

I don't think Forester is for people who look for a luxurious interior. Some interior materials even feel cheap — it's simply not a luxury car. But it offers the best value in its class and provides comfortable rides. I'm a person who favors function over form, so it would be a good choice for me.

轮到你了 It's Your Turn.

▶ **Word Bank on This Topic**

试驾 test-drive	物品的外观 exterior
内部空间 interior	
车身的工艺 build quality（在这个固定短语里不要用 building）	
宽敞的 spacious / roomy	豪华的 luxurious
腿部空间 leg room	头顶空间 head room
车后部的储物空间 cargo room	性能 performance

[剑桥例句] High-performance cars tend to be expensive as well.

操控性能　handling　　　　　　　　　加速　acceleration

全驱　all wheel drive / the AWD feature（在冰天雪地或者路面湿滑的地方全驱很有用）

四驱　four wheel drive（对付雨雪天气这个也尚可）

前驱　front wheel drive（这个对付雨雪天气就会艰难一些了）

豪华车，高端车（固定短语）　luxury car

经济型车　affordable car

看重功能而不看重外型　favor function over form

转向性能　steering　　　　　　　　　反应很灵敏的　responsive

可以忍受的　tolerable

[剑桥例句] The heat in the room was still tolerable.

紧凑型 SUV　compact SUV　　　　　　房车　RV / motor home

古董车，"老爷车"　antique car

二手车的售出价格　resale value（有些人把"老外"全想象成富翁，其实在国外"负翁"也不少，在英美开二手车甚至五、六手车的励志哥也不在少数）

请参考Pat的思路，并适当借鉴这个词汇表里的单词，思考如果是您会怎么说

Pat 的海外生活英语实录

　　形容车的外观漂亮，有些孩子肯定会想到 gorgeous，这个词在国外生活里确实属于绝对的高频词，但是它的语气很强，有点像中文"超靓的"，并不适合像 CR-V，RAV 4，Tiguan 这类"一般好看"的车。那么请试试 **neat** 吧，它在实际生活中不仅可以用来指"干净的"，而且也常常被用来表示"挺好看的"的意思。

【剑桥例句】

（1）It's a neat little cottage.

（2）You've got such neat handwriting.

2. 物品之电子产品

> Describe something electronic that you use often.
>
> You should say:
>
> what it is
>
> where / when you bought it
>
> what you use it for
>
> and explain why you like it.

☆ **电子产品之** iPhone 6

Pat 指南

在这个答案里 Pat 汇集了在英美喜欢数码的兄弟们常说的几乎全部高频词汇，但如果您觉得实在记不住，那就看下面的数码相机那段吧。

难度指数：★★★★☆

Pat 的答案

I'm going to describe my iPhone 6. I waited in line for hours to get it. And I should say it's well worth all the waiting!

I've used many smart phones but the iPhone 6 is definitely the best, hands down. It's thin, fast and gorgeous, and its touch screen is bigger than that of the iPhone 5S. The Retina HD display is super sharp and accurate. The ring tones are also pleasant.

The operating system of iPhone 6 is very user-friendly. I felt comfortable with it right away. And I love the maps ... so vivid and detailed. The image quality of the 8 megapixel camera is amazing, and the panorama mode is really cool!

It also comes with other cool features, like Touch ID and the iSight camera. It's bigger than the iPhone 5S, but I can still easily slip my iPhone 6 into my jeans pocket. By the way, as a phone, its call and reception quality is perfect.

The only thing that bothers me a bit about this gadget is the personal assistant tool, because sometimes it causes connection problems. But anyway that's not much of a problem for me.

Some people complained about the battery life. It's fine for me though, like a full day or something like that...

轮到你了　　　　　　　　　　　　　　　　　　　　　It's Your Turn.

▶ **Word Bank on This Topic**

电子用品　electronic device / electronic gadget（后面这个数码迷们用得超多）

排队　wait in line（这个短语在英美生活里也极为常用，而且队伍很长时还经常会有人向你确认 Are you in line?）

值得这么等　well worth all the waiting　　智能手机　smart phone

轻松地超出竞争对手们　is the best..., hands down

触摸屏　touch screen　　　　　　　铃声　ring tone

"视网膜"显示屏　Retina display　　　　高分辨率，"高清"　HD / high-definition

操作系统　operating system　　　　　方便使用的　user-friendly

鲜明的　vivid　　具体的　detailed　　特色功能　features

有像 X，Y，Z 等等多种功能　has various features like X, Y and Z

[剑桥例句] Our latest model of mobile phone has several new features.

指纹传感器　fingerprint sensor　　　触摸验证功能　Touch ID

让人心烦　bother sb.　　　　　　　　柔顺光亮的　sleek

私人助理　personal assistant　　　　语音激活的　voice-activated

800 万像素的　eight megapixel

应用程序　application software（地道英语里经常被简称为 apps）

打出和接听电话的效果　call and reception quality

存储　storage　　　　　　　　　　　抱怨　complain

battery life 电池一次充电后的使用时间（容易只看字面而误解为电池的终生寿命）

……千兆内存 … GB（考试时对它的发音请说 gigabytes /ˈgigəˌbaits/）

其他的手机常见功能：

内置相机　built-in camera　　　　　　折叠键盘　folding keyboard

发短信　texting / text-messaging（而且生活里 text 也经常可以当动词用：I'll text you.）

和亲友保持联络　stay connected with family and friends / keep in touch with family and friends

限量版　limited edition / special edition（这两个很地道的英文表达最开始只是用在出版物的限量发行，但现在英美生活里已经被广泛地用于各种产品了）

世界上销量最大的智能手机　the world's top selling smartphone

请参考Pat的思路，并适当借鉴这个词汇表里的单词，思考如果是您会怎么说

Pat 的海外生活英语实录

　　在英美，数码爱好者们对于 **gadget**（它可以指任何小型的电子或者数码产品）这个词真的是情有独钟，几乎已经达到了"逢码必用的程度"。而另一个经常会与它伴随使用的词则是 **handy**（灵巧轻便的）：

【剑桥例句】

（1）Have you seen this handy little gadget?

（2）This handy gadget is great for storing important data.

☆ *电子产品之　数码相机*

这个简单给大家描述一下。

难度指数：★ ★ ★ ☆ ☆

Pat 的答案

I'd like to talk about my digital camera. It's a Nikon. I bought it in Hong Kong. I think it's cool.

It has a sleek black body and is light and handy. The 2.5 inch LCD screen is large and clear. The touch-screen menu control is very convenient.

And… what else? Oh, I almost forgot. It's a 10X-zoom camera so the photos look great.

It uses an SD card so I can download everything onto the hard drive of my PC.

Most importantly, the 8 mega-pixel sensor gives me sharp pictures and the colours are always extremely accurate…

轮到你了 It's Your Turn.

> ▶ **Word Bank on This Topic**

光亮的　sleek

请注意听音频里朗读下面品牌的英文名称:

Nikon	Canon	Lenovo	Kodak	Fuji
Sony	Samsung	Ricoh	Olympus	

方便易用的　handy

能很方便地放在口袋里的　pocket-sized（反义词：笨重的 bulky /ˈbʌlki/）

触摸屏　touch-screen

变焦　zoom（光学变焦叫作 optical zoom，而数码变焦则是 digital zoom）

百万像素　megapixel　　　　　　　感光器　sensor

精确的　accurate

[剑桥例句] We hope to become more accurate in predicting earthquakes.

请参考Pat的思路，并适当借鉴这个词汇表里的单词，思考如果是您会怎么说

Pat 的海外生活英语实录

（1）英文里的相机叫作 camera，摄像机是 **video camera**，监控录像机叫 **surveillance**（它的读音是/səˈveiləns/）**camera**。但网络聊天时用的"摄像头"地道英文又叫什么呢? 不能叫 computer camera ✗，而要说 **webcam** 才够地道。另外还要提醒大家一下：出国后当您看到 CCTV 这个缩写，千万不要以为是央视驻英国记者站，其实它在英美生活里是指"闭路电视"。而"有线电视"在国外实际生活里就是被很简单地称为 **cable**（TV）才最地道。

【剑桥例句】Webcams allow moving pictures and sound to be broadcast on the Internet as they happen.

（2）如果一部照相机或者摄像机所捕捉的色彩非常逼真，那么在地道英文里会说 It captures true to life colours. 而如果一部照相机或者摄像机所产生的图像很锐利，则可以说 It takes razor-sharp images（"像剃须刀一样锐利"的图像）.

IN SKATING OVER
THIN ICE...
OUR SAFETY
IS IN OUR SPEED.

也许这对您来说根本不是一个问题，但 Pat 在中国时却真的多次遇到学生很困惑地问在英语里面是不是可以说某个物品 has sth.，因为老师教的是英语里只有一个人才能说 has sth.。Pat 的答复很明确：地道英语里完全可以很自然地用 has（复数当然是 have）来说手机、汽车、照相机、笔记本电脑（laptop）等等有零件以及具体功能的东东。

【剑桥例句】My mobile phone has a long battery life.（在地道英语里说一个手机的 battery life 其实常常是指它的待机时间）

Time to Branch Out.
推而广之

Describe a gift you received.

Describe something that you lost.

补充弹药

It's the thought that counts. （固定习语）重要的是心意。

thoughtful　体贴的　　　　　thankful　感激的

precious　珍贵的　　　　　look high and low for...　到处找……

upset　心烦的

regret doing sth. / having done sth.　后悔做某事

Extra Ammo

☆ **电子产品之** iPad Air

Pat 指南

早在 Pat 还上大学的时候 Apple 就已经掳得了相当多北美大学生的倾心。每次做集体 presentation 的时候放眼望去尽是一个个闪亮的 Mac 大白苹果，"果粉"们（Apple fans）和"果黑"们（Apple detractors）之间的争论也一直都没有停止过。现在，Apple 则又通过 iPad 进一步加固了它在年轻人心目中的崇高地位（exalted status）。虽然 Pat 躺在沙发上用 iPad 的时候经常被砸到鼻子或者门牙，可还是痴心不改。但现在我们最需要关注的并不是 Tim Cook 高调"出柜"（came out of the closet），也不是 42mm silver aluminum case 的运动版 Apple Watch 到底值不值 519 美刀，甚至不是 iPad 怎样迎接 Android-based tablets 的挑战，而是咱们怎样才能用最浅显的英文来描述它们。

难度指数 ★ ★ ★ ☆ ☆

Pat 的答案

To get my iPad Air, I waited for more than five hours in line. So you can imagine how excited I was when I finally got my hands on it!

It's super slim, nothing like my bulky laptop, and light as well. I can easily carry my iPad Air with just one hand. The Retina display is super sharp. And the chip is so speedy it loads websites even faster than my laptop.

And I have to say … the iSight camera on my iPad Air is almost toooooo good for a tablet. The picture quality is awesome (= extremely good) and the iSight camera can also record high-definition videos.

What else? Oh, the battery life… Well, I can spend a whole afternoon on my iPad Air and still don't need to recharge the battery, so can't complain, I guess.

I should say the iPad Air is an amazing device. No friends of mine who own an iPad Air regret having bought it.

轮到你了   It's Your Turn.

▶ **Word Bank on This Topic**

排队等候　wait in line	平板电脑　tablet

纤细的，苗条的　slim（这个词在当代英美生活里经常也被用来形容超薄的电子产品，如果只是想平实地说 iPad 很薄当然说 very thin 也可以）

笨重的　bulky　　[剑桥例句] The book was too bulky to fit into her bag.

笔记本电脑　laptop / notebook（但在日常的英美对话里 laptop 这个词远比 notebook 更常用）

第三方软件　third-party software / third-party app（在英美日常生活中谈到电脑或手机里的应用程序时 app 这个单词极为常用，而且它还可以有复数 apps）

便于携带的　portable（它的反义词是笨重的 bulky /ˈbʌlki/）

处理器　processor（在日常聊天时经常被简称为 chip）

[剑桥例句] Computers become lighter and more portable every year.

快速的，迅捷的　speedy　　　　　　加载网页　load websites

抱怨，不满　complaint（请注意这是名词，动词则少一个 t 是 complain）

不错的　decent（这个词在英美日常口语里其实和"体面的"真没啥关系，反倒是很像 quite good）

[剑桥例句] Are there any decent restaurants around here?

充电　recharge　　　　　　　　　设备，仪器　device

[剑桥例句] Rescuers used a special device for finding people trapped in the building.

高清晰的　high-definition

粉丝　an avid fan of...（当仅仅用 fan 已经不能表达出对于某事的狂热程度的时候，在 fan 前面再加个形容词 avid 可以充分表达出"给跪了"的决心，但请注意听音频里 avid 的发音）

上网速度非常快　Web browsing is lightning-fast（lightning 是闪电，is lightning-fast 当然就是形象地说"像闪电一样飞速的"，地道英文里还有 is fast as lightning 这个成语也很常用）.

同系列产品当中在它之前出现过的产品，"前身"　predecessors

[剑桥例句] The latest Ferrari is not only faster than its predecessors but also more comfortable.

电子游戏机　game console / game device（在英美家庭玩得比较多的是 Wii /wiː/，PlayStation Vita，Xbox One 和 Nintendo 3DS）

请参考Pat的思路，并适当借鉴这个词汇表里的单词，思考如果是您会怎么说

Pat 的海外生活英语实录

平心而论，Apple 的很多产品已经超出了生活必需品（necessities）的范围，而成为奢侈品（luxuries）。它们的主要意义已不再是满足人们对功能（functionality）的需求，而是给我们提供了更多的休闲选择。"休闲"的动词，除了 relax，还有个相当常用的口语词叫 **unwind**（发音/ʌnˈwaind/）。如果您觉得这个表达不好理解那么可以这样想——英文里的 wind up 是把东西拧紧，而 **unwind** 则是让绷紧的弦彻底放松下来。而"休闲"的名词除了 relaxation，则还有 **leisure** 和比较正式的 **recreation**。

【剑桥例句】

（1）A glass of wine in the evening helps me to unwind after work.

（2）Tim's busy schedule leaves little time for leisure.

☆ *电子产品之   优盘*

难度指数：★ ★ ★ ☆ ☆

Pat 的答案

I just bought a USB disk yesterday. Actually it's just like any other USB disks, tiny, light but sturdy. It has a storage capacity of 1 Gigabytes.

What I really like about this USB disk is it has a fast transfer rate, fast as lightning.

How do I use it? Well, I just connect it to my computer via a USB port and all set. It's compatible with both Microsoft and Mac systems...

It's a keeper.

轮到你了 ///   It's Your Turn.

▶ **Word Bank on This Topic**

电子用品   electronic device / electronic gadget

坚固的   sturdy   储存容量   storage capacity

输送速度   transfer rate

像闪电一样快（这是一个很地道的英文成语）　fast as lightning

通过……（传输）　via（*prep.*）　　　　　接口　port

一切就绪。　All set.　　　　　　　　　　　兼容的　compatible with...

[剑桥例句] This new software may not be compatible with old operating systems.

苹果的操作系统　Mac / Macintosh　　　　值得保留的东西　keeper

一张图片可以说明一千个文字才能说明的问题（常用成语）
A picture is worth a thousand words.

请参考Pat的思路，并适当借鉴这个词汇表里的单词，思考如果是您会怎么说

Pat 的海外生活英语实录

　　除了 USB disk 之外，优盘有时在生活里也有人会说 **USB drive**。这个似乎不好理解，但在实际生活里大家就这么说。那么电脑的"硬盘"又应该叫什么呢？严格来说应该是叫 hard disk，但是在实际日常生活里绝大多数人却都是用 **hard drive** 来指"硬盘"，也许不够严谨，但对于交流来说却已足够有效。英语在欧洲语言里没有法语优雅，没有德语严谨，也不像希腊语那样"富于哲理"，但它最终还是凭借其实用性成为了全世界最通用的语言。忽视英语在现实生活里的实际用法去闭门造车，只会导致更多的沟通不畅。

　　【剑桥例句】The hard drive is fixed inside your computer and stores a large amount of information.

3. 照片

☆ 照片 之 与人合影

Describe a photo that you like.

You should say:

what the photo is

when it was taken

why you like it

and explain whether you still keep it.

Pat 指南 🔊

很多同学喜欢 Ed Sheeran 的那首 *Photograph*，但是用英文描述一张照片要比听懂一首关于照片的英文歌更有挑战。有很多同学觉得这道题即使用中文说也绝难说到 1'30" 以上，而且即使勉强说了一点也会很生硬（mechanical）。Pat 仔细想了一下，确实即使让考生用自己的母语描述一张 photo 也很难，因为照片是平面的（two-dimensional），放大过之后也就那么大，只能从照片的一个 corner 描述到另一个 corner。其实说 wedding photo 不错，因为可以顺便把明天我们要学到的 wedding 扯进来，不过如果你自己还没结婚却是总惦记着人家的 wedding photo 可能就稍有点怪了（weird）……

无论怎样，我们的选择还是很多的，比如说你与一个朋友怎样一起拍合影（合影的地道英文就是 a photo of... and me）就不会很难，或者说无意中（by chance）拍到了一个名人（celebrity）的照片也不错，至少可以合理合法地把这个名人描述 2 ~3 句（不要太多 Less is more.）。

难度指数：★★★★☆

┌─────────┐
│ Pat 的答案 │
└─────────┘

My favourite photo is a photo of... (Put the celebrity's name here.) and me. It was taken a couple of months ago while I was at the Hong Kong airport, waiting for my flight.

It was like... I was chatting with some friends of mine. All of sudden, I spotted a guy who looked exactly like... (the celebrity's name again), which made me curious.

... is... （这里很自然地加入 2 ~3 句介绍这个 celebrity 的句子，不要长，但注意这部分可以用现在时）

So I just went up to approached him and asked if he was... You know what? He smiled politely and nodded yes! I was so excited and asked if I could take a picture with him.

He was like, " Sure!" And he even said "cheese" and made a V sign... He really made my day!

After I returned home, I got the picture framed and hung it on my bedroom wall. Honestly, I really didn't expect such a famous person to be so approachable...

轮到你了　　　　　　　　　　　　　　　　　　　It's Your Turn.

▶ **Word Bank on This Topic**

航班　flight　　　　　　　　　　　　看见　see / spot

[剑桥例句] If you spot any mistakes in the article just mark them with a pencil.

好奇的　curious　　　　　　　　　　点头　nod

"茄子"　cheese（请注意中文照相说茄子，而英文照相说 cheese "奶酪"）

放松的　laid-back　　　　　　　　　放在镜框里　frame

值得回忆的　memorable　　　　　　好接近的，平易近人的　approachable

[剑桥例句] Graham's very approachable — why don't you just talk the problem over with him?

捕捉　capture　　　　　　　　　　　珍贵的瞬间　precious moments

"玩儿自拍" take selfies（一张自拍照当然就是 a selfie 了）

集体合影　a group photo

V sign　　V 形的手势（Pat 在中国时惊讶地发现有国内同学们一致认为 V 形手势代表
　　　　　victory，但是 Pat 的多数英美朋友都认为手掌心向着对方的 V 形
　　　　　是代表 peace）

（某人或者某事物）让我一整天都很开心　... really made my day！
（这个说法在地道英文里实在太常用了，可以替代国内同学们爱说的
You made my day happy！）

请参考Pat的思路，并适当借鉴这个词汇表里的单词，思考如果是您会怎么说

Pat 的海外生活英语实录

　　说人"很上镜"，不能说 good on a camera ✗，而要说 He/She's very **photogenic**.（它的发音是/ˌfəutəuˈdʒenik/）。如果照片照得比真人好看，要说 It's **a flattering photo**. 而照片把人的缺陷无情地全都给拍出来了，则要委婉地说 The photo looks quite **candid**. 说一个人"不喜欢照相"在地道英文里则要说他/她"面对镜头害羞" He's / She's **camera-shy**.

　　【剑桥例句】Freya is very photogenic. She has the type of face that looks attractive in a photo.

Time to Branch Out.
推而广之

Describe an important letter you received / you wrote.

补充弹药

Extra Ammo

a nice surprise　惊喜　　　　　emotional　动情的

convey　（v.）表达　　　　　moving　感人的

be moved to tears　被感动得流泪

4. 手工制作（handicraft）

☆ **手工制作之　风筝**

> Describe something you made yourself.
>
> You should say:
>
> what the thing was
>
> how you made it
>
> why you made it
>
> and explain whether you still have this thing today.

Pat 指南

　　北京给我印象最深的是什么？不是 the Forbidden City，也不是 the courtyard houses，更不是 Peking Roast Duck，而是晴天时北京天空上的风筝，那么自由，那么悠闲（carefree）。世界各地的城市我去了很多，但就是没有一个城市的人像北京人这么爱放风筝，这是简单的快乐（simple pleasures of life）。上课练习的时候，让很多孩子描述 making a kite，但是怎么听都像在背百科辞典（encyclopedia）。Let me give it a try. 我一点也不怕话题跟你重复，只要我用的英语比你的简单。

　　难度指数：★★★☆☆

Pat 的答案

I made a simple kite for my cousin last week. Since I'd never made a kite before, I'd thought it must be tricky. But it turned out that making a kite was actually just a breeze.

I decided on its shape first. You know, I just chose a flat one because obviously it was the most basic form and could be easily carried around. Then I got a sheet of coloured paper and cut out the shape.

My cousin found some thin plastic strips for me. I tied them together with a string, which, apparently, would be the frame of the kite. After that, we made the "bridle", which connected the frame to the control line. Finally, I glued the paper to the frame.

All set. Ready for the "maiden flight".

It flew pretty well. Our hard work paid off.

I have no idea what happened to it later — maybe it got thrown away. My cousin is just an 8-year-old, anyway...

轮到你了   It's Your Turn.

▶ **Word Bank on This Topic**

表弟/表妹/表姐/表哥　cousin（一个词有这么多可能的选择，这样的"万能"词汇可以提高你在考试时的快速反应能力）

一张纸　a sheet of paper　　　　　　不容易做的　tricky

简单易行的事情　It's a breeze.（国内考生普遍熟知 It's a piece of cake.，却对这个使用频率同样很高的习语缺乏了解）

[剑桥例句] You won't have any problems with the entrance exam — it's an absolute (绝对的) breeze.

一条　strip　　　　　　　　　　捆在一起　tie... together

绳子	string（这里最好不要用 rope）	明显地	apparently / obviously
框架	frame	粘贴	glue / stick

细的 thin（这也是个万能词，还能表示瘦的，薄的，稀的，甚至夏天穿的衣服少也可以叫 thin summer clothes）

一切就绪了。 All set.（这个句子在国外生活里实在太常用，不论在学校、餐馆，还是体育场，都经常能听到）

有回报	pay off	首航	maiden flight
螺丝刀	screwdriver	剪刀	scissors
镊子	tweezers	钳子	pliers
把……拧弯	twist	把……弄弯	bend

[剑桥例句] Make sure you bend your knees when you're picking up heavy objects.

支架	bridle	折纸	paper folding
剪纸	paper cutting	刺绣	embroidery

缝制 knitting（其实有不少英美老奶奶也挺喜欢"打毛衣"的）

拼贴	collage /ˈkɒlɑːʒ/	陶艺	pottery

> 请参考Pat的思路，并适当借鉴这个词汇表里的单词，思考如果是您会怎么说

Pat 的海外生活英语实录

    handicrafts 如果只是业余玩玩儿可以像咱们这样自学成才，但如果要成为高手（pro）那可就要付出艰苦的努力了。艰苦的努力，多数考生会用 hard effort，strong 或者 painful effort 这样的表达，但其实 **arduous effort** 才是表达这个意思最为精确的一个短语。不少国内朋友看过 Donald Trump 的 *The Apprentice*（学徒）那档节目，就能深刻体会"学徒"得需要付出多少的 **arduous** effort 才能变成"师傅"了。在地道英文里还有一句习语叫 It's **a long and winding road.** 同样也是用来形容实现目标的艰辛过程。

    【剑桥例句】The journey was long and arduous.

Time to Branch Out.
推而广之

Describe a toy.

Are kites toys? Well，it depends on how toys are defined. According to *Longman* and *Oxford* dictionaries，toys are just objects for children to play with. So…

And，be sure to check this out: www. barnesandnoble. com/u/Learning-Toys-Learning-Games/379003165/ 在 Shop by Age 一栏选择适合不同年龄段的玩具，绝对比你这辈子见过的玩具都多，而且每个玩具的 Overview 下面还有 More details. 可以让你充分地享受一次 "返老还童" 的感觉😊

补充弹药

run around　到处跑		flip（*v.*）　翻滚	
high up in the sky　在高空		laid-back　放松的	
kite-flying（*n.*）　放风筝			
Rubik's Cube　魔方（注意在地道英语里 "拼魔方" 叫作 solve a Rubik's Cube）			
puzzle　拼图游戏		Lego blocks　乐高积木	
educational toys　益智玩具			
marbles　注意当它指玩具时并不是指大理石，而是指玻璃弹子			
toy car　玩具汽车		toy mobile phone　玩具手机	
remote-controlled cars / radio-controlled cars　遥控汽车			
Barbie doll　芭比娃娃		stuffed animal　填充玩具	

Extra Ammo

5. 服装

☆ 服装之　旗袍／唐装

Describe an item of clothing you like.

You should say:

what the item is

> where / When you bought it
>
> what it looks like
>
> and explain when you wear it.

Pat 指南

雅思口语中还有一个题目是描述 your favourite traditional clothing。所以建议大家准备旗袍（Chi-pao）或者唐装话题，这样就把两个题一起准备了。唐装有很多种翻译方法，但是大多数的英文听着特别扭（They sound awkward.）。我会叫它 Tang suit，至少这个听着还算自然。说旗袍和唐装除了历史不一样，其实多数内容还是一样的，不过 Pat 个人感觉唐装比较宽松（loose-fitting），所以它的效果主要是让男士看起来更富贵（well-heeled / well-off），而不是像紧身的（tight-fitting）旗袍那样让女士看起来更优雅（elegant/graceful）。

难度指数：★ ★ ★ ★ ☆

:··· **Pat 的答案** ···:

Let me talk about my Chi-pao. It was a birthday gift from my parents.

It's essentially a one-piece dress. But it looks unique because of the fabric, I mean, the silk. The bell-like sleeves and the slits on the sides also make it different from regular dresses.

My Chi-pao is pretty easy to slip on and really comfortable to wear. I guess that's exactly why chi-pao is so popular these days.

I wear it during the Spring Festival and other family occasions like family reunions.

Now let me share with you something about the history of Chi-pao. (*Pat's note: If you don't think you'll have time for this, just skip it and go straight to the next paragraph.*) It was popular among the Manchurian women in the Qing Dynasty. But now it represents the traditional Chinese clothing in general and is often considered a national treasure.

The only complaint I have about my Chi-pao is that many waitresses wear Chi-pao in restaurants too. So sometimes it can be really confusing or even embarrassing...

轮到你了   It's Your Turn.

▶ **Word Bank on This Topic**

本质上 essentially	连衣裙 a dress（这时候它是可数的）
独特的 unique	面料 fabric
刺绣 embroidery	像铃铛那样的 bell-like
袖子 sleeves	窄缝 slit

普通的，常规的 regular

[剑桥例句] Her heartbeat was regular.

穿上 slip on / put on	紧身的 tight-fitting
场合 occasion	家庭团聚 family reunion

[剑桥例句] We're having a family reunion next week.

喜庆的 festive	代表 represent
国宝 national treasure	让人困惑的 confusing
抱怨 complaint	优雅的 elegant
让人羞愧的 embarrassing	复杂的 complicated
花纹 pattern	制服 uniform
鲜花（图案）的 floral	丝绸 silk
庆祝 celebrates	棉布 cotton
绒布 velvet	皇族 the royal family
满族的民族服装 Manchurian costumes	身份的象征 status symbol
民族服装 ethnic costumes	

套装 suit（中文里所常说的"西装"在英美就被称为 business suit，有时直接简称 suit）

衬衣（男式） shirt	衬衣（女式） blouse
牛仔裤 jeans	牛仔上衣 denim jacket

毛衣（正面不带扣子的套头毛衣） sweater

毛衣（正面有一排扣子的毛衣） cardigan

适合春秋穿的长袖运动衫 sweatshirt

"帽衫儿" hoodie

请参考Pat的思路，并适当借鉴这个词汇表里的单词，思考如果是您会怎么说

Pat 的海外生活英语实录

适度注意着装是必要的，甚至还可以成为竞争时的一个优势（a competitive edge）。但如果一个人过度地追求时尚，那么就会沦为时尚的受害者（**a fashion victim**）了。

【剑桥例句】Ellie is a fashion victim. She always wears trendy clothes even if the clothes sometimes make her look silly.

雅思口试中偶尔还会咕咕冒出一张卡片：

Describe an item of clothing / a piece of jewellery（首饰）you like. 如果真赶上这个卡片，那真的要好好反思一下考前自己是否虐待过小动物或者坐公车没给老年人让座了。点点 www.jewelinfo4u.com 上面的一堆链接也许是个不错的选择，对各种首饰的解释都细致入微。但 ad 就可以跳过不必看，出国之后欣赏好首饰的机会是无穷无尽的，先赶紧把考试过了再"小资"不晚。

下面是最有名的一些时尚名牌，很多还没有标准的中文翻译，请大家仔细听音频中的发音。它们中大多数都不是英语，发音都是很容易错的哦。

BURBERRY	FENDI	CHANEL
GUCCI	CHOLE	HERMES
BVLGARI	DOLCE&GABBANA	LOUIS VUITTON
VERSACE	SALVATORE FERRAGAMO	MARC JACOBS
ANNA SUI	SWAROVSKI	

Do you know what amazes me more than anything else? The impotence of force to organise anything.

—Napoleon Bonaparte

想听起来更地道么？那您得知道 X-ish！

在英美日常生活里描述一个物品的颜色、形状、数量等的时候，如果想表示"差不多是……的"，"多少有点儿……"的意思，除了可以使用 kind of + 形容词或者稍正式一些的 somewhat + 形容词等表达之外，还经常会用一个形容词 +ish 形成一个新词来表达。这种"-ish 构词法"在英美生活里实在是太常用了，如果你当地朋友多的话几乎可以天天"遇见-ish"，例如：reddish（接近于红色的），roundish（差不多是圆形的），thirty-ish（三十左右的）等等。当然，在 IELTS 口试里也不要用得过于频繁，否则就没效果了，如果能自然地用上 1~2 次就已经很好了。

6. 双语感悟之 自行车 Random Reflections on Biking

Describe an invention（before the age of computers）.

计算机之前的发明，bicycle 也许绝对是最值得我们继续使用同时也最环保的一种了。

首先，It was invented in the late 19th century by some Frenchmen. 然后，It became popular immediately because it was inexpensive and easy to ride. 立刻流行起来了，原因很明显啊。

Now millions of people ride their bikes on a daily basis.（"每天"也可以这么说的）Some people are bike commuters.（骑自行车上下班的人，commute 是每天上下班的过程。）Others just ride a bike for pleasure / recreation.（另一些人就是为了那种乐趣）I like biking because I love the feel of the breeze on my face.（微风吹着就更舒服了）

再了解一下 bike 的组成部分（parts / components）：

铃铛叫 bell，不过好像我在北京骑过的几辆车铃铛都不响。车把叫 handlebars，车闸叫 brake，横梁是 crossbar，车座叫 saddle，脚踏板是 pedals（所以英文也经常说 pedal my bike），链条叫作 chain，轮子当然就是 tyre（BrE）/tire（AmE）了。

有些比较贵的自行车还有变速器，这个东东在日常生活里老美们都管它叫 shifter 或者 gear control，但正式的术语应该怎么说还真不知道。

如果车很新就说 brand-new，很旧就说 worn-out/beat-up，已经很久没骑过了就说 It's gathering（or collecting）dust now.

在北京 biking 还戴头盔肯定会被认为是小题大做（make a fuss about nothing），但在英美骑自行车时戴头盔（wear a helmet while riding a bike）实在太常见了，美国有些州甚至明确规定 18 岁以下的孩子不戴头盔是违法的。所以如果说一句 I always wear a helmet while riding a bike, for the sake of safety. 会让考官觉得你这人特有责任感（You're a responsible bike rider.）。

另外，在 Day 7 里面我们讲过 biking 的好处也都可以拿过来说说，或者稍变化一下，比如 It's cool especially when the gas price is soaring（急速上升），because bikes don't need any fuel（燃料）.

biking 其实也可以叫 cycling，比如您就可以说 Cycling is ecofriendly because it's zero-emission（零排放），而且英美小朋友们有时候在早晨出门之前还会特期待地问，"Can I cycle to school today?"

上次回 Vancouver 的时候听说最新研发出了一种叫 e-bikes（网络自行车）的东东，这个我真的想不明白了（I reaaaaaaaally can't figure that out.）。不过 Google 都已经开始在美国本土推它的 driverless cars（无人驾驶汽车）了，这年头，一切皆有可能啊。

Time to Branch Out.
推而广之

Describe a car or a bicycle.

补充弹药

transform（*vt.*）=fundamentally change　彻底改变

profound influence　深刻的影响

altered the course of history　改变了历史的进程

user-friendly　方便使用的

Extra Ammo

另类话题　**Off-the-Wall Topics**

如果说奔驰（国内的同学们习惯叫它 Benz，但以英语为母语的人们都叫它 Mercedes）是身份的象征（status symbol），那么悍马（Hummer）在北京就是属于最有钱的那个群体了（the upper crust）。Pat 自己在加拿大开过一次 Hummer H3，除了感觉到了 "the wow factor"（让身边的人们惊叹的效果），就是感觉汽油在不停地烧，这种车真不是给我们这种需要考虑油价的人设计的。

下面这段是一普通人买了 Hummer 之后就像拿了个烫手山芋（英文里叫"烫手土豆"hot potato）的无比纠结的心态，请仔细体会用词简单却清晰易懂的效果，这才是每天人们在用的真实英文：

I bought this Hummer for my wife. She just loved it. But I hated it from the start. It was not comfortable for me to drive. As a matter of fact, I refused to drive it. I would rather drive my Ford because it has a better ride and gets better mileage. Most ladies I have talked to enjoy it because they feel safe and yes it is a safe car to a certain point. We have had it for least a year and my wife and son both have had backing accidents due to the bad blind spots. If I had to drive it everyday, it would have a new home. But luckily I don't so it'll stay put till my wife also gets tried of it.

(*gas mileage: We've learned this in our Mini Cooper segment*, *right?*

backing: When you back up your car, *it goes backward.*

blind spot: The part of the road that you can't see when you drive a car.)

对本类话题有价值的网址

下面的网址对骨灰级 DIYer 准备关于物品类的常考题也会很有帮助：

家用电器：

http://www.dixons.co.uk/gbuk/index.html（It gives detailed descriptions of tons of home appliances）

手工制作：

www.allaboutyou.com/craft/craft-ideas-kids-crafts-beginners-guides

F　曾经沧海

Pat 解题　Pat's Decryption

这一节我们突破最后一大类卡片：经历。

描述经历的题中，有很多是关于 an event 的。要描述好 an event，我们首先要对什么是 event 做个定义：

"A social occasion or activity"，这是 Merriam Webster 对 event 的解释。

"something that happens, especially something important, interesting or unusual"，这是 *Longman* 对 event 的解释。

所以真的不需要担心得太多，只要是符合卡片要求的"事件"都可以介绍，一般来说卡片要求你描述的 event 本身已经带有一些特殊性了。

解决了关于 events 的担心，我还要再提醒您：说到 an event 或者 an experience 的时候经常会用到下面的词组（不一定每个都会用到，但是经常会用到其中的某几个）：At first, ...；But then, ...；So, ...；After that, ...；Then, ...；Next, ...；...shortly afterwards（很短的时间之后）；Finally / Eventually, ... 因为它们可以帮我们把顺序（sequence）讲清楚。

今天我们还会谈到人生中一个重要的 event — wedding。如果说东西方婚礼的差异，Pat 观察到的是西方的婚礼仪式（wedding ceremony）比较强调 spirituality（精神意义），仪式本身相对比较 simple（其实花钱也不少，但把钱主要都留给后面的 wedding reception 和更贵的 honeymoon 了），而中国的婚礼仪式则更务实（pragmatic）。比如"闹洞房"（The couple's friends mess around in their bedroom.）就有很好的喜庆效果，好玩儿。

展开本类话题的思路线索　Brainstorming Techniques
（熟悉下图可以确保你在拿到任何本类卡片题时都能有话说）

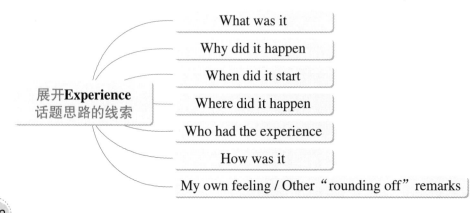

展开 **Experience** 话题思路的线索

- What was it
- Why did it happen
- When did it start
- Where did it happen
- Who had the experience
- How was it
- My own feeling / Other "rounding off" remarks

本类话题最新完整真题库　Recent Questions on This Topic

❋ Describe a sports event.

❋ Describe a special meal you had recently.

❋ Describe a difficult thing that you did well.

❋ Describe something you would like to succeed in doing.

❋ Describe a skill.

❋ Describe a happy family event.

❋ Describe a festival that is popular in your country.

❋ Describe a wedding.

❋ Describe a photo.

❋ Describe a birthday party.

❋ Describe an important change in your life.

❋ Describe an important stage in your life.

分级演示　A Spectrum of Sample Answers

1. 让人开心的事

> Describe a happy event.
>
> You should say:
>
> > what it was
> >
> > where it was held
> >
> > who went to the event
>
> and explain why it was a happy event.

Pat 指南

让人开心的事件选择挺多的，最重大的比如 wedding（今天咱们也要研究，因为 Part 2 官方题库里确实有 wedding 这道题，尽管多数去留学的烤鸭应该至今还没作为主角出席过 wedding，所以对 happy 的程度感受可能还不够深）；意义比较小的比如被特许参加了某个新游戏的"封测"（internal testing ／ alpha testing）。

不大不小又而最容易说清楚的，那就是毕业典礼了。不过在英美即使中学毕业典礼都是非常被家长们重视的（孩子自己倒不一定），也要"戴博士帽穿袍子"（cap ／ mortarboard and gown）。而在北美的很多大学里毕业典礼还有个意义深刻的说法叫 commencement（开始）。仔细想想挺对的，毕业典礼其实并不仅是上一个阶段的"毕业"，更标志着人生一个新阶段的"开始"不是么？

难度指数：★ ★ ★ ☆ ☆

Pat 的答案

Let me talk about my graduation ceremony. Actually the ceremony was very short and kind of too formal but still, it was a happy event.

On that day, my classmates and I were all dressed in caps and gowns and arrived early. Our parents and friends also came, with bouquets or gifts in their hands. After the guests were seated, we lined up in order and walked in. Then the principal and some guest speakers delivered speeches and some awards were presented.

The most important part of the ceremony was, obviously, the awarding of diplomas, when the students got called up to the podium, one by one, shook hands with the principal and received our diploma. Unfortunately, a couple of my classmates failed to get enough credits so they didn't get a diploma.

Then after the ceremony, I took lots and lots of pictures with my classmates, because I knew graduation would be the end of the years I shared with these wonderful friends of mine.

The graduation ceremony was not just a happy ending to a past academic experience, it also marked the beginning of a whole new stage, probably an even more challenging one, in my life...

轮到你了   It's Your Turn.

▶ Word Bank on This Topic

有点　kind of

正式的　formal

毕业典礼用的"博士帽"和"袍子"　cap and gown（这是在英美校园里最常听到的说法，如果想显得正式一点则可以说 mortarboard and gown）

花束（请注意听音频里它的发音）　bouquet

就座　be seated

[剑桥例句] Chris sent Evelyn a bouquet when she was ill.

排成队　line up in order

中学校长　principal（大学校长则多数被称为 president）

做演讲　deliver a speech

发毕业证书　the awarding of diplomas

演讲台　podium

两三个　a couple of

学分　credit

一个好的结局　a happy ending

学术的　academic

标志着　mark / represent / symbolise

阶段　stage

高兴的　delighted / elated（后面这个词较为正式而且语气很强，但偶尔在日常生活里也还能听到）

[剑桥例句] I was delighted by your news.

场合　occasion

请参考Pat的思路，并适当借鉴这个词汇表里的单词，思考如果是您会怎么说

[剑桥例句] We met on several occasions to discuss the issue.

Pat 的海外生活英语实录

　　如果要说一段经历是自己人生里的"转折点"，同学们多数会用 It was a turning point for me. 其实这个说法本身挺不错，但用的人过多容易被考官 takes it for granted。其实还有另外两种说法在地道英文里也很常用，但国内考生几乎从来不用：It **altered my lifestyle.** 和 It was **a watershed moment** in my life.

315

【剑桥例句】

(1) Giving up our car has altered our lifestyle.

(2) The year 1969 was a watershed in Madison's life — she changed her career and changed her partner.

2. 体育事件

> Describe a sports event.
>
> You should say:
>
>   what it was
>
>   where it was held
>
>   who went to the event
>
> and explain why it was special.

Pat 指南 🔊

最容易准备、不需要特别的专业知识的，肯定是 the Olympic Games。权威的朗文词典对 the Olympic Games 的英文定义就是：a modern international sports event in which people of all nationalities...完全符合这个题目的所有要求。奥运会是符合题目要求的，关键是你怎样描述最清晰。

难度指数：★★★★☆

┌────────────┐
Pat 的答案
└────────────┘

I really enjoyed watching the London Olympic Games.

I planned well ahead to make sure I could watch as much of the Olympics as possible. The opening ceremony showed us the amazing contributions the British made to the world. I particularly like Mr. Bean's hilarious performance and Paul McCartney's performance of *Hey Jude*. Some friends of mine complained that the opening ceremony was not well organised. But I think it was just a more creative

way to present a great culture.

During the London Olympics，more than 10，000 world-class athletes competed for their nations. Swimming was one of my favourite events because I'm a pretty good swimmer myself. And I was soooooo excited Sun Yang captured the gold medal in the men's 400-meter freestyle final. He really reminded me of the Olympic motto — "Faster，Higher，Stronger".

Watching the athletes from different countries competing against one another in a fair manner is uplifting. Bias still got in the way from time to time. But the Olympic spirit was respected by most of the participants.

It was a shame I didn't make it to London. I wouldn't be able to afford tickets to the games anyway …

轮到你了   It's Your Turn.

▶ **Word Bank on This Topic**

超级搞笑的　hilarious	决赛　final
半决赛　semi-final	四分之一决赛　quarter final
金牌　gold medal	银牌　silver medal
铜牌　bronze medal	

闪电般的速度　lightning speed（地道英文里还有 "as fast as lighting" 的说法）

夺取　capture

奥林匹克格言　the Olympic motto（"Faster，Higher，Stronger"）

奥林匹克公园　Olympic Park	奥运村　Olympic Village
奥运场馆　Olympic venues	令人振奋的　uplifting
很激励人的，很励志的　inspiring	偏见　bias
参加者　participants	参加　participation
特别精彩的部分，"亮点"　highlight	主办城市　the host city

国际奥委会　The International Olympic Committee（IOC）

激励一代人（伦敦奥运会的口号）　Inspire a Generation（the official slogan for the 2012 London Olympics）

吉祥物　mascot　　　　　　　　　　　奥运会的五环　the Olympic rings

距离开幕式 100 天的倒计时　100-day countdown

开幕式　the opening ceremony　　　　达到某人的期望　meet sb.'s expectations

完全没有达到某人的期望　smash sb.'s expectations

奖牌榜　the Olympic medal count / the Olympic medal table

奥运火炬传递　the Olympic torch relay　　点燃奥运圣火　light the Olympic Flame

主题　theme　　　　　　　　　　　　获奖运动员　medalist

竞争极为激烈的比赛　a fiercely contested competition

势均力敌的比赛　an evenly matched game　击剑　fencing

射击　shooting　　　　　　　　　　100 米短跑　100-meter sprint

摔跤　wrestling　　　　　　　　　　跨栏比赛　hurdle race

柔道　judo　　　　　　　　　　　　铁人三项　triathlon

排球　volleyball　　　　　　　　　艺术体操　artistic gymnastics

花样游泳　synchronized swimming　　射箭　archery

田径项目　track and field events　　　水球　water polo

马术比赛　equestrian events　　　　　跳水　diving

残奥会　Paralympics / The Paralympic Games

体育比赛的观众　spectators

[剑桥例句] They won 4-0 in front of over 40 000 cheering（欢呼的，加油的）spectators.

志愿者　volunteers　　　代表他们／她们的国家　represent their countries

感受比赛的气氛　enjoy the atmosphere of the games

报道　report / coverage（*n.*）

[剑桥例句] What did you think of the BBC's coverage of the event?

……是很让人遗憾的　It's a shame（that）…（注意：在地道英文里，It's a shame.
这句话不是"令人羞耻"的意思，而是"太可惜了"的意思）

[**剑桥例句**] It's a shame（that）the concert had to be cancelled.

独特的　unique　　　　　　　见证　witness

体育迷　sports buff　　　　（某个地方）人潮涌动的　be teeming with people

伦敦碗　the London Bowl

开幕式的各国运动员走队　the Parade of Nations（领队的旗手：the flag
bearer）

完成大满贯　complete the Grand Slam

请参考Pat的思路，并适当借鉴这个词汇表里的单词，思考如果是您会怎么说

Pat 的海外生活英语实录

"激烈的竞赛"，基础好的考生一般都知道 fierce competition 这个短语。但地道的英文口语里还有个说法，用来描述体育比赛的激烈程度属于当仁不让的好词：**a cliffhanger**。想象一下被悬在悬崖上的感觉多么让人紧张，就知道这样的比赛会是多么"扣人心弦"。

【剑桥例句】

（1）It looks as if the election is going to be a cliffhanger.

（2）Netherlands beat Kenya in a cliffhanger in the World Cup warm-up match.

3. 英语课堂演示

☆ *英语课堂活动之*　presentation／an interesting speech

> Describe an activity in an English lesson.
>
> You should say:
>
> what the activity was
>
> what you learned from this activity
>
> why you enjoyed it
>
> and explain whether you would like to do a similar
> activity again.

Pat 指南

国外大学在教学形式上有很多和国内不一样，有些 Pat 一直没想清楚应该怎么翻译成中文，比如 seminar 和 term paper，还有一个特别常见的就是 presentation。我把这个答案写得比较长，其实用词并不难，希望您没出国之前就能提前体会一下国外课堂的"轻松"气氛。

难度指数：★★★☆☆

> **Pat 的答案**

Last week, our English teacher asked us to prepare for a presentation on the differences between some British writers and their works. He told us how we should structure our presentation and then divided us into pairs.

After class, my teammate and I went to the library and checked out some books on those writers. After that, we read the materials thoroughly and figured out what we should present. Then we started making Powerpoint slides to make the information more organised and memorable. We also made some note cards to remind ourselves of the information we were going to present.

During the actual presentation, my teammate did the introduction first, then I presented our findings while he managed the slides. At first, I was a bit nervous. But gradually I began to feel at ease. When I forgot what I should say, I just glanced down at the note cards for clues.

My teacher and my classmates were very impressed with our presentation. After we finished it, some of them came up to us right away to compliment us on our presentation.

I learned a lot from that experience, like preparation could really make all the difference between a good and a bad presentation.

I'm looking forward to our next presentation now...

轮到你了   It's Your Turn.

▶ **Word Bank on This Topic**

课堂演示   class presentation   作品   works

[剑桥例句] The museum has many works by Picasso as well as other modern painters.

详尽地   thoroughly   借书   check out books

想出   figure out   感觉适应的，不感到紧张的   feel at ease

有规律的，有秩序的   organised   容易记忆的   memorable

低头很快地看一眼   glance down at   夸奖   compliment sb. on sth.

带来实质性的差异，获得实质性的效果   make the difference between... and...

有效的   effective   团队精神   team spirit

提示自己用的小卡片   note cards   PowerPoint 幻灯片   PowerPoint slides

(做演示时提示自己用的) 视觉提示工具   visual aid

集体讨论   group discussion   辩论   debate

团队合作   teamwork   预先"排练"   rehearse

听众   audience

请参考Pat的思路，并适当借鉴这个词汇表里的单词，思考如果是您会怎么说

Pat 的海外生活英语实录

评价好的 presentation 有很多标准，比如 engaging（能够吸引听众注意力的），well-rehearsed（预先"排练"充分的），well-structured（结构合理的）等。但其实说到底，唯一的标准就是 presentation 够不够 **informative**（可以提供很多有用信息的）。

【剑桥例句】

（1）This is an interesting and highly informative book.

（2）The dietician's（营养学家）talk was very informative.

Time to Branch Out.
推而广之

Describe a success.

Describe a skill.

补充弹药

rewarding　有回报的

boost my confidence　提升我的自信

uplifting　令人振奋的

When the going gets tough, the tough get going.（谚语）

这个其实很像中文的"坚持就是胜利"了。

Extra Ammo

　　口语题库里的一道神题 **Describe a foreign language（not English）you want to learn.** 给很多考生带来了严重的挫败感——英语考场上居然又让人再用英语去描述另一种外语，这对于根本就没学过"二外"的烤鸭来说无异于集体屠杀。theeasiestlanguagetolearn. com 给出了十种最容易学的语言排名，英语高居第二位。从少年时代就一直在跟英语较劲的同学可能会觉得这纯属"恶搞"。但这个网页上方的 interactive chart 还是有点意思的。一个事实是：跟世界上的多数主流语言比起来，英语确实还算是比较容易"上手儿"和"上嘴儿"的，只是要想真正学好、学精，那您就得好好努力了。

4. 一场表演

☆ **一场表演之　音乐会**

> Describe a performance or a show.（such as a dancing or singing performance）
>
> You should say:
> 　　what kind of performance / show it was
> 　　when and where you watched it
> 　　who you watched it with
> and explain how you felt about it.

Pat 指南

Pat 自己从高中就开始组织车库乐队，刚回北京的时候还在三里屯的几家酒吧唱过歌。在其中一家唱了一个月后经理就找我们谈话，说他们的啤酒销量那个月下降了 40%。还有一家在我们唱了 7 天之后，酒吧倒了（went bust）。不过我仍然很热爱音乐，这里给大家写一段去看 rock concert 的经历吧，您可以体会一下怎么用英文描述那种热烈的气氛（exciting atmosphere），估计这个话题大家掌握起来比其他表演容易点。这个答案掌握一半的内容后再描述摇滚音乐会就得心应手（feel at home with it）了。

难度指数：★ ★ ★ ☆ ☆

Pat 的答案

I went to... (*Put the band's name here.*)'s concert last Friday night. It was held at the Workers' Stadium. I'd long been a big fan of them so when a friend of mine got me a ticket to their concert, I was like, "WOW!" and felt like I was on top of the world.

I just couldn't wait till Friday came around. My friend and I made a huge poster with the members' names on it, to hold up during the concert.

It turned out that not just young people went there. The concert attracted people of all ages. One more reason for me to feel proud of the band... The stadium was totally packed!

When the band actually took the stage, we went wild. Some fans got so excited they cried and some even passed out at the sight of the band.

The band members were all amazing performers. They played songs from many of their albums, including their latest album, and even played some acoustic songs. That was pretty much the highlight of the concert. The live music and the thrill of just being there were amazing.

We knocked into one another, sang along with the band and screamed their names at the top of our lungs. And you know what? The band members did notice our poster and even waved at us when they were on stage...

It was a blast!

▶ **Word Bank on This Topic**

体育场　stadium　　现场的音乐　live music（请您注意听 live 当形容词时的正确发音）

海报　poster

挤满了人的　packed（其实在英美口语里这个词比 crowded 更常用，要是想进一步突出拥挤程度的话还可以说 jam-packed）

登台　take the stage　　　　　　疯狂的　wild / crazy / fanatical

[剑桥例句] Her enthusiasm for aerobics（有氧健身操）was almost fanatical.

兴奋的　excited / thrilled

昏过去了　pass out（这些词都是英美年轻人聊 rock concert 时超级常用的词汇）

专辑　album

纯演奏版（就是不用 MIDI 合成的那种，爱玩儿摇滚的朋友们肯定明白）
　　　　acoustic version

最精彩的部分，"亮点"　highlight　　尖叫　scream

大声的，高声的　at the top of our lungs

弯下腰去和粉丝握手　bend over to shake hands with their fans

超级好玩儿，玩得太"劲爆"了　It was a blast! / We had a great time.

氛围　atmosphere / ambience　　　现场音乐会　a live concert

嘉宾的演出　guest performance　　　激情　passion

灯光　lighting　　　　　　　　　　高分贝　high-decibel levels

不去不行，非去不可　be dying to go to...

请参考Pat的思路，并适当借鉴这个词汇表里的单词，思考如果是您会怎么说

Pat 的海外生活英语实录

　　如果要说演唱会上歌手和观众之间的"互动"，基础好的同学都能想到 **interaction**。的确，the interaction between the singer / the band and the audience（有时也简称为 the singer / band — audience interaction）就是这个意思。

但如果问您演唱会上歌迷挥的"荧光棒"英文怎样说您能回答么？**glow sticks** 就是口语里的"荧光棒"，而"挥舞"则还是 **wave** 那个动词。不过在英美有些歌手和 DJ 最近还联合发起了一场 *Ban the Glow Sticks* 的运动，也算是为环保做点小贡献吧。

5. 婚礼

> Describe a wedding you have attended.
>
> You should say:
>
>   when it was
>
>   who got married
>
>   what happened at the wedding
>
> and explain this was a typical wedding.

Pat 指南

William 与 Kate（在英美生活里一般是简称他们为 Will and Kate）当年的 royal wedding 在全世界获得了 20 亿观众的收视率，现在 Will 和 Kate 都已经生"二胎"了，可见婚礼永远是一个让人向往的主题。

这道题是说中式婚礼好还是说西式婚礼好呢？ To be or not to be. 那是个问题。其实这么想可能会比较清楚：如果两种都能说得很流利很明白，肯定两种都很好，而且中式的应该更好。但如果本来英文就不够流利，发音也不地道，表情还不自然，再给考官说一堆他/她根本不了解的概念，会是什么效果？如果说西式婚礼至少考官的"听懂率"还能高一点。

说 wedding，掌握一下顺序（sequence）的描述还有一些专门词汇能掌握就差不多了，也没必要说得"过好"，毕竟咱们谁也不是每天参加婚礼玩儿的人。

难度指数：★★★★☆

Pat 的答案

A friend of mine got married last month. I went to her wedding ceremony. It was held in a church and began at 9 in the morning. It was a typical Western-style ceremony.

There were around 150 people at the ceremony, including the bride's and the groom's family, and their friends and colleagues. We were all dressed up for the occasion.

After the opening remarks by the MC, the groom, in a black tuxedo, made his way to the altar with the best man and waited there.

When the Wedding March was played, the bride's attendants entered, including the maid of honor and the flower girl. My friend, you know, the bride, entered last in her white wedding dress, accompanied by her father.

I was sooooo moved watching my friend walking down the aisle. At the altar, the couple exchanged wedding vows and wedding rings. Then they kissed each other and were pronounced husband and wife.

The wedding reception was held at the Sheraton Hotel. It was like a big party, when all the guests celebrated the marriage with the bride and groom. Lots of food and wine were served…

轮到你了   It's Your Turn.

▶ Word Bank on This Topic

仪式	ceremony	典型的	typical
开场白	opening remarks	司仪	MC / master of ceremonies
新娘	bride	新郎	groom
同事	colleague	穿上正装	dress up
伴郎	best man		

男士晚礼服（一般在非常正式的场合才穿） tuxedo / tux

神坛	altar	婚礼进行曲	Wedding March
随从	attendants	伴娘	maid of honor

[剑桥例句] The Prince was followed by his attendants.

花童　flower girl(s)　　　　　新人　the new couple / the newly-weds

陪伴　accompany　　　　　　婚纱　wedding dress / wedding gown

交换　exchange

结婚誓言　wedding vow（也就是那段 Hollywood 电影里经典的：

> *"… from this day forward,*
> *for better, for worse,*
> *for richer, for poorer,*
> *in sickness and in health,*
> *to love and to cherish,*
> *till death do us part…"*)

很正式地宣布　pronounce（在这里它不是"发音"的意思）

祝酒　propose a toast　　　　祝贺　congratulations

切蛋糕　cake-cutting　　　　　蜜月　honeymoon

扔花束（据说拿到花束的女孩就是下一个会结婚的女孩）　toss the bouquet

（婚礼仪式之后的）婚宴　wedding reception / wedding banquet

向新婚夫妇撒米或者纸片　shower the couple with rice / confetti

祝酒　propose a toast

吃到一份（蛋糕）　get a slice of the wedding cake

请参考Pat的思路，并适当借鉴这个词汇表里的单词，思考如果是您会怎么说

Pat 的海外生活英语实录

如果描述一次婚礼，每个考生估计都要说十次以上的 get married。其实地道口语里可以代替这个短语的表达不胜枚举，但是其中的多数在语义或语气上并不适合出现在 IELTS 口试的答案中。一个适合出现在考场里的替换方案是 **tie the knot**，用一个结把两人牢牢捆起来，可见爱得真挺瓷实的。

【剑桥例句】

（1）So when are you two going to tie the knot?

（2）Evie's going to tie the knot with her German boyfriend next June.

Pat 最近在一本介绍中国文化的书里看到一段英文，专门描述中国文化中人生的四大喜事，挺有意思，请看看您能不能猜出来分别是什么：

Marriage is known as one of the four happiest things in one's life. The other three are achievement in examinations, meeting old friends away from home and rainfall after a drought (a long period of dry weather).

6. 节日

☆ 节日之　端午

> Describe a festival that is popular in your country.
>
> You should say:
>
> what the festival is
>
> what people do during this festival
>
> whether people celebrate this festival in the same way
>
> and explain why this festival is important.

Pat 指南 🔊

无数人描述过端午节，这是我的版本。它没有别的好处，唯一的优势是考官一定能听懂。对背景知识则没必要太 "死磕" (hung up on)，因为即使你说错了估计考官也不知道，英文对就是真的对。

难度指数：★ ★ ★ ☆ ☆

> Pat 的答案

The Duan Wu Festival has become even more popular since it became a public holiday in China.

This festival has long been associated with a famous poet in history, who was so worried about his country that he drowned himself. During the festival, people all across China eat rice dumplings (or in Chinese, *zong zi*), to pay tribute to this poet. We all respect people who love their country, right?

Another thing often associated with this festival is the dragon boat races. It's like a number of teams rowing and competing against one another. To be honest, I've only watched boat races on TV. It seems like such races are rare in cities. But from what I saw on TV, I could tell they were very vibrant and exciting events.

As I see it, the Duan Wu Festival is about vitality, about the circle of life.

轮到你了 It's Your Turn.

▶ **Word Bank on This Topic**

和……联系到一起　is associated with

[剑桥例句] This brand is associated by most people with good quality.

跳河自尽　drown oneself	起源　origin
向……表示敬意　pay tribute to...	划船　row
竞争　compete	罕见的　rare
有活力的　lively / vibrant / dynamic	生命的活力　vitality
（粽子、元宵或饺子里面的）填充物，"馅儿"　stuffing / filling	
豆沙　bean paste	竹叶　bamboo leaves
历史悠久的传统　a time-honored tradition	节日庆祝活动　festivities
中秋节　the Mid-Autumn Festival	月饼　mooncakes
元宵节　the Lantern Festival	驱难避邪　ward off evil spirits
灯展　display of lanterns	年三十　the Lunar New Year's Eve
压岁钱　lucky money	红包　red envelope
饺子　dumplings	放鞭炮　set off firecrackers
阴历　the lunar calendar	
标志着　mark / represent / symbolise	许愿　make a wish
午夜倒计时　count down to midnight	

请参考Pat的思路，并适当借鉴这个词汇表里的单词，思考如果是您会怎么说

7. 双语感悟之 人生里一个积极的变化

Random Reflections on Positive Changes

> Describe a positive change in your life.
>
> You should say:
>
> > when this change happened
> >
> > what this change was
> >
> > why it was positive
>
> and explain how this change has influenced your life.

Pat指南

首先要注意的是：讲这个题目一定会用到很多过去时！然后请想一想什么样的 change 算是 positive change？比如一次 basketball game 之后你的 teammates 让你意识到自己的问题在哪里；又比如一次家长生病了，你人生里第一次真正懂得应该照顾自己的父母；还比如你学开车考路考（took a road test），比过去更遵守交通规则了；再比如第一次离开家去别的城市上学，您不得不开始自己叠被子了（made your own bed）。以及决定出国读书后自己的种种变化也可以考虑……只要不紧张，找准话题往下讲就不会觉得太困难。有些地道的套话（clichés）是描述 change 的时候经常用的，比如：

英文	中文
This experience **changed the course of my life.**	这次经历改变了我的人生道路。
At first, I felt really **nervous** and **frustrated.**	刚开始我感到很紧张也很沮丧。
My teammates' encouraging words really **cheered me up.**	队友们的鼓励话语让我振作起来。
My driving instructor's **sound advice** led to a major change in my performance.	驾车教练的忠告让我的表现提高了很多。
It not only improved my skills, but solved my **attitude problem** as well.	这不仅仅提高了我的技术，也让我改变了自己心态上的问题。
For the first time in my life, I found my father so **vulnerable** and so **helpless.**	有生以来第一次，我感到父亲这么脆弱无助。

（续表）

英文	中文
This experience had a **great influence** on my life.	这段经历对我后来的人生有深远的影响。
I became a **caring** and loving son/daughter.	这件事情以后，我变成了一个更关心父母的孩子。
It **made** me start working on my **agility** and **team spirit**.	这件事促使我提高了我的灵敏程度和团队精神。
That was pretty much **a milestone** in my life.	这段经历可以说是我人生道路上一个新的里程碑。
It made me **tougher** and more **determined**.	这让我变得更坚强，更有决心。
Nothing endures but change.	（这是古希腊哲学家 Heraclitus 的名言，在英美生活中仍然经常被大家引用）世界上唯一不变的是改变。
I saw the **light at the end of the tunnel**.	（困难时）我终于看到一线光明。

⌐临时抱佛脚

有个卡片话题由于内容不好想一直被视为难点中的难点：

Describe an important letter you wrote.

可 Pat 真觉得准备这道题最不需要花时间：既然申请留学或者申请移民当然是要递交申请信的（申请信的英文说 application letter 或者 letter of application 都行，但现在也很时髦在申请资料里单独再写一封 covering letter*）。即使这封申请信并不是您自己写的那么找 agent 把信要一份过来看两遍也就熟悉了，而且今后万一大学或者移民官要面试您也会更清楚应该怎么说，是一举两得的好事不是么（kill two birds with one stone）？

不管你的申请信是如何写的，在描述时都一定能够用到下面几个单词和句型：

I'd like to talk about an application letter /a cover letter I wrote to...

（※申请材料中放入的简短自我介绍信在英国叫 covering letter，而在美国则被称为 cover letter）

My letter was made up of / consisted of... parts. 这封介绍信包括几个部分⋯⋯

I explained how and where I learned about（了解到）their programme / the position and the reason for my application. 接下来还可以大概说说你申的到底是哪个 programme 或者什么 position，即使英语再不好介绍一下自己申的相关专业或者职位肯定还是能扯几句的；

I described my personal and educational / professional qualifications. 这里也可以大概说说自己的教育背景或者工作经历，比如自己的 experience, skills, major... 等。而这些都是国内孩子们在去 English corner 的时候最爱聊的内容，肯定能说得很流利。"最高学历"的英文叫 highest academic qualification，比如 I hold a Master's Degree in...；

I expressed my desire（在书信里是愿望的意思）for an interview.

I indicated（给出了）how I could be contacted.

I then thanked the reader for reviewing my application and expressed my interest in getting a reply even if it was not what I hoped for.

在结束对这个卡片题的描述之前你还可以再谈谈这封信可能将带来的结果。如果申请结果根本无法确定则可以告诉考官 But everything is still up in the air...

Pat 的海外生活英语实录

如果问我"班长"这个词英文怎么说，我只能很老实地回答："Beats me."（俺答不上来。）因为在英国和北美的中学里根本就没班长。让老师指定（appoint）一个学生当班长的做法，即使学生不提出抗议（protest），家长们肯定也不干（They will be up in arms about it.），因为如果这样的话老师的权力（authority）就太大了，在 PTA meeting（家长会，北美的 PTA meeting 在很多中学里每两到三个月就开一次）家长们肯定要向校方直接提出投诉了（file a complaint）。

在英美比较被接受的方式是 student council，这其实并不是学生会，中文大约翻译成"学生政府"比较适合。它是一个很完整的机构，设有 president, vice president, secretaries, treasurer（有点像财政部长，负责管钱的，防止 student council 里的 president 出现经济犯罪）等职位（posts）。

【剑桥例句】

（1）They didn't have the authority to examine the company's records.

（2）We received several complaints about the noise.

（3）Teaching posts are advertised in Tuesday's edition of the paper.

下面这段简单的英文，可以让大家更深入地明白这个 student union 的 "ins and outs"，并且进一步领略"小词"在真实国外生活里的表现力。

Reasons to Run for Student Council

Student government might be a good activity for you if you:

- Like to bring about change.

- Would enjoy a career in politics.

- Enjoy planning events.

- Are outgoing and sociable.

- Have time to attend the meetings

Steps to run for student council:

- Read all the campaign rules carefully. They will differ from school to school.

- Make sure you meet academic requirements.

- Complete the application in a professional way. No messy handwriting or lazy answers. Teachers and advisors will be more supportive if they think that you are serious.

- You may be required to collect a number of signatures from fellow students, teachers, and administrators.

- Find a certain problem or policy that is meaningful to your classmates and make it part of your points. Create a catchy (=easy to remember) slogan.

- Find a friend who can help you create material. Just be sure to follow school rules.

- Prepare a campaign speech.

- Remember to play fair. Don't destroy, or cover over other students' campaign posters.

- Use the Internet and email in your campaign.

都是很简单的英文不是吗？如果对国外学校中的 student union 还想了解更多，请记

得一定要看看 *Election* 这部电影，Matthew Broderick 的表演绝对 phenomenal，Reese Witherspoon 演的 Tracy Flick 也真够强势的（pushy），而最神的（wacky）却是它让人没想到的结尾（unexpected ending）…

The Ultra-Short Track

　　刚开始在国外大学上课时，很多中国孩子都注意到国外的"叫兽"们布置各种论文时经常会明确地交待写论文需要遵守的 format（排版格式），但由于大家在国内时从未接触过这类英语经常会看不懂要求。而且近期的一道口语新题：**Describe something you did on a computer.** 也需要运用这方面的知识。www. baycongroup. com/tutorials. htm 是个在这方面很有用的网站，因为它提供了所有常见电脑软件英语操作的免费教程。点击 Word，Excel，PowerPoint，Macromedia Flash 8. 0 等之后就可以开始学习了。不仅可以用它来准备好这道考题，而且也可以为大家了解国外大学里常用的论文排版术语打下基础。

Day

激辩 Part 3
Don't let it become your Achilles' heel.

I talk of freedom

You talk of the flag

I talk of revolution

You'd rather brag

and as the final sunset rolls behind the earth

and the clock is finally dead

I'll look at you, you'll look at me

This will be what we said

Yes, this will be what we said

* *http://blog.ted.com/2010/06/17/audio_podcasts/* *

雅思口语 Part 3 的话题比较正式,并且经常要求权衡利弊、对比今昔或者展望未来,甚至和雅思写作的某些话题已有相似之处。而且,口语 Part 3 的用词也要比 Part 1 和 Part 2 更加正式,像 involve(涉及到),participate in(参与)等写作常用词同样也是雅思口语 Part 3 里的"神器"(详见 p.345)。同时,您还应该经常登陆本页上方的这个 TED 网站。这些录音文件几乎已经覆盖了 Part 3 的所有常见话题,而且 TED talks 的用词风格也很接近 Part 3 高分答案的用词风格,认真听吧。

* *http://www.bbc.co.uk/worldservice/learningenglish/general/sixminute/* *

与 Part 1 和 Part 2 不同,IELTS 口语的 Part 3 很少涉及你个人的"私生活",而是更加关注社区、城市、社会、国家甚至国际层面上的问题。BBC 著名的"6 Minute English"也为烤鸭们提供了准备口语 Part 3 的好工具,而且全都是用标准英音讲的,尽情地模仿发音也不需要担心"走火入魔",对略有难度的词还很绅士地给出了注释,连查字典的时间都省了。

▶ *We take the test very seriously, but we'll take a laid-back approach to it.*

准备 Part 3 应该做什么？

"趴睡"（Part 3）的任务是集中考查考生进行讨论（discussion）的能力，我们必须给予足够的重视。同时，Part 3 也是有明显的规律可循的。我们今天就从题型、用词和句式等方面深入地研究怎样回答好口语 Part 3。

Part 3 的高分答案长什么样

Part 3 是深入讨论，所以答案通常会比 Part 1 部分的答案要长一些。从答案的结构来说，通常是：

（1）明确地回答考官提出的问题；

（2）具体展开。展开时既可以使用 because, so, for example, such as, like（比如⋯⋯），if, and, also, even 等逻辑关系词（如果不确定用法请您及时复习 Day 4 和 Day 5），也可以使用 they, I, we, it, that 等代词，或者再次使用前一句话里已经使用过的关键词，都可以实现句子之间流畅、自然的衔接。

请看《剑 10》Test 3 里的"趴睡"高分答案：

> **How important do you think spending time together is for the relationships between parents and children?**
>
> It's extremely important. Spending time together helps parents and children build strong family bonds. For example, doing housework together gives them the chance to help each other. And when they eat meals together, they can have conversations and share ideas and opinions. Things like playing sports together and going on holiday together are also great ways to build good family relationships.

再来看《剑 10》Test 1 的 Part 3 高分答案：

> **Which kinds of jobs have the highest salaries in your country? Why is this?**
>
> The CEOs and managers of large companies get the highest salaries in my country. They work hard and help their companies make huge profits. Their high salaries are a reward for their hard work and contribution to their companies.

《剑 10》Test 1 的 Part 3 还对上面的问题进行了无耻的"追问",但只要英语清楚、流畅,咱们就能对严刑拷打泰然处之。

> **Are there any other jobs that you think should have high salaries?**
>
> Yes, I think there are. Primary school and secondary school teachers should also be well paid. They work for the good of society and they help children and teenagers develop important skills, such as reading skills, writing skills and maths skills. I believe they should earn more than they do now.

《剑 10》Test 2 里面的这个 Part 3 问题不谈国家和社会,但与社区有关:

> **Do you think local businesses are important for a neighbourhood?**
>
> Yes, they're very important. Local businesses make life more convenient for people who live in the neighbourhood. They also create jobs for local people and give local people a strong sense of community. For example, many people like to meet their friends at local cafés.

再请看《剑 9》Test 3 的 Part 3 高分答案:

> **Can travel make a positive difference to the economy of a country?**
>
> Yes, it can because travellers spend money on accommodation, food and transport. That also helps to creates jobs in the transport, entertainment and service industries, which can contribute to the economy of a country as well.

可见,与轻松活泼的口试 Part 1 答案相比,Part 3 的高分答案已经有点儿"写作"的味道(当然还不像 IELTS Writing 那么正式)。

下面这道《剑 9》Test 4 的 Part 3 考题则考到了社区和人民政府:

> **Who do you think should pay for the services that are available to the people in a community? Should it be the government or individual people?**
>
> I think that really depends on what kind of services they are. If the services can benefit most people in a community, like the community library and local school,

then <u>they</u> should be paid for by the government. <u>On the other hand</u>, community services like children's summer camps and art classes should be paid for by individual people <u>because</u> many community members don't use <u>these</u> services.

下面这道《剑 9》Test 2 Part 3 的考题要求你进行"心理分析",但你根本不必挖空心思去想弗洛伊德怎么说,能多少讲出点道理就已经不错了,只要英语表述得清楚、流利就成,牢记 IELTS 的本质永远是一个语言考试。

Why do you think some people like doing new things?

That's <u>because</u> doing new things is more fun than doing the same old things all the time, <u>which</u> is boring. When people do new things, they feel challenged and excited. It's almost like an adventure. <u>And</u> doing new things <u>also</u> leads to opportunities to learn new skills.

我们再来看更多的 Part 3 高分答案实例:

Why do many people like going to concerts?

I suppose there're different reasons for different people. Some people want to experience good music first-hand. Others want to get closer to the musicians they like. There're <u>also</u> people <u>who</u> go to rock concerts just to make friends.

与《剑 10》Test 3 的 Part 3 一样,下面这道题也是考父母和孩子之间的关系:

Do you think parents should help their children make decisions?

Yes, they should. Parents have more experience than their children and they know their children very well, <u>so</u> they can usually give their children sound advice. <u>But</u> I also think it's important that parents don't make decisions for their children.

对于需要口语 7 分的同学来说,今天后面您即将学到的"290 个 Part 3 高分词汇"可以满足回答 Part 3 问题的全部用词需求,而且对您今后的海外留学经历也将颇有裨益。

有效提高 Part 3 实力的 6 步
（A Six-step Approach to Success in Part 3）

A　回答"比较区别类"的题目有哪些必备句型？

　　为了把比较题准备熟练，请一定熟记下列句型，但是每组最多只要记 **1～2** 句即可，"大牛"们看看就行，自己能说最好。

There're a couple of differences between them.

There're several of differences between them.

I would say there are a lot of differences between them.

It seems to me like they are totally different.

The main differences are...

　　如果你真感觉考官让你比较的两种东西根本"风马牛不相及"，英文怎么说呢？那么请用地道的英文告诉他/她你的这种感觉，然后再讨论，"That's like comparing apples and oranges." 像这样有针对性的评价是具有沟通的实际意义的，而非 Pat 在国内见到过的大量"自说自话"的口语模板。我们在 Day 1 里已经综合了多位真实剑桥考官的看法，充分证明了考官们的核心任务是测试你的英语。你完全可以有和考官不一致的看法，但却不可以没有能力用英语去表达自己的看法。

接下来给出第一点区别的常用语：

The main one is...

The most fundamental one is...

The most important one is...

The most obvious one is...

Unlike..., ...

Compared with..., ...

接下来给出第二点区别的常用语：

Besides, ...

Apart from that, ...

A second difference would be... (请注意这里不要说 The second difference...)

> 另外，我们在 Day 4 里学过的 while / by contrast 这样的连词也可以用在对两种事物的描述句中间，表示这两种事物的对比。这些词组的语气用在 Part 3 相当合适，并不会显得过于正式，请放心使用。

Note:

对于"今昔对比"或者"展望未来"（比较 现在 vs 过去，或者比较 现在 vs 将来）的考题，一定要特别注意过去、现在和将来的时态变化。而且，您将会发现下面的词组也很有用。

In the past, ...

Traditionally, ...

People used to...

In the future, ...

Maybe in the future, ...

It's very likely that people will...

These days,

Today,

Now,

Currently, ...

回答 Part 3 里的"比较区别类"考题经常会用到形容词比较级。在 Part 1 和 Part 2 里面，如果要修饰一个形容词的比较级来表示"远远更……"，我们可以用 much / far / a lot 等 + 形容词比较级的结构，比如 much stronger, far more expensive, a lot better 等。

但在口语的 Part 3 里，你完全可以再试试 significantly + 形容词比较级（如果要用那么考前就得多练几次 significantly 的发音，以确保舌头不会"转筋"）。比如 significantly stronger / significantly more expensive / significantly better 等等，都会让你的答案"远远更"接近 Part 3 的用词风格。☺

[**英美实例**] Adults with kids are significantly more stressed than adults without kids.

如果感觉考官要求比较的两方其实真的很相似，那么也完全可以用下面的句型如实回答：

Actually, they have a lot in common.

Well, it seems to me like they are very similar.

Honestly, I don't think there's much difference between them.

> 描述将来的目标常会用到一个动词：
>
> fulfill（实现）：
>
> e. g. fulfill their dreams / fulfill our potential（潜力）/ fulfill their promise / fulfill their responsibilities

B　回答 causes / Why 原因类问题应该熟悉的句型

要求仍然是每组最多知道 1~2 句就好了。

That's because...

The main reason is that...

There're several causes of this trend.

Several factors contribute to...（请您注意地道英文里的 contribute to 并不一定是"做贡献"的意思，它的后面也完全可以跟负面的现象）

I believe a number of factors are involved here.

As a result, ...

As a consequence, ...

Pat指南

回答原因类题目有三个很常用的词组：

☆ **to the best of my knowledge** 和 **as far as I know** 这两个词组可以帮助你适度缓解谈

论你不太了解原因的现象时的无助感：

e. g. Hmm, **to the best of my knowledge**, those languages are dying out because of the spread of English.

☆ **is closely linked to** 这个词组可以表示"（某个现象）与……联系密切"

e. g. The 2007 financial crisis（金融危机）**was closely linked to** the subprime loans（次贷）.

C 回答"solutions/How should…?"类问题的常用句型

Solving the problem requires（需要）…

Solving the problem calls for（需要）…

To solve this problem, … should…

Some measures can be taken to tackle the problem.

The most effective way to tackle（解决）this problem would be…

Pat指南

回答解决方法类问题一个极度好用（但国内同学们基本从来不用）的句型是：Ideally, … **But in reality**, …（理想状态应该是……可实际上……）。听到你这么真诚（sincere），考官也会是一声叹息（sigh with sympathy）。

例：**Ideally**, all cars should be eliminated from this world because they are causing so many problems for us. **But in reality**, the number of cars just keeps increasing.

类似功能的地道英文句型还有两个，一旦有机会准确用到，必定拿分：

（1）**In theory**, … **But in practice**, …

（2）**Ideally**, … **But in practice**, …

D 回答 advantages 常用的词汇和句型

在 Part 3 的答案里，一旦考到 advantages 就必然要多次用到此含义，所以 advantages 可以适当地用 benefits 替换，以避免重复用词。

下列句型经常用来回答和 advantages 有关的问题：

Clearly, the advantages include...

The main advantage is...

The most obvious benefit is...

E　回答 disadvantages 类考题我们经常需要用下面的词汇和句型

如果感觉您的答案里 disadvantages 出现得过于频繁，可以用 drawbacks 来替换。

下面的句型可能会有用的（come in handy）：

There're some disadvantages.

A possible drawback is...

The main problem is...

The main concern is...

F　口语 Part 3 必备的高分词汇

☆ 这个词汇表里的多数单词其实大家都已经认识了，但是不一定会想到去用。对于确实想说出有一定复杂程度答案的考生，花些时间熟悉这些词汇是一定不会让你后悔的。

☆ 对口语词汇来说熟练特别重要，如果只是像 reading 的词汇那样看见之后才认识的单词在口试里面是一点用处都没有的。熟练掌握词汇最好的方法就是多复习并且积极地使用。Keep in mind that if you see a word three times in your life, it's yours forever.

☆ 即使在第三部分难词也不要用得太多。这些加分词汇在回答 Part 3 问题时，如果能用到 5~8 个，你的 Part 3 答案就已经有绝对足够的难度了。

☆ 过去 8 天学过的 good words & phrases 还可以继续用，这些词只是对您现有词汇的继续补充。

Pat 归纳的 290 个 Part 3 拿分词汇 (7 分词汇)

290 Words That Can Help You Build a More Powerful Vocabulary for Part 3

1	abstract	*adj.*	抽象的 (回答和 art 有关的题目用, 反义词是 concrete／realistic)
2	abuse／mistreat	*v.*	虐待
3	accurate	*adj.*	准确的
4	achieve	*v.*	完成, 实现 ≈fulfill
5	acid rain		酸雨
6	acquaintance	*n.*	认识的人 (感情色彩上没有 friend 那么亲近)
7	adopt	*v.*	采用, 采纳 (在 Part 3 里面表示接受某种方法、采用某种技术或者采纳某种生活方式时经常使用 adopt)
8	a double-edged sword		这个应该不用解释了吧, 写作里面用这个表示有利有弊太恶俗了, 但在口试里面它还是一个实用的表达
9	affluent	*adj.*	有钱的 ≈wealthy (在 Part 3 里指贫困的人们也可以委婉地说 people in need)
10	a healthy diet		健康的饮食
11	ambience	*n.*	气氛, 氛围 (Part 3 中经常用来代替 atmosphere)
12	ancestors	*n.*	祖先 (这个词一般用复数)
13	animal rights		动物权益
14	approach	*n.*	做某事的方法、解决某个问题的途径 (Part 3 中很多时候可以代替 method)
15	appropriate	*adj.*	恰当的, 合适的 ≈proper
16	approximately	*adv.*	大约
17	aspirations	*n.*	志向, 理想 ≈ambitions
18	attempt	*v. & n.*	努力尝试 ≈ effort
19	attractive	*adj.*	有吸引力的, 吸引人的
20	available	*adj.*	可以使用的, 可以利用的 (如果要说能够利用某种资源, 则使用短语 have access to…)

（续表）

21	avoid	v.	避免（后面跟 noun / verb-ing，但是不要说 avoid to do sth.）
22	backstabbing	n.	出卖朋友（经常用来回答 friends 类题目，"为朋友两肋插刀"英文则是 would give you the shirt off his back）
23	barrier	n.	障碍
24	be concerned about		关注（后面跟某种不太好的事情，Part 3 中很多时候可以代替 pay attention to）
25	behavior	n.	行为（经常在说 children 时用到）
26	biased	adj.	有偏见的（描述 media 时常用）
27	blockbuster	n.	大片儿
28	boost	v.	提升，促进（可以跟 efficiency / the standard of living / economy 等等）
29	budget	n.	预算（紧张的预算叫作 a tight budget）
30	burden	n.	负担
31	candidate	n.	候选人
32	career path		职业的发展道路
33	casual	adj.	随意的，休闲的（比如 casual clothing，说某人很随意的则可以用 easygoing 或者 laid-back）
34	celebrate	v.	庆祝
35	celebrity	n.	名人 ≈famous people
36	characteristics	n.	特征（这个词很常用但是发音比较有挑战，如果练习多次还是搞不定那就忘了它吧，或者改说 features）
37	charities	n.	慈善组织（这个词多数时候用复数）
38	cherish	v.	珍视，珍惜（在 Part 3 里 value 也经常被用作及物动词，表示很重视某事物）
39	chronic / persistent	adj.	长期存在的（后面跟某种坏现象，比如 pollution，poverty）

（续表）

40	clash	*n.*	冲突（性格不同导致的冲突可以叫作 personality clashes）
41	cloning	*n.*	克隆
42	combine	*v.*	结合，更正式的说法则是 integrate
43	commonly-used	*adj.*	被广泛使用的（经常跟某种工具或者语言）
44	communicate with		沟通，交流
45	community	*n.*	社区，经常会和 individuals（个人）一起用到
46	compete	*v.*	竞争（极度常用，和反义词 cooperate 合作都要背熟）
47	complicated / complex	*adj.*	复杂的
48	comprehensive	*adj.*	广泛的，覆盖面广的
49	computer-savvy	*adj.*	精通电脑的，（...-savvy 都是精通……的）
50	concentrate on / focus on		集中在……上面
51	confident	*adj.*	自信的（名词 self-confidence 自信和 self-esteem 自尊也很常用）
52	consequence	*n.*	后果，结果（Part 3 中经常用来代替 result）
53	conservative	*adj.*	保守的（也可以作名词当保守派讲，对比 the elderly / young people 常用）
54	constantly	*adv.*	持续不断地（Part 3 中经常用来代替 always）
55	contemplate	*v.*	考虑（Part 3 中很多题目可以用来代替 consider）
56	conversation	*n.*	谈话（比 chat 适用范围更广，不管轻松的还是严肃的谈话都可以叫 conversations）
57	corruption	*n.*	腐败
58	cultural heritage		文化遗产（有时也说 national heritage）
59	curious	*adj.*	好奇的（+ about something）
60	customs	*n.*	风俗习惯（经常和 traditions 一起用）

（续表）

61	cut down on / curtail	*v.*	削减
62	decorate	*v.*	装饰（名词为 decoration，回答建筑题目时也很常用）
63	delightful	*adj.*	令人高兴的
64	democratic	*adj.*	民主的
65	desirable	*adj.*	好的，积极的，值得拥有的（在 Part 3 里形容事物时，这个词很多时候可以用来代替 good，"贼"好用）
66	determine	*v.*	决定（很多时候可以代替 decide）
67	detrimental	*adj.*	这个词略显正式，但在 Part 3 里可以代替 harmful 这个词
68	devastating	*adj.*	毁灭性的（语气比上面的 detrimental 强十倍，经常用来说 environmental issues）
69	digital	*adj.*	数码的
70	disabled	*adj.*	残疾的（中国同学们常用的 handicapped people 在英美常会被认为带有不敬之意，而 disabled people 则是当代英文里指残疾人时真正常用的说法）
71	discipline	*n.*	纪律（self-discipline 自制力）
72	discover	*v.*	发现（名词：discovery）
73	dishonest	*adj.*	不诚实的
74	distracting	*adj.*	形成干扰的，构成干扰的
75	distraction	*n.*	干扰（动词是 distract sb. from...，减少干扰则是 reduce distractions）
76	domestic	*adj.*	国内的（反义词是 international）
77	durable	*adj.*	耐用的（经常说某种工具）
78	dynamic	*adj.*	很有活力的（= vibrant）
79	eco-friendly	*adj.*	有益于生态保护的（the ecosystem 是生态系统）
80	economical	*adj.*	省钱的

（续表）

81	economy	*n.*	经济（一定要区分这三个词：economy 经济，economic 和经济有关的，economical 省钱的）
82	effective	*adj.*	有效果的，效果好的
83	efficient	*adj.*	效率高的
84	electronic	*adj.*	电子的
85	eliminate	*v.*	消除（后面经常跟 poverty 或者某种 barrier）
86	embarrassed	*adj.*	不好意思的，感到丢脸的
87	encourage	*v.*	鼓励（经常用来回答 children 有关的题目，它的名词 encouragement，以及形容词 encouraging 也很常用）
88	encouragement	*n.*	鼓励（经常在回答和 children 有关的题目时用到）
89	enigmatic	*adj.*	神秘的 ≈ mysterious
90	enjoyment	*n.*	享受，乐趣 ≈ pleasure
91	entertaining	*adj.*	娱乐性强的
92	entire = whole / entirely = wholly	*adj.*	Part 3 的 whole 和 wholly / completely 经常可以用 entire / entirely 代替
93	equality	*n.*	平等（形容词当然是 equal）
94	essential	*adj.*	非常重要的（Part 3 里代替 important 很棒）
95	establish	*v.*	建立（Part 3 中解决方法类题目的一个常用句型是 establish a mechanism for... 建立……的机制）
96	establishment	*n.*	这个词在 Part 3 的讨论里非常常用，基本上等于中文的"专用于某一特定社会用途的场所"，比如 entertainment establishments, business establishments, retail establishments, 真可惜我们的考生在 Part 3 里面用得太少了
97	an exception		一个例外
98	exchange	*v.*	交换（+ ideas / thoughts）
99	exhaust fumes		汽车尾气（可以用复数）
100	exhausting	*adj.*	让人筋疲力尽的（可以说 sports / work）

101	experience sth. vicariously		间接地去体验某事物（经常用来回答和 media 或者 future 有关的题目）
102	experienced	*adj.*	有经验的（经常用来描述谁给你 advice 的题目）
103	experiment	*n.*	实验（scientific experiments 科学实验）
104	expert	*n.*	专家
105	explore	*v.*	探索（说 traveling 或者 future）
106	extended family		几代人合住的大家庭
107	exterior	*n.*	外观（Part 3 里面经常用来回答与建筑相关的题）
108	extravagant	*adj.*	奢侈的（这个词很不错，但如果实在记不住那就说 posh，意思差不多但是更口语化）
109	facilities	*n.*	设施，这个词多数时候用复数，注意和 equipment（设备）区分，一般来说 equipment 规模体积比较小
110	factor	*n.*	因素（关键因素叫 key factors）
111	family bonds		（名词短语）亲情
112	family reunion		（名词短语）家庭团聚（常用来说 festivals）
113	fast-paced lifestyle		（名词短语）快节奏的生活方式
114	fireworks	*n.*	焰火（回答跟 festivals 有关的题目时常用，啪啪响的鞭炮叫 firecrackers，燃放焰火或者鞭炮叫 set off fireworks / firecrackers）
115	flexible	*adj.*	灵活的，机动的（反义词：rigid 僵硬的，无法变通的）
116	freedom	*n.*	自由
117	frugal	*adj.*	俭朴的（回答与老人相关问题时常用）
118	frustrated	*adj.*	失望的，沮丧的（名词是 frustration）
119	fulfill	*v.*	实现，完成，发挥
120	function	*n.*	功能（在 Part 3 里泛指某事物的功能时 functionality 是一个比较"唬人"的词，近年来在英美也比较火）

（续表）

121	generation gap		代沟（回答 the elderly / children 的题目时极度常用）
122	genetic engineering		基因工程
123	genetically-modified food		转基因食品
124	global warming		全球变暖
125	gradually	*adv.*	逐渐地
126	green	*adj.*	这个形容词在西方已经成了"eco-friendly"的同义词，非常常用
127	greenhouse effect		温室效应
128	guidelines	*n.*	指导原则
129	habitat	*n.*	动物的栖息地
130	handle	*v.*	处理，解决
131	harmonious	*adj.*	和谐的（名词是 harmony）
132	have a yearning for	*v.*	非常渴望得到……≈be dying for
133	risk / danger	*n.*	风险/危险
134	health-conscious	*adj.*	关注健康的，健康意识很强的
135	homeless（people）		无家可归的（人们）
136	hone …skills	*adj.*	有效地锻炼某种技能，例如 hone children's leadership skills, hone students' academic skills 等等
137	identify	*v.*	确认，确定，找出（Part 3 里很多句子中可以代替 find）
138	ignore / overlook	*v.*	忽视
139	illegal	*adj.*	非法的，违法的
140	imitate	*v.*	模仿……（经常在说到 children 的时候用到）
141	immediately	*adv.*	立刻 = right away
142	impair	*v.*	后面只能跟 health 或者身体的某种机能，其他的"破坏"不要用这个词

（续表）

143	an incentive		能让人去积极地从事某事的激励物
144	inconvenient	*adj.*	不方便的
145	independent	*adj.*	独立的（反义词是 dependent 依赖的，become overly dependent on 则是指过度依赖于某事物，在 Part 3 里也很常用）
146	indispensable	*adj.*	不可或缺的
147	inferior	*adj.*	劣质的，落后的
148	influential	*adj.*	有影响力的
149	information highway		Part 3 很多时候用来代替 the Internet
150	informative	*adj.*	信息量大的（说 media 时常用）
151	ingredients	*n.*	原料，聊 food 时常用
152	inhumane	*adj.*	不人道的（经常用来回答和 animals 有关的题目）
153	integrity	*n.*	正直的品格
154	intelligent	*adj.*	聪明的
155	interaction	*n.*	交流，互动（很多时候可以代替 communication）
156	interactive	*adj.*	互动的（很多时候可以描述未来的工具）
157	isolated	*adj.*	孤立的（说 globalization 或者 individuals 话题时常用）
158	lack	*v. & n.*	缺乏
159	massive layoffs		大规模的裁员
160	layout	*n.*	布局（说建筑、城市或者 media 题目时常用）
161	introduce legislation to …		通过立法来……（基本就是 pass laws to 的严肃版了）
162	loyal	*adj.*	忠实的（经常在回答与 friends 有关的题目时用）
163	malnutrition	*n.*	营养不良
164	media hype	*n.*	媒体的炒作
165	metropolitan area / metropolis (*formal*)	*n.*	大都市

（续表）

166	misleading	*adj.*	有误导性的
167	monitor	*v.*	监督
168	multimedia	*adj.*	多媒体的
169	natural habitats	*n.*	动植物的自然栖息地，毁坏动植物的自然栖息地英文就叫 destroy natural habitats
170	natural resources	*n.*	自然资源
171	non-governmental organisations（NGOs）		在英美很重要的一个概念，非政府组织，很多国际问题的解决，包括 environmental issues, poverty reduction 减轻贫困等等都需要 NGOs 的努力
172	normally	*adv.*	通常
173	nostalgic	*adj.*	怀旧的（经常用来回答与 photos 有关的问题）
174	nuclear family		只有父母和孩子的小家庭（反义词是 extended family, 好几代人住一起的大家庭）
175	nutritious	*adj.*	有营养的
176	obligation	*n.*	Part 3 中经常代替 responsibility
177	obtain	*v.*	获得（Part 3 中经常代替 get）
178	obvious	*adj.*	明显的 ≈ evident
179	occupation	*n.*	职业（注意和 employment 就业的区别，就业机会要说 employment / job opportunities）
180	offender / criminal	*n.*	罪犯
181	old-fashioned	*adj.*	（形式）老式的；（观念）过时的
182	opportunity	*n.*	机会
183	optimistic	*adj.*	乐观的（反义词是 pessimistic 悲观的）
184	option	*n.*	选择（Part 3 里代替 choice 的好选择）
185	organised	*adj.*	说事物是指"整齐的，有秩序的"，说人是指"做事有条理的"
186	overweight	*adj.*	肥胖的，超重的

（续表）

187	ozone layer		大气臭氧层（ozone layer depletion 是固定短语，指对于大气臭氧层的破坏）
188	paparazzi	*n.*	（复数名词）狗仔队
189	parenting	*n.*	家庭教育（反义词是 schooling 学校教育）
190	participate in		参与 ≈ take part in
191	pastime	*n.*	业余爱好（Part 3 里经常可以代替 hobby）
192	pattern	*n.*	模式（当表示"模式"时它远比 model 更拿分）
193	peers	*n.*	同龄人
194	pessimistic	*adj.*	悲观的
195	performance	*n.*	表演（但 academic performance 则是指学业表现）
196	personalised	*adj.*	个性化的，专为个人设计的
197	poisonous / toxic	*adj.*	有毒的
198	policy	*n.*	政策
199	portable	*adj.*	方便携带的，便携的（反义词是笨重的 bulky /ˈbʌlki/）
200	potential	*n.*	潜力（也可以作形容词，"潜在的"）
201	poverty	*n.*	贫困
202	practical	*adj.*	实际的，实用的
203	precious / valuable	*adj.*	珍贵的，宝贵的
204	preference	*n.*	偏好，偏爱的东西（personal preference 个人偏好）
205	preserve	*v.*	保护（后面可以跟资源、建筑、文化传统等等）
206	pretentious	*adj.*	爱慕虚荣的，浮华的（反义词：down-to-earth 务实的）
207	prevent	*v.*	防止（prevent sb. from doing sth. 或者 prevent sth.）
208	primary / principal	*adj.*	首要的，最主要的
209	prior to...		（时间上）在……之前发生，Part 3 里很多时候可以代替 before

（续表）

210	priority	*n.*	首要任务
211	process	*n.*	过程
212	is / are proficient in...		对于……（填入某种技能）掌握得很熟练地，在 Part 3 谈技能或教育问题时特别好用
213	promote	*v.*	促进
214	psychological	*adj.*	心理的（对比：physical 身体的）
215	radiation	*n.*	辐射
216	rare	*adj.*	稀有的，珍稀的
217	real-time communication	*n.*	实时交流（比如 Skype、QQ 都是）
218	recipe	*n.*	某个菜的做法（e. g. a recipe for hot and sour soup）
219	recreation / leisure	*n.*	休闲
220	recycle	*v.*	循环使用（经常用在跟 environment 有关的答案里）
221	reflect	*v.*	反映出
222	regulate	*v.*	（政府）对某事物进行严格监管
223	relieve	*v.*	减轻（后面可以跟 traffic congestion, poverty 或者 stress 等等）
224	repercussions	*n.*	造成的广泛影响，尤其常指负面影响（Part 3 里经常可以代替 negative impact）
225	replace	*v.*	代替（经常用来回答 future 和 Western culture / Chinese culture 的题目）
226	represent	*v.*	代表，体现
227	reputation	*n.*	名誉，声望
228	require	*v.*	需要（Part 3 里当主语是事物的时候这个词可以替换 need）
229	retirement	*n.*	退休（动词为 retire）

（续表）

230	reward	*v.*	奖励，回报（它的形容词 rewarding "给人回报的" 也很常用）
231	ridiculous	*adj.*	荒唐的，荒谬的 ≈absurd
232	rules and regulations		这两个词经常可以连在一起说，表示"规章制度"
233	a safety net		一个保护网，注意这个短语在 Part 3 里经常是讨论政府为公众提供的福利（benefits / welfare）时使用
234	satisfy the need of / meet the need of...		满足……的要求或需要
235	scandal	*n.*	丑闻（经常用来回答和 media 或者 famous people 有关的题目）
236	schedule	*n.*	时间安排，时间表
237	seek	*v.*	寻求
238	seniors / the elderly	*n.*	老年人
239	separate	*adj.*	单独的，分开的（副词形式是 separately）
240	settle	*v.*	Part 3 里表示解决某种分歧很常用，例如 settle the dispute, settle the differences
241	shortage	*n.*	短缺 ≈scarcity
242	siblings	*n.*	一个人的兄弟姐妹的总称
243	significant → essential → vital	*adj.*	三个词的语气一个比一个强，基本等于是 important → very important → extremely important
244	sleep-deprived	*adj.*	睡眠不足的
245	snobbish	*adj.*	势利的（贬义词）
246	social networking website		社交网站
247	sources of energy / energy sources		能源（alternative energy sources 替代性能源，例如 wind power, solar energy 等）
248	souvenir	*n.*	纪念品
249	spacious	*adj.*	宽敞的

（续表）

250	species	*n.*	物种（注意它的复数也是 species），濒危物种 endangered species
251	staff	*n.*	员工（需要注意这个词是员工的总称，一般不加复数，员工个人叫 staff members）
252	standard of living		生活水平
253	staple food	*n.*	主食
254	state-of-the-art	*adj.*	先进的，尖端的（在当代英美日常口语里这个词和 art 其实没有关系，反倒是经常被用来形容尖端的科技或者设备）
255	status symbol	*n.*	身份地位的标志（比如 Mercedes，奔驰其实可以这么说）
256	steady	*adj.*	稳定的
257	stressful	*adj.*	压力大的
258	strive for		努力争取……（后面加名词）
259	sufficient	*adj.*	足够的（在 Part 3 经常用来代替 enough）
260	subsidize	*v.*	补贴（经常用来说 government 话题）
261	sympathy	*n.*	同情心
262	tabloid	*n.*	小报儿（回答 famous people 相关问题时常用）
263	tackle	*v.*	解决（可以代替 solve）
264	target / objective	*n.*	目标
265	tax revenue		税收
266	taxpayer	*n.*	纳税人（在西方 tax 是非常重要的概念 Only two things in life are certain: tax and death.）
267	temptation	*n.*	诱惑（resist the temptation 抵抗诱惑）
268	tension	*n.*	紧张感（也可以描述国家间的关系）
269	population boom		人口激增 （人口过量则是 overpopulation）
270	the unemployment rate		失业率

（续表）

271	throughout	*prep.*	它在口语 Part 3 里经常可以用来表示时间上从头至尾、或者方位上遍及各处，而且特别强调"绝无例外"，注意它的后面跟名词或者名词短语（例如：throughout the building, throughout the country, throughout history, throughout the year 等）
272	time-consuming	*adj.*	非常耗时的
273	traffic congestion		交通堵塞
274	tranquil and serene		宁静的，安静的 ≈ peaceful
275	typical	*adj.*	典型的
276	undermine	*v.*	破坏（后面跟抽象的概念，比如 the relations between countries，但对具体物品的破坏不要用这个词）
277	unethical	*adj.*	不道德的
278	unwind	*v.*	≈ relax（请注意听音频文件中 unwind 的发音）
279	user-friendly	*adj.*	（产品）便于使用的
280	values	*n.*	价值观（复数名词，经常用来对比 the past 和 the present）
281	vehicle	*n.*	交通工具
282	veterinarians（vets）	*n.*	兽医（这个词要能听懂，在去年底的考题里出现过）
283	victim	*n.*	受害者
284	violate	*v.*	侵犯（后面常跟 privacy, the law 或者 rights）
285	offensive language, violence or sexual images		（媒体里的）侮辱性的语言、暴力或者色情画面
286	virtual reality		虚拟现实（很多时候回答与 future 有关的题目会用到一些 virtual-reality equipment）
287	virtue	*n.*	美德

（续表）

288	westernised	*adj.*	西方化的
289	worthwhile	*adj.*	值得的，它是一个很常用的形容词，请对比：worthless 毫无价值的
290	yet another		又一个，再一个，经常在 Part 3 用来引出另一个原因或者解决方案，比如 This is yet another reason why we should be cautious（谨慎的）。

Pat 指南

下面的四个名词在 Part 3 中经常用到，如果用到一定不要加复数，因为它们都是不可数名词：knowledge，research，equipment 和 information。

超短线
The Ultra-Short Track

对于时间紧却面对 L. R. W. S 四座大山的考生们来说，如果实在找不出时间去充分准备 the Speaking Test 的 Part 3 了，那么至少要好好听听剑 4 ~ 剑 10 官方真题里每套 Listening 的 Section 4 吧，您会发现它的语言风格酷似口语 Part 3 的答案。例如剑桥官方真题里这个关于 recycling 的段子的和近期口语 Part 3 中关于 recycling 的考题何其相似：

This high quality comes at a cost in terms of the waste produced during the process. Plastic causes problems because there're so many different types of plastic in use today，and each one has to be dealt with differently. One of the most successful activities is recycling plastic bottles to make containers which are used all over the country.

其中标出颜色的部分全都是我们在本书里学过的高分口语表达。

或者如果您连通过听力 Section 4 来提高口语 Part 3 的时间都没了，那么最后的一道防线就是直接利用你的 Writing 基础来准备口语 Part 3 的问题。虽然这两个考试还真有不少话题是相似的，比如 Environment，Animals，Culture，Government 等，但全凭写作功底回答出来的 Part 3 会显得有点过于正式了，所以只可以作为 last resort 的不得已之选。

Day 10

黯然消魂者
Never Say Farewell.
Say Bye.

The play is done; the curtain drops
Slow falling to the prompter's bell
A moment yet the actor stops
And looks around to say farewell

最后一天了。

江淹的《别赋》说："黯然消魂者，唯别而已矣。"

其实除了离别，还有 10 个口语的超难卡片题，也是一样消魂的，留到最后一天来强势推出。不过在正式启动前，先给大家吃点镇静剂（tranquilizer）吧。

今天（上）部分我们要看的 10 个题，难度都只有★☆☆☆☆甚至只有 0 星。这 10 个题也是最近常考的话题，包括近期常考的 a good law 的话题，而且把它们搬到其他题目去也相当容易搬。想展示给大家的是：即使是简单得让人难以置信的词句，也能描述清楚很难的话题。

这就是——口语 10 大弱智卡片题。

（上）雅思口语卡片 10 大弱智话题

1. Describe an occasion（场合）that you were late for. / Describe a traffic jam. 一次迟到的场合/一次交通堵塞

I'm going to talk about a job interview I was late for. A couple of days ago, I got an email from a company, inviting me to an on-site job interview. I applied for that job last month and really hoped I could get it. At first I felt excited. But then I got nervous. I slept little that night. So the next morning, I woke up late, like 8:30 or something. They asked me to get to the company at 9 am. In a great hurry, I took a taxi and told the driver to drive as fast as possible. But there was a serious traffic jam then in the city and we got stuck in traffic. We moved so slowly I got totally mad. I yelled at (=shout something in an angry manner) the driver but he told me there was really nothing he could do about it. I had no choice but to call the hiring manager of that company and told him that I would probably be late for the interview and really felt sorry about it. To my surprise, that gentleman was so nice and calm and told me not to worry about it. They would just wait for me. He even asked me to tell the taxi driver to drive safely. Finally I got there and had the job interview. I answered all their questions about myself and about my past experience very fluently and clearly. They were impressed by all my answers and... I got the job! I was totally excited. That experience was really special because I felt I was lucky. But looking back, I guess I should have said sorry to that taxi driver. I shouldn't have become mad at him although I would be late for an important occasion.

2. Describe an interesting subject.
一个有趣的科目

Let me talk about my favourite subject — English. I'm fond of this subject for a couple of reasons. The primary is that it helps me understand the Western culture better. English abilities enable me to read English novels, to understand Hollywood movies and even to appreciate English songs. Another reason I like this subject is that English is a beautiful language and I really enjoy the pronunciation of the words and their spelling as well. Most importantly, English helps me make more friends. There are tons of English learners in my university. We often chat with each other in English and we sometimes read English books and magazines together, which is really fun.

I learn this language primarily through the help of my English teachers. They are nice and patient. They often organise discussions in class. Through these activities, we get more used to speaking this foreign language and thinking in English. I also listen to English songs to practice my listening ability. Watching Hollywood movies helps me a lot as well. These days, if you can't speak English, it's hard for you to get a job in big cities in China and I guess that's another reason why I spend so much time learning this language.

3. Describe an important decision. / Describe an important conversation.
一个重大的决定 / 一次重要的谈话

Well, I guess the biggest decision I've made so far was the decision to go abroad.

Actually, it was a very tough decision for me because things in my life had been pretty organised (= well-planned) before I decided to go study in a British / an Australian university. You know, I was studying in a top university in China back then. And I had tons of friends here in China. I was sure I would miss them a lot if I went abroad. But the problem at that time was that I felt bored with all those things. My life was in a rut (=a situation that never changed) and I just wanted to get out of it. I felt it was time for a change. I hoped I could experience something new and exciting, maybe a different culture. So I just asked my parents and my friends for advice. My parents had an hour-long conversation with me and they were obviously concerned about me. They thought it wouldn't be worth it if I give up a steady (=dependable) path of life simply because I wanted a change. And they were worried that I would feel lonely if I were so far away from them. Some friends of mine were also against my plan because they thought I would have to make a lot of effort for it and lose many things. But I was determined to pursue my dream (=to make my dream come true). No one could talk me out of it. I started preparing for the IELTS test and went to the university English corner every weekend to improve my spoken English. I also read English novels to practice my reading skills. Little by little, I felt my English was getting better. This decision is really important because I'm sure it changed my life positively. As for the conversations I had with my parents and friends, of course they just wanted to help me but I believed the only person to depend on was myself. Advice is something that helps people to see things more clearly, not something for us to follow blindly.

Time to Branch Out.
推而广之

Describe an important stage of your life.

补充弹药

be torn between A and B 左右为难   be in a dilemma 处在两难的境地

[剑桥例句] The Prime Minister is clearly in a dilemma about how to deal with the crisis.

see the light at the end of the tunnel (很困难的时候)看到了一线光明

alter the course of my life 改变了我人生的道路

full of uncertainties 充满不确定性

[剑桥例句] Nothing is ever decided, and the talks are still full of uncertainties.

weigh the pros and cons 比较利弊   face up to the challenge 迎接挑战

Extra Ammo

4. Describe a festival.
一个节日

I'm going to talk about the Spring Festival, you know, Chun Jie.

It's by far the most important festival in the Chinese culture because it marks the beginning of a whole new year. On that day, young people return to their parents' home and celebrate the festival. On the eve of the Chinese New Year, people have big meals and drink a lot. We prepare tons of food to show our hope that the next year will be prosperous. Not just food, the clothes people wear on the Spring Festival are also pretty special. Many men wear traditional Chinese coats called Tang Suit and ladies wear chi-pao, a traditional Chinese dress. Children are very excited about the Spring Festival because they can get lots of candy, new clothes and hong bao, you know, red packets or envelopes, with cash, or "lucky money", wrapped in them. Many kids set off firecrackers on the Spring Festival to celebrate it. Traditionally, Chinese New Year celebrations could last up to fifteen days. Unfortunately, these days the Spring Festival is not as important to us as it used to be because we have more ways to get relaxed, like partying and clubbing. And Western festivals like Christmas and Valentine's Day are becoming extremely popular in China, especially among young people. But anyway, the Spring Festival is still one of the key things that make us Chinese.

5. Describe a good law in your country.

一部好的法律

I'm going to talk about the marriage law in China. It was first passed back in the 1950s by the National People's Congress, but then it was changed many times. The latest change to this law, as far as I know, took place in 2002, which was about the marriages between Chinese citizens and foreigners. Then, let me talk about the contents (内容) of this law. It is made up of six parts, or six "chapters", which are the general principles, the rules about family relations, the rules about marriages, divorces and responsibilities and also some recent changes to the rules. This law is so essential because there are many people marrying or divorcing each year. So we really need a law to control such activities. For example, as you may know, many young people marry in some rural areas before they reach the legal age for marriage, and that has brought many problems such as family violence or bad treatment of their kids. So you see, we need such a law. On the other hand, I guess there are still some problems with this law. A friend of mine married last year but he didn't get along with his wife. So they divorced. But they now have problems dividing their property (=things they own) and debts. And some recent changes to this law have caused a great deal of debate. So I suppose we still have a long way to go before we get a really effective and efficient marriage law in China.

6. Describe a foreign culture.

一种异国文化

Let me talk about the Korean culture. Korea is pretty close to China and its culture

*C*ivilization is the art of living in towns of such size the everyone
does not know everyone else.

—John Jay Chapman

is very similar to the Chinese culture. There're many talented Korean singers and songwriters and their music is very creative. Plus, a host of world-class directors and actors work in Korea. The Korean movies have quite a large following in China. My favourite Korean movie is called "*My Sassy Girlfriend*". Korean food is tasty. My favourite Korean food is the Korean barbecue and kimchi (韩国泡菜). Koreans are into sports. There are tons of soccer nuts and taekwondo buffs in that country. Besides, I guess the Korean architecture is pretty unique too because it blends the traditional Asian architecture and modern architecture very well.

7. Describe your favourite room in your flat.

公寓里的一个房间

My flat is on the fourth floor of an eight-storey building. It's kind of old. My favourite room in my flat is the bedroom. It's not big, just like 10 square meters. There's a single bed in the corner. The pillows are fluffy and comfortable. There's a bedside table next to it and the table is brand-new. I bought it last week. There's also a wardrobe in my bedroom and I put all my favourite clothes in it. There's also a desk in my bedroom. I often read and write or browse the Internet at my desk. My favourite part of my bedroom is actually the potted plants. They look gorgeous and they smell good, too. By the way, I decorated this room all by myself.

The reason I'm so fond of this room is that, you know, it's my own space. I can really enjoy my privacy there. It's also relaxing. I can enjoy the peace of the night in my bedroom. Sometimes I even spend the whole weekend daydreaming there. If you see it for yourself, you'll know how lucky I am to have such a room.

8. Describe an old piece of furniture. / Describe an old object your family has kept for a long time.

一件老家具 / 在家中保存了很久的一件物品

I'm going to describe an old chair in my living room. This chair is special because of its long history — it was made in the Qing Dynasty and was handed down to me from my great-grandparents (= grandfather's / grandmother's parents). This chair is dark red and the paint has faded (= lost its colour) a little. It has four legs and a backrest. There are some cracks in the chair simply because it's soooooo old. It makes some noise when someone sits on it. But I think it's gorgeous and perfect for my living room. That's because there are many old things in my living room, like old Chinese paintings and antique desks. This chair is valuable also because it reminds me of my great-grandparents. They were kind of famous in their time and many people admired them. This chair looks really unique. I guess it must have cost them a lot. Now it's worth like 10,000 RMB or something like that but I just won't sell it. I'll keep it in my living room to show my respect for my great-grandparents.

9. Describe an unhappy shopping experience. / Describe something that made you angry.

一次不愉快的购物经历 / 一件让你气愤的事

Let me talk about one of my recent shopping experiences. A couple of days ago, I went to a supermarket to buy some groceries. I saw some apples that looked great. I paid for them right away and went back home. But then I was so surprised to find that the apples tasted very bad. Actually they were totally gross. So I returned to the supermarket and wanted my money back. But the shop assistants just wouldn't listen to me, and they were like, "Well, you should have tasted them before you paid." I got so mad that I complained to the customers around me. But those salesclerks still refused to give me a refund. I was left with no choice so I called the Consumers' Association and complained to them about this matter. They promised me they would look into the whole thing. Yesterday I got a phone call from the supermarket and they told me they would give me a refund. That was an extremely upsetting shopping experience. But I learned a lesson from it. Now I know that I shouldn't be fooled by the look of things in stores.

10. Describe an open-air market.

一个露天市场

I'm going to talk about my favourite open-air market. It's located in the eastern part of my hometown. It's very big... huge. Its history goes back all the way to like fifty years ago and it's very famous in my hometown. Actually, everyone can tell you something about this market in that city. The market is made up of many parts, like the food section, the toy section and the clothing section. Many locals go there every day. Some of them buy stuff and some others just look around. Many people from out of town are also drawn to this market. They heard a lot about it and hope to get some exciting shopping experience. This market never gets them disappointed. You know, tons of stuff there and everyone can find the thing he or she wishes to get. Some others just enjoy chatting and bargaining there. That's exactly why it's always pretty noisy out there. My favourite part of this market is the clothing part. I can find many different kinds of clothes, like casual, formal and sporty clothes there. Most importantly, the price is always reasonable. In fact, I can always get a discount because I know all the salesclerks there. The atmosphere in that market is very laid-back. It feels busy but people are friendly to one another. They always wear a smile on their face and enjoy the experience of buying or selling things. This market is totally amazing in that although it's so big, it's very well-run. It is kind of noisy but I guess that's perfectly natural for an open-air market. I'm sure if you go and visit it yourself, you'll like it too.

＼（下）雅思口语 10 大消魂卡片

下面这 10 个题目确实需要不少专门的词汇，所以往往导致考生一旦被问到那么回家之后就立马准备报名下一次的考试了。但相应地，如果你能好好准备，反而能让别人的弱势变成你的优势不是么？

这十个考题分别是：

Describe a museum / art gallery.

Describe a sculpture.

Describe a small business.

Describe a concert hall.

Describe a special meal.

Describe a party you prepared for another person.

Describe a naughty thing you did when you were a child.

Describe something in your home that was broken or didn't work.

Describe a place with a lot of noise.

Describe things that you can do to help improve the environment.

面对这么诡异（bizarre）的题目，Pat 仍然坚信，"There's nothing to fear but fear itself."

Killer A

1. 美术馆 Describe a museum / art gallery.

Pat 指南

准备一个美术馆吧，就能把这两个很难的题一起都准备好了。

难度指数：★ ★ ★ ☆

Pat 的答案

My favourite museum is the Modern Art Museum in... (*Put the city's name here.*)

The museum is located in the city center. It's an enormous building but has few windows. The interior is very spacious, and it's divided into various sections, like Asian art, Middle-Eastern art, European art and North American art. My favourite part of the museum is Sculpture Garden where there are hundreds of sculptures on display.

This museum has a fascinating collection of modern artworks, and it always has some temporary exhibitions going on. Last week, it held an exhibition of Andy Warhol's Works, which attracted many visitors. On weekends, the museum holds special events for children, such as cartoon exhibitions and videogame exhibitions.

Thousands of people pass through its doors every day. But what makes this museum really special is that unlike many other museums, the staff there encourage non-flash photography. And that makes the viewing experience more fun. So you see, this museum is very visitor-friendly.

This art museum is so famous that it receives lots of government funding each year. It seems all the money has been put to good use.

The admission fee is like ... 25 yuan for adults and 5 yuan for children. Pretty reasonable, huh? It's a cool place. Be sure to check it out!

▶ Word Bank on This Topic

很大的   enormous   建筑或者汽车的内部空间 interior

[剑桥例句] The interior of the building is well decorated.

部分   section   雕塑   sculpture

迷人的   fascinating   收藏   collection

艺术品   artworks / works of art   临时的，非永久性的   temporary

宽敞的   spacious   展览   exhibition

展品   exhibit

[剑桥例句] The museum has a fascinating collection of exhibits.

安迪·沃霍   Andy Warhol (the Pop Art 最著名的代表人物)

不使用闪光灯的摄影   non-flash photography

观赏的体验   viewing experience   构图   composition

色彩的搭配   colour scheme   笔触   strokes

人像画   portrait   风景画   landscape painting

静物画   still life   会议   conference

很方便观众参观的   visitor-friendly

(地道英文里有很多形容词是这样构成，在雅思口语里还有两个很常用的是 user-friendly "方便使用的" 和 pedestrian-friendly "很适合步行的")

入场费   admission fee

[剑桥例句] The admission fee is £ 6 for adults.

给人很多启发的   enlightening   娱乐性很强的   entertaining

信息量大的   informative   当代艺术   contemporary art

漫步   wander around

[剑桥例句] We spent the morning wandering around the old part of the city.

由……组成   be made up of

请参考Pat的思路，并适当借鉴这个词汇表里的单词，思考如果是您会怎么说

Pat 的海外生活英语实录

多数博物馆和美术馆的采光都不是靠太阳光，因为同一天里阳光的强度变化很大，视觉效果不够稳定。相应的博物馆和美术馆里的光线就不可以叫 sun 乂，而是要叫作 **lighting**（照明）。

【剑桥例句】Don't strain your eyes by putting up with（容忍）poor lighting.

Killer B

2. 一件雕塑 Describe a sculpture.

Pat 指南

如果准备一个雕塑展当中你喜欢的雕塑，就可以同时搞定 "Describe an exhibition" 的话题，所以还是很值的（worth it）。

难度指数：★★★★★

Pat 的答案

I went to a sculpture exhibition last weekend. Actually I took lots of pictures there. But anyway, I'll describe the exhibition just with words.

It was held in the garden of the Modern Art Museum, and it displayed artworks by more than 50 sculptors. The theme of the exhibition was "The Environment". There were lots of plants in the garden, which suited the theme well.

What was really special about the exhibition was it not only displayed the sculptures but also showed the sculptors' working drawings.

A sculpture I really liked at the exhibition was a piece dealing with the subject of the damage caused by environmental problems.

It was a reclining figure which looked calm and peaceful at first sight. But when looking more carefully, I noticed it has many openings on its surface. It seems through the contrast between the solid part and the openings, the artist expressed concerns about the conflict between human development and nature.

I really liked the symbolism of this sculpture. It was very meaningful, not just something for the "shock value". I don't remember the title of the sculpture. But anyway, titles are not that important to understanding abstract art, right?

The exhibition was also pretty educational because lots of brochures about protecting the environment were handed out to the visitors.

轮到你了   It's Your Turn.

► Word Bank on This Topic

雕塑家　sculptor　　　　　展示　display　　　　　主题　theme

[剑桥例句] The theme of honour runs through most of his novels.

（艺术品）是关于某一主题的…… deal with... 躺着的形象，卧像　a reclining figure

开口，孔　opening　　　　　　　　　对比　contrast

关注　concerns　　　　　　　　　　冲突　conflict

自然界　nature　　　　　　　　　　象征　symbolism

轰动效应　shock value　　　　　　　标题　title

（艺术）抽象的　abstract　　　　　　抽象艺术　abstract art

小册子　brochure　　　　　　　　　分发　hand out

（艺术）具象的　representational　　　空间　space

三维立体的　three-dimensional

[剑桥例句] This picture has a three-dimensional effect.

青铜　bronze　　　　　　　　　　　石膏　plaster

粘土　clay　　　　　　　　　　　　大理石　marble

光滑的　smooth　　　　　　　　　　粗糙的　rough

直的　straight　　　　　　　　　　弯曲的　curved

优雅的　elegant　　　　　　　　　　有创意的　creative

探索　explore　　　　　　　　　　　题材　subject matter

[剑桥例句] The programme's subject matter is not appropriate for children.

请参考Pat的思路，并适当借鉴这个词汇表里的单词，思考如果是您会怎么说

371

Pat 的海外生活英语实录

　　Pat 在纽约的业余时间大约有四分之一是花在博物馆和美术馆里的，最爱就是 MoMA 里那些应接不暇的现代艺术展。classical art 和 modern art 的本质区别就是古典艺术是为别人做的而现代艺术是为自己做的，所以口试时承认你并不理解某个艺术品相当正常而且真实，只要英语对就没什么好怕的。但是"难于理解的"用地道英文到底该怎么表达呢？除了 It's hard to understand. 外，基础好的同学也许还知道 incomprehensible, unintelligible 等多音节大词，前者与听力（listening）comprehension 是同源词，后者则与 intelligent 同根。不过在考试的时候说这些大词存在舌头转不过来的可能。其实在国外真实生活里 **It's beyond me.** 才是说某事物令你费解的最常用表达，人人都能懂。

　　【剑桥例句】I'm afraid theoretical physics is totally beyond me.

Killer C

3. Describe a small business.

　　☆ 小生意之　餐馆（a restaurant）

Pat 指南　🔊

　　英文里面有两句著名的谚语叫"Small is beautiful."与"Less is more."——"小就是美，少即是多"。

　　说实话，国外的中餐馆里面"压根儿"就没有地道的中国菜（authentic Chinese cuisine）。因为白人比较喜欢口味重的菜（savory dishes），我们中国人喜欢的口味他们反而会觉得太淡了（bland）。反倒是 sweet and sour chicken, Mongolian beef 这样在国内很少见到的菜，在老英老美们眼里反倒以为就是地道的中餐（authentic Chinese cuisine），上了当还吃得特起劲儿。在英美吃中餐见得比较多的是 Cantonese Cuisine 和 Szechwan Cuisine，后面一个是 Sichuan 的另一种拼写方式。虽然"老外"们熟悉的中国菜在国内并不是最流行的菜，不过建议您考雅思还是多说考官们肯定能听懂的菜名儿吧，比如 sweet and sour soup（酸辣汤），Kung Pao chicken（宫保鸡丁），Ma Po tofu（麻婆豆腐），braised pork（红烧肉），stir-fried string beans（干煸四季豆），Wonton Soup（馄饨），General Tso's Chicken（这个左宗棠鸡很多海外中餐馆都有，但是在北京的餐馆里还真是找不到）。

难度指数：★ ★ ★ ★ ☆

Pat 的答案

My favourite restaurant is a Chinese restaurant on Nan Hu Street. I'm a regular there.

It's small... you know... tiny, not obvious at all until you pass it. But it offers a great selection of Chinese food. The chef is awesome.

Just order some dishes there like General Tso's chicken or Kung Pao chicken and you'll know what I mean. And the portions are soooooooooo BIG.

But people are attracted to this restaurant by more than just good food. It proves that "Small is beautiful." The owner knows most customers' names. The clean tablecloths and the neatly-set tables make it so different from many other restaurants. The seats are comfortable. The waiters and waitresses are always helpful. They even give customers free fortune cookies.

By the way, the lighting in the restaurant is very pleasant and the background music is relaxing.

It's warm and cozy, especially on a cold winter day...

轮到你了   It's Your Turn.

▶ **Word Bank on This Topic**

常客　regular

[剑桥例句] He's one of the regulars at the Rose and Crown pub.

提供很好的……选择　offer a great selection of... (描述服务行业很常用的表达)

餐馆的厨师　chef   菜量　portion

[剑桥例句] The portions are very generous in this restaurant.

吸引　attract   老板　owner

桌布　tablecloth

幸运饼 fortune cookie（这个也是只在国外的中餐馆才有的东东，是一个小饼干里放一张小纸条描述你未来的运气）

灯光，照明 lighting   舒适的 cosy

[剑桥例句] This room is nice and cosy in the winter.

室内装饰 interior décor（这个词请特别注意听音频的录音）

精致的 exquisite   无可挑剔的 impeccable

[剑桥例句] The standards of service are impeccable.

饭菜的香味儿 aroma   挤满了人的 packed（日常口语里比 crowded 更常用）

[剑桥例句] The restaurant was so packed that I couldn't find a seat.

美食家 gourmet   推荐 recommend

地毯 carpet   硬木地板 hardwood flooring

餐饮体验 dining experience

请参考Pat的思路，并适当借鉴这个词汇表里的单词，思考如果是您会怎么说

Pat 的海外生活英语实录

（A）每一个在餐馆吃饭的人都可以叫作 a customer 或者更正式地说 a diner（请注意这个词里 i 的读音不是像 dinner 里面的 i，而是要读成 /ai/），但却不是每个在餐馆吃饭的人都可以称为"美食家"。作为巨蟹座的代表，Pat 一直被身边的朋友们叫作"吃货"（foodie），深感美味的食物实在难以抗拒（irresistible）。"美食家"在地道英语里的说法可不是 eating expert ✗，而是 **gourmet**（请注意结尾的 t 不发音，这个词的正确发音是 /ˈgɔːˌmei/）。口试时一旦考到跟"吃"有关的话题，当用出这个单词的时候，你得到的绝不会是考官对于贪吃者鄙视的眼神，而是他/她对于你地道口语的敬意。

【剑桥例句】A gourmet is someone who knows a lot about food and cooking and enjoys eating high-quality food.

（B）small business 的特点就是老板通常都是"白手起家"的。要表达这样的意思，除了有个地道但比较难的英文词 **entrepreneur**，还有 **a self-made man / a self-made woman** 这样很好理解也很容易在口试时说出来的表达。

【剑桥例句】

（1）He was one of the entrepreneurs of the 1990s who made their money in dotcoms.

（2）Self-made men and women are rich as a result of their own work and not because of their family wealth.

除以上的答案外，也挺"消魂"的两个题 **Describe a successful small company.** 和 **Describe a friend of yours who is a business leader.** 还可以通过 smallbusiness. aol. com/ success-stories/ 上近百个小企业家的故事轻松过关。

Killer D

4. 音乐厅 Describe a concert hall.

Pat 指南

对于不喜欢 classical music 的人来说，这个题目考的根本就不是能力（skills），而是考耐力（endurance）。不过如果你能把 Pat 编写的这个答案掌握差不多 50% 左右的话，那么有两个最近经常出现的题目"Describe a place where you listen to music / Describe a leisure center."就可以一起准备好了。出国之后你会发现那边儿喜欢 classical music 的人可真多，而且其实如果经常听，还真的会发现它确实具有 pop music 所没有的深度（depth）。

建筑的 location 和 exterior（外观）这里 Pat 就不再赘述了，直奔音乐厅最有特点的 interior design（室内布置）吧。

难度指数：★★★★★

Pat 的答案

I'm going to describe the concert hall I often go to.

The building is old, but still in good condition. The main hall is very big. I would say there're probably more than 1,000 seats in it. The seats are comfortable, and it's easy to see

the stage from most of the seats.

The hall has high ceilings and wood flooring. It feels pretty cozy, and the acoustics are amazing. The sound is great from everywhere in the hall.

I've seen many concerts in that hall, from classical to jazz to folk. I've also seen some drama performances there ... Very impressed.

It's a great place for music lovers. The employees there are friendly and helpful. And the ticket price is pretty reasonable, like 80 *yuan* per person. And sometimes you can get cheaper tickets online ...

轮到你了   It's Your Turn.

▶ Word Bank on This Topic

状况很好　in good condition	舞台　stage
天花板　ceiling	（建筑或者交通工具）很舒适的　cozy
地板的材质　flooring	音质，音效　acoustics
古典音乐会　classical concert	爵士音乐会　jazz concert
民族音乐会　folk concert	戏剧表演　drama performance
合理的　reasonable	交响乐团　symphony orchestra
独奏　solo	气氛　atmosphere
男高音　tenor	男中音　baritone
男低音　bass	女高音　soprano
女中音　mezzo-soprano	女低音　alto
音乐剧　musical	咏叹调　aria
指挥　conductor	观众　audience
鼓掌　applaud	谢幕　take curtain calls

（英国摇滚乐队 Queen 有一首著名的歌叫作 *We Are the Champions*，里面有一句歌词就是 I've taken my bows, and my curtain calls.）

请参考Pat的思路，并适当借鉴这个词汇表里的单词，思考如果是您会怎么说

Pat 的海外生活英语实录

音乐 "令人陶醉的"，绝对不要说 The music made me drunk. ✗ 英文里有 attractive / fascinating 等单词都可以表示有吸引力的，但对音乐来说，最准确的则是 **enchanting** 这个词。

【剑桥例句】The audience was clearly enchanted by her performance.

Killer E

5. 双语感悟之　一顿特殊的饭 Describe a special meal / someone's cooking skill.

Pat 指南

准备过这个题目的孩子一定感受过用英文 "报菜名儿" 的苦恼。描述自己 cooked a meal 的过程应该是个好主意，但要特别注意真没必要说得太多，1'30"~2' 其实并不需要很多内容。

老外做菜最常用的工具是 roaster（烤肉的烤箱），toaster & oven（烤面包和蛋糕用的烤箱）和 microwave（微波炉，全称叫 microwave oven）。而使用 gas stove（燃气灶）时则通常是煮菜（boil），而炒菜（stir-fry）却不常见，因为国外房子里面的警报器过于敏感，炒菜的油烟就能让它响（go off）。

下面给大家介绍一下做菜的常用词吧，知道 50% 就够，不用说得 "过好"，否则那就不是描述一顿特殊的 meal 而是一个 cook 的求职简历了。看完这段咱就去吃饭，看着桌上的菜顺便复习。

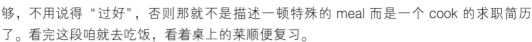

☆ 可以先介绍一下吃这顿饭的 "场景"，比如：

A friend of mine visited me a couple of weeks ago.

☆ 说说为什么做饭：

At first, we just chatted / did some catching up（这个我们 Day 7 已经学过了，"聊彼此的近况" 的意思）.

But then we got hungry.

Actually, there was some ready-made stuff in the fridge（冰箱）.

But I decided to cook a meal for him/her because he/she was my special guest

☆ 去哪里买原料（ingredients）

So we went to a grocery store / a supermarket and bought lots of stuff.

☆ 买了哪些东东（挑几个就可以了，两个正常人吃不了多少吧）

meats like pork, beef, lamb and chicken（注意表示不同种类的时候 meat 可以加复数）

vegetables like tomatoes, onions, potatoes, broccoli（西兰花，西方人认为吃这个非常 healthy，甚至在加拿大餐馆 Pat 还见过有人吃 steamed broccoli 清蒸西兰花的，真不知味道如何），green peppers（灯笼椒），eggplants（茄子），carrots（胡萝卜），mushrooms（蘑菇），cucumbers（黄瓜），spinach（菠菜），还有我的蔬菜最爱 asparagus（芦笋）…

seafood like shrimp（虾），lobster（大龙虾），tuna（金枪鱼），salmon（三文鱼），snapper（这个不知道中文该怎么讲，这三种鱼老外们特爱吃，因为它们 bone（鱼刺）少，而很多老外感觉餐桌上的鱼刺是 unappetizing 会影响食欲）

☆ 回家了

We went back to my place.

☆ 开始洗菜

rinsed out all the stuff（用水冲洗菜更多的时候不用 wash 而用 rinse）

☆ 切菜方法大全：

sliced the tomatoes and cucumbers（切成片儿）

peeled the carrots（削皮儿）

chopped some broccoli（这个还是西兰花）into chunks（切块儿）

shredded the pork（切丝儿）= cut the pork into fine strips

diced an onion（切丁儿）= cut the onion into cubes

☆ 如果是做沙拉还可以说搅拌

mixed the cucumber and tomato in a salad bowl

如果烤蛋糕可以说 baked a cake（西餐的面点叫作 pastry，做面点常用的发酵粉叫作

baking powder，请注意它与酵母 yeast 是不同的）

☆ 两种 "打鸡蛋"

break／crack an egg 是把蛋壳打破的动作而 beat（or whisk）the eggs 是把鸡蛋在碗里打匀的过程

☆ Pat "吐血" 奉献所有常见的做菜方法：

lit the burner（点燃 gas stove 燃气灶上的加热器）

boiled（水煮）and steamed（清蒸）the vegetables（国外吃蔬菜经常是吃 salad 或者清蒸）

stir-fried（炒）the onion with the ground beef（切碎的牛肉，我已经饿了……）in a frying pan（煎锅，咱们中国的圆底铁锅则叫 wok）

deep-fried（油炸）the fish fillets（鱼片，这个是法语词，发音请认真听录音）

braised the pork（红烧肉）

grilled the shrimp and the fillets（grill something 的过程类似于中文里的 "烤串儿"，而虾串儿的地道英文就叫 shrimp stick，在英美还有很多人用 shrimp skewer 的说法）

tossed in a handful of spices／herbs（放进去一把调味儿的东东，比如 pepper，撒盐英文是 sprinkled salt）

cooked it on high heat ＝ cooked it over a high flame（用大火，小火就把 high 改成 low 就可以）

When it started to boil（煮沸），…

I turned down（调低）the heat and let it simmer（炖）for like 10 minutes.

When the meat was brown, I turned off the burner.

还有一个法语词 sauté 是 "煎……"，有时候也能听到有人说说，比如 sautéed the chicken。

I put some noodle（面条，这里不要加复数）into the boiling water and boiled it until it was tender（面条软了）.

And then I ladled（用那种很长的大勺子舀）some sauce（在国外吃饭用得最多的就是 sauce，几乎无菜不放 sauce，很多刚去的朋友一开始都适应不了）over the noodle.

I poured some dressing（沙拉和 pizza 的调料）on the salad.

☆ 开始吃

My friend set the table.（放餐具）

served the dishes 端菜

We just helped ourselves to the food.

I made some coffee with the coffee maker.

After the main course，we had some ice cream for dessert（饭后甜点，我又饿了，写一个答案饿两次……）

We chatted over the meal.

He/She told me a whole bunch of funny things and they really cracked me up.（让我笑个不停）

☆ 还可以再说说吃完饭的事情

We took the serving dishes off the table.

And... cleared the table ＝ wiped the table off.

Put the leftovers in the fridge.（把剩菜放进冰箱）

Really memorable.（很值得回忆啊）

Bonus（附送内容）：

最后再给大家简单描述几句有中国特色的包饺子过程吧，不过太复杂的 Pat 真的自己也说不出来：

marinated the meat（把肉腌一下）

chopped up the vegetables（切菜）

mixed them into a paste（和在一起）and that would be the stuffing（馅儿）

mixed the flour（面粉）with water

and kneaded the dough（揉面团）

we rolled out the wraps（擀皮儿）

wrapped the stuffing（包起来）

put the dumplings into boiling water

ladled them out into bowls…

Yummy！虽然前几天跟大家说过回答考官的问题时不推荐用 yummy，但是这里用 Yummy！却是最合适的。

> 如果需要描述 **a cook**，您不妨看一看这两个网站：**www. gordonramsay. com/ corporate/theman/biography** 和 **www. jamieoliver.com**，网站名字上的这两个人都是目前在英国红得发紫的厨师兼厨艺电视节目主持人，甚至连 **Describe a TV presenter.** 这个题也可以"一锅端"了。

Killer F

6. 双语感悟之 一堂科学课 Describe a science lesson that you had in school or university.

Pat 指南

貌似很多孩子连中文的物理、化学都还没学好，居然被要求用英语描述这类课程，实在是 ridiculous！不过如果您在国外上过中学的 science class，就会深感这边的科学课完全可以用"吃喝玩乐"四个字形容。英美中学阶段的科学课不是像国内把物理、化学划分得那么严格，在有的学校甚至几门课就一个老师讲，所以一般 science 老师都比较好说话（怕家长投诉）。而且为了吸引大家的兴趣（其实是食欲 appetite），science 老师们还经常会拿可乐（coke），柠檬水（lemonade）、葡萄干（raisin）或者爆米花（popcorn）这类东西到教室做实验，有时微波炉（microwave）、烤箱（oven）这类厨具也会登场。最棒的是：因为这边的班级一般都比较小，也就十几个学生，所以做完实验大家往往就可以把剩下的 food & drinks 分了。最近在北美的中学科学课里还特时髦地用一些不可逆的（irreversible）化学反应来展示 *Harry Potter* 7 里的魔法是怎么变出来的，所以连 magic wand（魔法棒）和 potion（神水）这类演出道具都用上了，完全是最真实的 *Harry Potter* 3D 版。所以 Pat 非常建议大家把这个题目说得轻松点，如果一定把这题说得跟国内的理科课堂那么抽象，考官反而会感到文化休克（culture shock）。

而且这题也还可以在回忆上课过程的同时顺带着讲讲老师的特色，不能太长，但短短几句话肯定是没问题的。比如 Pat 给您简单回忆一下我自己中学时在加拿大上过的一堂科学课吧：

Well, that was when I was in grade 10.（北美讲年级的时候很少说高一，高二之类的词，一般都是像 grade 9，grade 10 或者 grade 11 这样讲的）. Back then, our science teacher was a really nice guy（请注意这个词跟中文的"家伙"不一样，其实只要是指某个男性在地道口语里这个词都巨常用）, you know, very patient and understanding（善解人意的）. And just like many scientists, he was kind of balding（快秃顶了）and wore thick glasses. But he was not a nerd（说"书呆子"最常用的英文词）because he always had some incredibly fun ways to make dead theories come alive（他能让枯燥的理论活起来）. I still recall（用这个词代替谁都用的 remember 怎么样） one of the most interesting science lessons he gave us. Our teacher came into the classroom with a huge beaker（烧杯）, a bag of raisins and a jumbo diet Pepsi（大瓶百事，还是不含糖的！）The whole setting made us thirsty and hungry! And he was like, "Guys！（今后对一堆人你就放心这么喊吧，即使有男也有女）Today I'm gonna show you some top secrets of density（密度）!" He opened the bottle and poured the Pepsi into the beaker and the soda（这个词可以泛指各种碳酸饮料，还有个词 pop 也差不多）just kept fizzing（嘶嘶嘶的响）in the beaker. Then the guy put a couple of raisins in the beaker. The raisins plumped up（变得胖大）because they were soaked（泡湿了）. "See?" Our teacher asked, "The raisins are sinking fast because their density is higher than that of the coke." Yeah, it was true. But then, right after the raisins hit the bottom of the beaker, they went back up! "That's because Pepsi is carbonated（含碳酸的）so it has lots of gas. Once the gas went into the raisins, the density of the raisins became lower, even lower than of the soda." He explained, in a matter-of-fact voice（这个中文我想不出怎么翻译，总之是讲 science 老师特别合适，只可意会，不可言传）. "But once the raisins went to the surface of the Pepsi, the gas in them was squeezed out（被挤出去）," he pointed to the beaker, "so their density became high again and so you can see that they're starting to sink again!"

Geez, he was right! The raisins just kept going up and down in the Pepsi, for nearly twenty minutes, while we were enjoying the rest of the raisins in the bag... ☺

轮到你了   It's Your Turn.

▶ Word Bank on This Topic

烧杯	beaker	实验	experiment
天平	balance	固体	solid
称重量	weigh	液体	liquid
悬挂	hang	加热	heat up
密度	density	冷却	cool off
质量	mass	元素周期表	the periodic table of the elements
体积	volume	化学公式	chemical equations
镊子	tweezers	化学反应	chemical reaction

勺子	spoon	显微镜	microscope
秤	scale	滴管	dropper
仪器	instrument	试管	test tube
仪表	meter	漏斗	funnel
搅拌	stir	温度计	thermometer

请参考Pat的思路，并适当借鉴这个词汇表里的单词，思考如果是您会怎么说

Pat 的海外生活英语实录

前文 Pat 已经说过，要描述音乐"令人陶醉的"，那么非英语里的 **enchanting** 这个词莫属。但如果要用这个词来形容一节课上得很精彩，那就有点拍马屁（butter up the teacher）的嫌疑了。地道英文里说一位老师讲课"引人入胜的"，最准确的表达就是 **engaging**，相应的它也可以用来形容 a speech, a TV show, a book 甚至 a childhood story（这些话题我们已经在 Day 8 里全都"无痛地"练习过了）。放心地跟 examiner 用吧。It'll make your answers very engaging. ☺

【英美实例】Although I was tired, I found the book very engaging, making me want to just stay up and keep reading it.

Killer G

7. 帮别人准备的一个聚会 Describe a party you prepared for others/another person.

Pat 指南

Pat 一直认为准备雅思口语最好的心态就是把它看成国外留学生活的起点。各位进到任何一所英联邦大学里都会立刻知道 party 是白人校园文化何等重要的一个部分了。即使已经工作的年轻白人如果是单身那么每个月也总会有 N 次机会去参加各种"派对"，只是这其中的分分合合到底给人带来的是消遣（recreation）还是更深的孤独感（loneliness）就要靠自己去体会了。

对于国内的孩子们来说，生日聚会是最容易说到"点儿上"的话题，而且 birthday party 用"小词"也可以说得很曲折（full of twists and turns）。

Last month, a good friend of mine, Mia's nineteenth birthday was coming up. I hoped it could be a really memorable birthday for her so I decided to organise a surprise birthday party for the birthday girl.

I called my friends Jillian, Chris, Evan and Matt who were also pretty close to Mia, and asked them if they'd like to join me in throwing a surprise birthday party for her. They were very delighted to hear my ideas and promised they wouldn't tell anyone about this "top secret". I also called Mia's parents to make sure they would be okay with my plan.

On Mia's birthday, we went to her apartment, helped her parents decorate the living room and got a big birthday cake ready. Then we went into hiding. About ten minutes later, we heard footsteps and Mia stepped into the apartment. All of us jumped out and yelled, "SURPRISE!" Mia was totally surprised and she was like, "Oh my goodness! What's going on here?" We said "Happy birthday!" to her in unison and then we brought out the cake and started singing the birthday song for her...

Mia told me it was the most special birthday she ever had. I felt my secretive planning really paid off...

（本节中的女配角 Jillian 将在 Pat 的另一本书《十天突破留学生活口语》中走到台前成为女一号，引领大家去深刻探寻一个长期被误读的真实西方世界）

轮到你了   It's Your Turn.

本文中所用的人名都是目前国外年轻人的常见名字

过生日的男孩/女孩　the birthday boy / the birthday girl

（某一时间）临近了　approach / come up / is just around the corner

[剑桥例句] If you look out of the window on the left of the bus, you'll see that we're now approaching the Tower of London.

很值得回忆的　memorable

为某人开一个"派对"　hold / throw a party for sb.

与某人关系很亲密的　be close to / be tight with

高兴的　delighted（口语考试中代替 happy 的优秀选择）

[剑桥例句] We'd be delighted to come to dinner on Friday.

绝对机密　top secret　　　　　　装饰　decorate

藏起来　hide / go into hiding　　脚步（声）　footsteps

大声喊　yell

天哪！　Oh my goodness！（比 Oh my God！略微含蓄一点的常用感叹方式）

异口同声地说　say something in unison

[剑桥例句] Try to sing in unison if you guys can.

秘密的　secretive　　　　　　　有回报　pay off

请参考Pat的思路，并适当借鉴这个词汇表里的单词，思考如果是您会怎么说

Pat 的海外生活英语实录

　　如果要说一个很成功的聚会是"精心策划"的，除了 **It was carefully planned / carefully organised / carefully arranged.** 这三个挺地道的表达之外，还有一个 Pat 从没听到过国内孩子用但在国外却挺常用的表达：**This was a well-thought-out party**.

【剑桥例句】

（1）The training schedule wasn't very well-thought-out.

（2）Nothing can be more fun than going to a well-thought-out birthday party.

超短线
The Ultra-Short Track

　　还有一道卡片题偶尔也会上来冒个泡儿：

Describe a show host（presenter）/ an educational TV programme.

　　其实准备这道题，最好想的素材就是说加拿大的"大山"了，因为可以直接扯到学英语上面去，而且用词也不会很难。比如可以挑一个由他主持的语言教学节目（language education programme），先说说他的外貌（tall，broad-shouldered，has pale skin 肤色浅，注意讲一个白人的皮肤白就不要用 has white skin 了，always wears a pair of glasses and a big smile，很有亲和力 very approachable / just like the guy next door…）。接下来就可以介绍"大山"的经历（born and raised in Canada，多伦多大学毕业 graduated from the University of Toronto），在北大学中文（studied Chinese at Beida / Peking University），又学习说相声（learned to perform the Chinese crosstalk comedy）等等。然后你还可以称赞他的中文说得多么多么完美（不一定要再用 perfect 那个俗词了，跟考官试试用 flawless 这个更拿分的词吧。Pat 在北京的时候不止一次地听朋友们说："大山"的中文比他们/她们自己的中文还好（His Chinese is better than mine！）。而且你还可以说他主持的节目给观众（the audience / viewers）带来很多乐趣（pretty entertaining），同时也很有教育意义（educational as well），甚至还可以说你希望自己今后也能像他那样能成为完美的"双语人"（to be perfectly bilingual），blah，blah，blah…

有些 TV show hosts 很靓（gorgeous），有些却外表平凡（average-looking / plain-looking）；有的 TV show hosts 很煽情（emotional / provocative），有些却是以理服人型（a calm，well-reasoned approach）；有的 TV show hosts 很"炫"（flamboyant），有些则很恭谦（humble / modest）。

不论主持人采用哪种风格，Pat 总结出了中外所有成功电视节目主持人全都具有的四个英文特点：talented / gifted（有才华的），energetic（精力充沛的），articulate（表达能力很强的）& engaging（确实能抓住别人注意力的）。

另外，下面这两个 TV show hosts 也都是 IELTS 考官们耳熟能详的，并且出国之后大家经常看到由他/她主持的节目 www. oprah. com/ ，www. simoncowellonline. com/

Killer H

8．小时候自己做过的一件淘气的事 Describe a naughty thing you did when you were a child.

Pat 指南

首先要提示的是：准备这道题时最好不要套用太多的大词或者长难句。如果您先跟考官说"我来说说我小时候做的特淘的一事儿哈"，紧接着却给出一个极为生硬的书面语答案，那就是明摆着告诉考官刚开始你伪装出的一脸轻松根本是给他/她挖的一个坑。

平淡是真（But you'll be rewarded for being unpretentious.）。

讲这道题的时候很多同学倾向于把 naughty 这个单词连续撸上 N 次，其实 naughty 有个近义词叫 mischievous（发音是/ˈmɪsɪtʃɪˌvəs/，请注意重音是在第一个音节）。这个词在国外的使用频率虽然还没有 naughty 那么高，但确实也是生活中经常能听到的词。

此外还有两个相关词组，用来描述自己小时候很调皮时有可能用到：an unruly kid 是指不服从管教的孩子，而 a disruptive student 则特指上课时违纪的学生。

如果想说自己小时候超级淘气、很不听话，动词的表达是 act up。请注意"不听话"在地道英文里不要说 I didn't listen to my parents' words.（这听起来更像是在说"我这人就特爱一意孤行"），而应该说 I liked to act up when I was little.

对于低年级学生来说，最经典的不听话行为莫过于逃课（对于西方考官来说"上课说话"可不能算是调皮，反而极有可能被视为优点）。在地道英文中逃课称之为 cut class 或者 skip school（请注意这个 school 前不能加 the），如果逃课就是很没出息地为了跟小男朋友／小女朋友出去疯玩儿，那么就说 I cut class / skipped school just to hang out with my little boyfriend / girlfriend；而如果逃课是为了去看电影那么当然就是 I cut class just to catch a movie / I skipped school just to catch a flick.

最 naughty 的逃课方式毫无疑问是在老师刚一点完名之后立刻无耻地溜出教室，那就可以用英语说（假设逃的是英语课）I went to the English class, got my attendance checked and then sneaked out of the classroom.

在美国，21 岁之前是绝不能买酒的，如果商家把酒卖给未成年人出了事故还要冒进监狱的危险。不过在北京时 Pat 倒是见过中学生把整箱啤酒往家搬的情况。和朋友们在酒吧喝高了当然也要算是 a naughty thing，除了 We got drunk in a bar. 这样的常规英文外，地道英语里有时还会讲 We got blasted drunk in a bar.

搞恶作剧捉弄别人，英文叫作 play pranks on sb.，也可以叫 play tricks on sb.，或者 play practical jokes on sb.（请注意这里的 practical jokes 并非"实用笑话"，而是恶作剧）。如果你的恶作剧让"受害者"（the victim）那一天都很不爽，则要讲 My prank reeeeeeeally ruined his / her day.

把一桶水放在门缝上面英文叫 put a bucket of water over a door；对方一推门水正好倒在他／她的身上英文说 He / She pushed the poor open. The bucket tipped over（翻了）and fell right on him / her. 浑身都湿透了叫 He / She got soaking wet. 水桶碰到头则要说 The bucket hit him / her on the head.

偶尔捉弄一下过于骄傲的某个同学（put a dent in his / her pride）倒也还是挺有社会意义的事情，但是必须要确保玩笑不能开得太出格了（I was lucky the prank didn't go too far.）……

如果你对别人做了恶作剧之后别人又找你"扯平"了，英文会讲 He / She managed to get even by doing sth.（get even 是个固定短语："扯平"的意思）。

Killer I

9. Describe something in your home that was broken or that didn't work.

近期被考到这道题的同学表示"鸭梨"很大……其实无非是被一个最简单的词忽悠了：broken。

Pat 指南

相当多的同学误以为说这道题必须要描述一件"被打碎的东西"，其实 broken 在地道英文里常用来指家电（home appliances）坏掉了。例如：

My iPad went broken but luckily, it was covered by Apple's warranty（保修）. 或者：My MacBook Air just arrived but sadly, it's broken...

了解了 broken 的含义，一切就变得豁然开朗了。下面 Pat 给您演示一下用高中程度的英语其实就可以把这道难题讲得非常清楚（简直是过于清楚）：

Let me talk about my laptop. It's a ThinkPad SL300. I bought it two years ago.

When I first bought it, everything was just fine... It was thin, light and super stylish. The screen looked gorgeous and typing on the keyboard felt totally comfortable. It also had a pretty decent hard drive that could hold lots of stuff and the battery could last up to four years.

But unfortunately it went out of order after I downloaded a file from an email attachment. I opened the file but ended up with a virus in my laptop. The virus was so powerful the operating system crashed right away and it destroyed the hard drive as well. The screen went black while the laptop was still running. So I turned off the laptop, only to find out it wouldn't even boot up anymore.

I began to worry that I wouldn't be able to get my valuable data back from the hard drive. And by that time, my laptop was not covered by warranty anymore so I took the laptop to a local computer store immediately. The people there fixed the problem and the hard drive data got saved as well.

And since then, I've always been extra careful any time when I pull stuff from the Internet...

这段话中的 email attachment 当然是指电邮的附件；operating system 是操作系统；

hard drive 在英文口语里就是电脑的硬盘，更麻烦的说法则是 hard disk drive，听起来很"严谨"，但是在英美生活里很少有人这么说；boot up 是一个与电脑有关的动词短语，（电脑）启动的意思；找回数据英文也可以说 recover data。

在使用某物品的时候操作错误，正式英文里叫 operated sth. improperly，口语里则可以说 I got it all mixed up. 如果自己在使用该物品之前压根儿就没看使用说明，则说 I really should have read（请注意 read 在这里是指过去，读成/red/）the user's manual / the user's guide first. 如果你在英语论坛上问了一个用户说明里其实明确写了但是你却没仔细看的问题，有些人就会用 RTM 来回复，意思就是 read the manual。

在很正式的书面语中，malfunction 可以用来指各种设备故障，这个单词也经常用作动词，比如可以写 It malfunctioned. 但在地道的英文口语里，电器出现小毛病则经常会用"调皮"这个拟人化的词来描述：It acted up. 短暂的失灵英文也可以说 It went on the blink；而电器工作不正常的情况极为严重时在地道英文里则说 It went haywire! 如果某个家电（home appliance）彻底报废，那么在国外日常生活里最常听到的一句就是 It was dead!

电视或手机的信号不好可以讲 The reception was awful. DVD 机"跳碟"叫 The DVD player skipped. 播放光盘时画面不流畅则可以说 The picture froze.（freeze 的过去时）

如果这道题您还是想说一个"被打碎"的东西，那么应该知道下面这些英文表达：

dropped sth. by accident 不小心掉了某物；

was broken into pieces 被摔成了碎片；

tried to glue the pieces back together 试着用胶把碎片粘起来；

It was precious to me. / It was invaluable to me. 某物对自己来说非常珍贵；

I just couldn't afford to lose it. 自己不能承受失去它。

可见，让一件物品 broken 的方式，在地道英文里其实远不止是 dropped it 或者 smashed it into pieces。

Killer J

10. 四道与环保有关的难题

Pat 指南

（i）**Describe a place where there was a lot of noise.**

噪声大的地儿，除了 airport（对于多数考生来说描述机场的挑战似乎有点大，即使用中文也难以说清）和 night club（让"小盆友们"描述这个也不是很合适），还可以有

shopping mall（是的，在国外多数 shopping malls 里面的地下层 lower levels 都设有 food court 美食街，而且地上的客流量也相当大，所以很多 shopping malls 并不安静）或者也可以说 an open-air market（今天上半部分里的弱智话题 10）。

此外，说这道题时您虽然不必知道 80～90 分贝到底有多吵，但却不妨了解一下 The noise level can be as high as 80-90 decibels /ˈdesɪˌbelz/ 这句很地道的英文。

尖锐的噪音叫 shrill noise，刺耳的噪音叫 penetrating noise，像金属摩擦泡沫塑料那样的摩擦噪音叫 grinding noise，而长期存在的噪音则叫 chronic noise。

说噪音"很烦人的"，形容词是 annoying，但是"长期持续烦人的"则要用 **depressing**，而"很烦人"如果改用动词则要说 It really **bothers** me. 此外还有个句型，叫 The noise really **drives me up the wall**. 比 The noise really **drives me nuts**. 要更加形象:)

（ii）**Describe a place that has been polluted.**

这个题目首先就可以先说一下这个地方曾经很美……

It used to be a beautiful spot.

blah, blah, blah...

可以用我们在前面 Day 8（C）学过的关于自然风景的内容说一会儿，然后就开始 complain 吧:

But now it has been seriously polluted. When I went there this past January. I just couldn't believe how this place had been ruined by pollution. The air was totally smoggy, so smoggy I guess the locals probably would suffer from respiratory diseases. And the water, which used to be crystal-clear, had become filthy because of the industrial waste dumped into the rivers. Plastic bags and disposable lunch boxes were scattered around or floating in the murky rivers.

The pollution was totally devastating to this place. Something must be done before the damage get irreversible...

轮到你了   It's Your Turn.

▶ **Word Bank on This Topic**

严重的破坏 ruin (v.)	烟雾重的	smoggy

[剑桥例句] Mexico City is one of the world's smoggiest capitals.

漂浮	float	非常透明的	crystal-clear
脏的	filthy / dirty	工业废料	industrial waste
倾倒	dump	一次性的	disposable（一定不要说 one-time...）
社区	neighborhood	分散	scattered around

[剑桥例句] I scattered the whole lawn with grass seed.

浑浊的	murky	呼吸系统疾病	respiratory disease
不可逆转的	irreversible	灾难性的	devastating / disastrous

[剑桥例句] The drought（干旱）has had devastating effects.

喷（烟）	puff（v.）	烟筒	chimney
浓烟	dense smoke		

请参考 Pat 的思路，并适当借鉴这个词汇表里的单词，思考如果是您会怎么说

WARNING 很投入地一口气打完这段话之后才发现自己 went overboard（过头了），把自己能想到的所有污染都给堆进去了，就差说 desertification（沙漠化）了。这样的地方大概只有 expedition team（探险队）才敢去。您别说这么多了，就从里面挑几种比较好记的记一下吧。Pat 很希望通过这个反例能让您明白一条真理：口语答案追求"高大全"其实更容易出问题 ☺。

（iii）**Describe a job that can make the world a better place.**

无数小将在考场里拿到这个话题之后当场晕倒——"能够让世界变得更美好的工作"话题太宏大了，让人完全丧失尺度感。其实现在英美年轻人最时髦的就是找"green-collar jobs""绿领儿"工作，也就是能为地球的环保事业做贡献的工作。www.renew-ableenergyjobs.com/content/what-is-a-green-job，点击这个页面上的任何一个工作，你就能立刻找到对它的详细描述和它所要求的条件。

（iv）**Describe things that you can do to help improve the environment.**

这个话题其实在 Writing 考试里早就考过无数次了，口语考试里描述时在前半段也可以先痛心疾首地讲一讲现在你所在的城市里污染已经严重到了何种程度。Pat 为您再简单地提示一下个人为环保做出的贡献常用的口语表达：

循环使用，当然是 recycle；自带购物袋则是 recycle shopping bags。

如果拒绝使用一次性筷子您可以说 take my own chopsticks to restaurants and decline disposable chopsticks（请注意这里的 decline 不是减少而是谢绝的意思）。

减少使用塑料制品可以说 cut down on the use of plastic bags and food containers；不乱扔垃圾叫 don't drop litter；把垃圾分类叫 sort out the household rubbish/household garbage。

多乘坐公交英文是 ride public transit/public transportation more frequently；总是骑自行车叫 always use a bike for short trips。

节约用水叫 save tap water（自来水），捐献旧衣服则是 donate my old clothes。

英文里"有益于环保的"有太多说法，比如 environmentally-friendly, environmentally-beneficial, eco-friendly，以及最简单却最常用的 clean 和 green。

此外，还有太多个人可以为环保做贡献的方法，比如有钱人少穿"皮草"（fur coats），苦孩子打印资料时用双面打印（double-sided printing）……等等。与"低碳生活"（low-carbon living）密切相关的更多英文表达如果您还有深入兴趣的话可以参阅《十天突破 IELTS 写作完整真题库与 6-9 分范文全解》的 Day 7。

附　录

Appendix

Pat's Guide
To The IELTS Speaking Test

Appendix A　雅思口语考试十大经典错误排行榜

Appendix B　老话儿的新生

Appendix C　紧张的 120 个小时

Appendix A

雅思口语考试十大经典错误排行榜

这是 Pat 自己在长期教学中总结出来的中国考生犯得过多的口语错误 chart 之 top 10 countdown。

Top 10　无视-ed 的存在 ✗

悍然忘记动词过去时的杀伤力非常强，因为一旦忘记必然就是接连说错一串儿动词的时态，特别是对于 Part 2 卡片题的描述。行之有效的避免方法是在 1 分钟的思考时间里就把-ed 写在你手中白纸上的醒目位置，而且字母写得大一点也没关系，在这方面不需要给剑桥省纸，反正 1850 已经垫进去了。

Top 9　he / she 之不知 ✗

有些孩子描述 an old man，一上来就是 she，但说了几个 she 突然又变成了 he... 我只能相信这位可敬的 old man 是一个 transsexual person。

Top 8　滥用……how to say... ✗

当一个中国孩子想不出该用什么词汇的时候经常会这么说，可惜这真心不是一个地道的英文插入语。下一次如果感觉被 "茬住了"，请改用 you know..., like...这样在国外确实每天都有人用的 fillers。

Top 7　用 I just stay home and relax myself. 麻痹考官 ✗

native speakers 不说 "relax myself" ✗。其实完全可以直接使用更加地道的 I just stay home and relax. √，或者 I just stay home and get relaxed. √。

Top 6　拿 climb the mountain 吓唬考官 ✗

这个倒算是正确的英文，可它的真实意思却是指用手去攀岩，属于极限运动的一种，难度相当大，普通人用脚徒步登香山的正确说法应该是 go on a hike in Xiang Shan Park。

Top 5　用 The colour is very suitable for me. 冒充领导 ✗ ◩

suitable 这个词在国外一般都是谈到正式的事情才用，日常生活里极少会听到人说 "The colour is very suitable for me." 这么沉重的说法，真不如就说 It looks right on me. 或者 It looks good on me. 口语的本质永远是交流，而不是"吓人"。

Top 4　"How are you?" "I'm fine, thank you. And you?" ✗ ◩

很多国内孩子们说这句的时候还要背着手，非常可爱。一个简单的 "Good. And you?"，再给人点儿笑容就比什么都强了。

Top 3　humorous　并不幽默 ✗ ◩

严格来说用这个词不能算是错误，但是在日常口语里形容一个人很幽默时，native speakers 真正常用的说法是 He / She has a good sense of humour. 或者 He / She has a great sense of humour.

Top 2　In a word, ...　自相矛盾 ✗ ◩

这个错得超多，包括看见过"范文"也喜欢用这个词开始一个长句子。其实在地道英文里，这个词组后面只能强调一个单词，比如 The movie was, in a word, bad.

Top 1　-s 之殇 ✗ ◩

单复数永远是最常见的错误。名词要不要加 s？动词要不要加 s（"单三"）？对这两个问题在考试前必须形成条件反射。一点儿也不夸张地说：您如果能把单复数错误完全改掉的话，你的口语成绩至少可以提高0.5分。遗憾的是，很多中国孩子根本就不觉得一个字母加不加还算个事儿，但是在英文里，加不加-s 却往往会带来句子意思的实质性差异，是一个"原则问题"。

最后还要提醒大家一下，"Long time no see." 其实是特地道的英文，而且有时候还可以在这个句子结尾用升调，引起对方的注意。

Appendix B

英语老话儿的新生

国外年轻人爱说的话跟老年人经常有差异，比如说一个简单的"晚上上床睡觉"，年轻人就不一定要说 go to bed，而可能会说 turn in。

不过有些老话儿却是老年人和年轻人都常用的，这就是 proverbs（谚语）和 idioms（成语）。

下面的 40 句话是 Pat 总结出来的雅思口试必备的 40 个 proverbs / idioms，不管考官是老 SG 还是小 MM 皆宜。

......

There's no place like home.	这个说任何涉及家或者住所的话题都很合适
He / She's a walking encyclopedia.	是活字典。形容知识很丰富
He's / She's a household name.	家喻户晓
He has the golden touch.	很会赚钱。形容成功人物常用
a whiz kid	神童
have two left feet	完全不会跳舞。Part 1 常用
get one's feet wet	意为"先尝试一下"，skill 技能话题常用
get the hang of it	初步掌握了……
know it backwards and forwards	精通……
Small is beautiful.	这是个俗语，可以用来形容任何可爱的小东西
It's a win-win situation.	是双赢的局面。Part 3 常用
have tunnel vision	目光短浅。Part 3 常用
not let the opportunity slip away.	别错过机会。
penny wise and pound foolish	小事儿聪明，大事儿糊涂。Part 3 常用

It's a dog-eat-dog world.	竞争很残酷。描述人的成功过程，Part 3 常用
give... the green light	批准……。
Variety is the spice of life.	多样是人生的调味料。leisure 话题常用
He's / She's sharp as a tack.	描述人反应很快，很精明
... is a notch above...	比……略胜一筹。很地道的英文
She's the apple of her parents' eye.	小孩是父母的掌上明珠。注意这里的 eye 不加复数
She's growing like a weed.	形容小孩长个儿快
Two heads are better than one.	这个 Part 2 说 advice 或者 a success 不错
... runs fast as lightning.	跑得像闪电一样。形容汽车或者人都可以
It fits like a glove.	形容衣服特合身儿
It's so quiet you could hear a pin drop.	别针掉在地上都能听见。这个形容安静的公园或者其他环境非常棒
It's smooth as silk.	形容人的皮肤、头发或者建筑和自然景观都可能用到
A dog is man's best friend.	这个说宠物不错，有的时候也会听到有人在 man 前面加个 a，都可以
in the first place	把这个短语放在否定句的句尾时很像中文的"压根儿"，比如 I didn't like that restaurant in the first place.
It's like putting the cart before the horse.	这个很像中文的"本末倒置"，不过在英文里它主要指做事情的顺序不对，应该先做的反而后去完成，很适合用在 Part 3 部分提出建议改变不良现状

When the going gets tough, the tough get going.

> 这里的第一个 tough 是 "困难的"，第二个 tough 是 "顽强的"，基本意思就是 "坚持就是胜利"。

... is a feast for my eyes/ ... is a great treat to me.

> 让我 "大饱眼福"，说艺术品或者自然景色都很好

It's the thought that counts. & It's always better to give than to receive.

> 这两个说 gift 非常好

He's a real Renaissance man. / She's a real Renaissance woman.

> 形容一个人多才多艺

of two minds about... / be born between A and B / in a dilemma / between a rock and a hard place / be in a bind

> 左右为难。Part 2 描述 decision 时可以用

Blood is thicker than water.

> 血浓于水。回答和 family 有关的题时常用

A man is known by the company he keeps.

> 这里的 company 不是公司，而是陪伴你的人。这句很像中文的 "人以群分"，说 friends 相关话题时常用

A fault confessed is half redressed.

> 敢于承认，错误就已经改正了一半。这句在 Part 3 提出 solutions 时常用

Prevention is better than cure.

> 预防比有病之后再治疗要好。用法同上

It's a blessing in disguise.

> 这句话很像中文的 "因祸得福"

If you want a friend, be a friend.

> 最后的这句最简单，但却最深刻，不仅在 friends 与 neighbour 话题里常用，到了国外也是生活的至理名言。

Appendix C

紧张的 120 个小时

The Hop，Skip and Jump towards the IELTS Speaking Test

在你即将奔赴战场之前，请允许我把 the IELTS Speaking Test 的实战过程介绍一下：

☆ 星期六下午第一个考生是 2：00 开始，星期日和星期一上午第一个考生是 8：00 开始，星期日和星期一下午第一个考生是 1：00 开始。星期六上午的笔试结束之后，你就可以开始准备 "蹲点儿" 或者 "网蹲" 的时间了。"网蹲" 其实也有它的好处，首先是安全，而且同一个半天里面全国的考题是同步的，在多数半天里中国大陆出现的卡片题达到了 21 ~28 张，但多数人考的是其中的 6 ~8 张。

☆ 口试之前 15' ~20' 必须进场，多数考场都是安排考生先到一个 waiting room 等候，会有中国监考官说一些考试纪律，看一下你的 ID。请确保在口试前关闭你的手机。(Your mobile phone must be switched off.)

☆ 到你的口语考试时间了，中国监考官会告诉你去你的考试房间，在多数考点考官会出门迎接你，但是也有些考点他/她会把门打开，考生自己走进去。

☆ 有时候会有简单的问候 "How are you?"，但有些考官现在把这个也省略了，还有可能问 mobile phone 是不是关机了。进到 interview room 后你才会真正明白 "套磁" 那些东东在实战时并不是很常用。

☆ 双方坐下。桌子上面会有录音装置，一定不要紧张，录音装置其实是为了保护你今后万一要申请 remark 的权利，是好东西。

☆ 常规部分，考官先说话：

Good afternoon/morning. My name is … Can you tell me your full name please? …

OK, can I see your ID card please?

☆ 正式开始问题部分，每部分都是考官先说话：

In this first part, I'd like to ask you some questions about yourself. So first of all let's talk about… (OK now I'm going to give you a topic and I'd like you to talk about it for one to two minutes…)

A Sample Topic Card

> Describe an important letter you received.
>
> You should say:
>> when you received this letter
>>
>> what this letter was about
>>
>> how you felt when you read it
>
> and explain why it was important.

OK, we've been talking about a letter you received and now I'd like to discuss with you some general questions related to this...

☆ 考试结束时，有些考官会送你出来，但是也有一些就偷懒坐在那儿跟你告别了。如果看他/她没有要再多说什么的意思，你也不一定要再多说告别的话了，一切自然最好。除了"Have a nice day."这样的说法，其实"Have a good one."在国外也极其常用，好处是你不用考虑是清晨还是快到黄昏了，挺万能的。而且不管是你先说还是考官先说，答案永远都是"You too."，不论怎样道别，你一定不要说的一句话是"I hope I'll see you again soon..."